Asset Allocation
and Private Markets

Asset Allocation and Private Markets

A Guide to Investing with Private Equity, Private Debt, and Private Real Assets

CYRIL DEMARIA

MAURICE PEDERGNANA

RÉMY HE

ROGER RISSI

SARAH DEBRAND

WILEY

This edition first published 2021

© 2021 Cyril Demaria, Maurice Pedergnana, Rémy He and Roger Rissi

Registered office
John Wiley & Sons Ltd, The Atrium, Southern Gate, Chichester, West Sussex, PO19 8SQ,
United Kingdom

For details of our global editorial offices, for customer services and for information about how to apply for permission to reuse the copyright material in this book please see our website at www.wiley.com.

Library of Congress Cataloging-in-Publication Data:

Names: Demaria, Cyril, author. | Pedergnana, Maurice, author. |
    He, Rémy, author.
Title: Asset allocation and private markets : a guide to investing with
    private equity, private debt and private real assets / Cyril Demaria,
    Maurice Pedergnana, Rémy He, Roger Rissi, Sarah Debrand.
Description: First Edition. | Hoboken : Wiley, 2021. | Includes index.
Identifiers: LCCN 2020056314 (print) | LCCN 2020056315 (ebook) | ISBN
    9781119381006 (cloth) | ISBN 9781119381013 (adobe pdf) | ISBN
    9781119380993 (epub)
Subjects: LCSH: Asset allocation. | Private equity. | Portfolio management.
Classification: LCC HG4529.5 .D45 2021 (print) | LCC HG4529.5 (ebook) |
    DDC 332.63/2—dc23
LC record available at https://lccn.loc.gov/2020056314
LC ebook record available at https://lccn.loc.gov/2020056315

Cover Design: Wiley
Cover Image: © Sielan / iStockphoto, © Vintage Tone / Shutterstock

Set in 10/12pt STIXTwoText by SPi Global, Chennai, India
Printed and bound by CPI Group (UK) Ltd, Croydon, CR0 4YY

10 9 8 7 6 5 4 3 2 1

To my family and friends, with a warm thank you for your support. Nothing would have been possible without you.

—*Cyril Demaria*

To Dr. Cyril Demaria for giving me the opportunity to work with him on this interesting project. To my family and my wife Yuchen, a warm thank you for your love and support.

—*Rémy He*

To my professor Cyril Demaria, a massive thank you for his consideration, time, and trust. I also would like to warmly thank my parents, Anne and Philippe, my three elder brothers, Mathieu, Thomas, and Quentin, and my fiancé Florent for their kind support.

—*Sarah Debrand*

Contents

Foreword

In *Asset Allocation and Private Markets*, Cyril Demaria, Maurice Pedergnana, Rémy He, Roger Rissi, and Sarah Debrand bring their academic background and real-world experience to bear for the benefit of readers wishing to understand the ins and outs of private markets investing, or so-called alternative investing. Relatively little has been written about this field, which has gone from an exotic investment specialty to an essential component of most investment funds. A book on this subject is sorely needed.

Fifty years ago, when people talked about "investments," they basically meant publicly traded stocks and bonds. While there's no standard definition of alternative investments, they can be understood as "alternatives to stocks and bonds" or simply "everything else," and decades ago they were largely unknown. (People were working in many of the fields that are now aggregated under the label "alternative investments," but they were few in number, the capital they managed was modest, and their activities were anything but the household word many of them have become).

The main categories of alternative investing came to prominence over the last 30–40 years. The biggest, now called "private equity," was called "leveraged buyouts" in the mid-1970s and grew many-fold in the 1980s, facilitated by the availability of high yield bond financing. Real estate investing, venture capital, and private lending joined private equity in more frequent use. And 15 or 20 years ago, the term "alternative investments" sprung up to describe them all.

Alternative or private markets strategies remained relatively obscure sidelines until roughly the mid-2000s. Then the poor performance of public equities in 2000–02 (the first three-year decline in the Standard & Poor's 500 equity index since the Great Depression) sent investors looking for alternatives to public stocks, and the reduction of interest rates to low levels to fight the Global Financial Crisis in 2008 vastly reduced the yields available on bonds.

Twenty or 30 years ago, most institutional investors such as pension funds, endowments, and insurance companies treated asset classes other than stocks and bonds as luxuries, a bit of which might be added to spice up portfolios. Now, with equities felt to be at full to high prices and bond yields at all-time lows, they have become indispensable portfolio components, and their use has grown exponentially. And yet relatively little has been written to establish their intellectual foundation.

Now, in their book, Cyril Demaria and his co-authors point out some of the aspects that require the serious investor's attention.

- As with interest rates (actually, due in good part to the low level of today's interest rates), the prospective returns on all asset classes—and certainly publicly listed stocks and bonds—are some of the lowest in history.

- And yet the returns desired or required by many institutional investors have not been reduced correspondingly.
- So-called beta markets have become increasingly efficient (that is, have become more "perfect" markets, where it is expected that the vast majority of investors' returns will be a function of the performance of the underlying market). Thus it is assumed that investor skill will contribute relatively little to investment returns there.
- Investors have concluded that (a) alternative investments are capable of providing returns that are at high absolute levels and superior to stocks and bonds, as they have in the past, and (b) part of this edge will come from the skill (or "alpha") of investment managers working in private markets, which are less picked over and thus are "less perfect."
- Thus, capital flows to alternative investments have surged.

The foregoing has raised some questions:

- To what extent did the past superior returns on alternative investments come as compensation for incremental risk borne, rather than as a "free lunch"?
- To what extent was it merely compensation for these investments' inherent illiquidity, and what are the ramifications?
- To what extent have the increased capital flows and increased attention on alternative investments rendered these markets more competitive and "perfect"— reducing investors' ability to demonstrate alpha and hampering the search for incremental return?
- To what extent have the factors mentioned added to these investments' riskiness?

Alternative or private markets investments present an interesting conundrum: Many investors face goals that require them to pursue high returns in today's low-return world. They have no choice but to turn to alternative investments for a good part of the solution. But alternative investments entail increased risk, reduced liquidity, and reliance on managers for skillful management (and thus the introduction of "manager risk").

Will alternative investments turn out to be a panacea or a pitfall? Because of the uncertainty inherent in investment and the competitive nature of the markets themselves, there cannot be an easy answer that applies to everyone. Skillful managers will help investors reach their goals in alternative investments, while the rest will frustrate their efforts. The risk and illiquidity entailed will be bearable for investors who approach the subject prudently and knowledgeably, but they may sink others. At a minimum, *Asset Allocation and Private Markets* by Cyril Demaria and his co-authors will help open investors' eyes to the considerations entailed in trying to be among the winners rather than the losers.

Howard Marks
Co-founder and Co-Chairman
Oaktree Capital Management

Acknowledgments

We would like to warmly thank the following persons for their kind support in the conception of this book.

First, this book would not have been the same without the unprecedented access to high-quality data. We would like to thank eFront, and namely Thibaut de Laval, for their continued support and the access to the eFront Insight (formerly Pevara) data. Our thankfulness extends to StepStone, and namely Thomas Häfliger and Marc Lickes, for their exclusive access to data regarding senior debt. It is thanks to this highly valued cooperation that our book can be more comprehensive in its coverage and hopefully more relevant to the readers. Any mistake or omission remains ours, as well as the conclusions drawn upon the use of the data.

We would also like to thank Thomas Meyer for his time, perspectives, and constructive conversations. We also owe a debt of gratitude to Gontran Duchesne, who provided invaluable support, helping us with some of the thorny mathematical aspects of certain questions. Often, the simplest questions are the most difficult to answer, and Gontran was always extremely helpful in finding out answers.

Finally, we would like to thank our publisher, John Wiley & Sons, and the team, for their patience and kind support in facing the multiple obstacles that the writers encountered in the process of drafting this book.

About the Authors

PROF. DR. CYRIL DEMARIA

Cyril Demaria is general partner and president of the Pilot Fish funds, a series of venture capital finder's funds for family offices and high net worth individuals. He was also partner and head of private markets at Wellershoff & Partners. Before that, he was in charge of private markets research at the Chief Investment Office of UBS Wealth Management. He also co-founded and was chief investment officer at Tiaré Investment Management AG, a Zürich-based wealth and investment management company. Previously, he created a multi-strategy fund-of-funds focused on environmental matters. He was also portfolio manager responsible for private equity fund investments at a French insurance group. As head of corporate development for a French IT firm, he managed four asset acquisitions and structured debt financing to do so. He started his career in a hybrid venture capital and funds-of-funds firm in San Francisco and Paris.

A French and Swiss citizen, Cyril Demaria is a graduate from HEC Paris, holds a BA in political sciences from the Institut d'Etudes Politiques (Lyon), master in geopolitics (Paris), master in European business law (Paris), and a PhD from the University of St. Gallen, with a thesis on the topic of "Alignment of interests of fund investors and fund managers in private equity," later published by Palgrave under the title *Private Equity Fund Investments*.

He is an affiliate professor at EDHEC Business School (Nice), and lectures at EADA (Barcelona) and other business schools. He collaborates regularly as an expert with the European Commission, Invest Europe, SECA, France Invest, the CFA, and the CAIA. He is the author of:

— *Développement durable et finance*, Maxima, 2003;
— *Introduction au private equity*, Revue Banque Editeur, 2006, 2nd ed. 2008, 3rd ed. 2009, 4th ed. 2012, 5th ed. 2015, 6th ed. 2018, 7th ed. 2020
— *Profession: business angel — Devenir un investisseur providentiel averti*, with Marc Fournier, Revue Banque Editeur, 2008
— *Le marché, les acteurs et la performance du private equity suisse*, with Maurice Pedergnana, SECA, 2009, 2nd ed. 2012
— *Introduction Private Equity, Debt and Real Assets*, John Wiley & Sons, 2010, 2nd ed. 2013, 3rd ed. 2020
— *Private Equity Fund Investments*, Palgrave, 2015.

He can be reached at: cyril.demaria@pilot-fish.eu, +41 79 813 86 49.

PROF. DR. MAURICE PEDERGNANA

Maurice Pedergnana heads the investment committee and acts as chief economist of Zugerberg Finanz AG (Zug). He is also the managing director of the Swiss Private Equity & Corporate Finance Association (SECA) and is a member of various boards of directors (Viability Consulting AG, IG Bank, Switzerland, and Uniserv AG). He is part-time professor at the Lucerne University of Applied Sciences and Arts (HSLU) since 2000. From 1999 to 2011 he was a member of the Bank Council of the Zürcher Kantonalbank. He also worked as a management consultant in the area of small and medium-sized enterprises. He lectured at the Zurich University of Applied Sciences in Winterthur (ZHAW) between 1997 and 2001. From 1989 to 1991 he worked as an assistant at the Malik Management Center at the University of St. Gallen, university where he studied economics from 1984 to 1988. From 1992 to 1993 he was a scholarship holder at Sophia University in Tokyo. Back at the University of St. Gallen, he completed his doctorate studies with a thesis on "Competitiveness and success factors of Swiss companies in foreign markets (using Japan as an example)."

RÉMY HE

Rémy He is an investment analyst at Obviam, a Swiss investment firm focusing on private markets investments in emerging and frontier markets. Before that, he was private market research analyst at Wellershoff and Partners. He was also a private equity consultant at Bennani and Marchal Associates, where he helped family offices, pension funds, and institutional investors setting up their private market investment strategy and risk monitoring. Previously, he was junior analyst in private market research at the Chief Investment Office of UBS Wealth Management. A French citizen, he holds a MSc in corporate finance and banking from EDHEC Business School.

ROGER RISSI

Roger Rissi is a lecturer at the Lucerne University of Applied Sciences and Arts (HSLU). His main teaching and research areas include advanced capital market and portfolio theory, corporate finance, risk management, and asset allocation with alternative investments. Previously, he worked in various functions of management support and control at UBS between 2000 and 2008. He has delivered several expert opinions for private sector companies, the European Parliament, and the European Commission. From 1994 to 2000, he studied economics with a major in finance at the University of Zurich.

SARAH DEBRAND

Sarah Debrand is a French capital markets analyst at Citi Bank, in London. She graduated from EDHEC Business School (Nice) with a double degree: a master in financial economics and a MSc in corporate finance and banking. She was on the EDHEC Dean's List, thus qualifying in the top 5% of her class.

In parallel to her studies at EDHEC, she completed diverse financial internships within the investment banking and accounting industries, where she developed strong and valuable analytical and communication skills.

Sarah has developed a keen interest in private equity and more generally in private markets, notably when following Cyril Demaria's lectures at EDHEC. Recognized for her attention to detail, understanding of the sector and critical approach, she was invited to co-author this book.

She can be reached at: sarah.debrand@edhec.com, +33 6 46 59 50 73.

Data Sources

Data sources are a particular topic of interest for private markets: there is no comprehensive database of activity and performance of private equity funds. Practitioners and academic writers access various complementary or competing sources, some of which are restricted and some are accessible to a larger public. Table 1 provides an in-depth perspective on the mosaic of sources available.

Databases with a restricted access are often provided to academic writers by fund investors or built by academic institutions (such as the Private Capital Research Institute[1]). We could access one of these sources for this book, provided by StepStone[2], a fund investor (see below). We are very grateful for this opportunity.

Databases accessible to the public can be sorted into two categories: bottom-up and top-down sources. Bottom-up databases rely on different sources of variable to low quality from voluntary disclosures by fund investors and fund managers, public information, and disclosures under the US Freedom of Information Act (FOIA) in the US. They usually lack historical depth, as they usually start at best from the mid-1990s. The geographical coverage is also uneven and difficult to assess in its representativeness. The advantage of these databases is that providers such as Preqin[3] and Pitchbook[4] provide full access to the data, down to single individual funds or investments. We have used the Preqin database for statistics of activity and to assess our own statistics on fund performance.

Top-down databases deliver an aggregate access to the underlying data, often collected directly at the source from fund investors and fund managers. These are essentially fund performance data. **eFront Insight, Cambridge Associates**, and **Burgiss** collect data about private market funds and aggregate them so that they are anonymized. Data is aggregated according to the year of the creation of funds (their "vintage year"). Data is homogeneous, of good quality, and delivers a good perspective on the cash flows and valuations of funds. For this book, we have had access to the data of Cambridge Associates and eFront Pevara (now Insight, see below). We are very grateful to eFront for having granted us access to this data.

---

[1] http://www.privatecapitalresearchinstitute.org/index.php.
[2] https://www.stepstoneglobal.com.
[3] https://www.preqin.com/.
[4] https://pitchbook.com/.

Therefore our sources combine high quality sources from eFront, StepStone, and Cambridge Associated (through Thomson Reuters Eikon, now Refinitiv). These data sources are further detailed below.

EFRONT INSIGHT

The eFront Insight database is generally considered as one of the most accurate and reliable sources of performance benchmark data in private markets. This database has been developed by eFront, a leading software provider specializing in alternative investments since 1999. Benchmarks based on the Insight database can be produced through eFront's software online. This software provides analytical tools supporting investors so they can make informed decisions, by quickly and easily benchmarking the performance of a portfolio, identifying market trends, and performing due diligence on potential investments.

This database contains information on more than 4000 funds, including the underlying cash flows. The source of the information is the data contribution of a wide variety of investors across the globe, including pension funds, funds-of-funds, and insurance companies, among others. The broad range of contributors makes the database diverse in terms of geographical coverage, investment strategies, and vintage, which in turn reduces the risk of bias. In terms of composition:

- North America and Europe account for 85% of the information contained in the database;
- Strategies include a wide range of private market strategies, from private equity (such as leveraged buyout, and venture capital), private debt (such as mezzanine and distressed debt), private real assets (private real estate, infrastructure, and natural resources), as well as secondary and funds-of-funds; and
- Vintages are rather well represented in the database from 1991 to date.

This data is sourced directly from the middle and back office software of the investors. Data (including data points on capital calls, distributions, net asset values, etc.) is collected directly from limited partners on a quarterly basis. Contributors provide data that is both anonymized and normalized, spanning from inception to date.

This data is cross-checked by eFront, thus guaranteeing the high quality and reliability of the aggregated data. Data consistency and reliability are ensured by a comprehensive series of manual and automated validation checks, run by a dedicated team of data specialists. These quality checks aim to:

- Identify inconsistencies in historical values or fund attributes;
- Detect gaps in data, duplicates, or null values;
- Identify cash flow issues;
- Neutralize currency effects; and
- Validate complete cash flow extraction by looking into PICC, DPI, and TVPI ratios.

STEPSTONE

StepStone is a global private markets investment firm focused on providing customized investment solutions and advisory and data services to its clients. Its clients include some of the world's largest public and private defined benefit and defined contribution pension funds, sovereign wealth funds and insurance companies, as well as prominent endowments, foundations, family offices and private wealth clients, which include high-net-worth and mass affluent individuals. StepStone partners with its clients to develop and build private markets portfolios designed to meet their specific objectives across the private equity, infrastructure, private debt and real estate asset classes.

StepStone Private Markets Intelligence (SPI), the firm's proprietary analytics platform, has gathered performance data on more than 10,000 investment managers and 26,000 private market funds. StepStone has accumulated through its research and due diligence activities performance data and cash flows on more than 65,000 private investments.

We have had access to its private debt loan database, which includes 124,000 tranches with up to 170 single characteristics. The cash flows are a generic replication of average private debts of different vintage years. Included in the construction are funds with a target size of 40–50 loans, where loans can be associated to a unique fund. After evaluating the database, 23 funds comprising approximately 1,000 loans were analyzed. Assumptions to replicate cash flows were[5]:

— 1.25% management fees and 15% carried interest over a 6% hurdle rate;
— Loans contributed to 90% of the fund sizes;
— Loans are drawn at launch and repaid at realization date;
— Coupons are paid assuming a gross yield equal to the internal rate of return; and
— The currency of reference is the USD.

CAMBRIDGE ASSOCIATES VIA THOMSON EIKON (NOW REFINITIV)

We also used the data from the consultant Cambridge Associates, accessed through Thomson Eikon (now Refinitiv). The data dates back to the 1970s and is one of the most established to date, covering private equity, some private debt (mezzanine and distressed debt), and private real asset strategies. Data is sourced directly from the middle and back office systems of investors, as well as in the due diligence process undertaken by Cambridge Associates when advising investors on their private market investments. Data is generally considered of high quality and reliable. Cambridge Associates declares capturing roughly 7,200 funds representing $4.6 trillion of capital across all asset classes.

---

[5]The following terms are further explained in detail in Chapter 3.

TABLE 1 Sources and categories of information in private markets

		Geographical coverage			Lat.-			Performance (benchmark) of general partners by strategy				Distr.	Senior	Pri-vate	Funds of	Infra-	Energy/ Nat.	Second-	Timber-	Farm-	Activity			Source Type		FOIA &	Funds
Category	Provider	US	Europe	MEA	Am.	APAC	Afr.	VC	Growth	LBO	Mezz.	Debt	Debt	RE	RE funds	structure	Ress.	aries	land	land	Index Mark.	Prim Mark.	Sec. Mark.	LP/GP back office	Voluntary	public data	# Funds covered
Database Providers — Fund and deal data level	Pitchbook	P	P	P	P	P	P	P	P	P	P	P	P	P	P	–	P	P	P	–	–	P	P	–	YES	YES	42 618
	Venture-Source (Dow Jones)	P	P	P	P	P	P	P	P	P	P	P	P	P	P	–	P	P	P	–	F	P	–	–	–	YES	35 000
	CEPRES	"ROW"	"ROW"	"ROW"	"ROW"	P	P	P	P	P	P	–	–	P	–	P	P	P	P	P	F	P	–	YES	–	–	6 400
	Merger-Market	P	P	P	P	P	P	P	P	P	P	–	–	–	–	P	–	–	–	–	F	P	–	–	YES	YES	10 400
Fund level data	AVCJ	–	–	–	–	P	–	P	P	P	P	–	–	P	–	P	P	P	P	–	F	P	–	–	YES	YES	12 000
	Preqin	P	P	P	P	P	P	P	P	P	P	P	P	P	P	P	P	P	P	P	F	P	P	–	YES	YES	36 000
	Eureka-Hedge	P	P	P	P	P	P	P	P	–	P	–	P	P	–	–	–	P	P	–	–	P	P	–	YES	YES	8 200
	PEI Connect	P	P	P	P	P	P	P	P	P	P	P	P	P	P	P	–	P	P	P	–	P	–	–	YES	YES	30 000
	Bison	P	P	P	P	P	P	P	P	P	–	–	P	P	P	P	P	P	?	?	F	P	P	YES	YES	YES	6 200
	Cobalt	BASED ON BISON AND HAMILTON LANE DATA - Platform powered by both Bison and Hamilton Lane																									
	eFront Insight	P	P	P	P	P	–	P	P	P	P	P	P	P	P	P	P	P	P	–	F	P	P	YES	–	–	3 900
Direct deal data	Dealogic	P	P	P	P	P	P	P	?	P	?	?	?	?	–	?	?	?	?	?	F	P	P	?	?	?	
	S&P Capital IQ	P	P	P	P	P	P	P	P	P	P	P	P	–	–	P	P	–	?	–	–	P	P	?	?	?	
	Zephyr (Bureau van Dijk)	P	P	P	P	P	P	P	?	P	?	?	?	?	?	?	?	?	?	?	F	P	P	–	?	YES	
	Cliffwater	P	–	–	–	–	–	P	P	P	P	P	P	P	–	P	P	?	?	?	F	P	–	?	YES	?	
Internat. and regional associations — Fund and deal data	EMPEA	–	P	P	P	P	P	–	–	–	–	–	–	–	–	–	–	–	–	–	F	P	–	–	YES	YES	3 200
Fund level data	ILPA	BASED ON CAMBRIDGE ASSOCIATES DATA																									
	Invest Europe	–	F	–	–	–	–	F	F	F	F	P	P	F	–	F	–	–	–	–	F	F	–	YES	–	–	8 000
	LAVCA	–	–	P	–	P	–	P	P	P	–	–	–	P	–	–	–	–	–	–	F	F	–	–	YES	?	?
	NVCA	F	–	–	–	F	–	F	–	F	–	–	–	F	–	–	–	–	–	–	F	F	–	–	YES	YES	?

Universities		PCRI	P	P	'ROW'					F	F	F					F		F						YES	–	YES	38 641
		CMBOR	–	P	–					–	–	–					P		–					P	–	YES	YES	YES	–
Intermediaries & gatekeepers	Fund level	Cambridge Associates	P	P	P					P	P	P			P		P	F	P			P		–	YES	YES	YES	YES	–	7 420
	Direct deal	Thomson VentureXpert					The database has been discontinued and replaced by an access to Cambridge Associates via Thomson Eikon																						
	Fund level data	Burgiss	P	P	P					P	P	P	–	P	P		P		P			P		P	YES	–	YES	YES	–	?
		Hamilton Lane	P	P	"ROW"					P	P	P	?	P	P	?	P		P			P		P	YES	YES	YES	YES	YES	?
		StepStone	P	P	P					P	P	P		P	–	?	P	F	P			–		–	YES	YES	YES	YES	?	?
		State Street	–	–	–					–	–	–		–	–	?	–	–	?			–		–	YES	YES	–	YES	?	?
		Greenhill Cogent	Global								–	–	–		–	–		–		–			F		F	–	–	?	?	?	?

Note 1: "F" refers to free offering, "P" refers to paying offering and "M" refers to member access only.

Note 2: Voluntary means that clients have accepted to give information on their own funds (LPs or GPs) in exchange of free access to data for example.

Note 3: LP/GP back-office means other than operators have access to data from clients.

Note 4: "FOIA" (Freedom of Information Act) means that the information is not available directly from public websites. It must be requested by American interested parties. We have grouped it with publicly available information data.

Note 5: Most of the sources offer some form of free index and a paying access to detailed data.

Note 6: S&P Capital IQ is a platform included in the S&P Global Market Intelligence offering. It has to be differentiated from S&P Global, S&P Global Ratings, S&P Global Platts and S&P Dow Jones Indices.

Note 7: Preqin and Pitchbook provide some form of free data based on their granular and detailed paying offering.

Note 8: The majority of professional associations (such as Invest Europe and ILPA) do not provide performance data but only activity data. However, some national associations (such as FranceInvest) provide both.

Note 9: EMPEA covers all emerging market regions. Farmland and Timberland strategies are included in real assets and there is no separate asset class for impact investing but they are considering this strategy.

Note 10: Preqin also covers hybrid funds and co-investments.

Note 11: MergerMarket's data includes information from Unquote.

Note 12: VentureSource provides an index based on venture capital transactions, not fund performance.

Source: Authors, based on public information, private discussions, and correspondence. As of December 2018. For clarity, we did not include data from national/local professional associations.

Abbreviations and Acronyms

AIFMD	Alternative Investment Fund Manager Directive
APAC	Asia Pacific region
AUM	assets under management
AVCAL	Australian Private Equity and Venture Capital Association
AVCJ	Asian Venture Capital Journal
bn	billion
bps	basis points
CEIOPS	Committee of European Insurance and Occupational Pensions Supervisors
CIO	chief investment officer
CMBOR	Centre for Management Buy-Out Research
CSR	corporate social responsibility
DCF	discounted cash flows
DCIIA	Defined Contribution Institutional Investment Association
DPI	Distribution to Paid-In
EBITDA	earnings before interest, taxes, depreciation, and amortization
EBRD	European Bank for Reconstruction and Development
EDM	emerging domestic market
EIF	European Investment Fund
EIOPA	European Insurance and Occupation Pensions Authority
EMPEA	Emerging Markets Private Equity Association
ESG	environmental, social, and corporate governance
EU	European Union
EUR	euro
EV	enterprise value
FCPI	Fonds Commun de Placement dans l'Innovation
FCPR	Fonds Commun de Placement à Risque
FIP	Fonds d'Investissement de Proximité
FLP	Family Limited Partnership
FO	family office
FPCI	Fonds de Placement en Capital Investissement
GBP	British pound
GP	general partner (manager of a private equity fund)
HNWI	high net worth individual

IFC	international finance corporation
IFRS	International Financial Reporting Standards
ILPA	International Limited Partners' Association
IOSCO	International Organization of Securities Commission
IPO	initial public offering
IRR	internal rate of return
IT	information technology
IVA	Israel Venture Association
LAVCA	Latin American Venture Capital and Private Equity Association
LBO	leveraged buyout
LP	limited partner (investor in a private equity fund)
LPA	limited partnership agreement
LPE	listed private equity
MENA	Middle East and North Africa
MFN	most favored nation
MFO	multiple family office
mn	million
NACUBO	National Association of College and University Business Officers
NAV	net asset value
NVCA	National Venture Capital Association
PE	private equity
PICC	paid-in to committed capital ratio
PIPE	private investment in public entities (or equities)
PM	private markets
PME	public market equivalent
ROW	rest of the world
RVPI	residual value to paid-in
SFO	single family office
SRI	socially responsible investments/sustainable and responsible investments
SWF	sovereign wealth fund
tn	trillion
TVPI	total value to paid-in
UNPRI	United Nations Principles for Responsible Investment
USD, $	US dollar
VaR	value at risk
VC	venture capital
VY	vintage year (year of creation of a private equity fund)

Asset Allocation
and Private Markets

CHAPTER 1

Sources of Capital: Nature, Constraints, and Objectives

In a Nutshell

This chapter will guide readers with background on investors and their asset allocation. Allocating assets can be challenging due to behavioral biases and an ever-changing macroeconomic and financial environment. Moreover, each investor is different. Taking into account their specific constraints is crucial for building a successful asset allocation, although those constraints are evolving over time.

I nvestors try to optimize the use of their capital to generate the highest financial performance possible within a set of identified constraints. Investors operate trade-offs to make the most of what is possible within these constraints. This task is called asset allocation (Chapter 2).

Setting up an asset allocation is challenging in multiple ways. First, investors are subject to behavioral biases (Section 1.1). Second, investors have to allocate their capital in an ever-changing environment: macroeconomic conditions, the performance and risks associated with specific investments, as well as demographic, regulatory, socioeconomic, and even psychological (investor's preferences) dimensions generate uncertainties about the outcome of an asset allocation.

Moreover, each investor is different and therefore has to carefully assess his own constraints to build an asset allocation (Section 1.2). These constraints evolve over time as well. Investors have to then revise their approach and their asset allocation. This can prove to be difficult, as investors tend to rely on the observation of the past to project themselves into the future.

1.1 BEHAVIORAL BIASES AND THEIR CONSEQUENCES

Behavioral biases affect every investor. This has been widely documented when investors look at listed markets. Behavioral biases apply also when investors plan to deploy capital in private markets (Section 1.1), although the consequences might differ. It is possible to address these behavioral biases (Section 1.2) thanks to specific actions.

1.1.1   Behavioral Biases in the Context of Private Markets Investing

Demaria (2015, Introduction), quoting Allen (2001), describes investors as agents of final capital providers, making decisions in the name and/or the account of the latter in private market funds. Fund investors are heterogeneous in their expectations and behaviors as well as irrational and subject to biases.

Demaria[1] explains that "in a context of low, asymmetrical, and incomplete information, **noise** can have significant consequences" on the behavior of private market fund investors. This noise can be rumors, outdated information, or partial information that fills the void. Demaria notably explains that the reputation of fund managers plays a significant role in private markets. Sorting information from noise can be challenging for fund investors.

Prospect theory applies to private market investors. As explained by Demaria (2015), an investor's expected outcome from an asset selection is determined by the gains or losses registered since the asset was acquired. Demaria mentions that private market fund investors do not fall into the usual trap of over-weighting recent information and under-weighting long-term trends. The conclusion of Demaria is that fund investors might, in fact, "under-react to information while they over-react on the stock exchange." Focusing specifically on losses, he explains that they are booked first as provisional (through the evolution of net asset values of funds) and then as effective losses. Fund investors tend to underreact to provisional losses, as they are judged only as an estimate. They also underreact to actual losses, as they have already integrated the information. Demaria also notes that losses booked by private market funds are the result of a process over which they have no control. Their potential actions are also limited.

Information on private markets is also subject to a significant time lag. Demaria mentions that as this information, notably about fund performance, is acknowledged, waves of investments are triggered and are fed by "belated knowledge and understanding of past performances." They are the result of **fashions**, **fads**, the **representativeness bias** (fund investors base their judgements on stereotypes), **aversion to ambiguity** (fund investors prefer the familiar to the unfamiliar), and **fear of the unknown**. As an illustration, investors have avoided strategies that recorded a loss, such as Western European venture capital after 2001. They missed the particularly high performance of these funds during the following years. Investors also tend to pile up on strategies that enjoyed significant and unexpectedly high returns, such as US venture capital in 1990–1997. A wave of capital inflow created an oversupply in the following years, resulting in a bubble and a crash in 2000–2001. Moreover, investors tend to over-weight their own experience and a limited number of recent events. They revise their beliefs with a certain time lag in front of new evidence, and with a relative lack of magnitude.

Demaria states that **home investing bias** affects fund investors, as they are a way to address the recurring lack of information mentioned above. US pension funds (Hochberg and Rauh, 2013) are a victim of this bias: public pension funds over-weight home-state private equity by 9.8 percent. Their in-state investments achieve a performance that is two to four percentage points lower than their own

---

[1]We refer to the Introduction of Demaria (2015) for more details (including detailed references to behavioral finance theories). The whole section is largely derived from it.

out-of-state investments and similar investments in their state by out-of-state investors. They conclude that over-weighting and underperformance in local investments reduce public pension fund resources by $1.2 billion per year.

Demaria also states that most investors are **overconfident**. They believe that they are better than average. They also overestimate the chances that future events will materialize as they expect and underestimate that they could be wrong. In private markets, overconfidence notably applies in the aptitude of investors to select the best funds (see Chapter 3), so-called top quartile funds, as notably analyzed by Harris et al. (2012). Fund managers exploit this bias by producing information that matches the expectation of investors. Demaria quotes Private Equity Online that surveyed fund managers in 2009. In this survey, 77 percent stated that they belong to the top quartile. Investors are also overconfident when backing emerging fund managers (Demaria, 2015, Introduction; Da Rin and Phalippou, 2013).

1.1.2 Avoiding Behavioral Biases

Knowing these biases should help investors to actively address them and avoid some of the negative consequences. A **self-assessment** is the first step in that process. Does the investor realistically possess some of the **know-how** necessary to invest in private markets? If so, to what extent? The **experience** of the investor, which is a **function of the time spent in the asset class and the network that was built**, can objectively be self-assessed. This experience is how **investors' skill** develops. The output is not binary but a matter of degree of know-how. Cavagnaro et al. (2019) estimate that a "one-standard-deviation increase in skills leads to an increase in annual return[2] of between one and two percentage points." Investors can then decide how to address their lack of experience and expertise, notably through outsourcing (Chapter 3).

The second step is to prevent behavioral biases from creeping back into the operations. For that, **asset allocation policies, investment decision guidelines,** and **processes should help**. Within these operational aspects, human resources play a specific role. The profile, which is the result of **recruitment policies** and the **tenure of the staff,** are important to keep in line behavioral biases. **Incentive policies** are crucial to frame the setup and execution of the asset allocation, notably when it comes to taking risks, as well as avoiding home biases and overconfidence. Internal incentives determine the final risk appetite of investors (Hobohm, 2010) and conflict with the effective target of investors (Demaria, 2015). These incentives are the result of **adequate resource management combined with sound investment objectives**. These investment objectives are the result of the assessment of the constraints by the investor, and the formulation of an asset allocation (Chapter 2).

Investors are often agents, acting on behalf of principals. These principals have implicit and/or explicit expectations. These expectations are interpreted by agents with

---

[2]Measured through the internal rate of return. The authors use a Bayesian Markov chain Monte Carlo method. The effect is higher in venture capital: a one-standard-deviation increase in investor skill leads to a 2- to 4.5-percentage point increase in returns. The effect declines as the sample period progresses (a consequence of the maturing of the industry, according to the authors). This higher performance is not related to a higher risk taken by investors.

the specific filter of their **beliefs**, which are difficult to tackle when it comes to behavioral biases and human resources. This is a wedge between theory and practice, which is difficult to identify, address, and minimize (or ideally eliminate). It is only through an active control, monitoring, and regular interactions between principals and agents that beliefs can be identified, discussed, and (if necessary) eliminated.

1.2 LAYING THE GROUND FOR AN ASSET ALLOCATION: ANALYZING INVESTORS

Mitigating behavioral biases is a bespoke effort, as investors differ significantly from each other. There is no equivalent of a unique set of policies that would eliminate these biases. Investors have to thus continue the self-assessment referred to above, this time to identify objective criteria which would help them lay the ground for their asset allocation. This is a multi-dimensional analysis (Section 2.1), which is visible when looking at categories of investors (Section 2.2).

1.2.1 A Multi-Dimensional Analysis

Investors can be classified according to different parameters that have significant consequences on their asset allocation.

The first one, and probably the most obvious when it comes to investing in less traded assets such as private markets funds, is their **time horizon**. Retail investors have probably the shortest one (from a few months to a few years), but they are de facto excluded from private markets for regulatory reasons (see Chapter 3). Institutional investors, such as banks and insurance groups, have a specific timeline, from one to multiple years. Pension funds and high net worth individuals[3] (HNWI) have a longer time horizon, varying from multiple years (in the case of ageing individuals) to multiple decades. The time horizon of family offices and sovereign wealth funds (SWF) spans at least multiple generations and could be even considered as infinite. Foundations and endowments can have infinite horizons by design (they are not allowed to spend their capital, just the proceeds of their investments), although some have a finite time horizon.

The second obvious dimension is the **regulatory pressure** under which investors operate, which itself is partially determined by the geographical location of investors (and thus the jurisdiction they depend on). The lowest regulatory pressure is probably on family offices and HNWI. Regulations are essentially set up to protect investors, but there is no specific requirement that they have to follow when allocating their assets and deciding where to invest. They are essentially unconstrained by regulations. SWF come next, with low to no regulatory pressure. Due to a lack of transparency, it is difficult to establish precisely the level of regulation they have to comply with. Endowments and foundations are lightly regulated. Most of the constraints come from their legal status as

---

[3] Defined as individuals which earn €200,000 or more per year or with a "liquid" wealth (excluding primary residence) of €1 million or more per year.

charitable institutions (or equivalent) and their tax exemption[4]. In some jurisdictions, this implies the undertaking of specific actions. In the US, for example, university endowments have an obligation to spend a certain percentage[5] of their total asset value every year. Pension funds, insurance groups, and banks have to comply with a high level of regulation. In Switzerland, for example, pension funds are not allowed to allocate more than 15 percent of their assets to alternative investments. In Europe, insurance groups and banks have to respect specific rules about their solvency and how to account each asset class they invest in using these solvency rules.

Although less obvious, the third parameter is the **size of assets under management**. Investing in private markets is an activity that is not easy to scale. This determines the asset allocation and the portfolio structure of investors. Small investors cannot easily replicate the asset allocation of larger ones (and vice versa).

A large size can have positive consequences. Dyck and Pomorski (2012) explain that Canadian pension funds with significant holdings in private equity perform better (740 basis points) than the ones with a smaller exposure, due to cost savings (25 percent of the gains) and superior gross returns (75 percent of the gains) that the authors attribute to the ability of investors with a larger exposure to "bridge the significant information asymmetries between investors" and fund managers. A large size can also have negative consequences. Large investors suffer from inertia (they respond more slowly to market changes) and suffer from higher home bias (Hobohm, 2010). This also leads to portfolio concentration, notably in large LBO funds.

Investors with lower assets under management can diversify more easily, notably in niche strategies. Their small size limits them in their ability to diversify geographically (lack of reach), as well as in terms of access to private market funds (the minimum threshold to invest in funds can be rather high). They do not benefit from economies of scale and lower costs. Smaller investors have been addressing some of these drawbacks. An easy way is to invest through funds of funds (see Chapter 3), although this adds to costs and prevents a tailored exposure. Another, assuming a sufficient amount to invest, is to set up an investment mandate (see Chapter 3), which provides a tailored exposure at a lower cost. However, this solution requires $25 to $35 million to invest in private markets and still adds up costs. Investors can also join forces to set up a joint consulting firm, as non-profit organizations did in the US with The Investment Fund for Foundations (TIFF Investment Management) in 1991.

Another parameter is the **experience (its length and diversity) of investors** in private markets (Lerner et al., 2007; Demaria, 2015). Da Rin and Phalippou (2013) explain that this is a function of the **total capital currently deployed in private equity**

---

[4]Since the Tax Cuts and Jobs Act of 2017, amended by the Bipartisan Budget Act of 2018, US endowments are in practice subject to an excise tax of 1.4 percent on endowment income if their universities welcome at least 500 tuition-paying students and the endowment has net assets of at least USD 500,000 per student (not adjusted for inflation). This could result in a readjustment of the asset allocation of endowments (Private Equity International, 2018).

[5]As explained by Dixon (2017), the US Internal Revenue Services issued a five percent payout guideline to private foundations in 1981. "It was broadly adopted by most non-profit organizations as a sensible baseline for spending."

(and by extension private markets). For them, it is what matters the most when sorting categories of investors, although in the context of asset allocation, this parameter is rather close to the size of the investor. The amount of capital to deploy will determine the financial resources that the investor can spend on analyzing private market investment opportunities (staff and due diligence). Investors deploying large amounts can have an influence on fund managers, assuming that they have the corresponding level of sophistication.

A long-standing presence of investors also determines the **access** to the best fund managers, which explains the outperformance of endowments in the 1990s thanks to their access to the best venture capital funds (Lerner et al., 2007; Sensoy et al., 2014). This access, combined with a persistence of performance (see Chapter 3; Kaplan and Schoar, 2005; Korteweg and Sorensen, 2017) is only one component of the overall skillset of investors. Cavagnaro et al. (2019) state that the "evaluation of [fund managers'] ability appears to be particularly difficult, consistent with [their] conclusion about the value of [fund investors'] skill."

Experience is connected to the **level of sophistication** of investors. This parameter is the result of accumulated know-how and knowledge, the access to qualified internal resources, and a clear vision and understanding of private markets. For example, "smart investors have already screened the market before a new fund is raised" (Demaria, 2015, and Hobohm, 2010). Unsophisticated investors are more likely to use agents, such as gatekeepers (see Chapter 3). This, in turn, will condition the asset allocation of investors, as agents tend to be conservative and focus on supposedly safe investments. This creates a quasi-systemic risk: herding, as agents tend to advise their clients along the same lines. Sophisticated investors can have a solid **reputation** as savvy private market investors, and thus have an influence on fund managers.

1.2.2 Categorizing Investors

Investors share a few investment constraints; others are specific to investors. Specific constraints can be **strategic**: the deployment of capital can support specific political goals, whether they are macroeconomic, social, or industrial, for example, in the case of governmental agencies or SWF. They can also be **voluntary**, as investors exclude investment sectors or promote environmental or social goals (see the General Conclusion of this book).

Some investors have to face **political pressure**. Hochberg and Rauh (2013) document that public pension funds, which are the ones most likely to be exposed to the negative political pressure of their board (Andonov et al., 2018), tend to concentrate their investments in local funds. Barber et al. (2015) found that some investors are pressured to invest in impact (that is to say ESG-compliant) funds. Both these practices lower returns (Cavagnaro et al., 2019).

As for common constraints, **liabilities** are one category: what the investor owes, when, and to whom. In effect, liabilities are the first order of investment constraint. They condition the whole asset allocation. Cornelius et al. (2013) and Winton[6] (2003)

---

[6]He states that "institutions with less frequent or less severe liquidity needs (such as pension funds and life insurers, according to him) have greater appetite for equity and for the debt of more risky borrowers." This is contradicted by the rest of this chapter.

state that the nature, structure, and duration of liabilities of each category of investor are driving their allocation to private equity. The payout schedule of the investor is part of its liability and a major constraint.

Regulations (see above), jointly with accounting rules (Cornelius et al., 2013), defining what is authorized, and defining what is forbidden are another category. This is a function of the location of the investor. They can have drastic consequences. Demaria (2015, Introduction) notes that the asset allocation of large institution investors is dictated by solvency and prudential ratios based on a standard method, which relies on modeling private equity fund investments by using some artificial historical risk and returns measurements. As he states, "The resulting ratios are artificially high" (Arias et al., 2010; Studer and Wicki, 2010; and Braun et al., 2014), as will be illustrated for insurance groups below.

Tolerance for risks (Demaria, 2015, Introduction), which is a function of the type of risk and the acceptable level of these risks, is also a source of constraint. **Expected returns**, in their level and frequency (if any), could also be seen as a constraint, although it is more often the result of the optimization of the three other sources listed above (liabilities, regulations, and risk appetite).

Hobohm (2010) groups investors in four categories depending on their return expectations:

– Institutional investors, which include pension funds and insurance groups. They are defined as "specialized financial institutions that manage savings collectively on behalf of small investors toward a specific objective in terms of acceptable risk, return maximization, and maturity claims."
– Investment corporations, which include asset managers and banks. They are defined as "in the business of investment management and investment advisory to generate returns for their shareholders." The Boston Consulting Group estimated that their global assets under management amounted to $62.4 trillion in 2012.
– Foundations and family offices, which include endowments.
– Governmental agencies, including sovereign wealth funds.

Hobohm analyzed the asset allocation of the different categories of investors (Table 1.1) over an extended period of time (1991–2005). Public pension funds differ significantly from the rest of the group in the high number of funds they invest in (35), and the use of external advisor (50 percent). Endowments and family offices, which are the smallest investors, come next in terms of number of funds they invest in and the use of external advisors. This is interesting, as they are very different from pension funds (notably as they are largely unconstrained by regulations).

Although this table supports some useful analysis, it is also unfortunately dated. Banks and insurance groups are no longer significant investors in private equity, as regulations prevent them from doing so (see below and Demaria, 2015). Therefore, this table should be seen as food for thought, but not as a current reflection of the situation of investors in private equity.

According to Deutsche Bank (mentioned in *Wall Street Journal*, 2018), the total global assets under management were estimated at $127 trillion as of 2014. Out of this total, pension funds represented $38.1 trillion, insurance funds $29.3 trillion,

TABLE 1.1 Investors in Private Equity (1991–2005)

	Public pension		Private pension		Banks		Insurance groups		Endowments		Governmental agencies		Family office	
	N	Mean	N	Mean	N	Mean	N	Mean	N	Mean	N	Mean	N	Mean
Investments	272	34.9	180	4.1	102	4.5	125	5.7	137	9.5	27	5.7	158	8.2
Years of experience	272	6.1	180	1.8	102	2.0	125	2.7	137	2.8	27	2.4	158	2.8
User of external advisor	272	49.6%	180	23.9%	102	1.0%	125	4.8%	137	34.3%	27	11.1%	158	16.5%
Average allocation to PE	191	4.8%	106	4.7%	36	13.0%	54	3.1%	80	10.1%	12	49.2%	67	13.0%
Location														
USA	272	60.7%	180	58.3%	102	28.4%	125	34.4%	137	92.0%	27	29.6%	158	87.3%
Europe	272	27.2%	180	30.0%	102	44.1%	125	46.4%	137	6.6%	27	9.5%	158	9.5%
Rest of the world	272	12.1%	180	11.7%	102	27.5%	125	19.2%	137	1.5%	27	48.1%	158	3.2%
AuM (USD bn)	264	15.9	155	18.2	80	280.3	98	66.3	125	2.0	20	38.7	135	2.2

Note: AuM refers to assets under management.
Source: Hobohm (2010).

and sovereign wealth funds $7.1 trillion. Although the details of this calculation are not available, this approach ignores some sources of capital such as family offices, endowments and foundations, and banks. Nevertheless, these estimates provide an order of magnitude of the importance of some sources of capital.

PwC (2017) stated that the total client assets amounted to $214.6 trillion in 2016, of which pension funds accounted for $38.3 trillion, insurance companies $29.4 trillion, SWF $7.4 trillion, HNWI $72.3 trillion, and mass affluent $67.2 trillion[7]. The penetration rate of the asset management industry was estimated at 39.6 percent. These figures are expected to increase significantly over the coming years.

We look at the different categories of investors and their challenges when it comes to including private markets in their asset allocation.

1.2.2.1 Family Offices, Multi-family Offices, and High Net Worth Individuals

Leleux, Schwass, and Diversé (2007) explain that "a single-family office generally manages the wealth of members of a single family made up of individuals sharing a common ancestry or surname and assets inherited communally. By contrast, a multi-family office [...] manages the pooled wealth of members of different families and allocates funds to investments either in aggregate or per family."

As mentioned before, they are the least regulated category of investors. The Securities and Exchange Commission (SEC) adopted a definition of a family office, which took effect on August 29, 2011[8]: a family office is any kind of entity that "(1) provides investment advice to family clients, (2) is wholly owned by family clients and controlled (directly or indirectly) exclusively by 'family members' and/or 'family entities' and (3)

TABLE 1.2 Total Assets and Evolution

Investor category	2016	2020(e)	2025(e)	CAGR 2016–2025(e)
Pension funds	38.3	53.1	64.6	6.0%
Insurance groups	29.4	38.4	44.7	4.8%
Sovereign wealth funds	7.4	10.0	13.6	7.0%
High net worth individuals	72.3	93.4	119.9	5.8%
Mass affluent	67.2	84.4	102.2	4.8%
Total client assets	**214.6**	**279.3**	**345.0**	**5.4%**
Global AuM	**84.9**	**111.2**	**145.4**	**6.2%**
Penetration rate of asset management services	*39.6%*	*39.8%*	*42.1%*	*0.7%*

Note: AuM refers to assets under management.
Source: PwC (2017).

---

[7]According to the authors, "Foundations and Endowments assets were not included as their total global assets represent less than one percent of all client assets".
[8]The Dodd-Frank Wall Street Reform and Consumer Protection Act inserted a clause exempting family offices from registering as investment advisers. The SEC was in charge of defining what would qualify a structure as a family office to benefit from this exemption.

does not hold itself out to the public as an investment adviser." Defined as such, they are unregulated in the US, and also in Europe (Leleux, Schwass, and Diversé, 2007).

Their liabilities range from regular short-term payouts for family members to live to long-term capital gains to increase the wealth of current and future family members. In that respect, the time horizon of investments can vary significantly from one family office to another.

Their appetite for risk is also very variable. It not only depends on the individual preferences of family members and their age, but also on how recent and how large the wealth is. The first or second generation of a wealthy family can be more risk-prone than the subsequent ones. The advisors also play a significant role as well as their incentives, as explained above. Some family offices emphasize non-financial goals, such as ESG targets. UBS and Campden Wealth (2020) mention that 34 percent of family offices are engaged in some form of sustainable investing (essentially through thematic investing).

As explained by Demaria (2015), the significant differences in these parameters (liabilities, appetite for risk) lead to the setup of specific targets, return expectations, and operational structures. The size of the clientele, its involvement, the connection to a family business, and the family background will determine the governance of the structure, and thus the type of investment mandate exercised. Figures 1.1 and 1.2 establish the connection between the size and structure of the family office and their appetite for risk.

As the structure evolves from single-family member, to limited member, to multi-generational family office, the risk appetite is reduced along with the entrepreneurial spirit. Leleux, Schwass and Diversé (2007) describe:

– Single family member offices: servicing a single individual, they separate wealth and business and can manage the intergenerational transfer of wealth.
– Limited-member single-family office: serving multiple individuals, they are set up for governance purposes. As there is little distance between current members and the original source of wealth, the members are thus "quite entrepreneurial and business-savvy and, therefore, tend to be more involved in the family office."

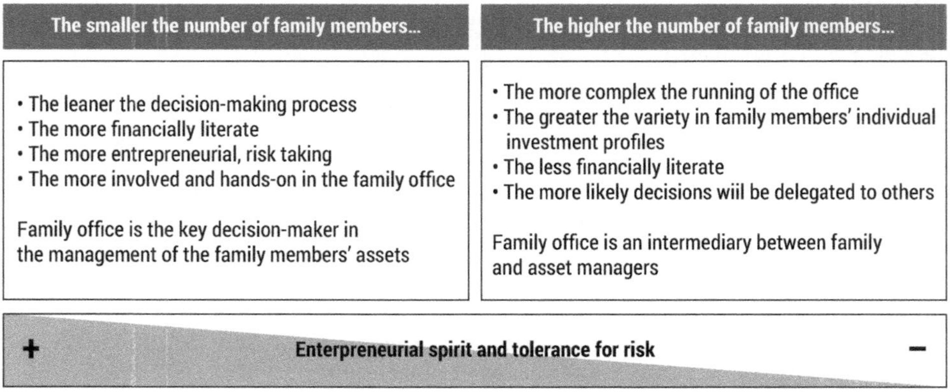

The smaller the number of family members...	The higher the number of family members...
• The leaner the decision-making process • The more financially literate • The more entrepreneurial, risk taking • The more involved and hands-on in the family office Family office is the key decision-maker in the management of the family members' assets	• The more complex the running of the office • The greater the variety in family members' individual investment profiles • The less financially literate • The more likely decisions wiil be delegated to others Family office is an intermediary between family and asset managers

+	Enterpreneurial spirit and tolerance for risk	**–**

FIGURE 1.1 Connection between family size, structure and tolerance for risk
Source: Leleux, Schwass and Diversé (2007).

	Low	Medium	High
Size	High number of family members	1st, 2nd generation	Founder only
Bonds, stocks, real estate	> 90% of assets	60–80%, reduction with time	50–75%, depending on volume of wealth
Private equity & venture capital	Limited < 10%	15–20%, increase with time	Up to 50%, depending on link to family business
Strategy	Allocation according to individual risk profile of family members	Increase in private equity as knowledge base increases	Invest because it is fun, more likely to co-invest or invest directly

FIGURE 1.2 Family office characteristics and risk appetite
Source: Leleux, Schwass and Diversé (2007).

– Multi-generational single-family office (close to a "single family private bank"), where there is a distance between the source of wealth and the office's clients. Governance is very important, as there is a significant discrepancy between the members' needs and investment time horizons. As a result, "there is a need for liquid, 'safe' investments to provide for current needs and also a need to undertake long-term, high upside, but high-risk investments for future generations."
– Multi-family office (MFO) and family office services.

The yearly cost of a single-family office is estimated at $1 million or more, making them attractive when managing investable assets in excess of $100 million[9]. UBS and Campden Wealth estimate that the costs were 113 basis points in 2018 and 117 basis points in 2019 for family offices.

It was estimated that in 2013, there were 5,000 US households qualifying for the $100 million mark. There are 100,000 households with $5 to 10 million in investable assets that are usually targeted by MFOs at the cost of 0.5 percent to 1 percent of assets per year. The Family Wealth Alliance estimated in 2010 that there were 2,500 to 3,000 active SFO managing $1.2 trillion (with assets size ranging from $51 million to 2.1 billion and an average of $605 million), and 150 MFO managing $400 billion (the range is from $36 million to 52 billion, with an average relationship of $51.5 million). Invest Europe estimated that there were 500 family offices active in Europe in 2007, of which 80 to 100 manage more than €1 billion. UBS and Campden Wealth (2020) estimate that the average family wealth is at $1.2 billion, and the assets under management of the average family office is $917 million.

The investment strategy of family offices varies depending on the characteristics of the family office. The share of private equity in the asset allocation depends on the risk appetite and the entrepreneurial spirit of the family members. Family offices are secretive. They are also lean and fairly simple structures (Demaria, 2015) illustrating "not

---

[9]See Steinberg and Greene (2013).

only the differences affecting investors within a given category, but also the evolution of investors over time." Demaria infers that these variations also affect each investor category in a similar fashion (although maybe not with the same amplitude).

As explained by Leamon, Lerner, and Garcia-Robles[10] (2012) and Demaria (2015, Introduction), family offices were the historical investors in private equity when private equity was indistinguishable from venture capital. However, as these family offices have evolved, notably in Europe, toward multi-generational family offices (or even MFO), their risk appetite has dropped (see Figs. 1.2 and 1.3). As family members age, their choices are focused on risk reduction (referred to as volatility reduction, assumed to be at portfolio level) and then return generation. Other criteria are important too but are secondary.

This prioritization is translated into a net preference toward LBOs (Fig. 1.4) followed by funds of funds and replacement capital. LBO presents an attractive investment profile, as it targets mature businesses (where the family most likely has some insights, either by exploiting one—or more—or having sold one) with a significant upside potential (see Chapter 3). Family offices do not target the highest risk/return profile (seed and start-up capital, and turn-around), but instead target the most familiar businesses. Replacement capital confirms this assertion: the specialists of this activity take over a participation in an existing mature company to replace an existing shareholder without structuring an LBO. The purpose is to offer an exit path to a shareholder rapidly and prepare a liquidity event (IPO, trade sale, and LBO). Underlying companies are often mature, profitable companies or growth companies with solid cash flows and

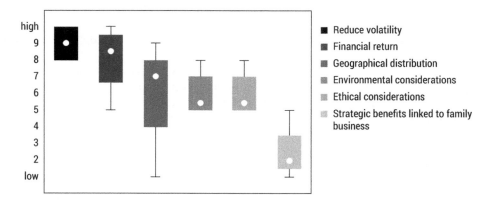

FIGURE 1.3 Main drivers of investment decisions for family offices
Source: Leleux, Schwass, and Diversé (2007).

---

[10]"In this nascent version of venture capital, the providers of capital—the LPs—were practically indistinguishable from fund managers [...]. Over time, the family offices hired individuals to manage the investment operation, but to a great extent the family oversaw the business, and the managers were salaried employees. All investments, regardless of the stage, were approved by a committee that generally included some family members."

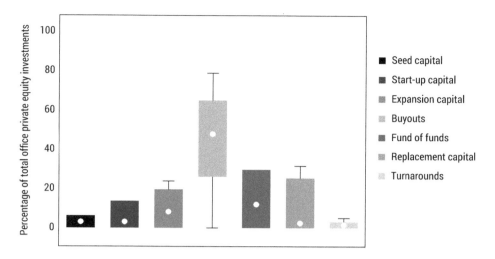

FIGURE 1.4 Allocation of family offices to private equity by investment stage
Source: Leleux, Schwass, and Diversé (2007).

businesses. The new owner structures solid guarantees through a series of governance and legal documents, notably to prepare its exit.

The common motivation of family offices is to "further the wealth of individuals" (Hobohm, 2010). According to UBS and Campden Wealth (2020), 56 percent of the family offices had a balanced agenda between wealth preservation, and wealth increased for their asset allocation in 2019. There were modest variations, depending on the geographical origin of family offices or their size. Globally, 19 percent were tilted toward wealth preservation and 25 percent toward growth.

A family office improves family governance. But it also serves to separate family wealth from family business, prepare intergenerational wealth transfer, and possibly prepare the sale of a family business (Leleux, Schwass and Diversé, 2007). Fig. 1.5 provides an idea of the underlying analysis for an asset allocation including alternative investments and namely private markets. Their approach is also opportunistic; changing over time or relying on mimicking the approach of other successful private market investors (with a delay) depending on their level of sophistication.

Family offices face **specific challenges** when integrating private markets in their asset allocation. First, they need to **balance the allocation around the existing anchor assets of the family** (or families) that they serve. If the family has built its fortune by owning private or listed firms, the asset allocation has to be established around these anchor assets. Although it is possible to analyze the characteristics of these anchor assets to isolate the features that are valuable and those that should be mitigated, these assets can shift in value abruptly and/or change their dividend distributions on short notice. As a result, the asset allocation has to be flexible to compensate these shifts. Chapters 4 and 5 address this issue with elements to build a portfolio of private market funds around these anchors.

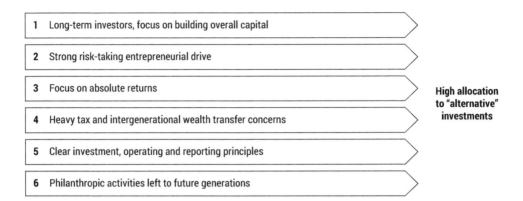

FIGURE 1.5 Underlying considerations of family offices integrating alternative investments to their asset allocation
Source: Leleux, Schwass, and Diversé (2007).

Second, family offices need to **accommodate shifting preferences and requests from the family members** (this includes panic and mood swings). In particular, unexpected payouts, or a significant change in expected payouts, can generate issues when assets are invested over a longer period of time (as it is the case in private markets). Unfortunately, there is no easy fix to this issue. Private market funds provide very few tactical instruments (see Chapters 3, 4 and 5) and they require time to be disposed of (direct investments) or to generate cash flows (secondary funds).

These shifts have to be planned as scenarios. Two main options can be identified. The first is to build cash reserves, which are, in essence, a reserve to absorb liquidity shocks. These cash reserves have to be distinctly held and are the counterweight of long-term exposures, such as private market funds. The second is to build a private market fund portfolio that generates distributions (thanks to direct lending, core real estate, or infrastructure; see Chapter 3 for definitions) and targets shorter exposures. This can be modeled and combined with cash reserves (see Chapters 4 and 5).

Third, family offices have to compose with their **fairly modest size**. They are the smallest type of investor—with assets under management of $817 million according to UBS and Campden Wealth (2020) and are even smaller than listed by Hobohm (2010) (see Table 1.1). The UBS and Campden Wealth study states that 11 percent of the assets under management were in direct private equity investments, and 7.7 percent were in private equity funds (and is expected to increase for 42 percent of respondents or stay the same for 44 percent). Direct real estate investments represented 17 percent, and timber and farmland amounted to 1.4 percent. There is no mention of other private market exposure.

According to this data, the average private equity fund program of family offices reaches $63 million. Their allocation tends to be focused more on LBO (see above), and these funds have seen their average size increase significantly. As a consequence, some funds might in effect be out of reach for family offices, as the minimum commitment requested by fund managers to access these large and mega LBO funds might be too high. The solutions are: to focus on the smaller end of the LBO spectrum (but this requires more resources to scout for these funds), or to pool capital with other like-minded investors (for example, through funds of funds, but this entails costs; see Chapter 3).

1.2.2.2 Endowments and Foundations

Endowments and foundations are "usually philanthropic organizations that either financially support other organizations, or directly engage in philanthropic activities while relying on their financial endowments" (Hobohm, 2010). They are usually set up for an infinite time. They are not allowed to spend their assets, but only investment proceeds. Most of them are based in North America (Demaria, 2015).

Endowments and foundations are largely unconstrained in their investments, except for a mandatory annual payout and an excise tax to pay (see above). Their infinite time horizon and limited constraints allow them to focus on the maximization of their wealth, while still complying with a pre-planned spending rate to provide "stable support for the sponsoring organization" (Reale, 2010). Indeed, "foundations look to generate income, net of all fees, of at least five percent per year to at least maintain the endowment asset base" (Hobohm, 2010).

Some of them, especially the large ones, are thus able to invest in new and novel asset classes and therefore can have a different portfolio structuring than other investors (Swensen, 2000; Lerner, Schoar, and Wang, 2007; Lerner, Schoar, and Wongsunwai, 2007; Hobohm, 2010). Yale and Harvard endowments have paved the way to private equity with allocations above 20 percent of their total assets under management (Frei and Studer, 2011). However, according to D'Angelo (2010), there is a substantial discrepancy between target and current allocations.

In 2019, 786 US university and college endowments managed $642.6 billion according to the 2019 NACUBO-TIAA Study of Endowments. Some US endowments are large. As of June 30, 2019, Harvard University's managed $40.9 billion, while Yale's managed $30.3 billion. Most of them are of a rather modest size: 675 (87 percent) manage less than a billion, and 306 (40 percent) manage less than 100 million. According to NACUBO, in 2019 the average size of the endowments was $819.6 million and the median $148.8 million.

According to The Hauser Institute for Civil Society (Johnson, 2018), there are 91,850 foundations in North America, 154,271 in Europe, 859 in Latin America, 47 in Africa, 161 in the Middle East, and 13,170 in Asia. Global foundation assets reached $1.5 trillion in 2018, of which 60 percent ($890 billion) are in the US and 37 percent in Europe (the Netherlands hosts $108 billion, Germany $93 billion, Switzerland $88 billion, Italy $87 billion, and the UK $84 billion[11]). Over 90 percent of foundations reported assets inferior to $10 million (and 50 percent of less than $1 million).

This size discrepancy of endowments and foundations has a direct consequence on their asset allocation (Table 1.3): the larger the size of the endowment, the higher

---

[11] According to The Investment Association (2019) the total assets under management from non-profit organizations ("charities, endowments, foundations, and other not-for-profit organizations") reached GBP 99 billion in 2019, of which 47 are managed institutionally.

the allocation to private markets and other alternative strategies. While Hobohm (2010) and Lerner et al. (2007) argue that private university endowments are among the most sophisticated private equity investors (notably when selecting VC fund managers), this statement might only be valid for the large endowments. Institutions managing more than $1 billion allocated 22.6 percent to private equity (see Fig 1.3, "private equity" and "venture capital", see Chapter 3), while those with less than $25 million allocated 1.5 percent in 2019. In absolute value, large endowments allocated collectively $113.6 billion[12] to private equity. Small institutions allocated collectively $15.2 million[13]. Thus, although all endowments could benefit from the flexibility offered to them when investing (Swensen, 2000), "most foundations are, in fact, too small to maintain their own investment team" (Hobohm, 2010). The NACUBO states that endowments employed, on average, 1.6 persons in 2011.

Endowments managing up to $100 million allocated one to five percent of their assets to LBO and most likely outsource the management to third parties. From $101 million to 1 billion, the proportion is 9 percent to 14 percent, which lowers the cost ratio to 0.2–0.7 percent per year (see Demaria, 2015, Introduction). The size of assets under management, therefore, plays a role in the performance of the investments, as it determines the use of internal or external agents to perform the allocation.

The other relevant thresholds, besides $100 million, seem to be $250 million and $1 billion. When endowments reach $250 million, allocations jump from 12 to 18 percent of assets under management. This could correspond to the recruitment of a consultant to help the endowment to invest in the asset class. Over $1 billion sees a further strong increase (allocations jump from 21 to 36 percent) of the proportion of assets under management invested in the asset class, which could actually mean that the endowment has internalized the skills to invest in private markets. The median size of US university and college endowments was $148 million in 2019 (see above), hinting at potential significant shifts in asset allocations currently and going forward.

There is also a direct link between larger size and higher performance (Table 1.4). The NACUBO concludes that "the larger cohorts outperformed based on the strong results of their large exposures to buyout and venture capital investments." Lerner et al. (2007) and Swensen (2000) argued that endowments and foundations outperformed other institutions in investing in private equity, notably thanks to their skills and access to top venture capital managers. The more experience they have, the more they diversify out of LBO funds (referred to as private equity in Table 1.3).

Lerner, et al. (2008) state that endowment size and admissions selectivity are a better predictor of performance than the allocation to private equity itself. Hence, they warn against simply copying the investment strategy of the leading endowments and state that "the same strategies that have worked so well for the endowments in the past two decades may not do so in the future." Sensoy et al. (2014) and Hobohm (2010) state that this outperformance was transitory and, in fact, that "there are no statistically or

---

[12]22.6 percent of 502.75 billion managed by 111 endowments, or an average of 1.02 billion per endowment.
[13]1.5 percent of 1.01 billion managed by 61 endowments, or an average of 0.25 million per endowment.

TABLE 1.3　Asset Allocation of US University and College Endowments (for Fiscal Year 2018–2019)

Allocation (in %)	Total institutions (equal weighted)	Over $1 bn	Over $500 mn–1 bn	Over $250– 500 mn	Over $100– 250 mn	Over $50– 100 mn	Over $25– 50 mn	Up to $25 mn
Number of institutions	786	111	84	88	197	152	93	61
Listed equities	50.9	31.3	45.3	46.9	53.2	54.6	57.7	60.6
Marketable alternative strategies	11.7	20.5	16.7	16.0	11.2	9.6	7.2	4.1
Listed fixed income	16.0	6.3	10.2	11.6	15.9	19.8	21.6	25.3
Short-term securities/cash/other	1.1	2.6	2.8	3.0	2.9	2.4	4.1	3.8
Listed real assets	2.8	1.6	3.0	2.6	3.5	2.9	4.7	2.3
Other	1.5	1.8	0.8	1.8	2.0	1.5	1.1	0.9
Private equity	6.2	13.6	9.6	8.8	5.7	4.6	2.3	1.1
Venture capital	2.2	9.0	4.0	2.4	1.3	0.6	0.6	0.4
Private debt	3.0	1.2	1.5	1.1	0.8	0.9	0.7	0.7
Private real estate	2.6	6.2	3.0	3.2	2.3	2.2	1.6	0.6
Private energy & mining	1.6	5.1	3.0	1.8	1.1	0.8	0.2	0.2
Private agriculture & timber	0.3	0.6	0.3	0.8	0.3	0.1	0.5	0
Total private markets	**15.9**	**35.7**	**21.4**	**18.1**	**11.5**	**9.2**	**5.9**	**3**

Note: Private equity includes leveraged buyouts (LBOs), mezzanine funds, merger and acquisition (M&A) funds, and international private equity. Marketable alternatives include hedge funds, absolute return, market neutral, long/short, 130/30, event-driven, and derivatives. On-campus real estate is included in the Short-term Securities/Cash/Other category.
Source: NACUBO-TIAA study of Endowments (2020), Authors. Data is dollar-weighted unless otherwise specified.

economically significant differences in returns across types of LPs[14]" (Sensoy et al., 2014).

This decrease in outperformance of the largest endowments is not only the consequence of a fall of venture capital returns (Hobohm, 2010) but also of a relative decline of the unique value of their skills: other investors have caught up. In fact, reinvestment decisions in funds contributed significantly to the high endowment performance in Lerner, Schoar, and Wongsunwai's study (1991–1998). In Sensoy et al.'s study, this phenomenon holds true for 1999–2006, but the margin of outperformance related to reinvestment decisions has decreased. Moreover, other investors generate similar outperformance in their reinvestment choices. Endowments and foundations exhibit no

---

[14]Limited Partners; that is, fund investors.

TABLE 1.4 10-Year Returns of US University and College Endowments

	Average %	Lower 5th Percentile %	Lower 10th Percentile %	Lower 25th Percentile %	Median %	Upper 75th Percentile %	Upper 90th Percentile %	Upper 95th Percentile %
Over $1 Billion	9.0	7.3	7.6	8.4	9.0	9.6	10.4	11.1
Over $500 Million to $1 Billion	8.5	7.0	7.3	8.0	8.4	9.0	9.8	10.3
Over $250 Million to $500 Million	8.4	6.4	7.1	7.7	8.4	9.1	9.8	10.0
Over $100 Million to $250 Million	8.3	6.3	7.0	7.5	8.3	9.0	9.6	10.3
Over $50 Million to $100 Million	8.2	6.2	6.7	7.5	8.2	8.9	9.6	9.9
Over $25 Million to $50 Million	8.4	5.4	6.4	7.7	8.5	9.1	10.0	10.6
$25 Million and Under	7.7	−5.8	5.6	7.6	8.7	9.7	10.3	11.2
All Institutions	8.4	6.5	7.1	7.8	8.5	9.1	9.9	10.4

Source: NACUBO-TIAA study of Endowments (2020).

special skill when choosing among first-time funds where there is limited or no track record. As a conclusion, Sensoy et al. (2014) state that "their access, choices, and performances have been unremarkable when compared with other investors."

Why is the endowment model so much in high regard, then? Because of a semantic confusion. There is no "endowment model" as illustrated by Brown et al. (2007), who state that "despite their ability to implement relatively unrestricted investment strategy, [...] university endowments [...] hold remarkably similar levels of asset allocation, [...] ultimately hurting [their] performance."

There is only a "Yale endowment's unique asset allocation" (see Insert 1); not really a model. In fact, anyone willing to reproduce the Yale endowment's performance would struggle not only for the lack of scale, expertise, and access, but also because most investors are taxed, while for a long time Yale's endowment was not. Therefore, any investor willing to apply the Yale endowment's asset allocation with the same results would need a multi-billion wealth, have the same access to fund managers, deploy the same expertise, and have the same know-how in a tax-free jurisdiction.

Insert 1: Yale endowment's unique asset allocation

Yale's endowment approach, in the word of its Chief Investment Officer David Swensen (2000) is a combination of six axioms:

- Emphasize equity-like assets (as opposed to fixed income).
- Hold a well-diversified portfolio (but not over-diversified). Its allocation policy was 23.2 percent in absolute return assets, 16.4 percent in equity, 15.9 percent in LBO, 4.9 percent in natural resources, 10.1 percent in real estate, 21.1 percent in venture capital, and 8.4 percent in cash and fixed income. Given the lack of granularity, it is difficult to assess what is the actual private markets exposure of Yale's endowment, but its private equity exposure alone reached 37 percent.
- Opportunistically invest at attractive valuations and rebalance regularly but avoid market timing.
- Use low-cost index for mature strategies to avoid unnecessary fees and costs.
- Invest in alternative assets to exploit market imperfections, thanks to external fund managers. In that respect, Yale's endowment systematically invests in private markets through funds (unlike Harvard's endowment, for example).
- Align interests of outside fund managers with the endowments. Private markets favor long-term relationships with established US fund managers with strong alignment of interests. Yale's endowment is unique in that it has access to high quality fund managers that might not accept new investors (*The Economist*, 2011).

It has a flexible governance structure as well as a dedicated, experienced, and stable team of investment specialists dedicated to asset allocation and fund selection. The scale of Yale's endowment reduces costs, and its long-standing presence

(continued)

(continued)

in private equity helps mitigate information asymmetries through its accumulated knowledge. Its reputation as a savvy investor opens doors and helps with getting favorable terms.

There is much debate about the value of the asset allocation of Yale's endowment. In particular, its performance used to be comparatively much higher than for its peer group. As of June 2019, the ten-year performance of Yale was 11.1 percent (The Yale endowment, 2019), which is still significantly higher than its peers (Table 1.4), but not as high as it used to be.

A few factors could explain this reduction of outperformance.

First, from 2010 to 2019, listed stocks have soared in value as interest rates have declined to unprecedented levels. Any endowment with a significant allocation to domestic listed stocks would have benefitted from this appreciation. This is visible with small endowments in Table 1.4. Whether this appreciation of listed stocks is sustainable and will continue remains to be seen. It is, therefore, risky to conclude that Yale's unique asset allocation (which, according to Swensen, 2000, contributed 20 percent to its overall performance) is falling back. Private market funds have yet to realize their performance over time (see Chapter 3) while listed stocks immediately record their progression.

Second, other endowments have started to adopt some of the rules defined by Swensen for Yale. The asset allocation advantage of Yale has thus started to erode. The opportunistic investments are much more difficult to operate when financial markets have essentially sustained a long evolution with little change. Nevertheless, Yale's endowment ten-year return of 11.1 percent still outperforms a standard portfolio. Norway's sovereign wealth fund, the Government Pension Fund Global (Norges Bank Investment Management, 2019), invests 70.8 percent of its $1.1 trillion[15] of assets in listed equities, 2.7 percent in unlisted real estate, and 26.5 percent in fixed income. In that respect, it is the equivalent of an "anti-endowment model." For over 20 years (December 1998 to December 2017), the annual return of the fund was 6.1 percent (4.2 percent after costs and inflation). Over an equivalent period (June 1998 to June 2017), Yale's endowment net return was 12.1 percent.

One criticism of Yale's endowment is that it recorded a 24.6 percent drop in value in 2009 (Harvard's 31.6 percent, 22 percent for all endowments, 27.2 percent for the S&P 500, and 13.2 percent for a traditional portfolio[16]). This was only the second drop in value in its history[17]. During the 2000–2004 crisis, its size increased by 20 percent while the S&P 500 dropped by 33 percent. The drop in value that occurred in 2009 should not be an issue for unconstrained investors with an infinite time horizon. Indeed, the endowment had recovered to its 2008 value level by 2014.

---

[15] 10,088 billion kroner at the end of 2019.
[16] Composed of 60 percent of listed equity and 40 percent of listed fixed income products.
[17] The first was in 1988 with –0.2 percent.

The biggest challenge for the endowment is that, over time, the reliance of Yale University on its endowment to finance itself has significantly increased: a third of its budget is now paid by its endowment (Harvard's endowment faces the same expectation). This is a significant shift for Yale's endowment: a regular and significant annual payout is expected. Additional constraints are imposed on Yale's endowment. Its incapacity to fulfil this expectation in 2009 demonstrates that an active liquidity management, with significant reserves, is a collateral requirement for an asset allocation embedding a significant share of private market funds.

Endowments and foundations face **specific challenges** when integrating private markets in their asset allocation. The most obvious one is, for the majority of them, their **limited size**, which prevents them from operating at scale and accumulating expertise. As mentioned above, this parameter is crucial to successfully integrate private markets in an asset allocation. Endowments and foundations can apply the same solutions suggested for family offices: teaming up or delegating their allocation to a third party.

The second challenge is an increase in **political pressure**, notably from students (endowments) and stakeholders (foundations) to avoid specific sectors of investments (such as oil and gas), to reduce the compensation of executives, and even to eliminate some asset classes that have a negative reputation (such as hedge funds). Addressing such issues is delicate. Eliminating industrial sectors from asset allocations can reduce diversification and prevent investors from capitalizing on an appreciation in value of companies in these sectors. The incentive structure of executives is of particular importance, as previously explained, to entice agents to take the appropriate level of risk and generate the expected performance. A strong governance and transparency (notably in benchmarking compensations) should help monitor executives and provide stakeholders and students with reassurance that these organizations are well managed and that the incentives are appropriate. Justifying the choice of asset classes requires a significant amount of pedagogy, especially when the rationale of this choice is technical.

The third challenge is that endowments, such as Yale and Harvard, record **higher constraints, namely a higher payout,** not only because of the excise tax, but also because their alma mater increasingly relies on them (see Insert 1). This is also true for smaller endowments. In fact, endowments struggle to determine the correct spending rate as illustrated by the wide variety of spending rules (Franz and Kranner, 2019). This is a specific challenge in terms of asset allocation, as endowments have to thoroughly stress-test their portfolios to evaluate their capacity to finance universities and colleges.

1.2.2.3   Sovereign Wealth Funds and Governmental Agencies

Sovereign wealth funds (SWF) are also largely unconstrained (Bortolotti et al., 2010), although their investment strategy can—or, for some authors, should (Cummine, 2016)—embed a political agenda (Dyck and Morese, 2010). In that respect, they are close to governmental agencies. Cummine (2016) lists ten definitions of SWF. A common definition (Demaria, 2015) is that SWF are "state-owned [or controlled[18]] investment fund[s] or entit[ies] that [are] commonly established from balance of payment surpluses, official foreign currency operations, the proceeds of privatizations, governmental transfer payments, fiscal surpluses, and/or receipts resulting from resource exports. The definition [...] exclude[s] [...] state-owned enterprises in the traditional sense, government-employee pension funds [...] or assets managed for the benefit of individuals[19]."

SWF "are not scrutinized by any financial regulatory body or investors, and their only reporting requirements are to sovereign states or sovereign owners who, in some cases, prefer less transparency" (Johan et al., 2013). According to them, 60 percent of SWF invested in private equity as of 2011 on a domestic and international base. Cummine (2016) counts seventy-nine of them: ten in North America, ten in South and Central America, twelve in Europe and Central Asia, seventeen in the Middle East, nineteen in East Asia and Australia, and eleven in Africa. Fifty-two SWF are born out of commodity-related income, while twenty-seven are not. The oldest is the Texas Permanent School Fund,[20] which was created in the US in 1854. The majority of SWF were established after 2000 (Cummine, 2016). They collectively manage an estimated $8 trillion as of 2019 according to Pitchbook. Their size varies significantly, but only eleven managed less than $1 billion in 2016[21] (Cummine, 2016).

Public and governmental agencies have a specific agenda. International institutions such as the European Investment Fund (EIF), the European Bank for Reconstruction and Development (EBRD), and the International Finance Corporation (IFC) support financial organizations (notably private equity funds) in emerging or more mature markets. National institutions such as the US Overseas Private Investment Corporation (OPIC) or the French Proparco have the same target. Others, such as the Banque Publique d'Investissement (BPI) in France, Ekuinas in Malaysia, Finlombarda Gestioni Societa di Gestione del Risparmio in Italy, the Finnish Industry Investment Fund in Finland, and Capital for Enterprise in the UK aim at developing their home country.

SWF face **specific challenges** when integrating private markets in their asset allocation, although an SSGA Research estimate, using data from the Sovereign Wealth Center, estimated that 28.7 percent of their assets were invested in private markets (51 percent of which through funds, 31 percent directly, and 18 percent through a combination of both [Massi et al., 2017]).

As governmental agencies and SWF share common characteristics (Johan et al., 2013, Bernstein et al., 2013), the investment policies of SWF can have **conflicting items on the agenda**. **Political meddling** is a challenge that these institutions have to face. Priorities can also shift in terms of importance or even to and from the agenda. Hobohm notes (2010), "it remains in most cases opaque to outsiders how large these funds are,

---

[18]See Johan et al. (2013).
[19]http://www.swfinstitute.org/sovereign-wealth-fund/, last accessed 26/7/2020.
[20]Although France's Caisse des Dépôts et Consignations, created by Napoleon in 1816, could in fact qualify as the first SWF (Cummine, 2016).
[21]The size of five is unknown.

who controls them, and what their agenda is", with the exception of the Government Pension Fund[22] of Norway, which sets a standard of transparency in the sector.

The investment policies of SWF notably depend on the origin of the capital, the level of development where the SWF is headquartered, and the structure and governance of the organization (Demaria, 2015). The motivations of SWF when it comes to investing are (Johan et al., 2013):

a. Insulation of the sovereign state's budget and economy against resource price and supply swings.
b. Conversion and transfer of income from non-renewable resources to future generations as a diversified portfolio of assets.
c. The putting to work of foreign currency reserves.
d. Planning for future liabilities (pension and other requirements).
e. Increasing political influence through foreign investments.

Hence, profit maximization is part of the motivation (a, b, c, d), but not all of it (e). Bernstein et al. (2013) conclude that SWFs are prone to poor investment decisions (due to political or agency considerations or not). They tend to **negate the idea that SWF are involved in certain sectors to fit with the social needs of the nation**, as these funds invest domestically when equity prices are high (and thus when other sources of capital are available). They conclude that **SWFs are trend chasers**, investing at home and abroad when equity prices are higher.

Johan et al. (2013) state that SWFs exhibit a certain **home bias** when it comes to private equity investing as confirmed by Bortolotti et al. (2010) and Bernstein et al. (2013), notably for SWF where political leaders are actively involved. Moreover, SWFs are more likely to invest in target nations where investor protection is low, and where political relations between the SWF and the target nation are weak. Cultural differences play a marginal positive role when a SWF invests abroad. This differentiates SWF when investing in private equity from other institutional investors.

However, Johan et al. (2013) limit their analysis to direct investments. SWFs invest directly abroad only in private firms of a significant size in order to bear the time and resources necessary for an efficient monitoring (what Hobohm, 2010, labels the **constrained-attention hypothesis**); this is related to the **large size** of SWF (in general) and the **lack of resources**.

Unlike family offices, endowments, and foundations, SWF have to tackle the challenge of investing large amounts. Very few assets can accommodate the deployment of hundreds of millions per investment. The average SWF manages $101 billion and allocates $29 billion to private markets. Assuming that 60 percent go to private equity and are deployed over five years, this means that $3.49 billion have to be deployed each year. At $100 million per investment, the average SWF has to do thirty-five investments per year (at 50 million, it is 70). This is a significant amount of work. Over five years,

---

[22]The GPFG does not invest in private markets, except directly in real estate and renewable infrastructures.

the number of investments to monitor reaches 175 (or 350). This requires significant resources.

Moreover, this restricts the investment universe of SWF. Fund managers limit the weight of a single investor in a fund to 15–20 percent. If a SWF puts 100 million per fund, this means that the fund has to reach a size of at least 500–700 million. This excludes most of venture capital, growth capital, small LBO funds, and mid-size LBO funds. Hobohm (2010) notes that SWF tend to invest in large LBO funds[23]. However, as this sector of private markets tends to mature (and returns progressively decrease), this approach might reach its limits. To be able to invest smaller amounts, SWF would need to recruit experienced teams with the right incentives. However, this might go against the political agenda of the governments of the states they belong to.

1.2.2.4   Pension Funds

Impavido (2012) defines pension funds as "pools of savings accumulated during the working life of individuals. At any given point in time, they are the sum of the flow of the employer and employee contributions (in the specific case of occupational pension plan), investment income, and eventual benefits paid." In theory, pension funds should be an ideal match with private market investments: the long-term liabilities of the first allow them to invest over the mid- to long-term in the assets of the second. Indeed, if pension funds do not have an infinite or multi-generational placement horizon, they invest over the adult life of individuals. At times, individuals decide to liquidate their plan upon retirement, but others decide to keep their pension investment and require a regular payout to face their expenses. In the former case, the time horizon is the expected employment time of the individual. In the latter, it is effectively the expected lifetime of the individual. It was estimated that pension funds managed about $35 trillion of assets in 2016 (Binham and Jenkins). In 2019, IP&E stated that the assets of the 1,000 largest European pension funds reached €7.72 trillion (included in this total is the SWF of Norway).

According to Impavido (2012), the definition of pension plans "varies from country to country depending on the specific pension plan or scheme arrangement." The latter part of the definition is the source of the main challenge when characterizing what a pension fund is (or is not) and what are the constraints that apply to it. Occupational pension funds can be legally separated from the employer (the plan sponsor) or not (they stay on the balance sheet of the sponsor). In the latter case, the plan member can be affected by the bankruptcy of the sponsor. Pension plans can also be personal, and therefore autonomous.

Pension products can also be sold by insurance companies to sponsors or individuals. Collective pension funds pool assets of different sponsors; group pension funds

---

[23] As for direct investments, the study of Johan, et al. (2013, Appendix A) shows that, with the exception of Temasek, GIC, and to some extent the Qatar Investment Authority, none of the SWF have a sufficiently high number of private equity investments to have built a diversified and balanced portfolio. Their strategy might be purely opportunistic or based on cherry-picking within co-investment agreements that they have set with specific funds in which they are invested (see Chapter 3 for more details and explanations).

pool assets of individuals or companies in the same pension plan. Individual pension funds do not pool assets and are based on individual accounts (such as voluntary 401(k) plans in the US). Pension funds can restrict (closed) or extend (open) membership to a specific group of individuals.

The diversity of pension funds and plans is compounded by the variability of the constraints they are subject to. One is the **regulations**, which vary a lot from one jurisdiction to another. Regulations notably explain that some pension funds invest in private markets, and others do not. Indeed, to add to the complexity, there are two categories of pension funds. Teall (2019) mentions that "defined benefit plans (DB) specify payments that employees will receive when they retire, and defined contributions (DC) plans define employer and employee contributions, but actual benefits depend on fund investment performance." Mendoza (2020) quotes Vanguard when stating that more than 100 million US citizens are covered by DC plans managing $7.5 trillion. As mentioned in Introduction, many US pension funds are underfunded.

The Defined Contribution Institutional Investment Association offers some perspectives about the integration of PE in the asset allocation of DC plans [Table 1.5].

The difference in performance between DB and DC pension plans over 18 years is estimated at 110 basis points (DCIIA, 2015) and can partially be attributed to the exposure of DB pension plans to private equity. DC plans have outperformed in stock selection. Employer stocks have also helped DC plans to generate outperformance (as the outcome is above the total average for both DC and DB plans). DB plans did better in fixed income than DC ones.

TABLE 1.5   Asset Mix and Returns of US DC and DB Plans (1997–2014)

Asset class	Asset Mix		18-Year Returns	
	DB	**DC**	**DB**	**DC**
Traditional				
Broad or large-cap stock	26%	30%	6.4%	7.9%
Small-cap stock	6%	8%	8.8%	9.8%
Foreign stock	23%	8%	4.5%	6.6%
Employer stock	0%	20%	n/a	8.6%
Fixed income	31%	10%	7.5%	6.1%
Stable value / GICS	n/a	17%	n/a	4.6%
Cash	2%	8%	2.6%	2.9%
Alternatives				
Real estate, REITS and other real estate	5%	n/a	9.5%	n/a
Hedge funds	2%	n/a	7.6%	n/a
Private equity	4%	n/a	11.1%	n/a
Total	*100%*	*100%*	*8.0%*	*6.9%*

Note: n/a means "not available."
Source: CEM Benchmarking and DCIIA (2015). 3,037 US DB plans and 2,020 US DC plan observations. Returns are the compounded average of the annual averages for each asset class. Asset mix percentages are the simple average of the 18 years of annual averages.

Overall, most of the outperformance of DB plans comes from alternatives, and first among them is private equity (followed by real assets and hedge funds). A joint study mandated by the Defined Contribution Alternatives Association (DCALTA) and the Institute for Private Capital concludes that "investing in private funds always increases average portfolio returns and reliably increases Sharpe ratios" (Brown et al., 2019). Using a sample of 2,515 US private equity funds (1,121 leveraged buyout funds and 1,394 venture capital funds, see Chapter 3 for definitions) to create simulated portfolios for the period 1987–2017 for DC pension funds, they identify a systematic and reliable outperformance of the portfolios including private equity funds.

Cornelius et al. (2013) explain that the secular shift from DB pension plans to DC have important consequences: defined benefits pension plans imply a transferability of the pension claims and thus a high degree of liquidity, as the benefits are not "portable from one employer to another." The portability is ensured by using cash. Assets, therefore, have to offer the option of being converted into cash at fairly short notice. This raises some difficulty, as private market funds or assets require fairly long and rather unpredictable holding periods. Thus, US DC plans were, for a long time, deemed unsuitable to welcome private market funds or assets. This has changed.

The US Department of Labor (DoL) issued an information letter[24] that states that DC retirement plans, such as individual 401(k) plans, may offer private equity investments in compliance with the obligations set up by the Employee Retirement Income Security Act[25] (ERISA). Indeed, if the owners of the plans can direct investments, it is the responsibility of the fiduciaries of the plan to select investments compliant with regulations. The letter of the DoL indicates that including private equity in a multi-asset class vehicle would be compliant and indicates the factors to select and offer such vehicle.

This is a significant change. Historically, the interpretation was that private equity investments raised ERISA fiduciary concerns, as they were not seen as prudent investments. High fees (see Chapter 3) as well as difficulties for private equity products to match ERISA valuation requirements and risk profiles raised concerns. The long-term horizon and the lack of liquidity mentioned above were probably the most pressing concerns. Cornelius et al. (2013) rightfully pointed out that the reliance on modern portfolio theories to manage risk places too much emphasis on historical asset return variances as a measure of risk and measures of correlations between asset classes. The result is too static and "gains from diversification often proved to be illusive." They recommend switching to less granular asset allocations with a higher emphasis on asset-specific risks. This reasoning is not limited to pension funds but applies to any investor willing to develop an asset allocation.

---

[24]US Department of Labor, Information Letter, June 3, 2020 (https://www.dol.gov/agencies/ ebsa/about-ebsa/our-activities/resource-center/information-letters/06-03-2020, last accessed 30/07/2020). Although the DoL letter refers to private equity investments, it is generally admitted that its principles could apply to private market investments at large.

[25]Enacted on September 2, 1974, the ERISA is an American federal tax and labor law which establishes standards for private pension plans, in order to protect employees, participants, and beneficiaries. It notably sets disclosure requirements and establishes standards of conducts for fiduciaries.

Pension funds face **specific challenges** when integrating private markets in their asset allocation. **Regulations**, already mentioned above, are one. They can define constraints in terms of asset allocation. In Chile and Switzerland, pension funds cannot invest more than 15 percent of their total assets in alternatives. In Mexico, pension funds can only invest through listed private market structures (CKD) that invest locally, reinforcing the **home bias** noted previously. Nigerian pension funds are also subject to **home bias** by regulation, as three of the five mandatory DC retirement savings accounts have to invest at least 2.5 percent of their assets in alternatives. One invests in private equity funds, which must invest at least 60 percent of their capital in local companies or projects. Chilean and Nigerian regulations also set criteria for the selection of private market funds, such as a minimum number of years of experience.

Another is **pressure on costs**. For example, in the UK, pension plans are subject to a 75-basis point cap on the total charges to an individual member. This effectively limits the exposure to private market funds, as they charge higher management and performance fees (see Chapter 3). A study from the British Business Bank (2019) shows that allocating five percent to venture or growth capital funds would not be expected to breach the charges cap. A review of this cap has been launched in June 2020 by the Department for Work and Pensions.

Swiss and Australian pension funds do not have to comply with charges on caps, but their boards (and the public) regularly **benchmark them in terms of performance and expenses**. The Australian Securities and Investments Commission has amended reporting regulations in November 2019 to simplify how fees and costs are reported as of September 2020. As the benchmarking is against the average of all their peers, and not against pension funds with similar asset allocations, this exercise can prove to be abrasive when it comes to expenses. This also applies to Swiss pension funds.

In Switzerland, expenses are measured thanks to the Total Expense Ratio (TER), which divides the total operating expenses by the average net assets (expressed in percent). If a pension fund invests a higher share in alternatives than the average, its TER will be higher than average, and the staff could be subject to criticism. The TER can also be magnified by the fact that private market funds deploy capital progressively (see Chapter 3) while managers collect fees on the full size of the fund. To avoid a sudden and significant increase of their TER when including private market funds in their portfolio, pension fund managers can negotiate a different fee schedule with private market fund managers (for example, by calculating fees on the capital deployed). This usually requires setting up a specific mandate, which requires a significant amount of capital (see Chapter 3).

The TER is also not performance adjusted. As explained by Morkoetter and Wetzer (2016), the average TER "of the participating [Swiss] pension funds is 0.6 percent, approximately 75 percent of which are portfolio management costs. [. . .] Costs of some private market investments, in comparison, are significant but [. . .] in private equity, average investments costs of 5.8 percent are overcompensated by gross returns of 12.1 percent; which results in net returns of 6.4 percent, the highest net returns of all major asset classes." Urdan and Gelb (2015) stated that "spending less on fees does not necessarily translate to higher net returns." They concluded that "if private investments can beat public equities by 300 bps per year (as commonly targeted), then shifting 15 percent of assets from public equities to private investments would boost a pension fund's total portfolio return by 45 bps per year."

Costs and TER are also related to **size of assets under management**. Dyck and Pomorski (2016) explain that DB pension plans "with significant holdings in private equity earn substantially greater returns than plans with small holdings [...]. A one standard deviation increase in PE holding is associated with 4 percent greater returns per year. Up to one third of this outperformance comes from lower costs as DB pension funds deploying larger amounts in private equity save on 'costly intermediation by avoiding fund-of-funds and investing directly.'" They conclude, in line with the beginning of this chapter, that "superior gross returns [are] only partially explained by access and experience." They conjecture that "larger PE investors have superior due diligence and ability to bridge information asymmetries."

Another constraint that pension funds face is **liquidity and capital requirements**. Broeders et al. (2020) describe liquidity requirements as the combination of "short-term pension payments and collateral requirements following margin calls on derivative contracts. The cash required for pension payments over the next year is well predictable." Regulations require DB plans to have "sufficient capital to manage the risks they are exposed to, such as financial market risks and longevity risk." The strategic asset allocation of a pension fund is an "optimization of the trade-offs between different risk factors for a given level of required capital."

Ang et al. (2014) show that an illiquidity risk defined as "the restriction that an asset cannot be traded for intervals of uncertain duration" leads to an increase in risk aversion. In particular, "uncertainty about the length of the illiquidity interval [...] is a primary determinant of the cost of illiquidity." For example, "investors are willing to forgo 2 percent of their wealth to hedge against illiquidity crises occurring once every 10 years." This could explain the rather low allocation of pension funds to private equity.

However, as explained by Bass (2014), if "pension fund executives [...] historically have been willing to pay a premium for liquidity", this "liquidity can be an illusion." Moreover, as we will show in subsequent chapters, it is possible to assess the illiquidity (as defined by Ang et al. above) of private market fund investments. This should reduce the anxiety of pension fund managers and provide them with a new perspective on the trade-offs they have to optimize.

Cagnati and Asfour (2017) address the question of pension payments and the time horizon. They offer a glidepath analysis, in which they differentiate an accumulation phase (when the individual is aged 25 to 45), a transition phase (aged 45 to 65) and distribution (aged 65+). These brackets could be refined but are illustrative. They decide to allocate 20 percent of the portfolio to private markets in the first phase; then decrease progressively to 15 percent during the second; and then to zero over 15 years in the third. In line with other studies above, they identify a 40 to 80 basis point increase of performance for the portfolio including private markets with a lower risk.

An additional challenge might be **political meddling**. An example was the pay-to-play scandal in the US (Demaria, 2020, Chapter 7): board members of public pension funds favored investments funds placed by specific agents in exchange for financial contributions to their political campaigns by these agents. As a result, placement agents are banned in specific jurisdictions. This is an illustration of the potential risks associated with the governance of pension funds. Similarly to endowments, pension funds might be subject to the pressure of their stakeholders (current or future pensioners), for example, to avoid asset classes or apply extra-financial criteria.

1.2.2.5 Insurance Groups

Insurance groups are another group of constrained investors who are driven by **liabilities** and thus the risks that they cover. They face **specific challenges** when integrating private markets in their asset allocation. Property-casualty insurers usually have to provide defined amounts upon the materialization of an event, while life insurers offer retirement benefits and wealth accumulation features. For Hobohm (2010), property-casualty insurers behave like DB pension funds in many respects. Life insurers behave more like DC pension funds according to him.

The **focus on liabilities** is a **defining feature**. The asset allocation of insurance groups depends on the matching of assets and liabilities in so-called asset and liability management (ALM). This exercise consists of managing liquidity, interest rate, credit, and operational risks to optimize investment decisions. The core challenge of insurance groups is to meet future expected claims while generating a satisfying performance from investments.

This means that **insurance groups have a structurally higher allocation to fixed income** products. Cash flows have to be relatively predictable, and if possible, recurrent. One of the current challenges is to execute such a mandate in a context of low interest rates (see Introduction). Real estate has emerged as a preferred route, as it delivers recurring income (rents) that is usually protected against inflation. It also provides interesting features such as the predictable depreciation of its book value and the potential appreciation of its market value.

As for pension funds, insurance groups are sensitive to **duration risk** (referred to as illiquidity risk in the previous section). In particular, the standard approach of private markets through closed-end funds (see Chapter 3), implies that they will be limited to no distributions during the first years of the program (see Chapter 5). This could be addressed by blending direct lending and core real asset funds in higher proportion in the private market program than for other investors.

Regulations are also a significant constraint, notably as insurance groups have to match solvency ratios. It is difficult to describe comprehensively the regulations of insurance groups as they are generally country specific.

A few, such as the Solvency II Directive in Europe, provide an illustration of the nature and impact of regulations. The Committee of European Insurance and Occupational Pensions Supervisors (CEIOPS) and the European Commission have set up capital charges for private equity fund investments within the standard formula. It is 49 percent (plus or minus 10 percent for symmetric adjustments for taking into account market movements over the previous 36 months) for standard private equity investments (referred to as type 2 equities). Braun et al. (2014) noted that "private equity is overly punished by the standard approach" and that "life insurers aiming to exploit the asset class" potential may expect significantly lower capital charges when applying an [. . .] internal model." They concluded that "it can be less costly to increase the exposure to private rather than public equity." For equities listed on regulated markets in

EEA and OECD ("type 1"), the capital charge is 39 percent plus or minus a symmetric adjustment of 10 percent.

Barton and Kaur (2019) note that infrastructure equities are subject to a capital charge of 30 percent, and that infrastructure corporate equities are subject to a charge of 36 percent. Both are subject to an adjustment (respectively 77 percent and 92 percent of +/- 10 percent). Barton and Kaur (2019) also note that equity held through private equity funds qualify as type 1, thus reducing the capital charges. The capital charge is reduced to 22 percent for long term investments (also referred to as investments of a strategic nature, where the insurer owns at least 20 percent of the voting rights in a demonstrated stable and close relationship). Further changes to reduce the capital charge associated with investing in private European SMEs is being discussed at the time of writing.

Given the high proportion of fixed income investments, the challenge of insurance groups is to **invest in private markets at scale**. Indeed, if capital charges are becoming more favorable, insurance groups will still need to gain experience. An area where they can capitalize significantly is their modeling capacities. In particular, along the lines of what is developed in Chapter 5, they can plan and stress-test distributions. Given the fact that many of them never completely retreated (unlike banks) from private equity investments, they can also progressively ramp up their program and leverage their expertise and reputation. They also can use their data as an internal model (instead of using the standard one) to possibly reduce further their capital charges.

1.2.2.6   Banks

Historically, banks would invest on their own account or on behalf of their clients. In the first case, as they invest from their balance sheet, they would essentially be constrained by **regulations** and solvency ratios. Economies of scope are [...] particularly important for banks (Hobohm, 2010). Banks assume different functions: lending to economic agents, offering financing solutions (private placements, IPOs) and advice, arranging and handling transactions (M&A, brokerage), structuring products and offering services, and investing in companies; "The latter function can be done on their own balance sheet" (proprietary trading, private equity). According to Hobohm (2010), "in doing so investment corporations employ the same principles of asset allocation as others."

Brooke and Penrice (2009) explain that direct investments in private equity is not a natural function for a bank, which potentially leads to conflicts of interest if it acts simultaneously as a creditor and investor in the same company. To address this, Demaria (2015) notes that the US Bank Holding Company Act (1956) allowed banks to invest in companies as long as they did not hold more than five percent of voting rights and 25 percent of total equity. The Small Business Act (1958) allowed the banks in the US to invest through small business investment companies (SBIC) in private equity. The Gramm-Leach-Bliley Act (1999) allowed banks to set up holding companies to invest directly in companies (ten-year holding period for direct investments and fifteen-year period for investments through private equity funds).

More recent regulations are essentially preventing most of the banks from being investors in private market funds. The Basel II Agreements required a prudential coverage of private equity fund investments of 24–32 percent, which was dissuasive. The Basel III Agreements added a cap of 5 percent of their balance sheet for banks to invest in private equity. In the US, the Dodd-Frank Wall Street Reform and Consumer Protection Act[26] of 2010 (which came into effect in 2015) restricted the ability of banks to invest for their own account (notably in paragraph 619, also referred to as the "Volcker Rule") up to 5 percent. On January 30, 2020, the Federal Reserve suggested rolling back the rules that limit bank investments in venture capital. The changes were adopted on June 25, 2020.

Banks invest in private equity for benefits other than pure financial returns. There are, therefore, **extra-financial parameters** to their asset allocation. Lerner et al. (2007) and Ivashina and Kovner (2011) show that banks cross-sell other services generating fees thanks to their lending activity. This lending activity is done at a lower rate thanks to a reduction of information asymmetry and also as a means to generate these cross-selling opportunities.

Banks also advise their clients through mandates. Depending on who is the client, the asset allocation is adapted. Banks are agents in that context, with all the dynamics associated with this status. We refer to the elements above in that respect.

1.3 SUMMARY

Throughout this chapter, we have pointed out that investors operate trade-offs to generate the highest financial performance possible within a set of identified constraints. This has to be done in a larger context, where heterogeneous investors handle behavioral biases.

In the context of private markets investing, that is to say of low, asymmetrical, and incomplete information, **noise** (rumors, outdated or partial information) can have significant consequences on the behavior of private market fund investors. Information on private markets is also subject to a significant **time lag**. **Home-investing bias** also affects fund investors. Finally, most of investors are **overconfident** and believe that they are better than average.

To avoid behavioral biases, a **self-assessment** by the investor is necessary. With an objective assessment of the knowledge of investments in private markets, the investor's experience, network built, and time spent in the asset class, an investor can identify gaps.

Then **asset allocation policies** and **investment decision guidelines and processes** (human resources, incentive policies, adequate resource management combined with sound investment objectives) should help to systematically prevent behavioral biases. Finally, investors can avoid biases through an **active control and monitoring of interactions between principals and agents**, notably to identify, discuss, and eliminate the beliefs of the latter.

---

[26]US Public Law No: 111-203 (http://www.gpo.gov/fdsys/pkg/PLAW-111publ203/html/PLAW-111publ203.htm, last accessed 16/8/2020).

Investors differ significantly from each other. **A multi-dimensional analysis** shows that investors can be classified according to different parameters that have significant consequences on their asset allocation:

- Their **time horizon**. Institutional investors have a specific timeline ranging from years to decades.
- The **regulatory pressure** under which investors operate. The lowest regulatory pressure is on family offices and HNWI, while the highest level applies to pension funds, insurance groups, and banks.
- The **size of assets under management**. Investors with lower assets under management can diversify more easily in terms of strategy, but their small size limits them in their ability to diversify geographically. They do not benefit from economies of scale and lower costs. Investors with large assets under management benefit from cost savings and superior gross returns but can suffer from inertia and portfolio concentration.
- The length and diversity of their **experience**, which is a function of the total capital deployed in private equity. The experience is connected to the **level of sophistication of investors**, which is the result of accumulated know-how and knowledge, access to qualified internal resources, and a clear vision and understanding of private markets. Sophisticated investors can have a solid reputation and thus have an influence on fund managers.

Some investment constraints are **specific** to an investor. They can be strategic or voluntary (ESG) but can also be political. Other types of constraints are **common** but apply at variable degrees: liabilities, regulation, tolerance for risks, and expected returns. The main categories of private market investors are:

- **Family offices, multi-family offices, and HNWI.** They represent the **least regulated category of investors**. Their **time horizon** can vary significantly from one family office to another as well as their **appetite for risk** as it depends on the individual preferences of family members, their age, and on how recent and large the wealth is. The differences in those parameters lead to the setup of specific targets, return expectations, and operational structures. The share of private equity in the asset allocation depends on the risk appetite and the entrepreneurial spirit of the family members. As the structure evolves from single-family member, to limited member, to multi-generational family office, the risk appetite is reduced along with the entrepreneurial spirit. Choices are focused on **risk reduction and return generation,** and this translates into a net preference toward LBOs followed by funds of funds and replacement capital. **Family offices do not target the highest risk/return profile.** They can face **specific challenges** as they might need to balance the allocation around the existing "anchor" assets of the family that they serve. They need to accommodate shifting preferences and requests from the family members. They have to deal with their fairly modest size.
- **Endowments and foundations.** Their **infinite time horizon and limited constraints** allow them to focus on the **maximization of their wealth**. Some of them, especially the large ones, are able to invest in new and novel asset classes and therefore can have a **different portfolio structuring than other investors**. The **size**

discrepancy of endowments and foundations has a direct consequence on their asset allocation: the larger the size of the endowment, the higher the allocation to private markets and other alternative strategies. **The size of assets under management** plays a role in the performance of the investments, as it determines the **use of internal or external agents to perform the allocation**. There is a direct link between larger size and higher performance, but we are currently seeing a **decrease in outperformance of largest endowments** as a consequence of a fall of venture capital returns but also a relative decline of the unique value of their skills. Endowments and foundations face **specific challenges when integrating private markets in their asset allocation:** their limited size, an increase in political pressure notably from students and stakeholders, and higher payouts.

– **Sovereign wealth funds (SWF) and governmental agencies.** SWF are close to government agencies and **largely unconstrained.** They are not scrutinized by any financial regulatory body. Their only reporting requirements are to sovereign states or sovereign owners. They face **specific challenges when integrating private markets in their asset allocation:** as governmental agencies and SWF share common characteristics, their investment policies can have conflicting items on the agenda, and they have to deal with political meddling. Profit maximization is part of the motivation for investment but not the only one. Some authors say that SWFs are prone to poor investment decisions and tend to negate the idea that SWFs are involved in certain sectors to fit with the social needs of the nation, concluding that SWFs are trend chasers investing at home and abroad when equity prices are higher. Unlike family offices, endowments, and foundations, SWF have to tackle the challenge of investing large amounts, and their investment universe is thus restricted (exclusion of venture capital, growth capital, and LBO funds).

– **Pension funds.** Their **diversity** is compounded by the **variability of the constraints** they are subject to and notably the **regulations,** which vary a lot from one jurisdiction to another and explain that some pension funds invest in private markets and others do not (two categories of pension funds: defined benefit and defined contributions). Pension funds also face **specific challenges:** the **regulations** can reinforce their home bias. The pressure on costs or benchmarking in terms of performance and expenses can create distortions. **Political meddling** can also be an issue.

– **Insurance groups** are driven by liabilities and thus the risks they cover. Their asset allocation depends on the matching of assets and liabilities (ALM). They are sensitive to duration risk. Regulations are also a significant constraint, as insurance groups have to match solvency ratios. Their challenge is to invest in private markets at scale. An area where they can capitalize significantly is their modeling capacities.

– **Banks.** If banks invest on their own accounts, they will be essentially constrained by **regulations** and solvency ratios. Recent regulations are essentially preventing most of the banks from being investors in private markets funds. **Banks invest in private equity for other benefits than pure financial returns,** and there are therefore extra-financial parameters to their asset allocation. Banks also advise their clients through mandates, and depending on who is the client, the asset allocation is adapted.

CHAPTER 2

Asset Allocation: Models, Limits, and Adaptations

In a nutshell

This chapter will notably explore the "standard asset allocation approach," the most frequently used when constructing a portfolio of assets, and its friction points with private markets. Indeed, private markets do not fit neatly in this standard framework. To be creative, investors have to follow simpler, less precise but rather robust principles of asset allocation.

As seen in Chapter 1, investors are subject to common and specific constraints in their effort to deploy capital and generate returns. This effort is largely determined by the investors' liabilities, particularly their future payouts. An asset allocation is the result of the investors' effort to match these liabilities with expected returns, while managing the risks associated with this effort. The CFA Institute refers to asset allocation[1] as "both the process and the result of determining long-term (strategic) exposures to the available asset classes (or risk factors) that make up the investor's opportunity set." In that respect, the strategic asset allocation (SAA) is "the first and primary step in translating the [investor]'s circumstances, objectives, and constraints into an appropriate portfolio [...] for achieving the [investor]'s goals within the [investor]'s tolerance for risk."

As explained by Marston (2011), the "trade-off between return and risk is central to all asset allocation," leading to the construction of a portfolio of assets. For that purpose, assets are analyzed individually in their various characteristics. We will refer to this as an **intrinsic analysis**. Assets are also analyzed in relation to each other. According to Marston (2011), "The correlation between one asset and another is central to this exercise." We will refer to this as a **comparative analysis**. Then, the combination of intrinsic and comparative analyses is tested under various market and economic conditions. We will refer to this as an **external analysis**.

---

[1] *Principles of Asset Allocation*, Introduction (https://www.cfainstitute.org/membership/professional-development/refresher-readings/2020/principles-asset-allocation, last accessed August 7, 2020).

Theoretically, different asset classes should be significantly uncorrelated and thus react differently to market and economic events. The diversification embedded in a portfolio of non-correlated assets reduces the risk of losses for the investor. As a result, the portfolio is more resilient. Cleverly combining assets should then lead to the generation of a specific level of returns for a corresponding level of risk.

This approach of asset allocation is an "asset-only" exercise. It is the application of a so-called mean-variance approach, which uses the average past performances of assets (returns) and the variation of these performances (risks) to build optimized portfolios. Although heavily criticized (as summed up by Marston, 2011, and the CFA Institute[2], 2020), this approach is the most frequently used and will be referred to as the standard asset allocation framework in this chapter.

This framework assigns a percentage of the overall pool of capital to each of the asset classes. This triggers the following questions: What is an asset class? Do private markets qualify as one? (Section 1). In practice, yes, but private markets do not fit neatly in the standard asset allocation framework. This creates frictions (Section 2). As a result, investors have to be creative and follow simpler but rather robust principles of asset allocation (Section 3).

2.1 ARE PRIVATE MARKETS AN ASSET CLASS?

Academic literature, and notably Markowitz (1952), identified two categories of assets: listed stocks and listed bonds. They are usually categorized as "traditional assets," to which cash can be added. Subdivisions have appeared over time as assets behave differently under stress and depending on specific market conditions.

For example, listed stocks are subdivided (see, for example, Marston, 2011), in large capitalization, mid-sized capitalization, small capitalization, and even micro capitalization; or growth stocks and value stocks. As for bonds, they can be subdivided into investment grade and high yield, sovereign or corporate, as well as short term or long term.

Investors can also split traditional assets according to their geographical origin, between local and foreign, illustrating the creeping home bias that permeates even academic literature, or more commonly, developed, emerging, and frontier markets.

Alternative assets regroup non-traditional assets such as real estate, infrastructure, foreign currencies, gold, commodities (natural resources, precious metals, nonferrous metals, agricultural products), derivatives, insurance products, and hedge funds. Private markets are also classified as alternative assets.

However, the classification of some these assets as alternative is debatable. For instance, real estate firms can be listed on the stock exchange. Real estate can then

---

[2]Criticisms include the issue that asset allocations are highly sensitive to small changes in the inputs and are highly concentrated in a subset of available asset classes. Moreover, the mean-variance optimization does not take into account skewness and kurtosis, or costs and taxes. Worse, while the asset allocations may appear diversified across assets, the sources of risk may not be diversified. Another criticism is that the mean-variance optimization has no direct connection to the factors affecting liabilities or payouts.

be traditional (through listed real estate investment trusts, for example) and alternative (as direct holdings or through private real estate funds). Hedge funds are in essence investment strategies, using traditional and alternative assets as instruments to operate. For some of them, their approach can be replicated thanks to exchange-traded funds. Some hedge fund strategies can thus be either traditional and passively replicate a set of investment rules or alternative and actively managed.

Private markets include private equity, debt, and real assets (Chapter 3). Dealing with non-listed assets, it could be argued that, indeed, they are part of the universe of alternative assets. A counterargument is that private equity belongs to the world of stocks, private debt to the world of credit (as bonds do), and real assets, which encompass real estate, infrastructure, energy, and a few other assets, to their respective investment niches. The proponents of the latter position argue that private markets could be seen as a series of investment strategies, like hedge funds.

2.1.1   The Asset Class of Private Markets

Asset allocation is about identifying and exploiting investment opportunities. Investors identify areas of the economy where value will be created and try to capture some of this value creation. For that purpose, they provide the financial resources to the agents that will operationally create the value and will be compensated for the risk that this process entails.

If private market investments are seen as a unique way to unlock the potential for value creation, then they are an asset class. If they are seen as an extension of an equity or credit risk, then it could be argued that they are not as such an asset class.

Private markets are usually considered as an asset class given their specific value creation and their ability to finance assets that listed markets do not usually cater to (see Chapter 3). For the rest of the book, we will focus on private market funds (see Insert 1).

Insert 1 – A Focus on Private Market Funds

It is important to note that throughout this book, we will exclusively focus on private market funds. This choice is motivated by multiple reasons:

- If data is scarce for funds, it is even scarcer at the underlying level. Some initiatives such as EDHECInfra[3] have managed to document underlying infrastructure assets and tackle the challenge of fair value. This approach is stimulating. Assuming that it can be applied to the whole private markets' universe, the method would deliver a wealth of information and facilitate the process of asset allocation. However, to our knowledge, there is no equivalent to EDHECInfra available for private equity and private debt. The closest source is

---

[3]https://edhec.infrastructure.institute/.

probably CEPRES's database, which provides some data on underlying private market investments.

– Value creation is, so far, documented at fund level. Moreover, investors are privileging funds for their private market investments. Direct and co-investments are growing, but they still represent a fairly small portion of investors' allocation (see Chapter 3).

– Funds are not just a technical instrument. Their setup, management, and operations have consequences in terms of performance, risk, and liquidity (see Chapter 3). As investors use funds or funds of funds to deploy capital in private markets, we will focus on this type of instrument.

These three reasons have led us to using the fund level for our approach of asset allocation with private markets. As more granular data becomes more available in the future, this framework could be adapted to include them.

Still, data quality and availability in private markets is not satisfactory (see Introduction, as well as Chapters 3 and 5): fair values are not transactional but appraised by fund managers, available with significant lag (usually three to six months), and the result of a conservative application of different valuation methods (summed up in the IPEV, see Chapter 3). We acknowledge these limitations, as well as those of the benchmarks, and advise readers to keep them in mind when reading this book and applying some of the techniques.

There are, nevertheless, positive features associated with the data we use in this book. First, we use three main sources, which are complementary. The main source is Cambridge Associates' database, which offers high-quality data, over long periods of time. Our complementary source is eFront's database (Pevara), which offers an equivalent level of quality but over a shorter period of time. This source provides a different geographical emphasis and allows us to cross-check results and run additional tests. The third source is StepStone's database of senior loans. Given the relative lack of coverage of senior/direct lending in the databases of Cambridge Associates and eFront, this source helps us document this specific strategy and cross-check our results.

The complementarity of our sources and the opportunities to cross-check results should limit one of the recurring issues with private market data: these three sources are, to some extent, individually affected by some **selection bias**. None is a total market index or benchmark. Cambridge Associates selects and monitors private market funds for its clients and thus sources data directly from managers and investors. It also tracks funds in which its clients did not invest. These funds can be added or removed from the database if managers start or cease to cooperate. This is why sample sizes and data can vary over time. eFront gathers data from fund managers and investors and aggregates them. The selection bias comes from the perimeter of its client pool. StepStone also gathers data on underlying loans, but its access is limited to the products it selects and invests in on behalf of its clients.

It is not possible to technically combine these three sources. Cambridge Associates' and eFront's data are provided as aggregates. Combining them in a sample would lead to double counting some funds and possibly aggregate data

(continued)

(continued)

that is extracted differently[4]. As for StepStone's data, it is more granular, focusing on underlying data. We have modeled funds with the underlying data, but it is delicate to integrate the result with actual funds from Cambridge Associates and eFront.

Another positive feature of the data we had access to is that it is largely unaffected by **survivorship bias**. In private markets, data is captured and saved regardless of the final performance of funds that are closed-end. The only exception is when data are collected from managers on a declarative basis. If the manager stops to report, the data provider will eliminate the fund. In effect, this drop is the result of a selection bias (see above) more than a survivorship bias.

2.1.2 Factors and Private Equity

This debate is not only theoretical but also has practical consequences. Some asset allocation models use factors to classify investment instruments. As explained by Bender et al. (2013), "A factor can be thought of as any characteristic relating a group of securities that is important in explaining their return and risk." This essentially applies to listed stocks in the long term. Factors represent an exposure to systematic sources of risk and are compensated by a premium.

Essentially applied to listed stocks, factors isolate groups of securities that react specifically to macroeconomic and market situations. These predictable reactions can be exploited to build a portfolio with specific characteristics in terms of expected risk and return. Bender et al. (2013) explain that "the number and nature of these factors [are] likely to change over time and vary across markets. Thus, the challenge of building factor models became, and continues to be, essentially empirical in nature."

Factors cannot be directly observed. They are determined once specific stock characteristics are identified as having a strong and lasting explanatory power in understanding the behavior of a broad range of stocks. As noted by Bender et al., "The market[5] can be viewed as the first and most important equity factor." Six more are identified: value, small size, low volatility, high yield, quality, and momentum (see Bender et al., 2013, for more details). They enter in three categories: macroeconomic (surprises in inflation, GDP, or yield curve), statistical (principal component analysis), and fundamental (industry, country, valuation ratios, technical ratios).

The logical consequence is that private equity, specifically, will prove to be very challenging to screen for factors. Private equity funds operate out of the stock exchange.

---

[4]For example, classifications of funds can vary between Cambridge Associates and eFront in terms of geographical exposure, strategy, size, and sectors. Moreover, the determination of their actual formation (their vintage year, see Chapter 3) leaves room for interpretation.
[5]The "market" is defined as an exposure to the returns of the capitalization-weighted index portfolio.

The companies in which these funds invest are traded irregularly and infrequently. Therefore, factor analysis cannot be applied as it is logically impossible to identify factors indirectly because of a lack of trading activity.

As we will see in Chapter 4, a value bridge analysis supports the identification of the elements that contributed to the performance of a fund. This is not a market-related approach but an intrinsic analysis. The value bridge analysis could be considered, to some extent, as a distant relative of a factor analysis. Measuring separately the impact of the financial leverage and the multiple increase in the performance of LBO investments (see Chapters 3 and 4) could be compared to measuring the excess return associated with specific factors.

Thus, factors are used to analyze the performance of active managers on the stock exchange, and value bridge analysis is used also to analyze the performance of an LBO manager. These two approaches still remain separated, and a factor analysis cannot, to our knowledge, be currently applied in private equity.

2.1.3 The Challenge of Building a Unified Asset Allocation

Thus, private markets do not fit neatly in the standard asset allocation framework, as unfortunately it is difficult to compare the characteristics of private market funds with traditional assets.

In particular, as we will see in the next chapters, **measuring the risk** due to price volatility does not work with assets that are sparsely traded. Analyzing returns is also challenging, as the unused cash of funds creates a performance drag that has to be taken into account (in Chapter 5, we will look at over-commitment strategies to try to address such issues).

Moreover, it is close to impossible to **run correlation tests** to see how unique private markets are and how much they diversify an investment portfolio. Swensen (2009) states that "private assets constitute separate asset classes because they behave in a fundamentally different fashion from marketable securities, making dependence on high short-run correlation between private and public markets an internally inconsistent, potentially dangerous strategy."

It is very difficult to run correlations between private and listed assets because:

– Information on private assets is poor and heterogeneous. Listed assets are well documented, as data is usually of high frequency and quality.
– Pricing points in private markets are limited in number and heavily depend on the context. Listed stocks are usually fungible (unless there are two classes of shares) and can be traded freely at low cost. Private stocks are bespoke, can be subject to specific duties (restrictions on trading such as pre-emption rights), or benefit from specific rights (such as liquidity rights). If a shareholder has the majority of the political rights in a private company, the shares are more valuable than those of the minority. However, if the minority has negotiated exit clauses and forced sale rights, its shares might have the same value as the majority (or at times a higher value if this is combined with liquidity rights).
– The minimum time horizon of the analysis diverges substantially from listed markets. The standard framework of modern portfolio theory assumes by default a

yearly framework during which capital is fully invested. This does not apply to private markets, which are accessible essentially through funds that deploy progressively their capital (over three to five years, see Chapter 3) over an indefinite period of time (usually three to eight years, see Chapter 3).

Some empirical evidence shows that there is a link between private investment strategies and some phases of the macroeconomic cycle. For example, distressed debt funds tend to perform better when they deploy capital in a recession. Venture capital funds benefit from the recovery phase following a recession.

LBO funds capitalize on times of economic stress for businesses (this can be sector-specific). This type of investment strategy capitalizes on opportunities that are relatively cheap (the multiples of EBITDA tend to be lower) and in need of significant change. LBOs tend also to be more lucrative when they use debt after interest rates have been falling down (economic agents are still adjusting to lower interest rates, which gives LBO funds an advantage).

Nevertheless, as ultimately listed companies also react to macroeconomic factors, there is some form of co-evolution between private equity investments and listed investments. The challenge is to quantify this co-evolution and see how much of it is synchronous. For example, performance data of LBO funds demonstrate that favorable conditions for investments are during a recession or in early recovery. This is also true for listed stocks. It would be logical to conclude that LBO and listed stocks do not diversify a portfolio in this specific context. However, the investment rationale can be very different. An LBO fund might refocus companies, while listed groups might engage in a wave of consolidation. Both will generate performance, but the sources of the performance are quite different. They diversify the risk of the investor while still performing well jointly under specific market conditions.

Assessing correlations is also challenging because private markets are evolving fast. In particular, funds have quickly gathered a lot of capital to invest (see Chapter 3). Over the course of the last 20 years, fundraising has been in tune with the macroeconomic evolution of developed markets. Simply put, fundraising has been pro-cyclical. As a consequence, the investment activity of funds has also been at least partially pro-cyclical. Since investors also invest on listed markets pro-cyclically (at least in most of the economic cycles), this creates a co-movement and some form of correlation. Whether this reduces the diversification of a portfolio remains to be assessed.

Finally, correlations have increased as private markets matured. Information asymmetries and market imperfections have decreased. To price private assets, whether to buy or sell them, the reference is often listed assets. The more frequent the reference to stock prices and the more efficient the pricing of private assets are, the higher the correlation between private and public prices will be. However, as mentioned previously, the longer duration of private investments relaxes de facto the correlations between private and listed assets.

An option would be to run correlation tests over longer and variable periods of time (as we do as an example in the next chapters). Nevertheless, this remains challenging and might not provide the expected results to establish an asset allocation.

A multi-year approach requires significant adjustments to the standard asset allocation framework and might not be compatible with the mandatory yearly performance reviews of investors.

2.2 FRICTIONS BETWEEN ASSET ALLOCATION AND PRIVATE MARKETS

The standard allocation framework combining the intrinsic, comparative, and external analyses of assets produces a target asset allocation. Investors then acquire listed assets accordingly. The actual allocation and the target one are a match. As the price of these assets fluctuates, the actual allocation diverges from the target one.

Investors then have a few options:

  i) If they believe that this divergence is temporary, they can wait until it resolves itself.
 ii) If they believe that this divergence is a lasting one, they can correct the actual allocation by rebalancing the assets. This consists in selling the assets that appreciated and buying the ones that did not.
iii) If they believe that the divergence is a lasting one but that rebalancing is not sufficient, they can revise their strategic asset allocation.

Investors can also proactively change their actual allocation without amending their strategic asset allocation. For example, they could adjust tactically their asset allocation to face specific events that might last only for some time. This tactical asset allocation provides flexibility to the investor, to seize investment opportunities or avoid an emerging risk, without changing the long-term course of the investments. Allocating assets tactically is possible when assets are listed and easily tradable.

This is not the case with typical closed-end private market funds (see Chapter 3), which cannot be easily sold or bought (see the section on secondaries in Chapter 3). In fact, one could argue that tactical adjustments are effectively made by the managers of private market funds (Chapter 3). The consequences are significant for portfolio construction (Section 2.1) and in terms of rebalancing (Section 2.2). Nevertheless, using open-ended funds as a proxy can support the definition of target allocations to private market funds (Section 2.3).

2.2.1 Managing Structural Under-Allocations to Private Markets

Combining public and private assets creates a permanent tension between the target asset allocation and the actual one. On one hand, the price of listed assets is in constant flux, reacting immediately to information and investor expectations. Some of these movements can be excessive and for an extended period of time.

On the other hand, the changes in the price of private assets are irregular and infrequent. At best, private market fund managers estimate the price of each of their holdings on a quarterly basis. These appraisals reflect the operational evolution of private assets and the shift in market conditions over a quarter. They also take into account the nature of the political and economic rights negotiated by the fund manager when investing.

Fund managers tend to appraise the value of private holdings rather conservatively (see Chapter 3). The valuations of private assets are available with at least a 45- to 60-day delays after the end of each quarter.

As a consequence, the evolution of the valuation of private assets systematically lags behind their listed comparables. That can lead to misunderstandings in terms of performance and exposure analysis.

In terms of performance, there is the equivalent of an optical effect: listed assets always appear as being ahead of private ones. Between January 2, 2010, and December 31, 2019, the value of the S&P 500 grew from 1,073.87 to 3,230.78 points. This represents an annual growth of 20.1 percent. According to eFront Insight, the 10-year rolling IRR of all private market funds as of Q4 2019 was 11.5 percent. It would be easy to conclude that public markets outperformed private ones, but this would be mistake.

Private market funds that are less than five years old are still investing and building their portfolio. As of Q4 2019, private market funds that are five to ten years old are still holding more than half of the capital they used as unrealized investments[6]. The value of these investments does not reflect their full potential: they are still held and valued conservatively (see Chapter 3). It is only upon an exit (a "realization") that the value of each of these investments will fully materialize.

In terms of exposure, the actual asset allocation also tends to systematically lag behind the targeted one. When listed stock prices see a prolonged period of sustained growth of their valuation, as between 2010 and 2019, their relative weight increases substantially in the actual asset allocation and might exceed the targeted weight. Other assets are under-weighted. Private markets are structurally among them, due to the conservative appraisal (see above and Chapter 3) over an extended period of time (the duration of the underlying investments of the funds) and the time lag of the reporting. We call this structural under-allocation to private markets the **"numerator" effect**: in a benign environment, investors recurrently undershoot their target exposure to private markets.

If they have an excess of cash, investors can try to increase their exposure to private market funds (or rebalance; see below) to catch up with listed stocks. Private market funds render this operation triply difficult.

First, funds deploy capital over an extended period of time (their investment period of two to five years; see Chapter 3). So an increased commitment to funds will not immediately translate into an actual exposure to private assets. Moreover, such increased commitment might be pro-cyclical and potentially reduce the performance of investors.

Second, the assets will still remain conservatively appraised. Even if the investor manages to ramp up his exposure to private market funds, the valuation of the assets in the portfolio will not increase in the same proportion as for the listed peers—until the actual exit. The gap between target and actual asset allocation will thus persist.

Third, funds regularly sell (or list) assets and distribute the proceeds to investors, thus reducing the actual exposure to private assets.

A solution could be for investors to **accept that the actual private markets exposure lags behind the target**. However, this defies the overall project of an asset

---

[6]Their residual value (or net asset value) represents between 55 and 95 percent of the capital they used (the paid-in). See Chapter 3 for explanation and details on these metrics.

allocation. The target becomes nominal, and trying to reach it in practice becomes an exercise in frustration.

Another solution could be to **independently value private assets to fully reflect their market value and reintegrate the output in the asset allocation**. This independent valuation is a challenging task given the lack of information on private assets. The European AIFM Directive (see Chapter 3) states that managers must provide investors with an independent valuation of their assets. This, however, did not materially change the overall results. Managers themselves have limited or no insight as to the potential timing and value at exit of private investments. Fund investors (or their advisors) have even less. Any effort to independently value private assets is akin to shooting in the dark.

A third solution could be to **specifically and formally separate listed assets and private markets**. A specific proportion of assets will be assigned to private markets, even though this quota could not be tested within the Markowitz framework. Investors would manage two separate allocations (the standard framework and a dedicated private market allocation) and reconcile them only when a revision of the strategic asset allocation is necessary. When possible, progressively ramp up or wind down the exposure to private markets; this solution is coherent with strategic revisions, which happen every three to five years. Setting a relevant allocation to private markets will be discussed below (Section 3). Chapters 4 and 5 follow this approach, as we independently model portfolios of private market assets.

2.2.2 Limited Rebalancing Options: the Case for Allocation Brackets

The counterpart to the "numerator" effect is the much dreaded **"denominator" effect**. There are scenarios in which investors are temporarily and substantially *over-allocated* to private markets. This happens when listed stocks see their value drop significantly over a short period of time.

A case in point was 2007–2009 when the S&P 500 dropped from a peak of 1,561.80 points on October 7, 2007, to 683.38 points on January 3, 2009. Listed stocks saw their prices correct by 40 to 60 percent, while the value of private market funds did not move initially; when it did, it was moderately. In practice, the *relative value* of their private market funds increased significantly (as a proportion of total assets). Moreover, these funds continued to draw down and deploy capital as investment opportunities arose, further increasing the actual allocation to private markets.

Investors then overshot their target exposure with no easy recourse. The temptation was high to sell other assets and buy these listed stocks. Investors who panicked sold stakes in private market funds on the secondary market at a 50 to 70 percent discount—if they could at all.

As they discovered, an asset allocation embedding private markets is much more difficult to rebalance than a portfolio comprising only of traditional assets. This can be a blessing in cases of temporary divergence (the first hypothesis above at the beginning of Section 2).

Indeed, on April 18, 2010, the S&P 500 had recovered to 1,217.28 points. As stock prices recovered sharply, these panicked investors were suddenly massively under-allocated to private markets. The price of listed stocks rebounded so quickly and sharply (in a V-shaped recovery) that eventually these investors could have been caught buying stocks during their fast recovery and ended up being over-allocated to them.

"Steady" investors who stayed put and waited out for listed markets to settle before taking action could see listed stocks recover. They were spared this expensive rebalancing activity.

When an asset allocation embeds private markets, panicked investors learned an important lesson: it is necessary to define **brackets around the target allocation**. Indeed, it is possible, to some extent, to reduce the exposure to private markets rapidly on the secondary market but at a very high cost to the investor, due to the heavy discount on the conservative NAV of these funds (see above). It is even more difficult to ramp the exposure back up through the same secondary market. Indeed, it is not possible to predict the supply of opportunities, which might not match the need of the investor in volume, quality, and price.

Steady investors would for example set a 5 percent allocation to private markets, plus or minus 200–300 basis points. To some extent, these brackets can be used to make opportunistic acquisitions if conditions are attractive on the secondary market for private market fund stakes. More crucially, they provide investors with some time to reassess their asset allocation and decide any adjustment.

However, if the divergence between target and actual asset allocation is a lasting one, the set-up of asset allocation brackets prevents the full use of tactical instruments (at least in proportion of the use of private markets). Rebalancing might also be slowed down, which reduces the attractiveness of this approach. As for reviewing the strategic asset allocation, private markets create some inertia that is difficult to compensate. As we will see (Chapters 4 and 5), investors should not try to time the market with their private market investments, so this inertia is not prejudicial to investors.

Fast tactical adjustments and rebalancing are in effect almost impossible in private markets. Moreover, the exposure is only gained gradually. This goes against the grain of the standard allocation framework. Thus, a portfolio embedding private market funds gathers a significant inertia. Any effort to amend the target asset allocation or to shift the actual allocation will require time to bear fruit.

2.2.3 A Possible Proxy to Define Target Allocations: Open-Ended Funds

Still, some investors want to use their standard framework to test assumptions and define a threshold of allocation to private market funds. A solution could be to use open-ended private market funds (also known as evergreen; see Chapter 3) as a proxy. These funds, provided by managers such as StepStone, LGT, Partners Group, Black-Rock, and Brookfield, provide an immediate exposure to investors. They are theoretically always accessible, and investors can theoretically exit at will. In practice, there are significant limitations[7] to enter and exit. This proxy is, thus, useful for refining a target asset allocation but less for the actual capital deployment.

---

[7]Evergreen private market funds are structured differently from their closed-end brethren. They do not distribute capital, either the principal or the dividends, or interest generated by the investments. Investors willing to invest in evergreen structures have to buy out an existing one or contribute to the fund (assuming that the manager wishes to collect more capital to invest). The

Evergreen funds can be used in the standard asset allocation framework: at cruise speed, they are fully invested. The manager can, therefore, provide annualized performance figures calculated along the same lines as for traditional assets. Performance figures include the performance drag of the unused cash. A "volatility" of the value of the fund can be measured as well, although it is quite limited. The annual performance and the volatility figures can be used in a portfolio optimizer fashioned according to modern portfolio theory.

This approach will result in allocating a very high proportion of assets to evergreen private market structures, as risk is very low and performance tends to be higher than for traditional assets. It will then be necessary to introduce constraints and variables taking into account the expected payout and time horizon of the investor.

The drawback of using evergreen funds is that they are not pure products. They usually blend different investment strategies and instruments. They also provide a limited geographical coverage of private markets. Their fee structure is usually much higher than for standard private market funds. Investors are also restricted in their movements and, most importantly, do not get distributions. Nevertheless, these instruments can be a bridge between the standard asset allocation framework and private markets.

2.2.4 Alternative Approaches

Some investors, such as Suva[8] in Switzerland, have decided to take a different approach. For them, it makes sense to **blend traditional and alternative assets into larger categories**. These investors consider that equity, debt, and real assets can embed different and complementary durations. They integrate private equity to their equity allocation, private debt to their fixed income allocation, and private real assets to their real estate, commodities, and other allocations. As a matter of illustration, the asset allocation of Suva for 2016–2020 was 38.5 percent to fixed income, 7.5 percent to credit (of which 0.5 percent was to private debt), 32 percent to equities (of which 7 percent was to private equity), 13 percent to real estate, and 9 percent were "skill-based."

The Swiss Bankers Association (SBA) followed suit and suggested that the investment guidelines for the Swiss pension schemes should be amended along the same lines than Suva's. It proposed that asset classes would be broken down into equity, debt, real assets, trading, and resources, with private assets assigned to these headline categories (Table 2.1). For the SBA, pension funds should adjust their asset allocation to invest more in alternative assets (Investment & Pensions Europe, 2017). Regulations deter allocation to alternative assets due to the categorization of assets. The SBA estimated that

---

manager paces the admission of new investors. Likewise, managers control the exit of investors. Unless a potential buyer wishes to buy out an existing investor, the manager will provide some liquidity under strict pacing and volume conditions to investors (a process known as gating).

[8]https://www.suva.ch/en/the-suva/finanzen-und-immobilien/suvas-investment-strategy, last accessed August 13, 2020. Suva is the largest provider of accident insurance in Switzerland (2 million employees in 120,000 enterprises). It is a nonprofit company, with a board composed of 16 representatives of employees, 16 representatives of employers, and 8 representatives of the federal government. Its total assets reached CHF 51 billion in 2017. The average liability has a time horizon over 15 years.

TABLE 2.1 SBA's Proposal for Categorization and Limits for Investments for Pension Funds

Investment category	Breakdown	Existing limit	Suggested new limit
Equity		—	**75%**
Listed	Domestic and foreign stocks	50%	75%
Private	Private equity		15%
Debt		—	**100%**
Listed	Domestic and foreign bonds	100%	100%
Private	Swiss mortgage securities	50%	50%
	Private debt		15%
Real assets		—	**50%**
Listed	Domestic and foreign real estate	30%/10%	50%
Private	Domestic and foreign real estate, Infrastructure	30%/10%	50% 15%
Trading and resources		—	**15%**
Trading	Hedge funds		—
Resources	Commodities		—
Other	ILS, etc.		—
Unhedged foreign currencies		**30%**	**30%**

[*]Currently subject to a total 15 percent limit for alternative investments
Note: private infrastructure is currently under review to be taken out of the 15 percent limit for alternative investments
Source: SBA (2016).

the Swiss second pillar assets would increase by around CHF 8 billion if pension fund portfolios were more diversified. In that respect, Swiss pension funds lag behind those of other countries in terms of investment performance.

Blending traditional and alternative assets presents multiple advantages. First, it is very flexible and rather agnostic to the instrument chosen to get exposure to equity, debt, or real assets. Second, the volatility of listed assets is diluted by private markets. To some extent, this reduces or eliminates the need to hedge volatility risks.

The difficulties associated with such an approach are that it is necessary to carefully manage investment durations and match them with expected payouts. Moreover, such an approach can create imbalances in the exposure of investors that might be more difficult to compensate due to the inertia associated with private market funds. This is of particular concern when it comes to assess value creation (and thus the performance drivers) and the sources of risk (and thus the effective diversification of the portfolio).

The asset allocation can alternatively **focus on liability-management or be goal-based**. Jost and Herger (2013) suggest a two-step approach that focuses on what they call "robustness[9]." They advise to minimize risk and maximize diversification, as this approach "generally produces more stable models." Then, they focus on maximizing returns by "superior fund selection." Risk is defined as "negative shocks (losses) [...] in a way that is analogous to the semi-volatility or downside volatility." They then allocate the risk to the market weight of each private market strategy.

Although this approach appears to be suited to private markets, it is unclear if it applies to other asset classes. Moreover, the authors assume that the market weight of each strategy is coherent with the constraints and ambitions of all investors (which might not be true; see Chapter 1). Finally, they seem to assume that the changes to the resulting target allocation can be forecasted and applied seamlessly. This remains to be proven.

2.3   SETTING UP PRIVATE MARKETS ALLOCATION THRESHOLDS

Challenges and uncertainties abound when it comes to integrate private markets in an asset allocation scheme. The fact that private markets do not fit neatly in the standard asset allocation framework means that running optimization routines does not deliver a meaningful result. The practical question is thus: How to decide how much to allocate to private markets? As mentioned in Chapter 1, copying the allocation of a successful investor such as the Yale endowment does not necessarily bear the same result. Moreover, the specific constraints that apply to Yale are probably not the same as for any random investor. Replicating the allocation might effectively hurt the investor, especially during times of economic stress.

Nevertheless, it is tempting to have a look at the allocations of investors by category of investors to get a sense of how they converge or diverge. Surveys are issued regularly to try to capture this information. Fernyhough (2019) provides an example (see Fig. 2.1) for sovereign wealth funds, pension funds, and family offices.

There are significant differences between investor categories but also within categories. Strikingly, the Canadian pension fund CPPIB invests a very large portion of its assets in alternatives, more than in listed stocks. Only Yale's endowment deploys more in alternatives. Even the average family office looks more conservative than CPPIB. The local regulations and the nature of this institution might explain these choices. Swiss pension funds, due to the 15 percent cap on alternative investments, would not be able to replicate the CPPIB allocation, for example.

CPPIB managed CAD 409.5 billion as of March 31, 2020, the end of its fiscal year. Its net return for the year was 3.1 percent, generating a net income of CAD 12.1 billion. On a calendar basis (January to December 2019), its performance reached a 12.6 percent rate of return. Over ten years, its net annual return was 8.1 percent (9.9 percent on a nominal basis). The target is to generate an annual real rate of return of 3.95 percent above the rate of Canadian consumer price inflation, after all costs, during the 75 years following 2018.

---

[9]They define robustness as an "asset allocation process that [...] has to be stable over time, in the sense that two successive optimal allocations should not differ drastically."

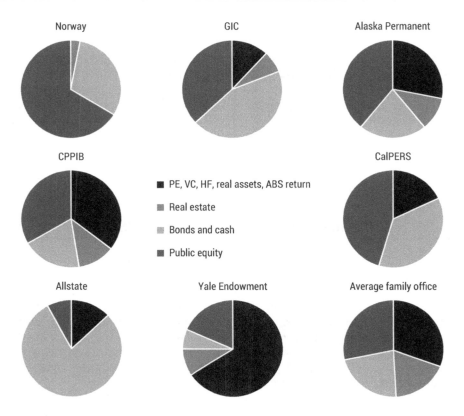

FIGURE 2.1 Asset Allocation for Select Categories of Fund Investors
Source: PitchBook (2019).

Note: Norway as of 2018, GIC as of March 2019, Alaska Permanent as of 2018, CPPIB as of June 6, 2019, CalPERS as of June 30, 2018, Allstate as of 2018, Yale Endowment as of 2019, family office as of 2017.

The asset allocation was dedicated at 21.4 percent to emerging market (net return: −1.1 percent) and the rest to developed markets (net return: 4.1 percent). Public equities represented 28.2 percent, private equities 24.7 percent, credit 12.4 percent, real estate 11.3 percent, government bonds, cash, and absolute return strategies 10.9 percent, infrastructure 8.6 percent, and other real assets 3.9 percent.

Six departments apply this asset allocation: Total Portfolio Management (CAD 180 billion), Capital Markets and Factor Investing (CAD 56 billion), Active Equities, which includes "private companies [and] externally managed funds focused on long-horizon structural changes" (CAD 61 billion), Credit Investments (CAD 40 billion), Private Equity, which "invests in global private equity suitable for large, patient and knowledgeable investors" (CAD 95 billion) and Real Assets (CAD 98 billion).

What distinguishes CPPIB from its peer group of large pension funds based in developed markets is its direct private equity investments. For example, it invested in

Merlin Entertainments in the UK (which notably operated the Legoland Parks), with a total transaction size of £5.9 billion. Likewise, it invested in large infrastructure transactions in Latin America. It also co-invested in Refinitiv, which subsequently merged with the London Stock Exchange in a $27 billion transaction.

2.3.1 Defining the Lower Band for a Private Markets Allocation

More generally, Ford (2019) quotes Willis Towers Watson stating that investors allocated 14 percent of their assets to private markets and that this should rise to 20 percent over the next 10 years. These are significant exposures to private markets. Clearly, investors have framed their allocations to take into account hard facts.

If the allocation to private market strategies is too small (below 3 to 5 percent of total assets), the overall result will be negligible in terms of contribution to performance and reduction of the portfolio risk. In fact, investing in private markets does not scale well but also implies a minimum consumption of financial and human resources that is significant. If the assets under management are modest and the allocation is minimal, the result could lead to a negative net contribution when factoring the direct and indirect costs of the private market program.

A small allocation is also an incentive to avoid deploying any effort or gain in sophistication. The allocation on private markets will stay on the fringes of the portfolio. As such, it is unlikely to generate attractive returns, except by luck (which might be assimilated as an uncontrolled risk) and, therefore, to trigger a higher allocation. For investors subject to significant regulations, such as insurance groups and banks, a small allocation also means that past exposure will be insufficient to support a switch from a standard model (which implies high capital charges as seen in Chapter 1) to an internal model (with probably lower capital charges). Thus, to make sense and kick-start a positive cycle of private market fund investments, it is necessary to deploy $15 to $25 million over three to five years. This should represent a minimum of 3 percent of the total assets under management. Below this amount and/or percentage, it makes sense to resort to a series of investments in funds of funds.

2.3.2 Defining the Higher Band for a Private Markets Allocation

Shukis and Thurston (2016), from Cambridge Associates, explore further the notion of allocation thresholds. They look at the asset allocation of endowments and foundations and state that "the median return of institutions with 15 percent or more of their assets in private investments was 3.6 percent for the 2015 fiscal year, and virtually all of these institutions had positive returns." This has to be compared with a performance of 1.3 percent for the whole sample, of which more than 25 percent had negative returns. Shukis and Thurston identify a "15 percent frontier" when it comes to allocating to private markets.

This "frontier" can be due to regulations. For example, Swiss pension funds can allocate up to 15 percent of their assets to alternative investments. Although this ceiling is currently being redefined, this still creates a hard cap. For insurance groups and banks, regulations also limit the options when it comes to investing in private markets.

The exploration of the higher band of asset allocation to private markets is, thus, subject to such regulatory hard caps.

Nevertheless, the exploration of Shukis and Thurston is fruitful. They find that crossing the "15 percent frontier" delivers strong results over the long term (they use data from their endowment and foundation clients from the 1970s onward). Over a horizon of ten years to June 30, 2015, the performance of the group that has crossed the frontier was 7.6 percent, 150 basis points higher than the returns of the group with less than 5 percent in private investments. Venture capital, LBOs, and distressed debt were the three best-performing strategies with respectively pooled average performances of 12.5, 11.9, and 10.8 percent. The average allocation to private markets of the best-performing portfolios over this period was 24.1 percent. The allocation of the worst-performing portfolios was 6 percent.

The authors confirm these findings for 15- and 20-year periods, with an outperformance that is "persistent and remarkably consistent": 180 basis points per year. They note that "there have been very few periods when the institutions with high private allocations underperformed those with low allocations, and when they did so, it was not by a wide margin [... and] in only six of the 20 years since 1996 [...]: 2001–2003 and 2009–2011." They add that "the shortfall was quickly recovered in subsequent years of strong private outperformance."

The authors note that other factors might have played in favor of the institutions with a higher private allocation: a longer-term horizon that prevented them from making poorly timed tactical allocations and more staff resources.

They address the three usual critics, which are the "illiquidity of private investments," the large size required for such investments, and the access to top funds. Along the lines of what is developed in our book, they state that "many institutions place a value on liquidity that exceeds their actual cash needs, even under worst-case scenarios" and especially when considering spending policies, cash sources, and credit facilities.

Shukis and Thurston also state that the "group with the high private allocation is not exclusively composed of very large institutions." This is also in line with what we develop in this book. Finally, they state that selection skills are important but that good funds are still accessible to managers.

The logical conclusion of the analysis of Shukis and Thurston would be that investors should maximize their exposure to private markets within their regulatory constraints (if any) and their payout schedule. However, a few additional considerations have to be taken into account. First, endowments and foundations could have accumulated know-how and contacts facilitating their investments in private markets that might not readily be available to any investor. Second, these institutions, as mentioned in the case of the Yale endowment, are tax exempt and benefit from low constraints.

2.3.3 Getting Started with a Private Markets Allocation

How should an institution start the exercise, knowing that correlation tests will not be of help, nor Sharpe ratios or the usual instruments used in modern portfolio theory?

A pragmatic approach could be to bypass the carefully crafted approach applied with listed assets and use a naive asset allocation as a first step. Investors would carve allocations dedicated to private markets with thresholds such as 5, 10, and 15 percent, and if regulations allow it, 30, 45, 60, and 90 percent. Within these thresholds, the allocation to private equity, private debt, and private real assets is constant (for example 33 percent each, or a market-neutral weighting replicating the relative weight of these strategies in the economy). To run such exercises, it is advised in a first approach to use open-ended products as described above. They provide a proxy with monthly/quarterly data points.

It is then possible to run these portfolios under different historical scenarios, such as 2000–2003 and 2008–2010 for stress times, but also favorable conditions such as 1995–1999 and 2004–2007 and analyze the output for each component of the portfolio, as well as for the overall portfolio. These outputs can then be used to explore a potential rebalancing strategy that would only apply to listed assets while steering the whole portfolio. In that example, unlisted assets act as a portfolio anchor that listed assets (and cash) balance.

This approach also helps refining the percentage allocated to private markets. As open-ended funds usually blend different strategies (LBOs, growth investments, infrastructure, real estate), geographical regions, and levels of intermediation (primary and secondary fund investments, as well as direct investments), they do not easily support the fine-tuning of the private market allocation. To do so, it is necessary to focus on the percentage of each strategy within private markets and thus to use closed-end funds.

For that purpose, a different approach and a specific model are needed (additional ideas and elements are provided by Cornelius et al., 2013, and Meyer and Mathonet, 2005). They are explored in Chapters 4 and 5. Reconciling the results of Chapter 5 with a standard framework is not possible, which is why an intermediate step using open-ended funds as a proxy can be helpful. This output-driven approach has the advantage of providing meaningful and empirical performance results.

There are significant limitations. This approach adopts the back-testing tilt that characterizes modern portfolio theory. Historical data cannot be fully relied on when setting up an asset allocation for the future. With private market funds, the history stops seven to ten years before the current date as assets mature slowly and get sold progressively.

Another limitation is that risk cannot be measured with volatility, which generates additional challenges when assessing the output. Value-at-risk can be used but is not always compatible with the requirements from the institution running the analysis.

A specific limitation to such an approach is that using open-ended funds is only a distant proxy to actual private market funds. These funds include a non-negligible idiosyncratic risk in asset allocation that should rely on market indexes. When switching to private market fund modeling (see Chapter 5), this limitation decreases, but investors face another challenge: it is not possible to "buy the market." Their model will then use capital-weighted averages, but their operational deployment will depend on their selection skills. Put differently, the process described above will introduce statistical noise at each successive step.

The positive aspects of such an approach are nevertheless very attractive. First, this is one of the few options to actually bridge public and private markets in a single exercise. Second, despite their limitations, the open-ended proxies and the private market non-investable indexes are actual market data. They deliver consistent and rich information, even though it is with a certain level of noise. Third, the multi-stage approach can support a double optimization: of the thresholds themselves and then within the private market thresholds of the payout, risk, and performance variables.

Such an empirical approach will probably frustrate highly quantitative optimization tools used with listed assets. These tools can still operate on this part of the portfolio and might be open to integrate specific constraints concerning the exposure to private markets. Regulations already impose such constraints. Integrating additional ones is thus possible.

Swensen (2009) states that "market returns stem from three sources—asset allocation, market timing, and security selection—with each source of returns providing a tool for investors to use to satisfy institutional goals." The approach described above addresses asset allocation with a set of practical steps and leaves the selection of private market funds in the hands of investors. As we will see (Chapters 4 and 5), market timing should not be on the mind of investors when considering private markets. Therefore, despite its focus on empirical steps, the approach described might be a useful first step toward more complex approaches integrating public and private assets.

2.4 SUMMARY

Throughout this chapter, we have pointed out that the standard asset allocation approach—which uses the average past performances of assets (returns) and the variation of these performances (risks) to build optimized portfolios—remains difficult to apply to private markets. Investors have thus to follow a more pragmatic approach.

Private markets are usually classified as alternative assets, but this classification remains debated. We argue that private markets are an asset class given their specific value creation and their ability to finance assets that are usually not catered to by listed markets. We focus on funds as value creation is documented at this level and investors are privileging them for their investments. Funds are not just a technical instrument: their setup, management, and operations have consequences in terms of performance, risk, and liquidity.

Factors are used to analyze the performance of active managers on the stock exchange. They cannot be directly observed and belong to three categories: macroeconomic, statistical, and fundamental. In private equity, factor analyses cannot be applied for a lack of trading activity. Value bridge analyses are used to analyze the performance of LBO managers. This solution supports the identification of the elements that contributed to the performance of a fund.

Nevertheless, it is challenging to build a unified asset allocation as it is difficult to compare the characteristics of private market funds with traditional assets. Measuring the risk due to price volatility does not work with assets that are sparsely traded. Analyzing returns is also challenging, and it is very difficult to run correlations between private and listed assets. Though there is now a form of co-evolution between private equity investments and listed investments, the challenge is to quantify this co-evolution and see how much of it is synchronous, which is not easy as private markets are evolving so fast. Correlations have increased as private markets matured, and information asymmetries and market imperfections have decreased. An interesting option would be to run correlation tests over longer and variable periods of time.

The standard allocation framework combining the intrinsic, comparative, and external analyses of assets produces a target asset allocation, and investors then acquire listed assets so that the actual and target allocation are a match. But as the price of these assets fluctuates, the actual allocation will sometimes differ from the target one. Investors can adapt by allocating assets tactically when assets are listed and easily tradable. This is not the case with private market funds, which cannot be easily sold or bought.

Investors have thus to manage structural under-allocations to private markets. Combining public and private assets creates a permanent tension between the target asset allocation and the actual one as the changes in the price of listed assets is in constant flux while the prices of private assets are irregular and infrequent. Fund managers tend to appraise the value of private holdings conservatively, and thus the evolution of valuation of private assets lags behind their listed comparable companies, which leads to misunderstandings in terms of performance and exposure analysis. The solution would be for investors to accept that the actual private markets exposure lags behind the target; or another could be to independently value private assets to fully reflect their market value and reintegrate the output in the asset allocation. Finally, the last one could be to separate listed assets and private markets.

When an asset allocation embeds private markets, investors need to define brackets around the target allocation. These brackets can be used to make opportunistic acquisitions if conditions are attractive on the secondary market. They provide investors with some time to assess their allocation after a major event and decide any adjustment. Fast tactical adjustments and rebalancing are almost impossible in private markets. Portfolio embedding private market funds are expected to gather a significant inertia.

Open-ended funds are useful for refining target asset allocation and can be used in the standard asset allocation framework, but they are not pure products. They blend different investment strategies and instruments, provide a limited geographical coverage, record higher fees, and do not distribute. They are thus only possible proxies.

Alternative approaches consist in blending traditional and alternative assets. The volatility of listed assets is then diluted by private markets, but it needs careful management of investment durations matching them with expected payouts. This approach can also create imbalances in the exposure of investors, difficult to compensate due to the inertia in private market funds. Another solution could be to focus on liability or goal-based management by minimizing risk and maximizing diversification with more stable models, but it presents some challenges as well.

Ultimately, the main question is how much to allocate to private markets. Replicating the allocation of a successful investor does not necessarily bear the same result, but studying the allocations of investors can be a valuable source of information. If the allocation to private market strategies is too small (below 3 to 5 percent of the total assets), the overall result will be negligible in terms of contribution to performance and reduction of the portfolio risk. The higher band is often a "15 percent frontier," often due to regulations. In general, investors should maximize their exposure to private markets within their regulatory constraints (if any) and their payout schedule.

A pragmatic approach could be to bypass the approach applied with listed assets and use a naive asset allocation. Investors would carve allocations dedicated to private markets with thresholds such as 5, 10, 15, 30, 45, 60, and 90 percent. Within these thresholds, the allocation to private equity, private debt, and private real assets is kept constant. It could be useful to use open-ended products, notably to run these portfolios under historical scenarios. This output-driven approach helps refining the percentage allocated to private markets and providing meaningful performance results.

There are some limitations: historical data are not perfectly reliable, risk cannot be measured with volatility, and using open-ended funds is only a proxy to actual private market funds. However, this approach remains one of the few options to bridge public and private markets in a single exercise, it addresses asset allocation with a set of practical steps, and it leaves the selection of private market funds in the hands of investors. It could be a useful first step toward more complex approaches integrating public and private assets.

CHAPTER 3

Private Markets Investing[1]

In a nutshell

This chapter will notably provide readers with definitions of private markets. As private markets financing can only be an active investment strategy, intermediation and delegation are widespread in private markets. Choosing which type of instrument and strategy to adopt is of particular importance. Understanding the benefits and the challenges of this type of private equity, private debt, and private real assets investments supports the process of allocating assets.

Private markets (PM) investing aims at financing private (that is, not listed on the stock exchange) companies or assets through the provision of debt and/or capital (Fig. 3.1). PM financing targets the full range of equity and liabilities of a private company or asset, by providing equity, convertible debt, and debt. Equity investments in private companies are classified as private equity (PE), debt provision to private companies as private debt (PD), and capital and debt provided to finance private assets are classified as private real assets (PRA) investments.

There are exceptions to this definition: some assets listed at the time of investment will eventually be acquired and delisted (public-to-private LBO, see Section 3.1.2). Private companies financed by PE can eventually be listed. In some cases, such as private investments in public equities (PIPE[2]), a company financed by PE is and will remain listed. These companies tend to be small or mid-sized and show very low (or even no) volumes of daily share trading. In many respects, these "listed" companies are comparable to their private equivalent.

Figure 3.1. shows a series of instruments to invest in PM. These instruments can be a source of innovation. For example, convertible debt combines features associated with debt (for risk management) and equity (for performance generation) investment instruments. These instruments can be adjusted to specific investment cases but rely on the existence of an adequate and enforceable legal environment (Demaria, 2020). Other PM instruments, notably in the real asset sector, are rather recent and some are still in the making[3].

---

[1] We would like to thank Markus Benzler and Erasmus Elsner for their comments.
[2] See section 3.2.1 on growth capital for further elements on PIPEs.
[3] For example, in intangible real assets financing, singer David Bowie issued a bond whose collateral was the music rights of his existing catalogue in 1997. The royalties on songs supported the

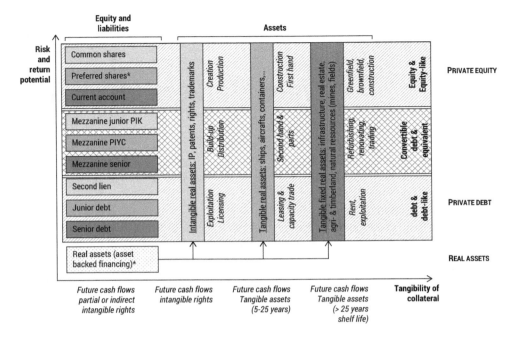

FIGURE 3.1   Private markets: instruments and landscape
* Available in specific jurisdictions only.
Note: "PIK" refers to "payment in kind" and "PIYC" to "payment if you can."
Source: Authors.

Therefore, investors have a large choice to fine-tune the design of their instruments according to their needs and the analysis of investment opportunities. This was not always the case. For a long time, instruments were limited to equity and some form of debt instruments. PE (and, to some extent, PRA strategies) pre-dated for a long time the creation of the first stock exchanges[4]. In fact, the concepts of corporation, corporate ownership, and capital (Demaria, 2020) date back to the Code of Hammurabi of 1750 BC. Venture capital (VC), which finances emerging businesses (start-ups), was in effect created by this Code. Assuming that the long-standing existence of an asset class on the market is associated with a deeper knowledge of its workings and that this knowledge increases the likelihood of investing, PM should logically represent a fairly large proportion of the portfolio of investors.

This is not the case. The majority of investors lack a thorough understanding of private markets. There are, however, exceptions. Rich families often own one or

bond yield. More recently, the producers of singer Eminem announced the listing of a structure that will provide investors with yield from future royalty income of songs (Nicolaou, 2017).
[4]Antwerp set up an exchange in 1531, specialized in bonds and promissory notes. London set up a stock exchange in 1773.

multiple private companies that represent a significant share, if not virtually all, of their wealth. For a long time, investing in private companies was executed only at arm's length, and investors would be the entrepreneurs themselves and their relatives. Later, in the 13th century, the emergence of the structure of the joint-stock company opened private companies to investments by industry specialists, merchant banks, or wealthy families. Shares would only exceptionally change hands, as these assets were the core wealth of investors. These direct holdings were expected to pay dividends supporting the daily life of investors.

As we will see in this chapter, active investment strategies call for delegation and intermediation (Section 1). Multiple instruments, such as funds, funds of funds (FOFs), and mandates support this process. The benefits are a combination of enhanced performance and risk diversification (Section 2). However, the challenges are related to a lack of transparency, and significant asymmetries of information are compounded by the principal-agent dynamic. Intermediation and delegation in private market investing generate their own challenges. Risk, return, and liquidity in private markets will be explored in detail when examining each sub-strategy (Section 3). As we will see, each one can match specific investment criteria for portfolio construction purposes. Strategies can overlap, as the borders between private market strategies are blurry, as well as between private and public markets (Conclusion).

3.1 ACTIVE INVESTMENT STRATEGIES CALL FOR DELEGATION AND INTERMEDIATION

Direct PE activities are often seen as the operational, day-to-day, work-related activity of families or individuals—but not necessarily as investments. They are framed in a different mental category, due to the active involvement and perception of control by investors. Indeed, investing in private companies and assets is essentially a **local activity** (for VC, for example, see Chen et al., 2009). This requires a constant and significant presence on the ground.

Therefore, direct private investing **requires significant expertise and know-how**, and **can only be an active investment strategy**. Knowing applicable regulations, being connected to the right network to generate investment opportunities, and understanding the local business culture is crucial to succeed in what remains one of the riskiest investment activities. Among the obstacles to overcome, besides the competition between investors, are the lack of transparency of private companies and assets, the asymmetry of information between entrepreneurs and investors, and the limited and modest protection offered to investors (notably minority investors) in private companies when compared to investors' rights in listed companies. On top of these common factors, each PM strategy has its own requirements, such as an industry expertise (VC financing start-ups) or an aptitude to restructure a company (distressed debt and turnaround capital investing). Thus, PM investing **cannot be a passive investment**.

3.1.1   Investment Instruments

To mitigate risks, different investment **instruments** can be used (Fig. 3.2). For example, PE investors can use common and preferred shares depending on the result of their analysis of a company. Preferred shares can embed different political and economic rights. These rights are negotiated between investors depending on their perception of the risks and profit potential offered by the investment opportunities. As a result, shares are not necessarily equivalent and fungible: for example, some are potentially worth a lot more than others depending on the realization (or not) of certain events.

This reasoning applies also to PD, as the seniority of the debt held determines its likelihood to be repaid. Accordingly, lenders set amounts, durations, interest rates, and covenants[5] based on their analysis of the opportunity. On this basis, investors negotiate

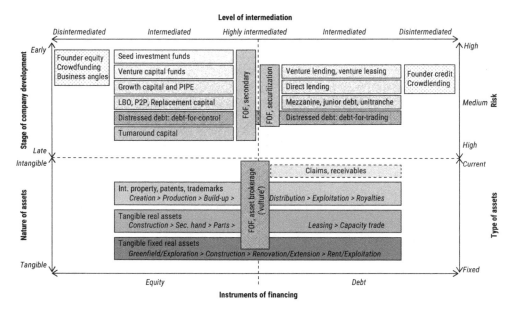

FIGURE 3.2   Private markets: classification of investment strategies
Notes: This panorama does not include direct active investments by investors themselves. "Sec." refers to "second." "PIPE" refers to "private investments in public entities." "P2P" refers to "public-to-private." "Int." refers to "intangibles." "FOF" refers to "funds of funds."
Source: Authors.

---

[5]Debt covenants can be defined as monitoring and action clauses in a lending contract, which aim to protect the lender by imposing certain restrictions on the activities of the borrower. The aim is ultimately to prevent the borrower to act in a way that would be detrimental to the lender. Debt covenants are used to mitigate the agency problem between the borrower, the lender, and the owner of a business. For example, negative covenants can prevent a borrower from undertaking

these terms. They can also add specific features, such as conversion rights into capital, to reward the risk they take: for example, the long duration of the debt, the subordination of its repayment, or the repayment at the end of its term only (repayment *in fine*).

As for PRA, debt and equity instruments can be used. Investing in PRA requires placing assets in corporate structures such as special purpose vehicles (SPV). These SPVs are structured with equity and debt. Assets can have specific features: they can be tangible or not, fixed or not, and exhibit different levels of maturity. For that reason, PRA usually cover the full range of equity and debt instruments applied to real assets.

Figure 3.2 shows that equity and debt strategies can mirror each other in the sense that they finance companies at different stages of their development. The risks and potential returns associated with each private market intervention determine the type of instrument (equity, debt, or a mix), as well as the strategy adopted. The strategic segmentation of PM between PE, PD, and PRA could appear as clear-cut, but in practice strategies can overlap.

For example, in business restructuring, it is possible to acquire the equity of a company (turnaround capital) often for a symbolic amount[6] or some of its debt to later convert it into capital[7] (distressed debt). Convertible debt itself is at the border between equity and debt investments. Moreover, PM investments can also target listed companies (to delist them, for example), or compete with hedge funds (in distressed debt investments, for example). As a result, the borders between public and private market investments as well as between PM strategies can seem blurry at times (see Section 2.4).

Figure 3.2 shows that at the higher end of the risk spectrum, debt strategies are nonexistent. The reason is that debt has to be serviced through the payment of interests (even if they can be differed), the repayment of the principal (which can be differed as well), and the establishment of a claim on a solid collateral.

Besides **direct** active ownership, there are tools to invest with relatively hands-off approaches (in a disintermediated way), such as crowd financing (equity crowdfunding and crowdlending). Both focus on the provision of capital (equity in the context of equity crowdfunding, debt in the context of crowdlending) to start-ups by any retail or professional investor via a website or an electronic platform. These two investment channels do not come close to representing the full spectrum of PM investments: they

---

the following action without informing and often requiring the prior agreement of the lender: take on additional long-term debt, pay exceptional or high dividends, deconsolidate or sell assets, undertake a merger. Positive covenants allow lenders to monitor the business leverage, cash flow, liquidity, and net worth and act on it.

[6] In certain instances, the "buyer" of the equity of a distressed company will in fact get paid by the seller to undertake the restructuring that the seller does not (or cannot) undertake.

[7] This form of distressed debt is described as "debt for control" (or "loan-to-own") while the form operated by hedge funds, for example, is described as "debt for trading." Distressed debt investing aiming at debt for control can only be effectively applied in countries with adapted national legislations, such as Chapter 11 of the US Bankruptcy Code or the equivalent, such as UK's Insolvency Act (Jones Day, 2007). See Section 2.2.1.

are restricted to projects of rather small size, relatively easy to assess and understand by investors who do not undertake thorough checks and analyses (so-called due diligence).

These instruments are recent and largely unproven. In particular, the lack of strong corporate governance rules, associated with light investor protection rules, limited information requirements, limited (or no) monitoring and control cast a shadow on these investment tools. Therefore, they do not meet the standard of professional investment programs. The viability of these instruments will be tested when the financed companies face the strains of an economic recession and have to tackle its challenges.

However, multiple strategies, such as LBO, distressed debt, and PRA, are not accessible through passive direct access (referred to as disintermediated in Fig. 3.2). Indeed, most PM investments are operated through intermediation and delegation.

3.1.2   Intermediation and Delegation: Funds

Historically, rich families and individuals (private wealth owners) were the very first to invest locally in very specific industries. However, they cannot—and in fact no investor, regardless of its size, can—professionally finance private companies or assets at every stage of their development in each country of the globe through equity and debt provision. To invest efficiently, it is necessary to diversify investments. Therefore, **intermediation** and **delegation** are necessary to PM investing. Levels of **intermediation** (Fig. 3.2) vary depending on the level of non-financial commitment (time, effort, and resources) of investors.

Until the emergence of **PM funds**, private investments remained at the margins of the investment world. Institutional investors, who represent the large majority of the sources of capital worldwide (see Chapter 1), operate differently from private wealth owners, as they usually do not invest (or lend) directly in firms or assets but invest largely or exclusively by delegating.

Thanks to funds, investment specialists opened private investing to institutional investors. This innovation unleashed modern PE. Investment specialists could manage third-party capital (Demaria, 2020; Demaria, 2015) by becoming fund managers (often referred to as general partners, or GPs). Fund investors (often referred to as limited partners, or LPs) in essence delegate to GPs the task of analyzing, selecting, monitoring, controlling, developing and ultimately selling private companies on their account (see Insert 1 for more details).

PM funds are a rather recent phenomenon, as it was only in the 20th century that these legal structures emerged (Demaria, 2020). As institutional investors were granted the right to invest in alternative investments over the course of the last four decades, PM funds started to pick up. They still represent in general less than 10 percent of the portfolios of institutional investors—and as little as 1 percent for Swiss pension funds.

Funds are the main conduit for intermediated investments[8] and are the focus of this book.

---

[8]See Section 2 for further discussion.

Insert 1—The functioning of PM funds[9]

To share costs, expertise, and risks, PM investors pool their capital in specialized structures: funds (Demaria, 2020; Demaria, 2015). These funds are set up and managed by fund managers on the account of fund investors. Most of the funds are accessible only to professional investors (accredited, qualified, or deemed to be sufficiently knowledgeable according to local regulations). Some jurisdictions also allow retail investors to invest in PM funds that are specifically designed for them[10]. Fund managers first design funds and then sell them to fund investors. Investors might decide to sponsor funds by providing a substantial initial commitment (they become "anchor investors"), as well as supporting the set-up and the marketing effort of the fund manager, possibly by associating their brand with the funds. In exchange, investors get a share of the economics of the funds they sponsor. The sponsorship has therefore a financial target and also usually addresses a gap in the asset allocation of the sponsor (or the clients of the sponsor if the sponsor is a financial intermediary, such as a bank).

Fund structures vary depending on the jurisdiction they are registered in. The most frequently used structure is the closed-end limited partnership. Fund investors (limited partners, LPs) commit to the fund at its inception. Fund managers (general partners, GPs[11]), upon reaching the target size of the fund, then close it to new investors. The only way for investors to get access to an existing fund is to acquire a stake on the informal secondary market (see below).

LPs are expected to hold their fund stakes during the lifespan of the fund ranging from eight (for some direct lending or other specific PD funds), ten (for PE, private energy, private real estate, mezzanine and distressed debt funds), thirteen (for funds of funds, timber and farmland funds) or even fifteen years (for infrastructure funds), often with the option of extending this lifespan (usually upon the agreement of fund investors) for two to three years[12]. Funds can be denominated for longer lifespans or even be open-ended (that is, with no pre-defined end date). In the latter case, they are called evergreen funds. PM closed-end funds and open-ended funds can be listed on the stock exchange.

(continued)

---

[9]This insert draws on Demaria (2015). We refer to the Introduction of his book for more details and references.

[10]For example, venture capital trusts (VCT) in the UK, and *Fonds d'Investissement de Proximité* (FIP) in France.

[11]For simplicity, we might refer at times to fund managers as GPs and to fund investors as LPs.

[12]The most frequent format is ten years except for private real estate (eight years) with up to two one-year extensions, according to Toll and Centopani (2017). In most of the cases, funds pay management fees during the extensions. These extensions are in general decided by the fund manager, possibly upon consultation with an advisory committee and/or a vote of the LPs.

(continued)

Funds do not have legal personhood and are represented by fund managers in all general and specific matters related to their activity. PM funds are blind pools: GPs do not know which assets they will invest in when creating funds. GPs, however, set a geographical scope, specific criteria to select investment opportunities, and a specific strategy to apply them to create value and performance. Contrary to certain views[13], the fund structure is of real importance: it provides the fund manager with the visibility (cash committed), flexibility (in terms of timing and decisions, see next paragraph), and mandate (signaling effect to the market) to select assets. It is the basis on which the portfolio of assets will be carefully constructed, balanced, and diversified. The fund is the unit of reference used by LPs to evaluate the performance of GPs.

The capital of funds is effectively deployed during the first three (direct lending, funds of funds, and some PRA funds) to five years (PE, private real estate, mezzanine, and distressed debt funds): the investment period. In most cases (Toll and Centopani, 2017), fund managers are allowed to recycle (that is, reinvest) early distributions during the investment period. This mechanism helps funds to compensate for the management fees and to reach an effective rate of 100 percent of capital paid in and invested. At the end of the investment period, funds are not allowed to do new investments (but can reinvest in existing assets if necessary, for example, in the case of venture capital funds). The capital is called by GPs (and "paid in" by LPs) as investment opportunities arise (and management fees are scheduled to be paid). LPs have to comply within 10 to 30 days after a capital call notice[14]. If they fail to do so, fund regulations (the Limited Partnership Agreement, or LPA) allow GPs to sanction LPs. Capital remains invested until there is an opportunity to sell the asset (or the investment is unsuccessful, written off, and the asset is liquidated). Exiting can take three to eight years (see Section 3.3 on liquidity). Upon the sale of an asset, the proceeds are usually distributed to investors immediately[15]. If the LPA allows it, GPs can reinvest early proceeds if funds are still in the investment period. Distributions are usually difficult to anticipate, and their timing can vary significantly. As a fund can only distribute cash, any asset remaining at the end of the fund's lifespan has to be sold. Fund managers can trigger an extension of the divestment period (see above) or sell assets on the direct secondary market.

PM funds do not offer redemptions: LPs are expected to remain invested in the fund until its full liquidation (which can happen at the end of its lifespan or, in rare cases, before). If needed, LPs can try to sell their fund stakes on the secondary market. There is no guarantee that LPs will be able to do so. The secondary market is informal and usually intermediated through specialists. When transactions happen,

---

[13]Braun et al. (2017) state, for example, that "funds, after all, are simply a legal wrapper around a sequence of underlying investments."

[14]For retail PE funds, the process is different: the capital is fully called upfront.

[15]In the case of an initial public offering (IPO), some rules apply for organizing an orderly divestment of PE owners.

the price of stakes is negotiated with a discount (usually of 15 to 30 percent, but the discount can go up to 50 to 70 percent in specific circumstances such as the financial crisis of 2007–2009) or sometimes a premium on the net asset value (NAV) of the fund. This net asset value is assessed quarterly by the GP, based on available information. Valuation techniques are determined by the IPEV guidelines (2015, updated in 2018), which state that assets should be valued at market value (marked to market) whenever possible. If this is not possible, then other techniques apply: for example, keeping assets at their historical cost and depreciating them if they do not develop as planned.

GPs have to commit a certain amount of their wealth to the fund, representing at least 1 percent of the fund size. They are compensated by yearly management fees[16] (paid quarterly in advance) calculated on the committed capital[17] of the fund (the fund size), or sometimes only the capital effectively deployed (the sum of capital paid in). Management fees are usually scaled down after the investment period by being calculated on the invested capital and/or according to a reduced management fee rate as time goes by.

GPs can collect transaction and other fees if this is planned by the LPA. These fees are usually partially or totally offset against management fees (Toll and Centopani, 2017). Organizational expenses of funds are also usually capped (normally at 1 percent of the fund size). Funds bear the costs associated with the analysis of investment opportunities that did not lead to investments (broken deal expenses).

Moreover, GPs are entitled to a performance fee (carried interest). It is calculated as a percentage of the profit of the fund (net of fees and expenses). PE funds usually pay a 20 percent carried interest to fund managers (Toll and Centopani, 2017), which has become an industry standard (this applies to 5 to 10 percent for funds of funds and 10 to 15 percent for direct lending funds[18] and some PRA funds). In some cases, fund managers command a 25 or even 30 percent carried interest[19]. Often, funds have

(*continued*)

---

[16]They range from 0.5 to 1 percent for funds of funds and 1 percent for direct lending funds (Jardine, 2017), as well as some private real asset strategies. For PE, mezzanine, and direct debt funds, the range is 1.5 to 2 percent. In certain cases, such as small VC funds or retail PE funds (sold to the general public), it can go up to 2.5 or 3 percent.

[17]According to McGrath (2017b), quoting Preqin, this is the case for 91 percent of LBO funds, 87 percent of growth capital funds, 84 percent of venture capital funds, 91 percent of funds of funds, 50 percent of direct lending funds, 63 percent of distressed debt funds, 71 percent of mezzanine funds, 52 percent of infrastructure funds, 64 percent of real estate funds, and 67 percent of natural resources funds. The rest charges the management fees on the invested capital.

[18]See Jardine (2017). According to Fixsen (2017), quoting Preqin, in 2016 the average management fee for private debt funds had fallen to 1.63 percent for 2016 vintage year funds. This encompasses the full spectrum of private debt funds.

[19]See Toll and Centopani (2017). LBO and VC funds that subscribe to this format often include the mandatory condition of hitting certain threshold returns (for example reaching a 2.5× cash-on-cash return before triggering a 25 percent carried interest).

(continued)

to reach a certain minimal performance before any performance fee is paid to GPs: the hurdle rate (also known as preferred rate of return). This rate is often determined as a minimum internal rate of return of 8 percent (Toll and Centopani, 2017) for PE funds (or less in the case of direct lending funds).

GPs have to raise the next generation of their funds regularly (usually every two to three years) to maintain their capacity to invest. The periodic liquidation of funds, and the necessity for GPs to raise capital, is theoretically akin to a democratic process: LPs get to reevaluate the work of GPs and to decide whether they renew their commitment (Demaria, 2015, Introduction).

In practice, the limited number of GPs with a track record of recurring and attractive past performances restricts the options of LPs. Moreover, GPs control the information that LPs receive. LPs have to engage in expensive and time-consuming due diligence on GPs. Once they pass the LPs' filter, GPs have a certain confidence that LPs will reinvest. In fact, LPs have also to pass the filter of GPs, looking for stable and long-term investors (Demaria, 2015). For LPs, switching to new GPs instead of investing in subsequent funds from GPs with whom they already cultivate relationships requires a compelling case. Not only does the case need to be solid to invest substantial resources to analyze a new relationship, but such a switch also implies that past choices from LPs were not optimal. LPs would recognize that they did not make the right choices in the past and would have to admit it to their own stakeholders. This admission would then have consequences on the career progression of executives involved, triggering agency issues (Demaria, 2015).

LPs delegate to GPs because the latter are **specialized**, as they have accumulated expertise and know-how. GPs are usually specialized geographically, by strategy (for example, VC, distressed debt, or brownfield infrastructure) or even sub-strategy (for example, early-, mid- or late-stage VC) and sometimes by industry (for example, software, semiconductors, oncology, or solar).

3.1.3   Further Intermediation: Funds-of-Funds, Mandates, and Securitization

Securitization and **funds-of-funds** offer investors a further degree of intermediation in PM investing. Securitization consists essentially in aggregating senior debt and loans (rated or not) into a large fund[20] and then to selling tranches of these funds. This

---

[20]This is done through Collateralized Debt Obligations (CDOs) and Collateralized Loan Obligations (CLOs). CDOs are created by fund managers who aggregate debt products such as mortgages, loans, and bonds (the collateral). Rating agencies assign a credit rating to CDOs, which can be guaranteed by a third party. CDOs are then divided in tranches that have different levels of seniority and therefore different priority in being repaid. The most senior tranches have a much lower risk of facing a default of repayment than the most junior or the equity tranche. The most senior tranches have therefore a better rating than the most junior ones, and thus pay a lower

technique can also apply to a portfolio of PM funds, used as a collateral to structure a CDO[21]. Funds of funds invest in a series of PM funds to provide investors with a high level of diversification, while targeting specific strategies and/or regions. These products prove to be particularly useful for investors with limited or no experience and resources to select GPs and fund managers. Funds of funds managers do this for them. As illustrated in Figure 3.3, for PE funds of funds, the chances of losses are limited (6.8 percent), as well as the losses given a loss (10 to 20 percent, measured in terms of internal rate of return).

As there is no passive investment instrument in PE[22], the closest equivalent to an ETF (or equivalent investable instrument) tracking PM "indexes" would be

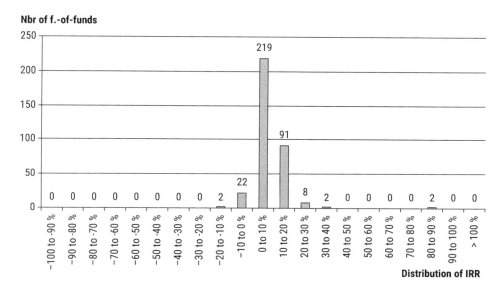

FIGURE 3.3   Performance of private equity funds of funds
Note: "f.-of-funds" refers to "funds of funds."
Source: Cambridge Associates (as of December 2016), Authors. N = 349 funds.

---

coupon. It is possible to assemble a basket of CDOs to further reduce the risk (in so-called CDO squared). CLOs are similar to CDOs but aggregate corporate loans with low or no rating, such as those used to finance LBOs. CLOs are neither rated nor guaranteed.

[21] In 2001–2002, Capital Dynamics jointly with Hamilton Lane and Rainer Marc Frey provided an illustration (*The Economist*, 2001). They securitized a portfolio of PE funds under the equivalent of a CDO named Prime Edge Capital for a total amount of €150 million. The product was guaranteed for its senior notes and liquidity by Allianz Risk Transfer. S&P rated the tranches. Capital Dynamics securitized in 2002 an existing portfolio of 64 funds from AIG in a $1 billion CDO with five tranches (Pine Street) and again, in 2006 a portfolio of 46 funds worth $810 million (Henzler, 2008).

[22] In particular, the LPX 50 is not relevant (Arias et al., 2010). This index tracks listed fund managers and holdings. As such, it does not provide any exposure to underlying assets and this index of listed private equity firms is, by design, distorted by the idiosyncratic risk of the firms that make up the index.

funds of funds. In effect, they provide a broad exposure, are diversified over time (their investment period is three years), track the pooled average performance of the industry, and are rather easily accessible with modest amounts to invest.

As funds of funds and securitization funds are rather generic and broad, some investors prefer to give a specific **mandate** (through segregated accounts[23]) to a fund manager or a consultant. This mandate is specifically set up according to the target and requirements of the investor. A minimum mandate size to invest in PE funds is €30 million. The mandate can be discretionary (the manager decides on the actual investments based on the criteria defined by the investor) or only advisory (the manager does the analysis, but the investor retains the final decisions). One of the benefits of mandates (Private Equity International, 2017) is that they help reduce fees and increase the transparency on costs and on investments. They also help reduce the number of GP relationships: this is important to LPs as monitoring GPs requires significant resources[24]. They also provide more control over the exposure of the investors, the portfolio, and the timing of investment.

The economics of the mandate change upon the choice of the investor. A discretionary mandate would probably include a performance-based commission, while an advisory mandate would probably not. Mandates, funds of funds, CDOs, and CLOs bear fees (and carried interest for funds of funds). They transform an indirect exposure to PM into essentially a highly diversified financial product.

3.2   BENEFITS AND CHALLENGES OF PRIVATE MARKETS INVESTING

The instruments described above were designed to provide institutional investors (see Chapter 1) with some of the benefits enjoyed by entrepreneurial families in their private investments, namely performance (2.1). PM investing also offers potential investment diversification. However, it remains challenging (2.2), due to a lack of transparency and information asymmetries. Some of these challenges are partially addressed by intermediation, which reduces some of the risks associated with direct investing (2.3) but implies higher costs and principal-agent dynamics.

3.2.1   Benefits: Performance and Diversification

Entrepreneurial families are drawn to PE investing for at least two reasons: they can exercise a certain level of control on it, and these investments can generate substantial profits. **Control** and **performance** are intimately linked. A family can set a strategy, then execute it or delegate the execution, monitor the progress, and adjust the strategy. The success materializes in financial proceeds.

---

[23] Also called separately managed accounts.

[24] To reduce monitoring costs, some LPs have decided to significantly reduce their GP relationships. By concentrating their capital in the hands of a reduced number of GPs, they also hope to negotiate better terms and generate economies of scale. An illustration was provided by CalPERS, the largest public pension fund in the US, which decided in 2015 to reduce the number of fund managers by half (from 212 to "about 100"; Martin, 2015).

Although institutional investors are drawn to **financial performance**, their will and resources to apply efficient direct control on private assets are usually limited. The result is that pension funds have exhibited poor direct investment performances in PE (Nielsen, 2010). This is confirmed by Fang et al. (2015), who analyzed seven large institutions with 20 years of experience in direct PE investments and state: "While solo transactions outperform fund benchmarks, investors' ability to resolve information problems appears to be an important driver of solo deal outcomes." Despite their long experience, these large institutions with substantial resources only perform in direct investments if they have the specific skills and resources for that purpose.

Therefore, institutional investors delegate not only the operational development of private assets but also the selection and control of private investments themselves (see Section 1 above). Fund investors exercise a limited level of control on fund managers (Demaria, 2015). PM provide institutional investors with a source of **investment diversification** in the construction of their portfolio. The value proposition is therefore attractive, combining higher financial performance with portfolio diversification, the latter not reducing the former as explained below.

Measuring Performance: IRR, MOIC, and PME

Before delving into performances and the debates about them, it is necessary to clarify how they are calculated and measured. Three measures of performance are used to assess PM investments: the internal rate of return (IRR), the multiple of invested capital (MOIC), and the public market equivalent (PME). Each has its own advantage but suffers from significant drawbacks. These performance indicators can be presented net or gross of fees.

Gross returns help investors in assessing the value creation of fund managers. However, most returns communicated by database providers and sought by investors notably for benchmarking purposes are net of any fees and costs. Net returns are the only reliable way to assess and compare the performance of a fund manager. However, the returns are only net of any fee and cost paid by the fund. In certain instances, such as in LBOs, underlying assets sometimes pay fees[25] to the fund manager. According to the industry's best practices, these fees should be offset against management fees. For the purpose of this book, and unless disclosed otherwise, all fund performance figures used are net of any fees and costs.

---

[25]For example, monitoring fees, which can be "accelerated" to be collected in full by the fund manager in the event of a sale or an IPO. This practice has triggered investigations from the SEC, which sanctions fund managers for this practice. For example, in December 2017 TPG settled with the SEC for $13 million (including a $3 million penalty) over such charges that were done without proper disclosure to limited partners (see Bradford, 2017). The best practice is currently that either fees paid by the underlying assets to the fund manager are forbidden (as the fund manager is already compensated by the fund with the management fees for such effort) or, if such fees are paid to the fund manager, they have to be offset against management fees. It is up to fund investors to check the practice of each fund manager and ensure that best practices are applied.

Internal Rate of Return (IRR)

Despite its flaws (see below), the internal rate of return[26] (IRR) is probably the most commonly used metric to assess the performance of PM funds. Suited to the evaluation of multi-year investment projects, this annualized measure of performance factors the effect of time on investments. Expressed as a percentage, it supports the immediate comparison of two similar investments to determine which one is the best.

The IRR therefore seems a good candidate to measure the performance of PM funds. However, it suffers from various significant drawbacks:

1. The IRR measures the performance of capital effectively invested and not the capital committed. For institutional investors, this means that there is a discrepancy between the measure of the cost of capital (measured on the full amount committed) and the measure of return on capital (on the capital effectively invested). Indeed, as PM funds call their capital as needed (see Insert 1), the IRR starts with the capital call and stops as the capital is refunded. If this is appropriate for comparing simple investment projects, for institutional investors the use of IRR raises some challenges. The uncalled capital (capital that is reserved for PM investments but not yet invested, also named dry powder) represents a performance drag that is challenging to anticipate and compute[27]. Moreover, institutional investors get to deploy on a net basis a maximum of 60 to 65 percent of their commitment. The first distributions of a PM fund usually compensate the capital calls happening at the later stage.

   To approach a maximum exposure close to 100 percent, some investors engage in a practice of over-commitment: they commit for a higher amount than they effectively plan to deploy. This practice indeed helps investors hit their operational target in terms of capital deployment, but the risk is that the pattern of distributions is delayed due to an economic or a financial crisis. PM funds would theoretically continue to draw down their capital, and investors could be in effect over-allocated (or worse, they might have to default on their commitment).

2. The IRR is a time-sensitive instrument that is particularly affected by the timing of cash flows. It can be easily manipulated to show magnified performances. At least two instances demonstrate the weaknesses of this instrument:

   a. Fund managers can be tempted to generate cash inflows as quickly as possible. Early cash flows will boost the fund's IRR. For that purpose, fund managers might:

      i. Give up on part of the absolute performance of the fund they manage in exchange for early proceeds. They might sell a company at the first occasion instead of trying to maximize its value. As the IRR does not offer alternative

---

[26]Calculated as: ((cash inflows) / (−cash outflows))^(1/duration of investment) − 1

[27]The cost of uncalled capital is also difficult to offset. This uncalled capital could be placed on money markets, but this falls short of the cost of capital of institutional investors. Even optimizing the duration of this uncalled capital to match the expected drawdowns of PM funds with modeling (see Chapter 5) can go only so far.

scenarios in its calculation, there is no sanction for fund managers who give up on some additional cash proceeds.

ii. Be tempted to take on more risks to distribute early proceeds[28]. As the IRR is not risk-weighted, there is no penalty for the fund manager to do it.

Distributing proceeds early in effect exacerbates the issues of institutional investors willing to deploy more capital, for a longer time, and willing to maximize their performance in regard to the cost of capital associated to PM investors.

b. Fund managers can also delay capital calls (or anticipate distributions) by using credit lines. This shortens holding periods and boosts IRRs. For lenders this is a profitable activity, and there is a low credit risk[29] as fund investors will eventually pay their capital call or face hefty penalties (Demaria, 2015). For fund managers this is an attractive practice that helps magnifying time-sensitive IRRs. For fund investors, this is a detrimental practice that compounds existing issues. First, their capital stays even idler than in the scenario without credit lines. Then, their absolute performance is reduced as the fund effectively pays interests. Finally, this practice muddles further the interpretation of IRRs. In particular, it is difficult to separate value creation from pure financial leverage. As the use of credit lines is becoming more commonplace, forecasting PM fund cash flows becomes more difficult for investors. These forecasts are precisely necessary for leading a policy of over-commitment or simply to minimize the performance drag of uncalled capital. The result is that funds are becoming more leveraged, and fund investors might also use leverage. This could compound risks, especially in a downturn scenario where liquidity is scarce, as demonstrated in 2008–2009. The Institutional Limited Partners Association (ILPA, 2017) recommends a full disclosure by fund managers on their use of credit lines, to limit the use to a certain percentage of the uncalled capital (15–25 percent) and for a maximum of 180 days outstanding.

---

[28] For example, through a "dividend recap" of a company under a leveraged buyout (LBO). This operation consists of a fund manager borrowing money against a company that the fund owns and then distributing the proceeds from this loan to fund investors. The company is supposed to refund progressively the loan by distributing dividends. This magnifies the IRR as fund investors collect capital fast but increases the risk associated with the investment: if the company fails to repay, creditors can exercise their right to take control of the company, sell it and get their principal back. For its owner to avoid this scenario, the company has to undertake whatever is needed to repay the loan. It might have to divert some of its resources to do so, possibly damaging its development, growth prospects, or its position on the market.

[29] However, tail risks are high as illustrated by the following example. A fund manager launches a fund and decides to make significant investments by drawing on a credit line backed by a first closing. Building this first pool of assets could help the fund manager to reduce the fear that many investors experience when investing in a blind pool. However, the value of assets could drop in case of adverse events. Not only new investors would shun the fund, but existing investors might decide not to pay their commitment, as the penalty for such action is ineffective. As a matter of fact, the penalty for defaulting fund investors is to reduce the value of their actual commitment by half and ultimately exclude them from the fund. As the fund did not draw on commitments, this penalty is irrelevant. The lender could seize assets, but fund managers could also be liable for such a scenario.

3. The IRR assumes that capital refunded can be reinvested immediately at no cost at an identical rate. This is never the case. Distributions from PM funds are essentially unpredictable as they depend on the sale of private assets (a process which may span many months and is never disclosed in advance). Institutional investors cannot reinvest them immediately in PM funds from the same manager, as managers raise funds for a given strategy every two to three years. Moreover, capital is called as needed (see previous point). Significant costs are also incurred to operate a complete due diligence on fund managers.
4. The IRR does not take into account the context of investment. Although the MOIC suffers from the same limits, this is of particular importance in the case of the IRR. As the IRR is time sensitive, particularly favorable economic and financial conditions can significantly lift a fund performance without any specific extra effort from the fund manager.

As PM become more efficient, performance dispersion of fund managers decreases. Competition between fund managers to attract capital increases correspondingly. Fund investors routinely benchmark fund managers by comparing the performance of their funds with their peer group. The peer group is constituted of the funds created the same year and applying the same strategy in the same geographical region. Funds are ranked by performance into quartiles. Fund investors decide to invest in upcoming funds depending on the ability of a fund manager to place past funds in the top, or upper, quartile of the peer group. Being part of the top quartile can sometimes be related to minor performance differences. The incentives to manipulate the IRR of a fund by accelerating cash inflows or delaying capital deployment increase correspondingly. The temptation for fund managers is real.

IRRs should therefore not be taken at face value but recalculated by fund investors to understand how they were generated and whether some of practices described above were applied. If so, they may recalculate them to harmonize fund performances and be able to compare them. The ILPA (2017) recommends that fund managers provide such information and has come up with a template for that matter. IRRs should also be interpreted in combination with other performance metrics such as MOICs. Moreover, fund investors can use the time-zero IRR formula (also known as MIRR) to reduce the artificial impact of early cash flows on the performance of a fund. They could also input money market interest rates as the variable of reinvestment for PM fund distributions to compute their MIRR.

Multiple of Invested Capital (MOIC)

The multiple of invested capital[30] (MOIC) is also a commonly used metric to assess the performance of PM funds. It became over time the main reference in private markets. One of its main advantages is that it focuses on the absolute performance of funds. It is expressed in "multiples of" represented by an × (as in 1.0×, for example, for an investment which just breaks even). MOICs are by construction agnostic to the amounts

---

[30] Also referred to as paid in.

used as a basis of calculation, which facilitates comparisons of fund performances. The main MOIC used in PE is the "total value to paid in" (TVPI). This ratio is the result of the division of the sum of distributions and value of assets in a portfolio (the total value), on one hand, and by the total capital called by the fund manager, on the other (the paid in). If the paid in includes fees and costs, then the TVPI is net. If it does not, then it is gross.

The TVPI is the sum of two other ratios: the "distributed to paid in" (DPI), which is the result of the sum of distributions divided by the total capital called by the fund manager, and the "residual value to paid in" (RVPI), which is the sum of the value of assets in a portfolio[31] divided by the total capital called by the fund manager. These two ratios are complementary. When a fund is launched, the RVPI increases as the fund invests. At the early stage of a PM fund, the TVPI equals the RVPI only. Then the fund starts to dispose of certain assets. The RVPI then decreases, and the DPI usually increases, although not necessarily by the same amounts. If the fund sells a given asset at a higher price than for what it was kept in the fund, the DPI increase will be higher than the RVPI decrease. Vice versa, if the sale happens at a lower price than what the asset was accounted for, the DPI increase will be lower than the RVPI decrease. If the asset is a full loss (write-off), then there will be no DPI increase corresponding to the RVPI decrease. At the end of its lifespan, the TVPI equals the DPI only.

The TVPI captures in one figure the current situation of a given fund. The RVPI isolates the value of assets in the portfolio and reflects the potential for future performance of a fund. The DPI reflects the proceeds distributed to investors and is an indication of the maturity of the fund. The three ratios can be compared to a historical or current average.

Figure 3.4 provides a perspective on the TVPI of PM strategies and the dispersion of this TVPI (spread of top 5 percent and bottom 5 percent) as proxy for risk. According to this risk-return scatterplot, riskier strategies are—not surprisingly—potentially the more profitable ones. Financing start-ups (VC) ranks among the riskiest but also possibly the more lucrative investment activity. An investor in American VC funds could multiply his investment by 1.72 (on a net pooled average basis). This multiple could be as low as 0.33× (a multiple achieved by the bottom 5 percent of the sample) and as high as 5.30× (achieved by the top 5 percent of the sample) depending on which fund the investor would have selected.

The TVPI has been criticized as a measure of performance. It partially relies on NAV calculations by fund managers[32], who could be tempted to inflate the valuations of their portfolio companies[33]. Brown, Gredil, and Kaplan (2013) have indeed found

---

[31] As estimated by the fund manager according to the best practices detailed in the International Private Equity and Venture Capital Valuation Guidelines (http://www.privateequityvaluation .com/valuation-guidelines/4588034291, last accessed 2/1/2018). See Insert 1.

[32] See Insert 1 for more details about NAVs and their estimation by fund managers.

[33] At least two reasons could explain this behavior. First, when fund raising, a fund manager relies on his track record, which notably includes active funds. Inflating valuations of active funds might help to appear as successful and therefore trigger commitments to the next generation of funds. Second, during the divestment period, most of fund regulations set the management

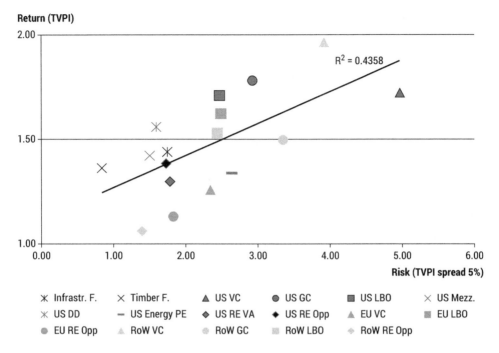

FIGURE 3.4 Return (TVPI)-risk (5 percent spread) profile of private markets strategies "Infrastr. F." stands for global infrastructure funds, "Timber F." for global timberland funds, "VC" for venture capital, "LBO" for leveraged buyout, "Mezz." for mezzanine debt, "DD" for distressed debt, "RE" fore real estate, "VA" for value add, "Opp" for opportunistic, and "RoW" for rest of the world.
Source: Authors, based on Cambridge Associates data published in December 2016 (data as of Q2 2016). Funds' performance only. Vintage years record fully realized funds and active funds that are largely realized (up to 2008).

"evidence of managers boosting reported NAVs during times [of] fundraising [...]. However, this behavior is mostly limited to firms that are subsequently unsuccessful at raising a next fund [, which] suggests that investors see through the manipulation[34]. In contrast, [they found] evidence that top-performing funds under-report returns. This conservatism is consistent with these firms insuring against future bad luck that could make them appear as [...] NAV manipulators." Therefore, there is a reporting risk (see below, section on risks), but it tends to be limited. Nevertheless, throughout this book, we will refer often to DPIs to cross-check our results and assumptions.

---

fees as calculated as a percentage of the NAV of the fund. The higher the NAV is, the higher the compensation of the fund manager will be.
[34]This is confirmed by Johan and Zhang (2016), who state that "endowments are systematically associated with less pronounced differences between realized returns and subsequently realized returns. Moreover, endowments receive more frequent reports from their PE funds, implying more stringent governance [...] Higher reporting frequencies from PE funds are correlated with a lower tendency for the limited partners to receive overstated performance reports."

An alternative is to rely only on DPIs, which is our approach whenever this is possible. DPIs cannot be manipulated as they are cash-on-cash calculations. The issue with relying only on DPIs is that to be fully meaningful, this ratio requires liquidated funds. Often, these DPIs reflect performances generated in very different conditions than the ones expected in the future. Figure 3.5 illustrates this statement with US VC. According to it, the performance of US VC is outstanding and should trigger a wave of allocations to this investment strategy. Indeed, thanks to US VC, some large US endowments have, for a while, been performing very well compared to other institutional investors (Lerner et al., 2007). However, these historical performances faded after 1998, and over 1999–2006 endowments did not outperform anymore (Sensoy et al., 2014). US VC performances of 1991–1998 are not likely to be reproduced going forward (the section on VC in Section 3 illustrates this point). Strategies with relatively shorter holding periods, therefore reaching distribution stages faster, are also favored by a DPI analysis, especially when including active funds (as Fig. 3.5 does, with vintage years until 2008).

Moreover, more mature strategies and geographical regions (such as the US) are better documented and therefore appear as more attractive. This is the case in Figure 3.6 with the US: local private market strategies are the most mature and exhibit the highest DPI.

Figure 3.7 provides a different perspective by setting a single and recent time period: 1999–2008. Unfortunately, not all the strategies considered have data for each of the considered vintage years[35]. This approach shows that US VC is no longer an exception—or that VC funds from the rest of the world could be the exception this time. The hierarchy of equity, debt, and real assets remains valid. The correlation between risk and returns remains valid but is weaker. Many of the funds captured in the sample, especially on the real asset side, are in the making (Fig. 3.8). This is because the maturity of strategies differs significantly (Fig. 3.9). In particular, private debt exhibits the highest maturity and therefore the fastest time to liquidity. It is followed by growth and LBO strategies in private debt, while private real assets exhibit the slowest pace to maturity. As mentioned above, Figure 3.9 shows that VC funds from the rest of the world are still very much in the making and that the TVPIs that measure performance in Figure 3.7 are still essentially estimates.

MOICs are probably the most reliable indicators of performance. They cannot easily be manipulated. To compare PM funds, multiples are robust and support rigorous analysis. The flipside is that they require interpretation from fund investors for the following reasons:

1. They do not take into account the effect of time and cannot be easily annualized. MOICs do not include any time-discounting mechanisms. Comparing PM funds with funds applying other alternative or traditional investment strategies can therefore be difficult. In particular, as PM funds are not rapidly and fully invested, it is even more difficult to compare their performance with other asset classes. To do so, it is necessary to factor in holding periods, which materialize the duration of investments. The Public Market Equivalent methodology supports this approach (see next section), but MOICs do not.

---

[35]Global infrastructure and RoW RE Opp. encompass only vintage years from 2003 to 2008; and EU GC only vintage years 2000, 2001, 2005, 2006, 2007, and 2008.

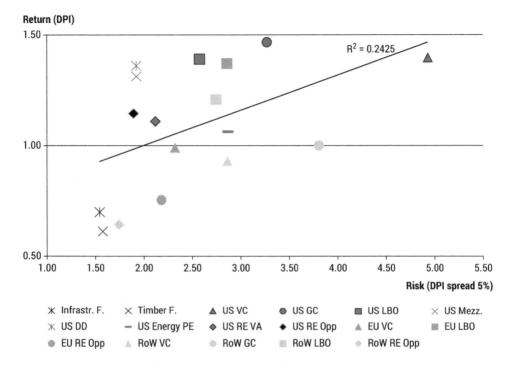

FIGURE 3.5 Return (DPI)-risk (5 percent spread) profile of private markets strategies
Note: Return is measured thanks to the pooled average Total value to paid-in ratio (TVPI) of
sample funds. The total value of funds is the addition of proceeds distributed from the sale of
investments (distributed), and the unrealized value of investments still in portfolio (residual
value). The paid-in is the sum of capital called and invested by funds. Risk is measured by the
difference of performance (TVPI) between funds belonging to the top 5 percent of the sample
and funds belonging to the bottom 5 percent. Samples for each strategy cover different time
periods until 2008.
"Infrastr. F." stands for global infrastructure funds, "Timber F." for global timberland funds,
"VC" for venture capital, "LBO" for leveraged buyout, "Mezz." for mezzanine debt, "DD" for
distressed debt, "RE" for real estate, "VA" for value add, "Opp" for opportunistic, and "RoW"
for rest of the world.
Note: Return is measured thanks to the pooled average distributed to paid-in ratio (DPI) of
sample funds. Risk is measured by the difference of performance (DPI) between funds
belonging to the top 5 percent of the sample and funds belonging to the bottom 5 percent.
Samples for each strategy cover different time periods until 2008.
Source: Authors, based on Cambridge Associates data published in December 2016 (data as of
Q2 2016). Funds' performance only. Vintage years record fully realized funds and active funds
that are largely realized (up to 2008).

Return (DPI)

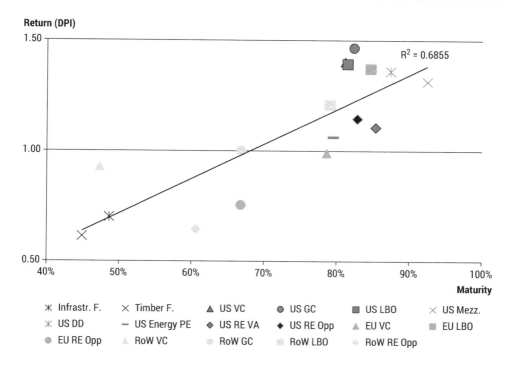

FIGURE 3.6 Return (DPI)-maturity profile of private markets strategies

"Infrastr. F." stands for global infrastructure funds, "Timber F." for global timberland funds, "VC" for venture capital, "LBO" for leveraged buyout, "Mezz." for mezzanine debt, "DD" for distressed debt, "RE" for real estate, "VA" for value add, "Opp" for opportunistic, and "RoW" for rest of the world.

Note: Return is measured thanks to the pooled average distributed to paid-in ratio (DPI) of sample funds. Maturity is measured by dividing the total distributions (DPI) by total value (TVPI). Samples for each strategy cover different time periods until 2008.

Source: Authors, based on Cambridge Associates data published in December 2016 (data as of Q2 2016). Funds' performance only. Vintage years record fully realized funds and active funds that are largely realized (up to 2008).

2. Like IRRs, MOICs do not take into account the context of investment. Investors have therefore to benchmark funds with their peers but also to look at macroeconomic and financial conditions to analyze the performance of fund managers. Given the fact that investment periods usually span five years and divestment periods five to seven years, it is difficult to separate value creation by fund managers from the effect of these conditions (as well as luck) (Korteweg and Sorensen, 2015).

3. MOICs as described above take into account the capital invested, not the capital committed. The performance drag associated with the uncalled capital is not integrated into MOICs. Fund investors have to apply specific calculations to integrate opportunity costs and cost of capital in the overall performance analysis based on MOICs.

Return (TVPI)

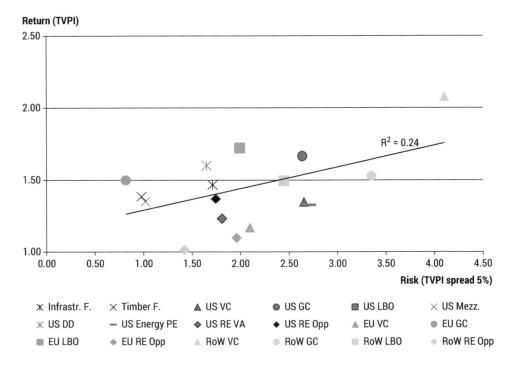

FIGURE 3.7   Return (TVPI)-risk (5 percent spread) profile of private markets strategies (1999–2008) "Infrastr. F." stands for global infrastructure funds, "Timber F." for global timberland funds, "VC" for venture capital, "LBO" for leveraged buyout, "Mezz." for mezzanine debt, "DD" for distressed debt, "RE" for real estate, "VA" for value add, "Opp" for opportunistic, and "RoW" for rest of the world.

Note: Return is measured thanks to the pooled average total value to paid-in ratio (TVPI) of sample funds. Risk is measured by the difference of performance (TVPI) between funds belonging to the top 5 percent of the sample and funds belonging to the bottom 5 percent. Samples for each strategy cover the same time period: 1999–2008.

Source: Authors, based on Cambridge Associates data published in July 2017 (data as of Q4 2016). Funds' performance only. Vintage years record fully realized funds and active funds that are largely realized (up to 2008).

   4. MOICs are not risk adjusted. Technically, it would be possible to compute a simplified Sharpe[36] or Sortino[37] ratio by dividing the pooled average TVPI (or DPI) by
   the TVPI (or DPI) spread. However, this delivers only a relatively imperfect proxy
   of the expected results for three reasons:

---

[36]The Sharpe ratio is designed to measure the excess return generated by an asset or a group of assets against the risk-free rate and divide the result by a measure of risk (usually the standard deviation of this excess return). The formula is therefore: Sharpe ratio = (asset(s) return – risk-free rate) / (standard deviation of (asset(s) return – risk-free rate)).

[37]The Sortino ratio is a variation of the Sharpe ratio. It is the result of the realized return minus the target/required rate of return of the investment strategy divided by the semi-deviation, which

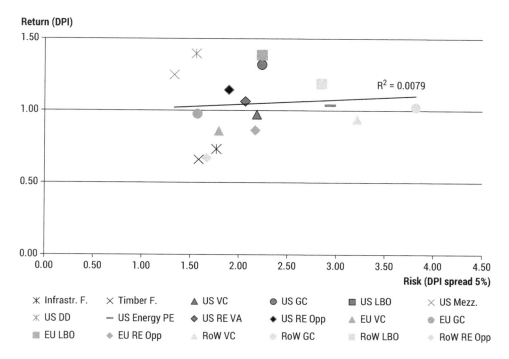

Return (DPI)

✻ Infrastr. F.	✕ Timber F.	▲ US VC	● US GC	▪ US LBO	✕ US Mezz.
✳ US DD	— US Energy PE	◆ US RE VA	◆ US RE Opp	▲ EU VC	● EU GC
▪ EU LBO	◆ EU RE Opp	▲ RoW VC	● RoW GC	▪ RoW LBO	◆ RoW RE Opp

FIGURE 3.8   Return (DPI)-risk (5 percent spread) profile of private markets strategies (1999–2008)

"Infrastr. F." stands for global infrastructure funds, "Timber F." for global timberland funds, "VC" for venture capital, "LBO" for leveraged buyout, "Mezz." for mezzanine debt, "DD" for distressed debt, "RE" for real estate, "VA" for value add, "Opp" for opportunistic, and "RoW" for rest of the world.

Note: Return is measured thanks to the pooled average distributed to paid-in ratio (TVPI) of sample funds. Risk is measured by the difference of performance (DPI) between funds belonging to the top 5 percent of the sample and funds belonging to the bottom 5 percent. Samples for each strategy cover the same time period: 1999–2008.

Source: Authors, based on Cambridge Associates data published in July 2017 (data as of Q4 2016). Funds' performance only. Vintage years record fully realized funds and active funds that are largely realized (up to 2008).

    a. Funds are not fully and permanently invested; this would require detailed calculations about the actual exposure of funds. Not only does this require significant work, but this level of granularity of data is difficult to access (except for investors in single funds). As a result, it is difficult to deduct the risk-free rate as the standard Sharpe formula would require—PM funds are invested over multiple

---

is supposed to be a proxy of the downside deviation as the Sortino ratio assumes a normal distribution of risks. As shown previously, return distributions in private markets do not follow a normal distribution. Calculations such as Monte Carlo simulations, Sharpe ratios, and Sortino ratios are therefore in essence ineffective and require for the latter two adjustments to be of use.

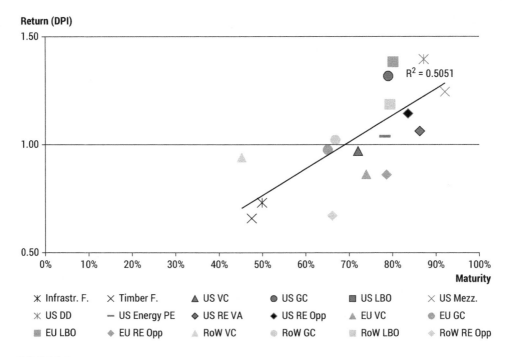

FIGURE 3.9   Return (DPI)-maturity profile of private markets strategies (1999–2008)
"Infrastr. F." stands for global infrastructure funds, "Timber F." for global timberland funds,
"VC" for venture capital, "LBO" for leveraged buyout, "Mezz." for mezzanine debt, "DD" for
distressed debt, "RE" for real estate, "VA" for value add, "Opp" for opportunistic, and "RoW"
for rest of the world.
Note: Return is measured thanks to the pooled average distributed to paid-in ratio (DPI) of
sample funds. Maturity is measured by dividing the total distributions (DPI) by total value
(TVPI). Samples for each strategy cover different time periods until 2008.
Source: Authors, based on Cambridge Associates data published July 2017 (data as of Q4 2016).
Funds' performance only. Vintage years record fully realized funds and active funds which are
largely realized (up to 2008).

years during which the risk-free rate changes. Moreover, as the actual underlying exposure of PM funds fluctuates over time and reaches a usual net maximum of 60–65 percent for PE funds, it would prove to be difficult to compare
Sharpe/Sortino ratios with funds from other asset classes, which are usually
rapidly deployed and remain essentially fully invested.
  b. Sharpe and Sortino ratios rely on a definition of volatility that does not really
    apply to PM funds (and which itself is criticized). Even though a TVPI (or DPI)
    spread can be calculated, assuming sufficiently rich statistical samples, it cannot
    be computed for a single fund.
  c. Sharpe and Sortino ratios are calculated assuming normal distributions, notably
    for risk measurement. This assumption is not satisfied for PM funds, which
    exhibit non-symmetric, fat tails.

Public Market Equivalent (PME)

The Public Market Equivalent (PME) is an attempt to address some of the criticisms formulated toward the IRR and the MOIC in a consistent and rigorous way. This rather recent method was designed as a proxy to compare PE fund investments with public markets. Initially designed as the "Index Comparison Method" by Kocis et al. (2009, Ch. 11), the method was further refined by Ljungqvist and Richardson (2003) and Kaplan and Schoar (2005) to become the PME. Originally, the PME method consisted in discounting the distributions of a PE fund by using the S&P 500 total return index. These discounted distributions were added up and then divided by the sum of all the discounted capital calls of the fund. A PME greater than one indicates the fund under consideration outperformed the listed index. Rouvinez (2003) refined it with his PME+ by adjusting distributions by using a scale factor applied to the sum of the distributions[38].

To be fully effective, the PME method requires a few adjustments. First, it is better applied to fully realized funds, as it requires distributions to be computed. Considering the NAV of funds as a distribution is misleading and renders the analysis moot[39]. Second, the approach of Kaplan and Schoar, which blends the paid-in, is not precise enough. This is due to the fact that available data from commercial databases is anonymized and aggregated. Although a precise PME would require matching each capital call to each distribution to effectively factor holding periods (and therefore eliminate time sensitiveness and liquidity from the list of questions), data does not allow it. Demaria (2015, Ch. 2) suggests computing a PME-DPI, which computes an average holding period and assumes that capital calls match distributions on this basis. However, this is an approximation, and it would be better to access the detailed cash inflow and outflow information to buy and sell the index and replicate exactly the cash-flow pattern of the fund(s) analysed with an index. To our knowledge, Cambridge Associates[40] is the closest to achieve a true replication of cash-flow patterns of PM funds thanks to an index. Its "modified Public Market Equivalent" (mPME) is therefore one of the best attempts at applying the PME method.

There are various advantages associated with the use of the PME. First, it considers the context of investment by neutralizing the economic and financial environment as reflected by the listed index chosen. In that respect, it supports the clear identification

---

[38]Focusing on IRRs and PME, Gredil et al. (2014) offered a further refinement of the PME+ by suggesting the computation of a "direct alpha." In their method, fund cash flows are compounded by the returns of the reference benchmark to the same single point in time. Their method in essence blends cash flows without reconciling them to single investments and focus on interim NAV. We do not support this approach, as we consider IRRs irrelevant, and a PME calculation should reconcile cash inflows and outflows for single investments and ignore interim NAVs to just consider the NAV at calculation time for active funds.

[39]The treatment of NAVs in the PME method triggers other methodological issues documented by the academic literature, such as excess remaining NAV. The PME+ method (Rouvinez, 2003) and PME-DPI method (Demaria, 2015) offer different solutions.

[40]Cambridge Associates, "About Our Investment Benchmarks," pp. 5–6 (https://40926u2govf9kuqen1ndit018su-wpengine.netdna-ssl.com/wp-content/uploads/2014/02/CA-PE-and-VC-Benchmarks-Overview-Definitions-and-FAQs.pdf, last accessed 3/1/2018).

of the value creation of a fund manager or a PM strategy[41]. Then, it neutralizes the debate about time sensitiveness or liquidity by setting a standard time framework for comparison.

Harris et al. (2014) describe it as a "market-adjusted multiple of invested capital." Robinson and Sensoy (2013) state that the PME does not measure the "true" risk-adjusted returns of PM funds. This statement is probably correct, especially since it is difficult to effectively measure risks associated with PM investing with one single metric. However, the PME comes close to solving many issues plaguing the analysis of performance of PM funds. Indeed, Sorensen and Jagannathan (2015) state that using the PME is "equivalent to assessing the performance of PE investments using Rubinstein's dynamic version of the CAPM" and that "one need not compute betas of PE investments, and any changes in PE cash flow betas [. . .] are automatically taken into account."

The flip side of using the PME is that the results are sensitive to the choice of the index. For many PM strategies, it is difficult to choose the right index or even identify one that could be relevant. For example, benchmarking PD strategies or private real estate ones is particularly challenging as there is only a limited supply of indexes, and they tend to track the same type of assets. Even benchmarking VC funds outside the US is challenging, as there is no real international equivalent to the Nasdaq composite (which gathers the closest listed comparable companies to technology start-ups in the US). Sorensen and Jagannathan (2015) advise that the "public market index used in evaluations should be the one that best approximates the wealth portfolio of the investor considering the PE investment opportunity."

Finally, the PME does not take into account the performance drag of the uncalled capital, although by tweaking it, this could be possible. The idea would be to assume that the capital is deployed at 100 percent in an index the first day of activity of a PM fund or regularly over six to twelve months and then sell the index as the fund divests. However, this could raise other methodological questions, especially if a PM fund does not fully invest the committed capital or invests more of the committed capital (by recycling early distributions, as sometimes allowed by the fund regulation to compensate the performance drag of management fees).

Performance and its persistence

Investors are interested in PM funds for their performance. PE strategies are on the higher risk / higher return end of the scatterplot exhibited above in Figures 3.4 and 3.5. They all exhibit a TVPI spread above 2.0×, while PD and private real asset strategies come next. Due to a lack of data, some investment strategies and regions are missing. In particular, more conservative strategies (such as direct lending or core real estate) are not documented[42].

---

[41] It could even be used to change some of the terms and conditions associated with the compensation of fund managers, setting up a flexible method to establish a hurdle rate and a carried interest (Demaria, 2015, Chap. 2).

[42] Possible reasons for this information gap are that some regions have only emerged recently as playing fields for some strategies. Other strategies are rather new or have evolved in their structuring (for example from open-end to closed-end funds). As a result, database providers do not have enough data to support an analysis.

Nevertheless, each PM strategy with sufficient data as tracked by Cambridge Associates delivers a positive performance on a pooled average net basis. Figure 3.4 (encompassing the full history of different PM strategies until 2008) and Figure 3.7 (covering only 1999–2008) deliver an important piece of information: none of the strategies exhibit a pooled average TVPI below 1.0×. This assumes that investors are able to invest in all the funds tracked by the database on a pro rata basis. The performance sought by fund investors and referred to at the beginning of this section is visible but requires patience and an ability to select (Demaria, 2015, Introduction) and to actively monitor (Johan and Zhang, 2016) funds.

According to Coller Capital's Global Private Equity Barometer of Winter 2017–18[43], 82 percent of fund investors expect to achieve annual net returns of 11 percent or more across their PE portfolio over the next three to five years. Only 17 percent of them expect to reach net returns of 16 percent or more. 60 percent of fund investors expect declining returns as the PE market matures[44]. Section 3 will provide more detailed elements about risks and returns for each investment strategy.

Why are investors so keen on reflecting on past performance, while financial theory usually explicitly states that past performance is not a predictor of future performance? The main reason is that, unlike in other areas of finance[45], historical performance figures matter in PM due to a phenomenon known as the persistence of performance of fund managers. Sensoy et al. (2014) note that "private equity performance continues to outperform public markets on average" over 1999–2006, as they did in 1991–1998, despite the general maturing of the industry[46]. Korteweg and Sorensen (2015), note that the persistence of performance remains factually true for high and low performers[47]. This persistence is partially related to:

- Long-term large spread of performance between top and bottom quartile PE funds (that they estimate at 7 to 8 percentage points annually net of fees).
- The overlap of contemporaneous funds. According to Korteweg and Sorensen, "Partially overlapping funds are exposed to the same market conditions during the overlap period. Even though these contemporaneous exposures are purely transitory

---

[43]Coller Capital, Global Private Equity Barometer, Winter 2017–18, p. 12 (https://www .collercapital.com/sites/default/files/Coller%20Capital%20Global%20Private%20Equity %20Barometer%20Winter%202017-18.pdf, last accessed 04/01/2018). Sample is 110 fund investors in PE funds, 40 percent of whom are based in North America, 40 percent in Europe, and 20 percent in Asia-Pacific.

[44]The Introduction provides some background to compare these returns with other asset classes. However, as explained in the next section, comparing annual returns with IRR is misleading.

[45]See Korteweg and Sorensen (2015) for a synthetic literature review encompassing mutual funds and hedge funds.

[46]Which "has transitioned from a niche, poorly understood area to a ubiquitous part of institutional investors' portfolio" (Sensoy et al., 2014).

[47]Kaplan and Schoar (2005) were the first to document the persistence of performance of private equity fund managers. Robinson and Sensoy (2013) confirmed it, while Harris et al. (2013) find that it declined for LBO fund managers after 2000. However, this is debated. Li (2014) found, for example, that LBO fund managers exhibit a stronger persistence of returns than VC fund managers. However, Harris et al. (2014) found additional evidence of persistence of performance of VC fund managers and a drop of in persistence for buyout funds after 2000.

[. . .], they induce a positive correlation in the performance of subsequent overlapping funds, which shows up as a spurious persistence." Empirically, this sounds rather implausible. First, PM funds are raised on average every two to three years according to the same sequencing. Fund managers compete with their peers with funds from the same vintage years. Good market conditions therefore benefit the whole peer group. When the tide comes in, all the boats are lifted accordingly. If one boat behaves differently, this means that the captain did something different. Second, fund regulations prevent successive funds from cross-investments to avoid conflicts of interests. Therefore, two successive funds do not invest together in the same deals. This means that even if two boats share the same captain, they are in effect at two different spots during the tidal cycle. The captain has to exploit the conditions and location of each boat optimally. What Korteweg and Sorensen describe as "spurious" is not empirically validated and might indeed be an expression of persistence of returns.

– Selection skills that they estimate as "modest." They conclude that luck plays a significant role in selecting good or bad performers. This point contradicts empirical knowledge and practice. It therefore deserves some additional comments.

Selection skills are assessed throughout the academic literature by a single approach: assessing the ability of fund managers to consistently rank in a certain quartile. However, this approach assumes that the dispersion of returns (and for that matter all else) remains constant. This is not the case. Sensoy et al. (2014) describe the maturing of the PE industry. This translates into narrower spreads of performance as illustrated by Figure 3.5 (which encompasses the whole history of PM strategies until 2008) and Figure 3.8 (which focuses on 1999–2008). The simple average of the DPI spread (5 percent) reflected is respectively 2.54× and 2.21×[48].

As the dispersion has narrowed, and fund managers have started to deploy strategies to optimize their IRRs, the analytical framework of the academic literature has shifted and does not account for these strategies. Therefore a fund manager can drop (or upgrade) from one quartile to another without actually losing ground in terms of value creation and performance generation. Performance persistence might look as if it is declining on the basis of a quartile analysis (Braun et al., 2013; Harris et al., 2014; and Korteweg and Sorensen, 2015) but might have in fact persisted by other measures.

Therefore, quartile analysis has to be used with caution, given the risks associated with misinterpretation (Harris et al., 2012). A recent illustration was provided by Antoinette Schoar in a conference (as reported by White, 2017 and Primack, 2017) during which she announced a decline in persistence of returns based on a quartile analysis. While the underlying academic paper is not yet available at the time of writing, Schoar states that same quartile persistence was of 33 percent during 1995–1999, 33 percent during 2000–2004, 25 percent during 2005–2009, and 22 percent during 2010–2013. According to the same sources, top-quartile persistence was 31 percent during 1995–1999, 28 percent during 2000–2004, 13 percent during 2005–2009, and

---

[48] Excluding Growth Capital Europe, which is not in the sample for Figure 3.5.

12 percent during 2010–2013. For Schoar, an explanation of this decline is the increase of fund sizes. She is quoted as saying, "When the fund size increases, the marginal return on the funds goes down. Research suggests this is something that has accelerated in the last decade." She also states that "this is a very strong relationship."

Though interesting, this analysis warrants some caution. First, it is unclear as to which date these figures were applicable. It is likely that the periods 2005–2009 and 2010–2013 include active funds that are still in the making and therefore could explain the declining figures. Second, peer groups have to be carefully constructed if a quartile analysis is done. In particular, there is a strong correlation between the size of funds and the size of operations they lead as well as the nature of interventions (Demaria, 2017a). It is therefore methodologically important to separate mega, large, mid-, and small-size LBO funds.

The fact that fund investors exhibit, depending on their skill set and resources, an ability to generate an outperformance thanks to their asset allocation (Swensen, 2009) and their fund manager selection (Demaria, 2015, Introduction) proves that the persistence of returns of fund managers remains a fundamental feature of PM investing. Looking at the underlying deals of LBO fund managers (only), Braun et al. (2017) conclude that there is a persistence of returns due to features of specific fund managers and that it has declined over time. They attribute this to the maturing of the LBO sector, the commoditization of financial and operational engineering instruments used in this area, as well as the move of professionals between GPs (or forming new ones). They also state that the increasing level of auctions has wiped out a large portion of proprietary deal flow, as well as competition for deals that have led to increased valuations (and lower valuation as well as lower persistence).

How can this persistence of returns be explained? Entrepreneurs screen investors to find the best by looking at investors' past successes as reported publicly but also through their network of fellow entrepreneurs (Hochberg et al., 2007). They seek qualified introductions to the investors they have screened. Investors give high importance to qualified introductions from a specific network of contacts, among them entrepreneurs (especially the ones with whom they had worked), trusted advisors, and fellow investors they co-invest with regularly. Entrepreneurs can agree to lower the valuation of their company to attract highly regarded investors (Hsu, 2004), especially individual figures (Ewens and Rhodes-Kropf, 2015) since attracting this kind of investor is a major signal to the potential and actual partners of the company. Finally, the experience and network of the investor can contribute significantly to the value of the company (Cai et al., 2014) and support a successful exit (Sorensen, 2007). Successful investors can invest in a broader range of companies at lower valuations and contribute more to the value creation in the company. Their performance is, therefore, likely to persist as long as their skill set remains relevant. This conclusion is particularly true for individuals, less for firms which have recorded a decreasing persistence of returns over time. Fund investors are, therefore, advised to carefully assess the individual contribution of past and present employees of fund managers in order to determine the generation of performance and the likelihood that it will persist.

Diversification

Looking at Figure 3.4 above, some PM investment strategies look rather unattractive, well below the regression line, such as opportunistic private real estate, or European VC. Other strategies, such as American growth capital and LBO, are far above the regression line and seem particularly attractive. Along these lines, why would institutional investors invest in the former category instead of only investing in the latter?

First, this snapshot is taken over different periods of time. As explained in the first pages of this book, there is no exhaustive database of performances, and some strategies (particularly the American ones) are particularly well documented but also suffer from selection biases: the clients of Cambridge Associates were historically essentially American institutions investing in the US. When the consulting group started to invest abroad on account of its clients, it started to also collect data. Macroeconomic factors could notably explain why US strategies appear so attractive: the decade of 1990 was particularly favorable for VC and LBOs, while distressed debt fell back (as illustrated in Fig. 3.4). Cambridge Associates' data exhibits a well-documented upwards bias (Demaria, 2015) in terms of performance. The consultant might also systematically exclude funds according to the standard selection criteria of the clients.

Second, each of these strategies performs at specific times in an economic cycle. Excluding one strategy from a portfolio on account of historical conditions that were not favorable does not make sense in terms of portfolio construction. Diversifying a portfolio by including strategies with lower historical performances would make sense, especially when assuming that cycles turn and conditions evolve over time. Performance drivers are different between the three sub-asset classes (PE, PD, and PRA), as well as within each of them (as detailed later in this chapter).

Third, Figure 3.4 was drawn by using a mix of funds ranging from fully realized to still active (although largely realized, we do not include funds created after 2008, as many funds are still active). This can bias the output, but focusing on fully realized funds might exclude too many funds to form a meaningful sample. Moreover, this might provide a picture of a situation too far back in time to be relevant at all.

Fourth, the figure will evolve depending on the risk and performance metrics that are chosen (see below, the section on performance measurement). Even choosing the relative weight of funds in a sample can significantly affect the output. For example, in this book we chose from the start to use the pooled average as a snapshot of the overall market, but the median or a simple arithmetic average could also be used. Along the same lines, we measure the dispersion of performance by looking at the spread between the top 5 percent and bottom 5 percent, but some observers might prefer a spread between the top 25 percent and the bottom 25 percent. Others might adopt a different risk metric, such as the dispersion of the pooled average (or median or arithmetic average) performance over time, for example.

Fifth, not all fund investors look for the highest return possible either because their tolerable risk threshold is lower or because they want more predictable and steadier returns even if this means lowering return expectations. For that reason, PD or PRA might appeal more to certain categories of institutional investors, especially if they combine yield distribution and capital appreciation, for instance. Pension fund managers might also want to diversify their broader portfolio of traditional assets by including PM assets that perform well when traditional assets do not.

Therefore, Figure 3.4 is only a partial perspective and will benefit from further analysis to structure a portfolio (see Chapter 5). At least five reasons would encourage investors to look deeper and further before drawing any definitive conclusions.

In the context of an investment portfolio, PM investing provides attractive drivers of diversification. First, it taps into a wider investment universe (Nadauld et al., 2017). There are more than 300 million private companies and roughly 52,000 that are listed globally (a pool that has been shrinking in the US over the last 20 years). PE funds can take private some of these 52,000 listed companies. They can also list previously private companies. Although not every private or public company (or asset) is a good target for a PM investment, in effect the investment universe of PM funds is the largest in the financial sector. This is a major source of diversification for portfolios of institutional investors, especially since the number of public companies has been shrinking over time.

Second, the range of industries that PM funds can finance is much more diversified than the one represented on the stock exchange[49]. VC funds provide an exposure to emerging industries, which are not yet represented on the stock exchange. LBO funds target companies focusing on niche markets (for example, providing specialized machines to a narrow industry) or markets that do not attract public attention (for example, funeral homes). Distressed debt funds target companies that might operate in commoditized sectors (such as the retail industry) or falling out of favor (for example, fax or dot matrix printers manufacturers) and which are less or not at all represented on the stock exchange. They might also be able to pick sectors that are often represented only through large listed conglomerates on the stock exchange.

Third, PM funds finance the equity need of companies, restructure their capital structures and liquidities, and provide asset-financing solutions. This can happen at every stage of the life of a company from inception to restructuring (Demaria, 2013) and even at the liquidation stage (leading potentially to asset financing projects or a company restart). Traditional financial markets tend to finance only mature assets, with specific characteristics and a significant size. In fact, as explained by Nadauld et al. (2017): "The elements [private market portfolio] companies [and assets] have in common is that they could not have been financed through traditional sources of financing because they require the involvement of a highly motivated investor who has substantial rights to make them profitable."

Fourth, PM funds offer institutional investors a wider geographical exposure, including notably an exposure to countries without a stock exchange (or in which the latter is under-developed).

As long as the legal, cultural, and entrepreneurial frameworks are in place and rights can be enforced, there is ground for applying some form of PM investment strategies. The financial and legal expertise, as well as the local financial and physical infrastructure, are in essence the main limits to the development of this kind of activity.

---

[49]This is true in developed markets (DM) but even more in emerging markets (EM). As stated by Lerner et al. (2016), "EM PE investments appear to focus on companies in high growth sectors that are underrepresented in public markets, thereby allowing limited partners (LPs) a more balanced exposure to a country's economic drivers."

However, risks are also significant and go beyond the standard framework that applies to traditional finance. This is true for direct private equity investments but also for fund investors.

Risk Measurements

Finance theory generally identifies two categories of risk: systematic and idiosyncratic.

Systematic risks include interest rate risk, market risk, and inflation risk. **Interest rate risk** is partially applicable to PM investments, especially since some strategies (LBO, direct lending, mezzanine/unitranche debt, private real assets) use financial leverage. Moreover, the reinvestment rate risk is significant, especially since investors have to wait for the next fund to be able to commit and later deploy their capital (see above).

Market risk is less applicable to PM as they are less liquid. Nevertheless, as private assets are appraised often thanks to listed comparable ones, there is an indirect impact of market risk on PM investments. Some of the market risks that can usually be hedged for listed assets cannot easily be in PM. A case in point is the risk associated with foreign exchange variations: as distributions from PM funds are often largely or essentially unpredictable and can happen over the course of five to seven years, investors have to bear this risk.

Inflation risk is largely hedged by PM strategies, notably as they either use variable interest rates (therefore hedging the inflation) or because their capital gain features are a natural hedge against it. However, major and sudden inflation increases are difficult to handle and can translate into foreign exchange risks, which PM investors cannot protect themselves from (see paragraph above).

Idiosyncratic risks include liquidity risk, credit risk, and operational risk. As mentioned in the Introduction, **liquidity risk** differs in PM from other asset classes. PE, PD, and PRA funds apply investment strategies with variable asset liquidity. This liquidity cannot precisely be calibrated in most of PM strategies, but it can be evaluated and estimated through modeling. Therefore, **asset liquidity risk** can be defined as the variation of duration around the average time to liquidity of a given asset. Funding liquidity in PM funds is handled by fund regulations. As explained previously (see Insert 1), **funding liquidity risk** cannot totally be excluded (except by setting up mandates or segregated accounts) but is drastically limited by the sanctions attached with a defaulting fund investor.

Credit risk applies to PM in two specific instances: recovery and event. **Recovery risk** implies that funds might lose part or all of the capital they lend or invest. This risk is diversified by the careful construction of a portfolio of assets that are thoroughly analyzed by fund managers. Even in the riskiest part of the PM investment universe, fund managers have demonstrated their ability to recover capital on a pooled average basis. Nevertheless, recovery risk applies to each investment made by a given fund manager and also to the fund itself. **Credit-event risk** could also indirectly apply to PM strategies with fixed income characteristics (such as PD) or including fixed income features (such as LBOs), as the contagion from listed instruments could extend to leveraged loans financing LBOs or to other instruments that are further refinanced in CDOs.

As for other credit risks, funds are less sensitive to them. **Settlement risks** exist in PM but are not equivalent to those associated with public markets. Transactions in PM are at arm's length and involve extensive due diligence, which notably establish the reliability of the counterparty, as well as the existence and the rightfulness of its legal claims.

Exchange rate risk can apply if a fund invests in different countries with currencies differing from the one it is denominated in. For example, this applies to funds denominated in dollars and investing in emerging markets with no currency peg to the dollar. Otherwise, there is no underlying exchange rate risk.

Sovereign credit risk does not really apply in the case of PM as funds do not lend to sovereign entities. If a sovereign investor invests in a PM fund, this is more a funding liquidity risk than a sovereign credit risk.

Besides these classic financial risks, we identify five types of risks. These risks are probably more illustrative of the nature of risks associated with PM investing, and support assessments of risk-adjusted returns.

Five Risk Metrics for Private Markets Funds: Macro, Selection, Reporting, Allocation, and Timing

We identify at least five types of risks associated with PM investing. These are novel measures that we designed as academic literature has not, to our knowledge, addressed the question so far. None of these measures is sufficient by itself to provide a sufficient perspective on risks associated with PM. Moreover, the precision and reliability of the measures depend on the quantity of data on which they rely. A lack of data can artificially exhibit a low or a high level of risk. It is advised to compute or score the level of confidence associated with the calculation with these measures of risk.

The general, or **macro, risk** associated with a given strategy measures the spread between the highest pooled average TVPI and the lowest recorded. Figure 3.10 provides a perspective for US VC funds. According to this measure, the risk is 4.86×. The calculation of the macro risk level is attractive as it provides a direct reading of the range of potential returns that an investor could expect to receive. It also supports a value-at-risk reasoning. As it uses the pooled average performance of a strategy, there is no bias associated with the selection of funds by the investor.

However, this measure is sensitive to outliers, such as the US VC returns of vintage years 1993 to 1996. These returns were exceptional, and few investors expect to reach them *on a pooled average basis* ever again. Using a multiple year rolling average or eliminating the outliers could help refine this spread. Moreover, it assumes that the investor can invest pro-rata in all the funds of the sample and at no extra cost (that is without the help of a consultant, a fund of funds or with significant internal costs). This is unlikely.

This is why it is worth also calculating a **selection risk** metric. Investors can significantly outperform or underperform the pooled average return of a given strategy depending on which fund(s) they have access to and invest in. Figure 3.11 provides perspective, with the performance of the top 5 percent, upper quartile, bottom quartile, and bottom 5 percent US LBO fund managers. A simple average of these four categories is also calculated. The difference between the average performance of the top

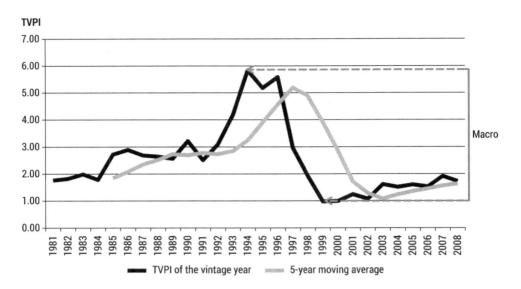

FIGURE 3.10   Pooled average TVPI of US VC funds by vintage year and 5-year moving average
Source: Authors, based on Cambridge Associates data published in December 2016 (data as of Q2 2016). Funds' performance only. Vintage years record fully realized funds and active funds that are largely realized (up to 2008).

5 percent and the bottom 5 percent could be described as the extreme selection risk that an investor takes. The difference between the average of the top 25 percent and the bottom 25 percent would then be the average selection risk.

This approach helps investors to identify the risk associated with inadequate resources and expertise to select fund managers. Figure 3.11 shows that the risk is not symmetrical: the amplitude of the fluctuations of the top 5 percent returns is much more significant than for the bottom 5 percent returns. The gap between the top 25 percent and the top 5 percent funds is higher than between the bottom 25 percent and the bottom 5 percent. This is confirmed by Weidig and Mathonet (2004), who find a relatively high positive skewness associated with VC and LBO returns.

As a consequence, a typical standard-deviation analysis would be misleading. Another consequence of this lack of symmetry is that Monte Carlo simulations used to generate randomized portfolios, which rely on the assumption that data is distributed normally, are in effect not applicable. A value-at-risk analysis based on selection risk should therefore focus specifically on the downside risk to be properly calibrated. For example, according to Weidig and Mathonet (2004), the probability of total loss of a PE (that is VC or LBO) fund is 1 percent, and the probability of a total loss of VC is 30 percent and 23 percent for an LBO fund.

As discussed above (see section on MOIC), the **reporting risk** is real but rather limited. Figure 3.12 plots the evolution of active funds versus the average of fully realized funds. This graph illustrates the difficulty of estimating the potential outcome of active funds. According to that figure, it appears that except vintage years 2010, 2012, and

TVPI

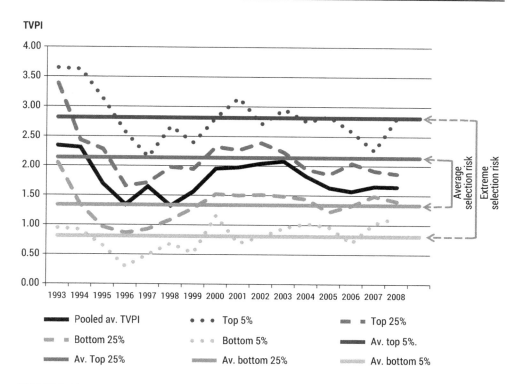

2014, most of the other vintage years are following the evolution of the historical average over time. This historical average itself witnesses some accelerations in terms of progression of performance, but the line does not recede except during the very early quarters when the MOIC is not representative (funds are drawing to invest and to pay management fees, which affect significantly the TVPI). Nevertheless, Figure 3.12 provides an interesting tool to monitor the performance of active funds. It supports the assessment of individual VY and then possibly of individual funds versus their vintage year and the historical average.

The last two risks are connected: **strategic** and **tactical asset allocation risks**. These risks are not specific to the PM asset class but apply differently when dealing with assets that are less liquid.

Risks Associated with PM Strategic Asset Allocations

Strategic asset allocation (SAA) risks are associated with a market neutral portfolio of PM funds and deviations from it. By "market neutral" we refer to a portfolio that replicates the breakdown by region and strategy of private markets (see below, notably

Mutiple (TVPI)

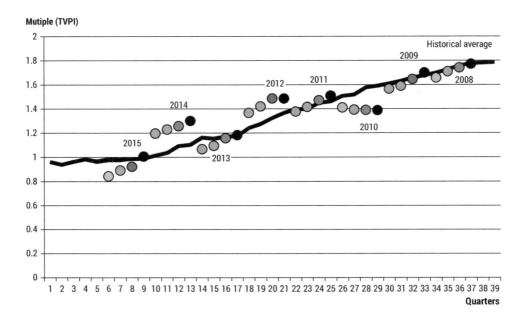

FIGURE 3.12 Compared quarter-on-quarter evolution of the TVPI active Western European LBO funds by vintage year and the average of fully realized funds
Note: The line records the average of fully realized funds (up to 2007). Each dot represents the evolution of the TVPI of active funds from three quarters ago (light grey) to the current quarter (black).
Source: Authors, based on Pevara (now Insight), data published in Q2 2017 (data as of Q1 2017). Funds' performance only.

Fig. 3.14). The market neutral portfolio itself has its own drawbacks. First, it requires significant resources to be replicated. Then, this portfolio is the result of the collective ambition of all investors (see introduction to Section 3 below for more details). It is not necessarily what they wish they would invest in, maybe because there is no fund on offer for that matter, nor is it the most desirable output, as some strategies seem to gain more momentum than others. As a result, there might be "white spots" on the PM investment map of investors, notably because there is no strategy available (for example distressed debt investing in Continental Europe).

By deviating from a market neutral portfolio, which would reflect the average weight of every strategy and region, an investor adds PM SAA risks. This has specific consequences in PM, as investors may not be able to **access funds to deploy capital as planned**. For example, fund managers might not be convincing by the standard of investors. Nevertheless, Swensen (2009) explains that 20 percent of the performance of the endowment of Yale is associated with its asset allocation (80 percent being related to the selection skills of the team[50]). This performance is 4.1 percentage points per

---

[50]The performance generated by the selection skills of fund investors was assessed by Cavagnaro et al. (2017). According to their study, "One standard deviation increase in skill leads to an increase in annual returns of between one and two percentage points" for LBO and between two and four and a half percentage points for venture capital. The authors use a Markov chain

year on top of the median of 8.5 percent realized over twenty years (ended June 2012) as measured by Cambridge Associates' index of endowments. If Yale had performed in line with the median in terms of fund selection while keeping its unique portfolio structure, it would have outperformed by 1.1 percentage points per year. The risks associated with building a dedicated PM strategic asset allocation bear potentially significant rewards.

Risks Associated with PM Tactical Asset Allocation Instruments

Not surprisingly, some investors might be tempted to anticipate market trends to generate additional performance. This **tactical asset allocation risk**, which is often described as **market timing risks**, is particularly difficult to handle in PM. As funds have five-year investment periods, fund managers have significant latitude to deploy their capital. Trying to time the market by investing in funds at a specific time does not guarantee that this capital will be deployed immediately. Therefore, it is advisable to avoid timing the market by investing in primary funds altogether. The best way to eliminate risks associated with market timing is in fact to invest in funds regularly and try to minimize the impact of events on specific vintage years. As illustrated in Chapter 5, capital should be deployed over five to seven consecutive vintage years.

Nevertheless, investors could be tempted to invest tactically in PM as certain economic conditions unfold. Two instruments are available: **secondary investments** and **co-investments**.

Risks Associated with Secondary Investments

Secondary investors aim at acquiring existing stakes in PM funds (or underlying assets[51]) from current investors. Secondary buyers assume the obligation to participate in future investments and pay upcoming management fees. This activity represented the equivalent of 2 to 8 percent of primary fund commitments over the period 2011–2016 according to Cambridge Associates. In 2017, transaction volumes reached $58 billion[52]. Secondary investing has proven particularly popular over time for multiple reasons (Demaria, 2017b).

Monte Carlo method, which seems methodologically relevant as it does not assume a normal distribution but includes the choices of the agents to define statistical distributions supporting the statistical tests. The authors state that the results are connected to the risk preferences of fund investors and that selection skills apply also in categories of fund investors as defined by their risk appetite. They also find evidence that some fund investors' "systematic outperformance goes well beyond established venture capital partnerships during [the 1990s], and appears to exist in first-time funds, in reinvested funds, in buyout funds and in other time periods as well."

[51]The secondary market also includes so-called direct secondaries, which represent 15 to 25 percent of the secondary market. Buyers acquire the stakes in private companies or assets held by private market funds instead of the stakes in these funds. These operations can help solving the issue of funds reaching the end of their lifespan while still holding one or a few companies or assets. By selling these companies or assets, the fund distributes its last proceeds and can then be liquidated.

[52]This total was up 57 percent on the $37 billion of 2016. These volumes are the NAV of funds after discounts and include unfunded commitments, which were recorded and surveyed by Greenhill Cogent. As a matter of comparison, 26 funds raised $38.3 billion in 2017 (compared with 33 billion in 2016).

First, unlike primary funds that offer to invest in blind pools, fund stakes offered on the secondary market are already partially or fully invested. Investors can therefore try to assess the value of the underlying assets. This gives them a sense of control. Moreover, secondary stakes in a portfolio of funds could provide investors with a broad diversification, as well as a privileged access to fund managers who might be otherwise inaccessible.

This assumes, however, that secondary investors have the resources and prior information necessary to do so, as the information provided by sellers of fund stakes is limited and the time to evaluate these stakes is rather short. Moreover, primary investors can plan on which fund to invest in, based on geographical, strategic, industrial, and other criteria. Investment opportunities on the secondary markets are **random in their timing and their nature**. Secondary investors bear significant **opportunity costs**, as attractive investment opportunities might not materialize at all, or these opportunities might not match their investment criteria.

Second, stakes on the secondary market are usually transacted at a discount[53] (on average 20 to 30 percent on the fund's NAV). This provides investors in theory with an extra return, but in fact, discounts compensate the risk that buyers take in transacting under **short timeframes** with **strong asymmetries of information** on the secondary market (Demaria, 2017b confirmed by Nadauld et al., 2017).

Demaria (2017b) shows that the secondary market is highly competitive and investment opportunities should carefully be assessed by investors. Discounts on NAVs can be significantly reduced at market peaks and be insufficient to compensate asymmetries of information between buyers and sellers. These discounts can even be replaced by premium as secondary investors struggle to deploy capital and fund stakes on offer are not numerous enough to satisfy the demand. Moreover, NAVs are no longer calculated conservatively thanks to the historical cost method. Instead, many fund managers use the fair market value method and mark their portfolios to market (with all the consequences associated with this practice; see Insert 2). Secondary investors might overpay their stakes in existing funds if portfolios are marked to market when the stock exchange peaks and then an asset price correction follows. Not surprisingly, Nadauld et al. (2017) conclude that the secondary market "can be characterized as one in which relatively flexible buyers earn returns by supplying liquidity to investors wishing to exit."

Third, secondary stakes provide in theory an attractive investment pattern. Investors get to deploy significant capital up front. Distributions happen relatively fast as funds gather a portfolio of assets, of which some are relatively mature and ready to be sold. This cash-flow pattern magnifies the IRR of these investments and therefore should lead to a careful joint assessment with MOIC. As explained above, IRRs can be highly misleading, especially since secondary buyers increasingly use credit lines to differ capital calls or anticipate on distributions. The consequence of the use of these credit lines (also called equity bridge financing) is to magnify further IRRs. Demaria (2017b) concludes that secondary funds do not outperform fund of funds, once their vintage years are reconciled.

---

[53]On average 20 to 30 percent of a fund's NAV. Nadauld et al. (2017) record an average of 13.8 percent over 2006–2014 and 9 percent out of the period of the financial crisis.

Insert 2—The IPEV and the Fair (Market) Value

In 2005, leading private equity associations[54] decided to form the International Private Equity and Venture Capital Valuation Guidelines Board (IPEV Board). The purpose was notably to provide guidelines to fund managers and fund investors valuing private equity investments. These guidelines were eventually released in 2007 and implemented over the course of the following years.

Before the IPEV, the rules to value portfolio companies were based on **historical costs**. In a usual transaction, a third party values a private company at the time of acquisition of part or all of it. This is considered the market price of the company. This market price is set as the reference valuation to which adjustments were made by fund managers on a quarterly basis. The rules diverged but essentially were as follows: if the company was on or above its business plan, the reference valuation was kept at par. If the company was behind its business plan, the fund manager would depreciate the reference valuation.

The only time the reference valuation would be revised upward (or downward without interpretation) would be if another third party valued it for a new transaction (for example in a subsequent round of financing for a start-up).

This method presented the advantage of being fairly conservative and to be rather simple. The drawbacks were that the quarterly valuation of portfolios was not representative of the potential market value of the companies in portfolio and that the fund managers had potentially too much discretion in defining the depreciation applied to the reference valuation. Moreover, there were uncertainties about the reduction of depreciations in case the company was catching up with its business plan or if the company revised its business plan to adjust it to market or business conditions.

The historical cost method was increasingly at odds with international accounting standards such as the IFRS and the US GAAP. These two sets of rules required assets to be accounted at their **fair value**, that is to say to re-evaluate them regularly to reflect their intrinsic evolution (including when they perform well) as well as the evolution of market conditions (a process known as mark to market).

The IPEV Board offers methods to value private equity companies in this framework: the **fair market value** (FMV). These methods are supposed to provide fund investors with a more reliable and precise perspective on the value of their assets. Since the application of the AIFMD in Europe, the application of these methods by the fund manager is checked by an independent valuation specialist (which can be a third party or an in-house independent function).

In order of importance, the first method is to compare private companies in portfolio with their closest private comparable companies recently the target of equivalent transactions. This approach presents the advantage to be simple and limit the

(continued)

---

[54]The *Association Française des Investisseurs en Capital* (AFIC, now France Invest), the British Venture Capital Association (BVCA), and the European Private Equity and Venture Capital Association (EVCA, now Invest Europe).

(continued)

distortions of valuation as companies are closely related (or even potentially directly competing with each other). The drawback is that private transactions are far and apart, exposing the valuation to stale pricing. Moreover, valuations are the result of a negotiation, the details of which are confidential, and are associated with specific rights (such as liquidation rights, exit rights, special voting rights, and many more) that can influence directly and significantly the valuation. These rights are gathered in the shareholder's agreement, a document that is usually confidential.

Not surprisingly, the use of listed comparable companies comes next and is usually the main method used to appraise the value of private companies. This method is simple, as listed companies provide a continuous stream of detailed information. However, this approach assumes that there are listed companies comparable with private portfolio companies and that they are sufficiently traded to provide meaningful pricing information. This method also assumes that private companies generate profits on which a valuation can be performed. It does not apply to companies with negative cash flows or earnings before interests, taxes, depreciation, and amortization (EBITDA), such as start-ups or distressed companies.

The next method sums the discounted future cash flows (DCF) of the company to assess its intrinsic value. This method is more complex but does not explicitly rely on comparable peers to execute the assessment. However, this method requires reliable mid-term projections of future cash flows, a discount rate to apply to these cash flows, and an infinite long-term growth rate. These elements might be available for infrastructures or monopolistic utility companies but are rather subjective otherwise.

The next method relies on the sum of the appraised value of the parts of a company, which provides an interesting insight into the firm but does not solve difficult questions such as the value of its activity going forward. Moreover, intangible assets, such as brands and patents, are particularly difficult to evaluate, and face the same challenges as the DCF method.

The last method is the historical cost described above.

The FMV presents some significant drawbacks. First, by forcing "thinly traded assets" (Longstaff, 2018) into a framework designed for listed assets, it creates discrepancies. For example, a company can be valued at a certain price, but the stakes in the company are not necessarily a pro-rata of this price. Premia associated with majority ownership or discounts associated with minority ownership have to be factored in. Specific economic and political rights must be factored in as well. Moreover, multiple discounts apply when valuing a private asset, such as the cost of lower liquidity, which was estimated to be 20–40 percent by Longstaff (2018) and confirmed empirically. However, in the advent of a take-private (also referred to as public-to-private), consisting in delisting a company through an LBO, the buyer routinely pays a *premium* of 25 to 30 percent on the market capitalization of the firm.

These discounts are the result of analyses and negotiations between buyers and sellers. These negotiations are contingent to the time, the place, and the parties involved. The fiction that they can easily be replicated on a regular basis is misleading. In fact, the concept of FMV and fair value are themselves a fiction, as they rely on the idea that the private company valued can be sold at that price at the time of valuation. Finding counterparties, negotiating, and reaching an agreement are time consuming (at least three to six months), expensive (so it would reduce the proceeds of the sale), and never guaranteed (so there might simply be no actual counterparty).

Happily, fund managers who have led these negotiations and are fully informed of the framework of each transaction benefit from a relative freedom to apply the FMV (recognized and granted by accounting standards such as FAS 157). This can be misinterpreted and has often led to the accusation of maligned intentions (Klein, 2016). However, Jenkinson et al. (2016) have demonstrated that in fact net asset values (NAV) of funds are "extremely good predictors" of their future cash flows and performance, especially by year three. Only weak fund managers artificially boost the NAV of their funds at time of fundraising, while most fund managers tend to be rather conservative.

Another major drawback of the introduction of the FMV rule to account for private companies is that it artificially increases the perceived risk of these assets. Private assets valued according to the historical cost method do not fluctuate frequently and substantially (unless a major event happens). For investors using the volatility of an asset as a measure of risk, private assets appear as stable and rather less risky. This is coherent with the low loss ratio, which effectively matters to investors.

Not surprisingly, given the nature of the method, the FMV also reduces the perception of the portfolio diversification benefits associated with private equity: public and private companies "co-move" (Welch and Stubben, 2018). The FMV imports the volatility of listed assets in the valuation of private ones. Investors will measure more changes in the valuation of private assets and consider them as riskier, despite the fact that the loss ratio remains unchanged. The direct consequence is that solvency and prudential costs associated with investing in private equity could increase substantially while the actual risk is unchanged. This can lead to hasty conclusions, such as increased correlations and lack of diversification (Welch and Stubben, 2018).

A sensible approach would be to drop the FMV and revise the international accounting standards. The next step would be to stop measuring risk by using artificial volatility as measured on stock exchanges. It would in effect recognize that the valuation framework for listed assets is not the absolute reference for that matter.

Risks Associated with Direct and Co-investments

PM funds and fund of funds have been set up so that investors can benefit from the expertise of fund managers, share the significant costs of investing in private markets assets, and diversify their investments. However, funds and fund of funds bear significant costs, such as management and performance fees, as well as transaction and setup costs, for example. Regularly, investors are tempted to eliminate these costs by doing direct investments.

Direct investing requires recruiting experts, competing with fund managers in that process. Fund managers offer an attractive compensation, combining relatively high fixed salaries and bonuses (thanks to the management fees they collect), as well as carried interest. Moreover, direct investing implies supporting the costs of investing and monitoring private market investments. This activity can only be profitable if the investor deploys enough capital to build a diversified portfolio of assets and amortizes the costs associated with direct investments. In practice, no investor can operate direct investments on a global scale. This often leads to **home-investing bias** and several other **behavioral biases** (Demaria, 2015, Introduction) that can be damaging for the performance of the investor (see Weidig and Mathonet, 2004, for an assessment of risks associated with direct investments in start-ups).

To avoid these biases and risks, investors have developed an alternative approach: **co-investing** directly in private companies and assets along PM funds. Although there is no standard practice, fund managers grant co-investment rights to usually reward large commitments in funds and/or fund investors committing early in the fundraising process (for example, in the run up to the first closing). The benefits for investors are twofold. First, they benefit from an additional control on how their capital is deployed: they have the choice to over-weight or under-weight specific companies or assets in their portfolio. Second, co-investing can help reduce the overall costs associated with PM investing.

On both fronts, the way co-investment rights are structured varies from fund to fund:

i) Access to investment opportunities:

    a. Some fund managers offer a systematic access[55]. Fund investors get the right to co-invest for a total amount of up to their commitment in the fund. In effect, the fund manager operates a pool of capital wielding potentially twice the size of the actual fund. This is probably the most favorable option for fund investors, though it requires them to decide fast (usually within two to four weeks) and with limited room for due diligence. Fund managers have to handle the uncertainty of additional capital contributions from co-investors and might be tempted to limit this option by transforming co-investment rights as a pure opt-in mechanism.

    b. Other fund managers offer access to investment opportunities only if there is additional investment capacity in the underlying asset. This might lead to an effective **adverse selection** for co-investors (Fang et al., 2015), as the fund manager might open a deal to co-investments only if there is extra capacity. As funds are structured for a given deal size (the sweet spot) and a given number of investments, an extra capacity means that the co-investment opportunities diverge from this sweet spot and therefore might not be the field of expertise of the fund manager (larger deals require different skill sets to execute successfully, notably when it comes to value creation). Braun et al. (2018) look at co-investments from a bottom-up perspective. According to their findings, there is no adverse selection, in the sense that if fund investors had invested in all the deals offered to them during the period analyzed, their performance would not have diverged from the fund performance. However, there can be an adverse selection because not every fund manager offers to every fund investor the option to co-invest. This is likely what Fang et al. (2015) have documented.

---

[55]Some fund managers, however, apply a minimum size threshold to invite fund investors. The World Economic Forum (2014) indicated that only a subset of the fund investors community can actually operate co-investments in LBOs (see below).

c. Finally, fund managers can offer co-investment rights exclusively to their current fund investors or to an enlarged universe of prospective fund investors. In the latter case, prospective fund investors get to know fund managers as they operate and might be incentivized to join the next fund to continue to benefit from such rights.

ii) Reduced costs and fees:

a. Some fund managers grant co-investment rights to any investor willing to pay fees (management, transaction, and/or carried interest). These fees are structured differently to those in a fund, as management fees and carried interest are nominally lower, but co-investors have to share transaction and due diligence costs.

b. Some fund managers provide co-investment opportunities in exchange for a lower management fee and/or lower carried interest or even for a simple flat transaction fee. These opportunities are usually reserved to fund investors (or in certain cases also to prospective fund investors). Co-investors may have to share some of the transaction and due diligence costs associated with investments.

c. Some fund managers provide co-investment opportunities at no cost to fund investors. The aim is to incentivize investors to commit (usually significant amounts) to the current and upcoming funds. As mentioned above, these co-investment rights might not be systematic but are determined by the extra capacity for capital deployment offered by select deals. This model is increasingly unlikely, especially since the SEC has launched investigations on the split of investment costs between funds and co-investors. The treatment of broken deal fees is contentious, as fund investors bear these costs, but co-investors could escape them. The SEC has imposed a rule of fairness in that matter (Dasgupta, 2017).

For funds investors co-investing systematically and pro-rata with the fund, the end result is to reduce the total fees and costs that they bear when investing in private markets. To facilitate such systematic and pro-rata co-investments, fund managers have even launched so called **co-investment funds,** which in essence replicate the fund structure at lower costs for large fund investors. This fund shields co-investors from risks associated with direct investing but implies costs. However, very large fund investors willing to save fees may negotiate separate mandates at lower fees, thus making co-investing less attractive.

Unless investors use co-investment funds, co-investing implies that they have the human, time, and financial resources to assess co-investment opportunities in a relatively short time frame. A lack of resources exposes them to the **usual investment risks**, essentially bad choices, compounded by behavioral biases and ultimately significant losses. This has been observed by Fang et al. (2015).

Co-investing also requires that investors have enough capital to deploy in order to diversify their direct exposure and that co-investors exercise a certain discipline in their co-investments; otherwise they are exposed to **investment concentration risks**. According to the World Economic Forum (WEF, 2014), only institutions with more than $25 billion under management and with a certain level of maturity co-invest (those above $50 billion invest directly alone). Around $700 billion was invested directly by

TABLE 3.1   Correlations of LBO fund investments and co-investments by deal sizes (2006–2016)

Deal sizes ($)	Correlation
Up to 25 million	0.42
25–99.9 million	0.58
100–499.9 million	0.49
500–999.9 million	0.38
1–2.49 billion	0.72
Above 2.5 billion	0.87

Source: Pitchbook, Wellershoff & Partners, 2017.

these institutions (WEF, 2014), representing roughly 20 percent of the total amounts they invested in private markets overall. Demaria (2017a) estimates that amounts available for co-investments represent 25 percent of the dry powder for private equity investments, essentially dedicated to large and mega LBO in the US, as there is a high correlation between co-investments and deal sizes (Table 3.1).

Doskeland and Strömberg (2018) estimate that the average co-investment fund accounts for 16 percent of the corresponding primary funds on a value-weighted basis. They conclude that "the unconditional size of the co-investment market accounts for 10 percent of the assets under management in PE funds, or around $200 billion." As for direct investments, for the years 2011–2016, they estimate that institutional investors "invested a total of $153 billion directly into PE transactions, representing 7 percent of the equity value of all PE transactions." In 2017, they estimated that this figure reached 9 percent. According to them, fund investors "are more likely to be direct investors in larger deals in general, and in the buyout segment in particular."

Unfortunately, the theoretical benefits of this discipline are not confirmed by reality. Co-investments tend to be **pro-cyclical** (Demaria, 2015b) and therefore to happen when asset prices are high. They also correlate with larger investments (Demaria, 2015b, Table 3.1), such as large and mega LBO deals (Demaria, 2017a) or infrastructure investments. This in essence leads to **increased concentration** of portfolios. Demaria (2015b) also confirms that co-investments are subject to **home-investing bias**.

Co-investing, as well as to a certain extent investing through "segregated accounts," which replicate a fund, can be subject to **adverse selection** ("lemon effect") as mentioned above. Unless co-investors have significant in-house expertise, it is difficult to eliminate this risk (which is particularly prevalent if fund managers invite co-investors in deals out of their sweet spot).

Co-investors also have to accept the **legal and reputational risks** associated with direct investing. In particular, funds limit the liabilities of investors to their commitment in the fund (they are "limited partners") while co-investing exposes them to liabilities associated with direct exposure, which are not proportional to the size of the co-investment.

Co-investing with funds provides investors with the access to investment opportunities, but the latter cannot materially influence the investment process and outcome. The investors' rights to invest alongside a fund are typically pre-negotiated, and there is little to no room for amendments. The role of co-investors is therefore to provide capital and to **remain largely passive**. This **entails significant risks**, as investing in private markets implies an active involvement from investors to mitigate and manage risks from investment to exit.

According to Fang et al. (2015), the combination of adverse selection, co-investing out of the sweet spot of fund managers, and lack of expertise in direct investing explain why co-investments underperform fund investments. Anecdotal evidence from the performance of CalPERS show that between 1990 and 2014, the $2.7 billion invested in direct and co-investments generated a 1.45× MOIC and 12.8 percent IRR[56]. The $60.7 billion invested in funds generated a 1.46× MOIC and 11.4 percent IRR. It is unclear if the performance of direct and co-investments factors in all the costs that CalPERS supported for that purpose.

3.2.2 Challenges

Direct and co-investment risks are a direct consequence of the challenges associated with investing in private companies. Chief among them is a generalized **lack of transparency**, breeding recurring and structural **asymmetries of information**. Private companies are unlike the listed ones. Public companies are required to provide recurring detailed information to the public. Regulators provide a detailed framework for this disclosure and enforce it. Third parties, such as auditors, independent analysts, as well as the shareholders themselves, check this information. Despite this scrutiny, and the active role of regulators, major frauds have occurred in the past in listed companies.

The risk is even higher in the case of private companies, where requirements in terms of information disclosure are much lower. Although some jurisdictions in Europe (such as France) require each company to disclose to the public its yearly financial statements, its bylaws, the structure of its board, the main events affecting it (such as a bankruptcy or a major amendment to its bylaws), most of jurisdictions only require the disclosure of the date of the creation of the company, the name of its officers able to sign on its behalf, and possibly some of the major events affecting it (such as bankruptcy or a change of its equity structure). Regulators have therefore only a limited role in the control of the information produced by private companies. Auditors are often not mandatory in private structures or have a limited role.

Investors want to avoid fraud and abuses. The challenge for them (principals) is to check and control the information about private companies provided by:

- Sellers in a transaction where investors are the buyers;
- The management (agent) once investors have acquired (or this agent bought into) an asset, to eventually sanction it. The management has an incentive to provide limited information, presented in a way that favors its agenda and rewards its effort.

---

[56]More recently (Private Equity International, 2016), the $1.8 billion invested directly returned 1.8 percent on a 10-year basis, while segregated accounts generated 4.1 percent and fund investments 10.2 percent.

To counter any information bias, prospective investors run a due diligence process, which consists of checking thoroughly the information provided to them by the owners and managers of a given private company. The due diligence process can lead prospective investors to co-produce information on that specific private company that might otherwise not be available. The result of this analysis conditions the **valuation** of the private company as well as the structuring of a **shareholders' agreement** (if multiple owners are involved) that will define the rights and duties of investors in the private company. The purpose of the due diligence process is to reduce (if not eliminate) asymmetries of information and compensate for the general lack of transparency surrounding the investments in private companies.

The **shareholders' agreement** relies on an effective legal system, where contracts such as these can be enforced in courts in a relatively fast, affordable, and predictable way. This is a condition for the emergence of a professional private equity industry and in general for any private market investment activity. This legal environment allows professional private market investors to exercise their rights, which are at the core of their activity. Michael Jensen described private equity investors as "organizations that run governance systems that run businesses." He previously explained (Jensen, 1989) that in fact, private equity, and specifically LBOs, was on the verge of eclipsing the public corporation. The cause is the discipline that private equity investors impose on their investments, notably due to the use of debt to acquire a business in an LBO and that has to be repaid from the profits generated by the acquired business.

The **valuation** of private companies is a recurring concern. The stock exchange provides in real time an estimate[57] of the valuation of public companies. There is no equivalent for private companies. The valuation of private holdings is nevertheless of particular concern to investors as they need to analyze their performance, their risk exposure, and the development of their investments and report on these analytical elements.

A few corporate finance methods can help current and prospective investors to determine the price of private companies, but each falls short in its own way in providing a definitive answer. Two main methods have emerged over time: the intrinsic method and the method by analogy.

The intrinsic method (discounted cash flows) implies that the value of a firm is the sum of its future net cash flows. This method assumes that a company has positive cash flows that can be predicted with a certain level of confidence and that we know

---

[57]The general assumption is indeed that a public company's worth (its market capitalization) can be determined by multiplying the number of shares outstanding by the spot price of these shares on the stock exchange. However, this reasoning can only be an approximation, for multiple reasons. First, public companies can have multiple classes of shares, which have different prices. Second, they regularly issue stock options, which make the calculation of the number of shares outstanding relatively more delicate than a simple reading. Third, there can be multiple spot prices for the same shares at a given time: blocks of shares exchanged on a dark pool are usually traded at a different price from the spot price. A majority shareholder will trade his block at a different price per share from a minority one. Fourth, if a company has to be sold as a whole, its overall price will diverge from the result of the simple multiplication above. For example, private equity firms routinely bid at a 30 percent premium on the market capitalization of a company.

what is the cost of time (discount rate) when future cash flows are far in the future. This is not always the case, notably in the case of start-up or bankrupt companies and of companies with high growth rates that will eventually slow and plateau (or even decline). Moreover, discount rates vary over time, depending on multiple macro- and microeconomic factors.

The valuation method by analogy (comparable company analysis, sometimes referred to as "public comparable method" or "multiples approach") compares public and private companies and relies on multiple assumptions. First, public and private companies can be relatively close in terms of size, activities, and geographical scope. Second, they should be at a relatively close level of maturity. Third, they have to exhibit similar financial structures. As difference appears, investors apply adjustments to the result of this valuation technique by applying discounts (or premiums), but this approach is not particularly rigorous and cannot be easily replicated over time.

Ultimately, the valuation of a private company (or asset) depends on *who* sells and *who* buys shares as much as *what* is for sale: the price is the point of equilibrium between two sets of values from the seller and the buyer. The valuation is the result of a due diligence process and of a negotiation. Given the intensity of the due diligence process in terms of time (multiple months) and resources, it is difficult to apply it frequently to generate a regular valuation of a private company. This means that replicating over time the intrinsic and analogical methods described above will not provide an accurate result: the information generation and negotiation processes will not occur, until there is a third party involved for a new transaction.

Therefore, valuations of private assets suffer from **stale pricing**: the historical valuation applied to assets is usually the reference point, sometimes empirically adjusted to reflect recent developments. Stale pricing is the result of the **lower liquidity level associated with private assets**. In theory, investors in private assets are willing to accept a lower level of liquidity, which is required to acquire, develop, and sell these assets. In effect, investors accept that their capital is locked up for a more or less predictable period of time, with limited (or no) sale option during that time. Therefore, stale pricing should not be an issue, as mid- to long-term investors in private assets do not plan to resell them at will.

The pain point with stale pricing is that it generates issues in terms of asset allocation. Many investors use a simple asset allocation model, based on relative target weights of their assets: for example, 60 percent of listed stocks, 30 percent of fixed income, and 10 percent of real estate investments. Assuming that real estate investments are not listed, they are in effect subject to stale pricing[58]. If listed stock prices increase (drop) significantly over a sustained period of time, and real estate prices do not follow the same valuation inflation (deflation), investors will in effect be under- (over-) invested in real estate. This phenomenon is called the **denominator effect**. To deal with these discrepancies between actual and target exposure, investors can set brackets

---

[58]This can be partially mitigated by regular independent appraisals. This approach is a costly exercise, and it does not eliminate valuation biases. In fact, independent appraisals are the equivalent of a delayed mark-to-market valuation exercise for real assets.

of asset allocation. This can help them if the sudden price shifts of listed assets are temporary. If these shifts are prolonged or permanent, they could in effect force investors to sell or buy assets at a bad time.

To handle some of the challenges associated with private assets investing, investors can delegate to specialists. This intermediation provides them with some benefits but also creates new challenges (2.3).

3.2.3 The Benefits and Challenges of Intermediated Private Market Investing

Direct PE stakes and real estate ownership belong de facto to the investment portfolio of many private investors, such as family offices, endowments, foundations, and even sometimes insurance groups, pension funds, or sovereign wealth funds. This can simply be the source of the wealth to be invested, the result of a legacy of direct acquisitions or investments, or an active policy of external growth. Sound and balanced portfolios should take into account these assets as part of the overall portfolio (in a "total wealth" approach) to diversify risks, such as investment biases (for example, home or industry) and detrimental portfolio concentration. To do so, it is usually necessary to delegate (see Section 1 above).

The benefits of intermediation in private markets investing are notably related to **lower risks**. Intermediaries, such as fund managers, provide expertise, which translates into a **low loss ratio**[59]. Using an investment vehicle pooling capital from different investors supports the construction of a **coherent and diversified portfolio** with **limited dilution of performance**.

Moreover, this expertise, if deployed through a fund gathering commitments from multiple investors, is less expensive as its **cost** is **shared among all investors**. Some investors expect to maximize further the benefits of sharing the costs of experts by co-investing with funds with all the risks and drawbacks associated with this approach (Section 2.1 above). A way to mitigate co-investment risks and costs is to set up co-investment funds but fund managers then charge management fees and carried interest (albeit at lower levels than in a traditional fund). These funds strip investors of the opportunity to tactically adjust their portfolio with private assets vetted by fund managers: they buy into a blind pool that complements the activity of the main fund providing investment opportunities.

Investors tend to be uncomfortable with blind pool investing due to the numerous unknowns associated with private asset investing for multiple reasons. First, they dislike the unknowns associated with the assets ultimately chosen by fund managers. Even though investors entrust fund managers with executing specific strategies in a particular geographical region (and sometimes in a precise industry), these investors are tempted to look beyond and form an opinion on the assets themselves.

---

[59] For an illustration in the UK, see Jelic (2011), who finds that only 3 percent of British LBOs end in liquidation. He finds that LBO failure rates are similar to other UK private companies. This is in line with Strömberg (2008), who "reports relatively modest bankruptcy rates of LBOs, similar to those reported for corporate bond issuers."

Private market funds are designed to provide significant freedom to fund managers to do exactly that, without anyone overseeing this effort. In fact, any overseeing from investors would defeat the purpose of delegation. As illustrated above (Section 2.1), the poor record on aggregate of direct co-investing by investors, despite the fact that assets are fully analyzed by fund managers, illustrates their lack of expertise and know-how. Some co-investors are doing better than others, notably those with an in-house expertise, but the overall disappointing track record of co-investors is the factual proof that they should not interfere with the work of fund managers.

Second, **investors dislike the fact that fund cash flows are difficult to predict**. Fund managers deploy capital over five to six years (see Insert 1), which might not be the pace that investors want. This gradual capital deployment (over six years in Fig. 3.13[60],

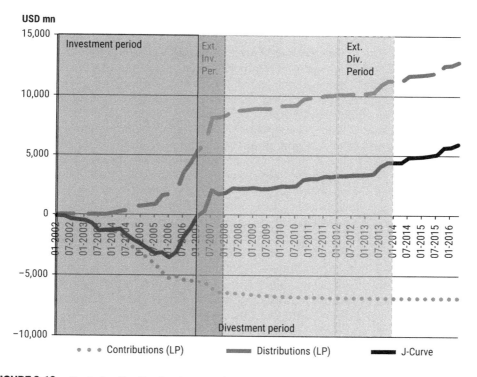

FIGURE 3.13 Capital calls, distributions, and cumulative net cash flows (J-Curve) of European LBO funds of vintage year 2002

Note: "Ext. Inv. Per." refers to a possible extension of the investment period of one year (see Insert 1). "Ext Div. Per." refers to the possible extension of the divestment period of two times one year (see Insert 1).

Source: Authors, based on Cambridge Associates data published in December 2016 (data as of Q2 2016).

---

[60]In this Figure, we chose randomly the vintage year 2002 for European LBO funds to draw the cumulated capital calls (or paid-in capital), distributions and net cash-flows of this pool of funds.

which corresponds to the investment period extended by one year, as most fund regulations allow managers to do) allows fund managers to optimize their investments and seize attractive opportunities. The experience of co-investing shows that investors tend to be pro-cyclical in their capital deployment. The rigor and discipline applied by fund managers, a direct consequence of the freedom provided by investment periods, is a source of performance.

Fund managers also distribute capital rather early, after two to three years (Fig. 3.13), and this also might not be the pace that some investors want. Some investors willing to generate relatively high performance (measured through IRR) expect shorter time to liquidity to reinvest capital more frequently and hopefully increase it faster. Investors willing to generate high absolute performance (measured through MOIC) expect longer time to liquidity, to let fund managers maximize the cash returns. Interestingly, investors break even at the beginning of the divestment period of these funds. Distributions are also visible at the end of the two-year extension of the divestment period (year 12). Some funds continue to distribute beyond that point, which means that they operate well beyond the usual lifespan of a European LBO fund (usually with the agreement of fund investors).

What probably rattles fund investors the most are the **principal-agent dynamic and the risk of abuses and frauds**. Demaria (2013, Chap. 7; 2015, Introduction) details and illustrates them with empirical examples. Abuses remain largely exceptional. They range from outright fraud to charging additional fees to underlying assets, to risking conflicts of interest by operating other activities such as mergers and acquisition advisory or equity capital market activities (such as initial public offerings). As fund managers increase the size and the diversity of their activities, they could increasingly have to face other types of conflicts of interest.

Let's consider the case of a fund manager financing a given private company simultaneously through equity and debt with two separate funds managed by two separate teams: a private equity team and a private debt team. These two teams work for the same manager (as they do for Blackstone or Apollo for example). If the company runs into trouble, the private debt team should react early and take action to protect the interest of the private debt fund. However, the private equity team, which belongs to the same fund manager, could argue that this could be detrimental to its track record as an equity investor and therefore could hurt the fund manager. This discussion would not happen if the private equity team and the private debt team were totally independent and belonged to two separate fund managers. Ultimately, the decisions taken by the private debt team on behalf of the private debt fund investors might not be in the best interest of fund investors. The alignment of interests of the team and investors is weakened.

Regulators have been looking into some of these conflicts of interest, but it is up to the fund investors to enforce their rights. As demonstrated by Demaria (2015, Introduction), the choice of fund investors is rather limited ("exit, voice, or loyalty"), and their fragmentation weakens their position when facing a single powerful agent. This agent is difficult to replace or its skill set is difficult to imitate, which underpins its power in its relationships with agents.

The principal-agent tension in private markets funds investing has evolved into a **debate about the actual value creation by fund managers**. To be more precise, a stream of practitioners and academic writers, probably willing to avoid the difficulties of private market investing and to preserve some of the myths patiently built in theoretical finance (such as market efficiency, transparent markets, risk effectively measured thanks to stock price volatility) took it upon themselves to demonstrate that LBO investing does not create value. For these authors, the aggregated performance of LBO investing can be replicated by investing in an index of listed stocks an amount composed of capital and half of it of borrowed money[61]. This reasoning is flawed at multiple levels.

First, these approaches compare the evolution of stock prices and LBO performance without factoring in the exact cash flow pattern of LBO funds and matching each cash outflow (investment and management fee pay out) with the associated inflow (realization of investment). Some of these authors consider that the cash committed to LBO funds is invested at a multiple of 1.5 from day one in listed stock indexes. This is not coherent with the pattern described above and in Figure 3.13. One of their arguments is that as fund investors commit the capital, the cost of this committed capital is running due to solvency and prudential rules. Investing it in listed stock indexes is therefore logical according to them. This reasoning however does not take into account that the committed capital not yet called by LBO funds does not sit idle on the balance sheet of investors but is invested. As will be shown in Chapter 5, the full return of called and uncalled capital can be calculated with a bit of effort.

Moreover, their assumption that capital should be deployed at all times is flawed. Investors invest when they assume that they will make a profit ("going in") and divest when they assume that they could lose money ("going out"). On the stock exchange, they assume that the market will be liquid enough to offer them ground for transactions. One could argue that the risk of the investor is associated either with bad timing in going in or out of the market or with the volatility of the price of assets if the investor remains invested regardless of the movement of asset prices.

The framework is different in private markets. As these markets are less liquid, investors have to carefully assess if the conditions are favorable to make a profit over the usual holding period[62]. They cannot divest at will and have therefore an incentive to be selective and invest only when the conditions promise a profitable investment. They risk, therefore, making an investment at an inflated valuation in an asset that ultimately does not fit the plan of the investor and that requires significant time and resources to be reshaped and sold.

---

[61] For recent examples, see Stafford (2017) and L'Her et al. (2016).

[62] We will refer to the concept of time to liquidity instead of holding periods. Holding periods refer to the time between an investment and its exit. This is a useful and interesting concept that helps notably, an understanding of the value creation of the fund manager. Time to liquidity refers to the time between the capital call corresponding to an investment (which can be delayed, as we will see, by the use of credit lines) and the distribution (which can be anticipated through a recapitalization, for example). StepStone (2018) analyzed 332 USD-denominated LBO funds of vintages years 1985 to 2007, which were liquidated or close to being liquidated. They found that the "average difference between cash flow duration [our time to liquidity] and performance duration [our holding periods] was 0.22 years." They also note that "high commitment amounts and booming markets led to a longer wait before capital was returned."

Second, leveraging the returns of listed stock indexes, because the underlying fund investments are themselves leverages, is puzzling. First, it assumes that the lender of the money used to invest in listed stocks accepts the provision of debt at a low interest rate. This means that the borrower has significant collateral to borrow against it. The cost of this collateral (and of the debt) should be factored in the performance reduction when investing in listed stock indexes through leverage. In the case of LBOs, the fund itself is not leveraged: it is the underlying asset, which is the collateral, and the cost of debt is negotiated accordingly and fully factored in the net returns of LBO funds. In essence, practitioners and academic writers leveraging listed stock indexes forgot the initial lesson of Jensen (1989) explaining that the governance associated with the LBO structuring is itself the source of some value creation in LBOs.

Third, the return comparison does not take into account the risks. Leveraging an ETF of listed stocks is possible but entails significant risks that usually only hedge funds are ready to take. These hedge funds are leveraged but are structured so that their losses can be controlled or stopped. They also have to take very short-term positions and frequently adjust them to cut losses (this entails costs). LBO funds, as mentioned above, have very low loss rates and present a radically lower risk profile.

Fourth, private market funds and stock exchanges have different investment universes. Listed assets tend to be larger, more diversified, and present specific characteristics that make them good support for a listing. Multiple strategies in private equity (venture capital), private debt (distressed debt), and real assets do not have any listed equivalents. Even in LBOs, this is not necessarily the case. The size of assets targeted ranges from small (enterprise value of $5–25 million) to mega (above $1 billion). To be listed, a company usually has to reach a certain size. Moreover, LBO invests in a large array of sectors, some of them not represented on the stock exchange. As the number of listed assets decreases[63], comparing public and private markets becomes increasingly challenging and less relevant.

Fifth, multiple analyses of reverse LBOs (RLBOs[64]) have demonstrated that these operations outperform other IPOs and the market. This effect has been analyzed and confirmed many times (Cao and Lerner, 2009; Cao, 2011) during benign economic times (Degeorge and Zeckhauser, 1993; Holthausen and Larcker, 1996) and crises (Chamberlain and Joncheray, 2017) and does not decrease over the long term. This outperformance is not related to the LBO duration, the sponsor reputation, or the level of leverage employed, and there is no evidence of time or industry effect. There is no correlation with the market capitalization either. The outperformance of RLBO can only be attributed to a long-term value creation by the LBO fund manager (Muscarella and Vetsuypens, 1990) thanks to its specialized knowledge (Leland and Pyle, 1977) and

---

[63]Wilson and Buenneke (2017) state that the number of listed companies decreased by half from its peak of 1996. They counted 3,671 companies listed in the US in 2016. Doidge et al. (2017) state that there were 8,025 listed companies in the US in 1996. Between 1975 and 1996, there were 27 percent more new listings than de-listings. Between 1996 and 2012, there were 84 percent more de-listings than new listings. McGrath (2017a) calculated that the average market capitalization per stock was "$6.3 billion at the end of 2016, almost double of what it was in in 2005."
[64]Operation in which a listed company that had gone private through an LBO is going public again.

monitoring (Diamond, 1984) during the time the company was private, such as investment and working capital optimization (Holthausen and Larcker, 1996).

3.3 STRATEGIES: PRIVATE EQUITY, PRIVATE DEBT, AND PRIVATE REAL ASSETS

It is difficult to quantify the total size of PM investments globally. First, because these investments include amounts dedicated to direct PE investing by private investors and families. Registries of commerce in many countries theoretically track these amounts, but there is no comprehensive database of these operations. Moreover, many of these investments are considered as entrepreneurial efforts and not third-party investing as such. They therefore do not qualify as PM investments.

Even after discounting active direct private investments by private investors and families, the task to evaluate PM investment activity worldwide remains difficult. Although most PM investors use funds, they can co-invest with these funds (by piggybacking). They can also use mandates. These two investment conduits remain largely below the radar of most databases.

Funds should theoretically be easier to track as they are marketed to third parties. This is only partially true. Some funds are formed in a very private and confidential way for investors that are not subject to disclosure requirements. Moreover, many jurisdictions do not track the activity of PM fund managers. For example, it is only recently that the SEC requested US GPs to register[65]. Even in the EU and in the US, small fund managers can remain largely under the radar of regulators if they do not manage more than a certain amount of aggregated capital. In many countries, there is no systematic tracking and accounting of how many funds are active on their territory.

Our estimate (Fig. 3.14), based on Cambridge Associates and Preqin databases, is that PE represents 56 percent of the PM fund investment universe, PD 17 percent, and PRA 27 percent. The US accounts for 67 percent, Europe for 20 percent, and the rest of the world for 13 percent[66] of PM fund investments. PE funds represent roughly 5 percent of the total market capitalization of listed companies (Doskeland and Strömberg, 2018, quoting a report commissioned by the Norwegian Ministry of Finance). Doskeland and Strömberg estimate that the total worldwide PE transaction volume over the five-year period 2012–2016 amounted to $1.8 trillion (in constant 2009 dollars), that is, 360 billion per year. This includes fund, direct, and co-investments.

---

[65]Since 2011, in the US, PE fund managers are requested to file a Form PF unless they are VC specialists or manage less than $150 million (https://www.sec.gov/rules/final/2011/ia-3222.pdf). In the latter case, they file a Form ADV (https://www.sec.gov/divisions/investment/guidance/private-fund-adviser-resources.htm). The purpose of the legislation is to provide the regulator with a clear picture of the systemic risk associated with leveraged operations.

[66]Lerner et al. (2016) tend to confirm this figure, thanks to statistics from the Emerging Market Private Equity Association (EMPEA). Over the period 2009–2015, PE funds in emerging markets raised capital representing between 10 percent (2009 and 2013) and 20 percent (2011) of the global total. Doskeland and Strömberg (2018) estimate that the US represents 54 percent of total PE capital, Europe 22 percent, and Asia (excl. the Middle East) 20 percent (in constant 2009 dollars) in terms of fundraising from 2012 to 2017.

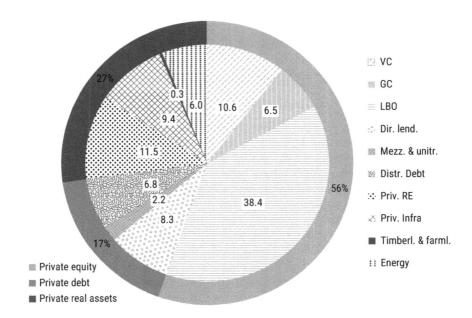

FIGURE 3.14 Relative weight of private market strategies, by amounts raised by funds (1981–2016)

Source: Cambridge Associates (as of December 2016), Preqin, Authors. These figures remain relatively stable. According to Preqin (2017), the aggregate capital raised globally by closed-end private capital funds between 2007 and 2016 was dedicated at 31 percent to leveraged buyouts ("LBOs"), 7 percent to growth capital ("GC"), 9 percent to venture capital ("VC"), 19 percent to private real estate ("Priv. RE"), 7 percent to private infrastructure ("Priv. Infra"), 9 percent to debt and special situations (mezzanine and unitranche debt, referred to as "Mezz. & unitr."; as well as distressed debt, referred to as "Distr. Debt"), 5 percent to funds of funds (not tracked above), 13 percent to other (co-investments, secondaries, natural resources, special situations, timber and turnaround). Preqin (2017) does not track in this study direct lending ("Dir. lend.," which we estimate through indirect clues). The graph above does not track co-investments and secondaries. We blended turnaround with distressed debt. Natural resources include our category "energy." "Special situation" might include certain distressed debt strategies.

According to the SEC's Division of Investment Management (2017), as of first quarter of 2017, 14,106 PE[67] and 2,422 private real estate funds were active in the US. Additionally, 4,448 "other private funds," which are defined by the SEC as not meeting the "definition of hedge fund, liquidity fund, private equity fund, real estate fund, securitized asset fund or venture capital fund," were also active. They might include PD and

---

[67] 10,350 "private equity" funds, 3,004 "Section 4 private equity" funds ('advised by a Large Private Equity Fund Adviser' as defined by the SEC, therefore managing at least USD 2 billion) and 752 'venture capital' funds. According to the American definitions, we assume 'private equity' funds as being LBO funds and 'venture capital' funds as being venture and growth capital funds.

other private real asset funds. A total of 1,441 PE fund managers[68] were registered, as well as 307 private real estate fund managers and 751 "other private fund" advisers.

The gross asset value[69] of PE funds[70] was $4,030 billion, $434 billion for private real estate funds, and $1,076 billion for "other private funds." Their net asset values, which are the values of assets in portfolio at the time of reporting, reached respectively $3,632 billion, $340 billion, and $983 billion.

These figures show the state of US private market funds, which are supposed to gather the lion's share of this activity globally (Fig. 3.15). However, the rather small number of fund managers that are actively reporting shows that the data from the SEC might not yet capture all the active fund managers on US soil. As a matter of

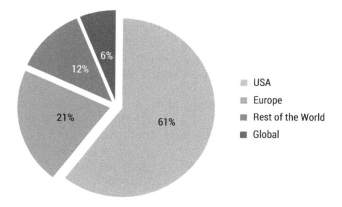

FIGURE 3.15   Geographical focus of private market funds, by amounts raised (1981–2016)
Source: Cambridge Associates (as of December 2016), Preqin, Authors. These figures remain relatively stable. According to Preqin (2017), the aggregate capital raised globally by closed-end private capital funds between 2007 and 2016 was dedicated at 56 percent to North America, 25 percent to Europe, 14 percent to Asia-Pacific, 2 percent to Latin America, and 3 percent to the rest of the world (Africa and Middle East).

---

[68] There were 1,084 "private equity" fund advisers, 249 "Section 4 private equity" fund advisers, and 108 "venture capital" fund advisers.

[69] Although this terminology does not apply to private market funds but to hedge and open-end funds, we assume that the SEC captures, thanks to this metric, the assets under management of private market fund managers, which would be the sum of the capital invested at the time of reporting and the capital committed but not yet invested ("dry powder"). This definition would explain the rather small difference between the gross and net asset value, the net representing 89 to 95 percent of the gross asset value for PE funds (LBO, growth, and venture). The figure is 78 percent for private real estate and 91 percent for "other private funds."

[70] $2,320 billion for "private equity" funds, 1,648 billion for "Section 4 private equity" funds, and 62 billion for "venture capital" funds.

comparison, Invest Europe (2017) declares that there are 1,200 active PE firms[71] managing €600 billion (funds only). Preqin (2017b) states that 7,509 "private capital"[72] fund managers were managing $4.6 trillion worth of assets as of December 2016, of which $2.5 trillion were in PE.

These figures are difficult to reconcile, notably due to differences in definitions (for example, the US does not capture funds of funds and secondary operators, while Invest Europe and Preqin do). According to the SEC, US PE fund managers were in charge of $4 trillion of assets. This exceeds the $2.5 trillion recorded globally by Preqin. Invest Europe declares that European PE fund managers were in charge of €600 billion worth of assets. Discounting assets from mezzanine funds (which belong to PD) and some exchange rate effects, this would represent roughly 20 percent of the $2.5 trillion recorded by Preqin. Our conclusion is that although Preqin does not exhaustively capture the activity of PM, it is a relatively useful proxy to assess the dynamics of the market. It might under- or over-estimate the relative weight of markets. In general, one should apply caution when making assumptions based on statistics, especially with market activity. Over time, with data collected by regulators, PM fund activity should be better documented.

The SEC's Division of Investment Management interestingly lifts the veil on a rather unknown corner of the market, managed accounts, therefore shedding a welcome light on this practice. Managed accounts are offered to investors by fund managers in at least two instances.

First, an investor plans to commit a very significant amount of capital with a fund manager. Usually, the investor wants to negotiate specific terms and conditions for this investment, including fee rebates and possibly specific rights such as co-investment or participation, with an advisory board. Under the standard fund regulations (such as a limited partnership agreement) and specifically the "most favored nation" clause, which grants to every investor the best conditions negotiated by any other investor, these special conditions would apply to everyone. The fund manager does not necessarily want this to happen and will therefore create a separate vehicle called a "managed account" for that specific investor. Even though this generates an extra administrative burden, the investor will get, in effect, a fully owned vehicle tailored to his needs. This managed account also preserves the equilibrium between investors of the fund: a large investor, who would own 20 percent or more of a fund, could jeopardize the whole fund in case of default. By isolating the large investor in a segregated account, the risk is limited to that account. The large investor also benefits from features tailored to his needs, such as possibly an ad hoc reporting. In this scenario, the managed account replicates exactly the investment strategy of a given fund.

Second, an investor wants to apply a specific investment strategy, possibly excluding some sectors, for example. The fund manager will therefore create a managed account that will fit exactly the criteria of the investor (assuming that this extra work makes economic sense for the fund manager). If the aim of the investor differs substantially

---

[71]That is, fund managers specialized in VC, growth capital, mezzanine, LBO, and turnaround.
[72]Which would correspond roughly to our definition of PM (PE, PD, PRA: PE, PD, real estate, infrastructure, and natural resources [Preqin, 2015]).

from the investment strategy of the fund, the investor will in effect give a mandate to the manager (which will become a gatekeeper in that case) to invest according to a specific strategy (see above, Section 1). In this specific case, the investor has to carefully negotiate the terms and conditions to ensure that interests are aligned. Among the possible risks are adverse selection: a fund manager might be tempted to put the best investment opportunities in the funds he manages first and in mandates if there is capacity only—or place the less promising opportunities in the mandates first. Fund managers usually get a higher compensation from the fund they manage and also communicate more effectively on the performance of their past and current funds (which are easier to benchmark as well) to raise the next generation (see Insert 1 above for more details).

The SEC (2017) provides more details about the first scenario. It was estimated by the consultancy Bain & Company (2017) that segregated managed accounts represented 6 percent of the capital raised in 2016 (up from 2.5 percent ten years ago). According to the SEC, managed accounts in PE totaled $51 billion (29 in "PE funds," 22 in "Section 4 PE funds," and none in "venture capital funds"), 6 in private real estate, and 1,529 for "other PE" funds. This represents respectively 1.26 percent, 1.38 percent, and 142.10 percent. Depending on how "other PE" is treated, managed accounts would represent between 1.3 percent and 28.6 percent of amounts managed in PM funds.

Investors usually include PM funds in their portfolio for two reasons: **risk diversification** and **capturing absolute returns**. The following sections detail PM strategies in these two dimensions. For simplicity, the US dollar was used as a reference currency. This choice introduces distortions in return analysis. A more in-depth perspective would rather use local currencies whenever possible.

3.3.1   Private Equity: Financing Private Companies

As explained by Demaria (2013), PE funds can finance companies at virtually each and every stage of their development. PE fund managers aim at solving specific issues affecting companies, which should significantly increase their value. Investors support entrepreneurs with capital, advice, contacts, know-how, and expertise. They act as a sparring partner in the governance of the companies they support. To capture this upside, fund managers acquire part or all of these companies before implementing the plan and then sell their stake when the company has executed the plan and its value increased. Two main types of operations are executed by PE funds: capital increases (2.1.1) and/or transfers of ownership (2.1.2). Database provider Preqin estimated that, as of December 2017, PE funds managed over $3 trillion, of which $1.1 trillion is committed capital yet not invested ("dry powder"). This figure is confirmed by Doskeland and Strömberg (2018), who estimate that the PE fund market represents 57 percent of the total private capital fund market.

3.3.1.1 Capital Increase

Private companies need resources to emerge (venture capital) and grow (growth capital). Investors acquire minority ownership stakes through capital increases and get reinforced investor rights, thereby joining existing shareholders.

Venture Capital (VC)

Definition

VC funds finance companies from inception (seed capital), prototyping (early-stage), industrialization (mid-stage) to commercial launch until they reach profitability or until they are acquired or listed on the stock exchange (late-stage, also known as expansion). VC represents roughly 19 percent of the PE fund investment universe and 11 percent of the PM investment universe. Doskeland and Strömberg (2018) estimate that the VC transaction volume varies between $40 and $70 billion per year (in constant 2009 dollars).

Risk-Return Profile: Performance Drivers

VC funds aim to generate high absolute returns by **pioneering new sectors** and/or aiming at **conquering significant market shares rapidly** thanks to transformative innovations.

This entails significant risks. VC finance start-up companies that are usually losing money, due to their young age and the heavy investment that they require. A significant number of start-ups fail. To mitigate these risks, VC fund managers operate extensive due diligence and audits, capitalizing on their specialization for that purpose. VC fund managers are specialized by industrial sector but also often by stage of development of the companies they support. Start-up financing is operated in stages (called "rounds of financing"): entrepreneurs collect a certain amount of capital to reach milestones. Once this is done, they collect more capital to reach the next ones. Start-ups can execute capital increases ranging from a few hundred thousand euros at seed stage to 20 million or more in late-stage financing.

Staging start-up investments helps investors to manage actively their risk by limiting their losses, notably when start-ups fail to reach the next milestone. If the company is unsuccessful, it is usually liquidated, and investors suffer losses. VC investors co-invest with each other, forming investment syndicates, to spread their risks. They can also reinvest in further rounds of financing of successful start-ups, therefore cutting their losses early and investing more in successful portfolio companies. Staging investments also helps entrepreneurs to manage the dilution of their own stakes in start-ups, as the value of start-ups increases substantially when milestones have been reached.

Use in a Portfolio Context

By targeting emerging industrial sectors and technologies usually not covered by traditional investments, VC funds act as a diversifier for investment portfolios. Moreover, as VC funds target young companies addressing notably emerging customer needs, they provide an exposure to fast growth companies that are rather rare on the stock exchange.

Performance

Very successful VC funds generate high returns compared to other PE strategies (Fig. 3.4 above). The performance is commensurate to the risk (Fig. 3.16).

Successful investors must identify them before they are too well known and get access to them. According to Cambridge Associates, 1,326 US VC funds created from 1981 to 2008[73], collectively represent $244.4 billion, generated a pooled average net IRR of 17 percent[74]. The multiple on invested capital[75] (MOIC) reaches 1.72× (on a pooled average basis). This has to be compared to a Public Market Equivalent[76] (PME) of 1.57×. The average time to liquidity is 3.47 years.

Top quartile funds on aggregate generated a pooled average net IRR of 15.8 percent (a 2.09× MOIC), the median was 6.4 percent (1.42×), and the bottom quartile −2.2 percent (0.87×). This illustrates the importance of top performing funds and their weight in the pooled average. The top 5 percent of funds generated an IRR of 64.9 percent (5.30×) and the bottom 5 percent of −16.3 percent (0.37×)[77].

However, US VC stands out because of the exceptional performance of the vintage years of 1990 to 1997 (Fig. 3.16). Once these vintages are excluded, the performances of US and European VC funds tend to be similar. During the period 2000–2008[78], US VC

---

[73] Although Cambridge Associates provides data of funds created after that date, we have chosen a cut-off date of 2008. Funds before that date are either fully liquidated or mature enough to provide performance data representative of their overall performance. Funds posterior to that date are still in the making and therefore distort performance figures. Data is provided as of June 30, 2016, as reported in December 2016.

[74] Figures are as of June 30, 2016 as accessed on Thomson Eikon in December 2016. This date applies to all Cambridge Associates figures mentioned in this chapter, unless stated otherwise.

[75] Also known as total value to paid-in (TVPI).

[76] The Public Market Equivalent aims to provide a rigorous comparison between PE investments (here VC) and an index of listed stocks (in this specific case, the Nasdaq Composite). The method consists in mimicking the cash-flow pattern of venture investments with the index. When a venture fund invests in a start-up, the equivalent amount is used virtually to buy units of the index. When the fund divests from that start-up, the corresponding virtual units of the index are sold. It is therefore possible to compare the actual performance of the VC fund manager and of the index, factoring in the holding period. The main difficulty associated with this method is to identify an index to compare the investment strategy with. To apply the PME, detailed fund cash flows are necessary, in particular to match cash outflows and cash in-flows (or write-offs).

[77] In Europe, 92 funds created between 1989 and 2008 and representing $15.4 billion generated a pooled average net IRR of 4.9 percent. The top quartile funds generated a net IRR of 8.5 percent and the bottom quartile −6.1 percent. MOIC are respectively 1.26× (pooled average), 1.53× (top quartile), and 0.66× (lower quartile). The PME of the pooled average is 1.39× based on the MSCI Europe. As for the rest of the world, 138 funds created between 1989 and 2008 and representing $16.5 billion generated a pooled average net IRR of 10 percent, the top quartile funds a net IRR of 14 percent, and the bottom quartile −2.6 percent. MOIC are respectively 1.97×, 1.97×, and 0.89×.

[78] Performance statistics as of June 30, 2017 reported in December 2017 by Thomson Cambridge Associates. This period covers vintage years after the technology boom of the decade 1990 and funds with a lifespan over ten years which are significantly or fully realized. The performance is however likely to be below the long term average as it records two major macro-economic downturns (2001 and 2008).

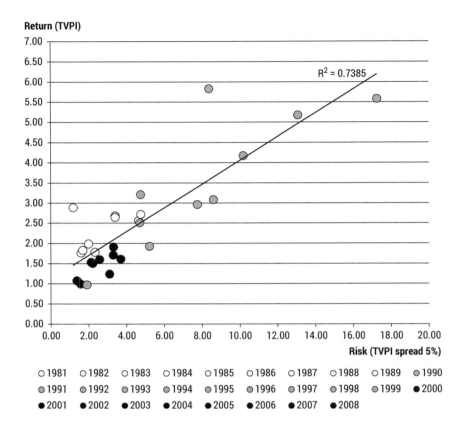

FIGURE 3.16   Return (TVPI)-risk (5 percent spread) profile of US venture capital funds, by vintage year

Return is measured thanks to the pooled average total value to paid-in ratio (TVPI) of sample funds. The total value of funds is the addition of proceeds distributed from the sale of investments (distributed), and the unrealized value of investments still in portfolio (residual value). The paid-in is the sum of capital called and invested by funds. Risk is measured by the difference of performance (TVPI) between funds belonging to the top 5 percent of the sample and funds belonging to the bottom 5 percent. Funds are sorted by their vintage year.

Source: Authors, based on Cambridge Associates data published in December 2016 (data as of Q2 2016).

funds generated a net pooled average IRR of 5.6 percent and a TVPI of 1.43×[79], whereas European funds generated respectively 2.98 percent and 1.22×[80].

---

[79]Despite the fact that funds in this specific sample are 10 years or older, they are still in the making as the DPI, which measures the actual proceeds paid to fund investors, is 1.02×, and the RVPI, which measures the value of assets still in portfolio, is 0.42×.

[80]With a DPI of 0.88× and an RVPI of 0.33×.

VC funds from the rest of the world (RoW) offer apparently the most attractive risk-return profile, according to Figure 3.3 (above) based on Cambridge Associates data. However, performance figures from these funds are skewed by very high performance from funds still in the making (of vintage years 2007 and 2008). Historical performance of fully realized RoW VC funds (that is, fully liquidated) is also in line with US VC funds.

Growth Capital (GC)

Definition

GC[81] funds finance companies already profitable[82] and engaging in major operations such as acquisitions, internationalization, or the launch of new products. These are corporate projects that banks do not usually finance and that these companies cannot fund by themselves. Companies increase their capital in a single operation of typically $25 to $75 million but also significantly more. GC funds obtain in exchange the ownership of usually 15 to 40 percent of the company and specific governance rights (which normally include board seats).

Companies financed by GC are private but can also be public. In the latter instance, the operation is a private investment in public equities (PIPE). The company remains listed and increases its capital through a private placement. The GC investor usually invests at a discount on the average stock price over the last three to six months in exchange for a lock up of 24 to 36 months. After that period, the investor recovers the ability to sell shares freely. At this point in time, the plan executed by the management–thanks to the additional financial resources provided by the PIPE–should materialize, and the stock price should reflect the positive impact of this plan on the company.

According to Cambridge Associates and Preqin, GC represents roughly 12 percent of the PE fund investment universe (6 percent of the PM universe), although this amount appears rather low. Given the fact that the risk-return profile of GC funds is rather conservative (see next section), they might fall more often under the radar of database providers that tend to advise and capture the behavior of institutional investors looking for higher returns. Our guess is that GC, therefore, represents a higher share of the PE and PM universes, but due to a lack of data we cannot more precisely assess what it could be. Doskeland and Strömberg (2018) estimate that the GC transaction volume varies between $60 and $80 billion per year (in constant 2009 dollars).

---

[81] Growth Capital funds are sometimes (for example, by Cambridge Associates) referred to as "growth equity" or more recently, "scale up capital." We use the former, but it is equivalent to the latter expressions.

[82] Cambridge Associates (Mooradian et al., 2013) define the targets of GC funds as sharing some of the following traits: they are owned by their founders, have no prior institutional investment, have a proven business model, substantial organic revenue growth (more than 10 percent), and are EBITDA-positive (or expected to be so within 12 to 18 months).

Risk-Return Profile

GC investing exhibits a different risk-return profile than VC investing. Given the fact that companies are already profitable, risks are more limited. According to Cambridge Associates (Mooradian et al., 2013), the loss ratio for US GC was 13.4 percent as of March 2012, to be compared to 35.4 percent for US VC[83]. However, companies growing at a robust pace and willing to execute a transformative event still face significant risks. For example, mergers and acquisitions can have disappointing results or negatively impact acquiring companies. This risk is particularly acute for small and mid-size companies which are usually absorbing comparatively larger brethren while facing intense competition. The distraction associated with managing a capital increase and the execution of the acquisition plan can also affect the growth of companies. Nevertheless, the prospect of losses on any given investment remains rather limited compared to other PE strategies, as portfolio companies are profitable, growing at a fast pace, and usually have limited to no debt. Given these characteristics, they usually tend to be priced rather richly when GC funds invest. This explains why fund performance is relatively constrained in this sector.

Use in a Portfolio Context

Due to its lower risk profile, compared to other PE strategies, GC is a source of risk **diversification** for investors' portfolios and an **attractive source of risk-adjusted returns**, notably in the US. (See Figure 3.4 above.) GC funds provide resilient returns even in challenging macroeconomic environments.

Performance

Although GC funds exhibit the lowest risk profile of the PE strategies, their performance generates relatively high returns, making them one of the most—if not the most—attractive of PM strategies (Figure 3.4 above). US GC funds exhibit much more consistent performance across time (albeit with a limited number of data points, see Figure 3.17[84]). According to Cambridge Associates, 109 US GC funds created from 1990 to 2008[85] and collectively representing $94.1 billion generated a pooled average net IRR of 19.3 percent. The multiple on invested capital (MOIC) reaches 1.78× (on a

---

[83] And 15.1 percent for US LBOs.

[84] Although the number of data points appears as relatively limited. Cambridge Associates provides data for 109 funds created between 1990 and 2008. 14 vintage years count three funds or more, thus providing performance data. However, our measure of risk requires eight funds or more per vintage year as we rely on the spread between top 5 percent and bottom 5 percent. Therefore, the number of data points falls to six only.

[85] Although Cambridge Associates provides data of funds created after that date, we have chosen a cut-off date as of 2008. Funds prior to that date are either fully liquidated or mature enough to provide performance data representative of their overall performance. Funds posterior to that date are still in the making and therefore distort performance figures. Data is provided as of June 30, 2016 as reported in December 2016.

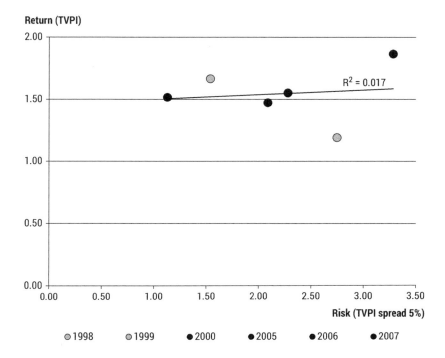

FIGURE 3.17 Return (TVPI)-risk (5 percent spread) profile of US growth capital funds, by vintage year

Return is measured thanks to the pooled average total value to paid-in ratio (TVPI) of sample funds. The total value of funds is the addition of proceeds distributed from the sale of investments (distributed), and the unrealized value of investments still in portfolio (residual value). The paid-in is the sum of capital called and invested by funds. Risk is measured by the difference of performance (TVPI) between funds belonging to the top 5 percent of the sample and funds belonging to the bottom 5 percent. Funds are sorted by their vintage year.

Source: Authors, based on Cambridge Associates data published in December 2016 (data as of Q2 2016).

pooled average basis). This has to be compared to a Public Market Equivalent[86] (PME) of 1.52×. The average time to liquidity is 3.28 years.

Top quartile funds on aggregate generated a pooled average net IRR of 19.1 percent (a 2.23× MOIC), the median was 10.1 percent (1.61×), and bottom quartile 3.5 percent (1.19×). The performance of bottom quartile funds is positive, which is an attractive feature of the strategy[87]. The risk profile of GC funds differs from the one of VC funds.

---

[86]The index used is the Wilshire small-cap growth index.

[87]This is not a geographical exception. A total of 163 funds from the rest of the world, created between 1989 and 2008 and representing \$52 billion, generated a pooled average net IRR of 8.1 percent. Top quartile funds generated a net IRR of 12.5 percent, and the bottom quartile -0.5 percent. MOIC are respectively 1.5×, 1.76× and 0.97×. The PME of the pooled average is 1.32× based on the MSCI World.

The top 5 percent funds generated an IRR of 44.8 percent (3.54×) and the bottom 5 percent of –8.2 percent (0.61×).

3.3.1.2 Transfer of Ownership

Once companies are profitable and have established their operations, they can self-finance their development. They have reached maturity. When needed, they have access to debt financing (notably from banks) and selectively to additional capital from their shareholders. Mature companies, whether public or private, face specific challenges.

First, mature companies tend to operate in established markets. To continue to grow they have to:

- Develop new or underserved market segments. They are vulnerable to emerging competitors and shifting client needs; and
- Gain market shares over their competition. To do so, they have to develop products/services that are more attractive than the competition's and provide the same at a lower price or with differentiated features.

Resource constraints remain a permanent—and one might argue necessary—challenge to be addressed by the management. These constraints force companies to strive for efficiency, gain in productivity, and to conquer new markets (or capture additional market share). Managers have to carefully allocate financial resources to the relevant projects necessary to execute the strategy of the company. If not successful in their strategy or the execution thereof, mature companies can lose ground.

In that context, a change of ownership can help companies to shift their strategy and implement a new plan. If the company is stable and needs fresh ideas to be more efficient or find relays of growth, a leveraged buyout (LBO) could be implemented to support this transfer of ownership. If the company is in difficulty, a restructuring can be undertaken by a turnaround fund.

Leveraged Buyout[88] (LBO)

Definition

The purpose of a leveraged buyout (LBO) is to manage and finance the transfer of ownership of a company by using a combination of capital and debt. The company can be listed (in the case of public-to-private) or not. The seller can be as diverse as a corporation (listed or not), a financial institution, a public entity, an individual, or a group of individuals. The sale process can be at arm's length or competitive (through an auction).

The buyer of the company[89] will borrow against future cash flows generated by that company (which is also the collateral of the debt). For that purpose, the targeted

---

[88]LBO is often mistakenly referred to as 'private equity'. Although LBO belongs to the PE sector, it is one of its sub-strategies.

[89]To structure the LBO, the buyer will set up one (or multiple) holding company(ies). The buyer will inject capital in the form of equity in a holding company. This holding company will borrow from banks or specialized credit institutions (such as mezzanine funds, see below). The total collected will allow the holding to acquire the target company from the seller.

company has to generate substantial and stable cash flows. The amount borrowed by the buyer can reach up to 60 to 80 percent of the price of the company, depending on the characteristics of that company. The rest is provided by the buyer in the form of equity.

The use of debt means that buyers use a financial leverage to acquire the company. This financial leverage can play in favor of the buyer, if the cost of debt remains below the yield generated by the company, or against the buyer, if the cost exceeds this yield. If the company fails to generate enough cash flows to regularly pay interests and repay the principal to the lenders, the use of this financial leverage might lead the buyer to lose the ownership of the company (and therefore the equity investment). Lenders have in effect the right to seize the ownership of the company if the debt is not serviced as expected.

The buyer also benefits from tax leverage, as the interest payments to lenders are deductible from the group formed by the holding (mother company) and its subsidiary (daughter company). Depending on local tax laws, tax savings can be more or less significant. In certain jurisdictions, such as the US, tax deductions of interest payments can be capped.

LBOs are essentially operated in developed markets (Demaria, 2013, Chapters 1 and 2), as this type of operation requires rather low interest rates and thus low inflation rates. It also requires an adapted tax and legal framework, as well as an efficient enforcement of legislation and court decisions. Moreover, it requires specialized actors and a certain level of sophistication from investors and lenders.

The buyer (or one of the buyers) of the company can be a fund (or a group of funds through a so-called club deal). The LBO is in that case "sponsored." However, in some cases, the buyers do not include funds or financial institutions, and the LBO is "unsponsored." Sponsored LBOs are akin to interim ownership. Given the limited lifespan of funds, the ownership is necessarily constrained to a three- to five-year ownership[90]. Unsponsored LBOs can last longer or even be indefinite depending on the investment time horizon of the acquirer of the company.

In its most classical form, an LBO implies that the buyer acquires the company in full, or a large majority, notably to benefit from the financial and tax leverages detailed above. However, in certain instances, the buyer can team up with existing owners and will be a significant minority shareholder.

Although no regulation prevents it, it is unusual that the financial institution providing the debt is also providing the equity for this acquisition. This could entail serious conflicts of interest if the LBO does not develop according to plan. The department of the financial institution providing the debt would have to exercise its rights and potentially evict the department providing the equity from the operation. On the other hand, the equity department could be tempted to use its clout in the organization to force the debt department to take a loss to avoid losing the investment.

There are different types of LBOs. The most well-known is probably the institutional LBO (IBO), which is often described simply as "LBO." It is by definition

---

[90] In that respect, some fund managers have launched funds denominated for a longer term (15 years). This allows them to hold the companies for longer (seven to ten years, for example). Longer holding periods support the execution of LBO plans (see below) requiring more time. Longer-term funds can potentially target a pool of companies out of investment scope for their shorter-denominated peers.

sponsored. In this variation, a fund or financial institution (or a group of them) acquires a company, simply replacing the seller and keeping the management in place. In instances of leveraged buy-in (LBI), the management of the company will be replaced by the new owner.

Management buyouts (MBO) lead the current management of the company to become the sole majority or significant minority shareholder. If the management is new (for example, in case of an owner-manager selling the company upon retirement), then the operation is a management buy-in (MBI). In that respect, an MBO/MBI can be sponsored (if the management teams up with a fund/financial institution to provide the equity to acquire the company) or unsponsored (if the management acquires the company alone).

Owner buyouts (OBO) lead one or some of the current owners of the company to acquire the company from exiting owners, in the run up to a divorce or a succession, for example. The owner-buyer(s) can team up with a fund (sponsored) or not (unsponsored). The proceeds from the debt (and possibly of the equity provision by the financial sponsor) are used to acquire the stake from exiting owners.

Each LBO should theoretically be associated with a specific plan to ensure that the value of the company will grow. The purpose of the buyer is indeed to resell the company with a significant profit. Although financial and tax leverages are an attractive feature of LBOs, they are not sufficient to generate the returns expected from such operations.

Value creation can be attributed to different sources, such as "top-line growth," meaning an increase of turnover. This can be achieved organically—by ramping up production, gaining market share, or launching new products—or by acquiring competitors. If fund managers are specialized in the latter case, their strategy is usually described as "leveraged build-up" (LBU). In that case, the fund acquires a first company (the "platform"), which then acquires smaller competitors or complementary firms (the "add-ons").

Another source of value creation is related to operational improvements. Although it is often summed up as cost cutting, it is broader as it can lead to refocusing the company on specific business lines or reviewing some of its processes (such as procurement practices or production). Operational improvements can unlock substantial value in conglomerates, for example, by divesting from less profitable activities.

A third source of value creation is related to financial engineering. It is not only due to the financial and tax leverage but also to a change in multiples of transactions[91]. This change in multiples can be due to luck, in which case the value creation is accidental and random. It can also be associated with negotiation skills but also a reflection of the transformation of the company. For example, a small company acquired as an

---

[91] Private companies are valued thanks to essentially two methods: discounted cash flows (DCF) and the multiple (also known as listed comparables) method. The latter one derives transaction multiples by dividing the market capitalization of comparable listed companies by their earnings before interest and taxes (EBIT) and sometimes depreciation and amortization (EBITDA). These transaction multiples are then used as a support during negotiation to discover the price of a private company, factoring discounts associated with size, lack of geographical or product diversification, financial structure, and multiple other factors.

LBU platform will be acquired at a rather conservative multiple: it is relatively vulnerable and does not command any market power. After acquiring and consolidating its sector, this company might have become the leader in its market. Its power has significantly increased, and its multiple will then increase, notably reflecting the reduction of its intrinsic risk.

Exploiting a source of value creation does not mean that an LBO extinguishes all the potential for change in a company. Therefore, multiple successive LBOs can be undertaken, with each a specific plan leading to an increase in the value of the firm. These subsequent (or secondary, tertiary, …) LBOs ultimately lead to another transfer of ownership and ultimately to a trade sale or an IPO. Some LBOs will eventually fail, although the rate of failure is rather limited as previously described. These failures can have a fairly high profile[92]. Some of them are associated with an excessive debt burden that the company cannot repay. This debt burden can vary over time and notably increase during the LBO by the practice of so-called dividend recapitalization (also known as leveraged recapitalization). The owner of the firm decides to increase the debt supported by the company and self-distributes the proceeds. This qualifies as a partial realization as the owner gets a distribution while retaining the full ownership of the company.

According to Cambridge Associates and Preqin, LBOs represents roughly 69 percent of the PE fund investment universe (38 percent of the PM universe). The breakdown between small, medium, large, and mega LBO funds is difficult to estimate, notably as the definition of these segments has evolved over time. Doskeland and Strömberg (2018) estimate that the LBO transaction volume varies between $500 and $600 billion per year since 2012 (in constant 2009 dollars). Assuming an average leverage level of 65 percent, the equity investments in LBO are estimated to be $150 to $250 billion per year.

Risk-Return Profile

LBO funds acquire stable and profitable companies. These companies are established in the sense that they have demonstrated their activity to profitably sell their products and/or services over multiple years. They often can count on barriers to entry generated by their know-how, their technology, their brand, their patents, their investments, and other factors, giving them an advantage. These companies may grow (organically or through acquisitions), record a stable (and maybe recurring) or a slowly declining turn-over. The risk associated with acquiring these assets is, therefore, moderate to low.

However, LBO funds aim at generating relatively high absolute returns by **using financial leverage** to acquire these companies and **implement a plan to change significantly the acquired company**. This plan has to be executed in relatively short time as the company is on average sold (or listed on the stock exchange) four to five years after its initial acquisition. This exit happens upon the materialization in the accounts of the company of this positive change.

---

[92]For an illustration, the largest LBO was a failure (WSJ, 2014). KKR, TPG Capital, and Goldman Sachs took Energy Future Holdings (formerly known as TXU) private in 2007 for a total of $43.8 billion (Hall, 2007).

The risks are therefore related to:

- The use of the financial leverage, which compounds the positive as much as the negative results of the plan introduced by the investors jointly with the management.
- The implementation of the plan. The higher the level of change, the higher the level of risks and the higher the level of potential returns. Therefore, the level of risk depends on the type of LBO executed, which itself determines largely the plan implemented in the company.

An absence of a plan to change a company under LBO is itself a major risk. To sell a company at a significantly higher price many years after it was acquired, and thus generate a profit, LBO funds cannot simply rely on the leverage effects. The financial leverage adds up the performance of the fund manager and imposes a strong governance and incentive framework (Jensen, 1989), but this framework is the instrument to implement the plan. Anecdotal evidence has indeed demonstrated that purely financial LBOs did not succeed, nor OBO, without any operational change.

LBO fund operators actively manage their risk by diversifying their investments across carefully selected industries. They leverage their specialization in terms of target size and type of plan implemented.

Fund managers target companies of a specific size. The size of companies itself determines the type of skill set required to analyze them and to implement a plan to successfully change them. LBOs are operated on companies with an enterprise value of €25 to €75 million ("small" LBO), €75 to €750 million ("mid-market" LBO, which can be subdivided in "lower mid-market" from €75 to €500 million and "higher mid-market" from €500 million to €750 million), €750 million to €1.5 billion ("large" LBO), and above €1.5 billion ("mega" LBO). These categories imply, respectively, equity investments of less than €15 million, €15 to €150 million, €150 to €300 million, and more than €300 million[93].

The type of plan implemented can vary–from refocusing the business (or shifting it to another market), growing it through acquisitions and/or internationalization, or increasing its efficiency. A plan usually focuses on a single major strategic shift with very specific targets to reach within a certain timeframe. Once the company has reached these targets, its value significantly increases, and it can be sold.

Use in a Portfolio Context

LBO is a staple of private equity portfolios: it is the largest segment of the private equity universe, targets companies whose business model and activity are relatively easy to understand and offers an attractive risk-return profile. Moreover, LBO funds can accommodate fairly large amounts of capital per fund. Investors can therefore **diversify** their portfolio by industry (LBO funds can focus on companies with no listed

---

[93]According to the classification of Invest Europe. These amounts and thresholds might vary depending on the geographical markets and can also evolve over time.

competitor) and size of assets (as small and mid-market LBO target companies below the radar of stock exchanges). However, LBO is largely operated in developed markets: financial leverage is generally not available in emerging markets, and the investment universe for control acquisitions is relatively limited.

Performance

Investors are also drawn to LBO by the performance of funds, notably when adjusted for risk. According to Cambridge Associates, 604 US LBO funds created from 1986 to 2008, collectively representing $674.2 billion, generated a pooled average net IRR of 12.8 percent. The multiple on invested capital[94] (MOIC) reaches 1.71× (on a pooled average basis). This has to be compared to a Public Market Equivalent[95] (PME) of 1.41×. The average time to liquidity is 4.46 years.

Top quartile funds on aggregate generated a pooled average net IRR of 19.2 percent (a 2.09× MOIC), the median was 11.9 percent (1.66×), and the bottom quartile 6.5 percent (1.34×). This illustrates the attractiveness of LBO: only the bottom 5 percent of funds lost capital on aggregate. The top 5 percent funds generated an IRR of 35.8 percent (3.18×) and the bottom 5 percent of –4.9 percent (0.71×)[96]. On a risk-adjusted basis, LBO funds generate an attractive performance with a very limited risk to lose capital. Their risk-return profile stands between venture and growth capital funds (Fig. 3.18 and 3.19).

Turnaround Capital (or Rescue Capital)

Definition

Turnaround capital (also known as rescue capital) consists in acquiring ailing businesses before they enter bankruptcy. This strategy is often blended in the same category as distressed debt investing (see below), but the former differs from the latter. New investors buy the equity of an ailing business for a symbolic amount or are sometimes even paid by the current owner to restructure the business out of court, thus avoiding an expensive and sometimes unpredictable outcome in bankruptcy courts.

The seller avoids the issues associated with a bankruptcy procedure, such as reputational damage, but also operational difficulties. One of the benefits of using turn-around capital funds is to sort business issues while avoiding the negative publicity associated with a bankruptcy procedure, which is a public legal process. Clients and providers of an ailing business can continue to work with the company operating as a going concern, while its issues are sorted out. Indeed, suppliers and creditors could be reluctant to maintain business relationships with the company under administration.

In some pre-bankruptcy procedures, the intervention of external administrators is supporting the restructuring. Sometimes, the arrangement between the company

---

[94] Also known as total value to paid-in (TVPI).

[95] The index used is the Wilshire 5000 total market index.

[96] In Europe, 311 funds created between 1988 and 2008, and representing $312.1 billion, generated a pooled average net IRR of 15.2 percent. Top quartile funds generated a net IRR of 22.2 percent, and the bottom quartile 4.7 percent. MOIC are respectively 1.61× (pooled average), 2.14× (top quartile), and 1.23× (lower quartile). The PME of the pooled average is 1.17× based on the MSCI Europe. As for the rest of the world, 120 funds created between 1995 and 2008, representing $65.9 billion, generated a pooled averaged net IRR of 9.4 percent, top quartile funds a net IRR of 19.6 percent, and the bottom quartile 1.5 percent. MOIC are respectively 1.53×, 2.02×, and 1.09×.

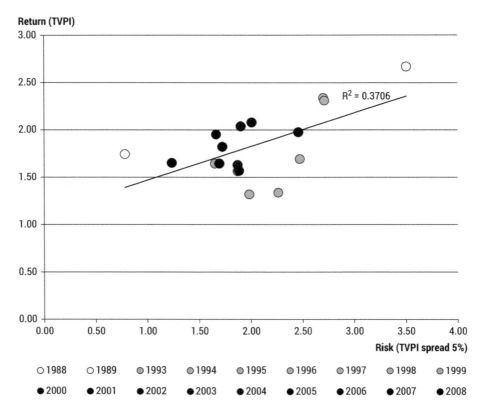

FIGURE 3.18 Return (TVPI)-risk (5 percent spread) profile of US LBO funds, by vintage year Return is measured thanks to the pooled average total value to paid-in ratio (TVPI) of sample funds. The total value of funds is the addition of proceeds distributed from the sale of investments (distributed), and the unrealized value of investments still in portfolio (residual value). The paid-in is the sum of capital called and invested by funds. Risk is measured by the difference of performance (TVPI) between funds belonging to the top 5 percent of the sample and funds belonging to the bottom 5 percent. Funds are sorted by their vintage year.
Source: Authors, based on Cambridge Associates data published in December 2016 (data as of Q2 2016).

and its creditors is approved by a court. This is the case, for example, in the UK, with the scheme of arrangement (also known as scheme of reconstruction). The arrangement altering the creditors' and shareholders' rights is therefore approved by a judicial authority.

One of the benefits for the buyer of an ailing business is that it usually has accumulated significant losses, which will become in effect a tax shield for the profits of the restructured business until these losses are fully compensated. Turnaround capital therefore benefits from a tax leverage close to the one described above for LBOs.

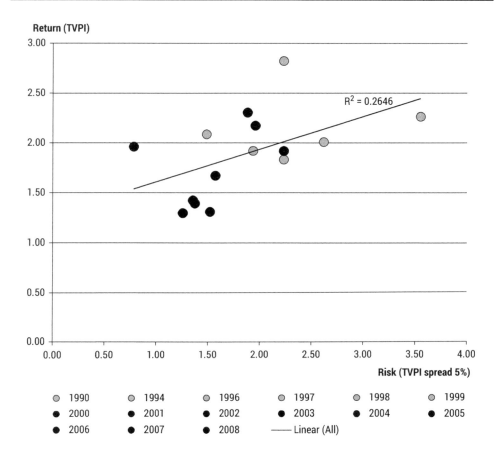

FIGURE 3.19 Return (TVPI)-risk (5 percent spread) profile of European LBO funds, by vintage year

Source: Authors, based on Cambridge Associates data published in December 2016 (data as of Q2 2016). Return is measured thanks to the pooled average total value to paid-in ratio (TVPI) of sample funds. The total value of funds is the addition of proceeds distributed from the sale of investments (distributed), and the unrealized value of investments still in portfolio (residual value). The paid-in is the sum of capital called and invested by funds. Risk is measured by the difference of performance (TVPI) between funds belonging to the top 5 percent of the sample and funds belonging to the bottom 5 percent. Funds are sorted by their vintage year.

Turnaround capital can be operated through funds, although the time required to successfully restructure a business might exceed the usual lifespan of this type of structure. Therefore, in various jurisdictions corporate structures with an open end (in effect holding companies) are used to execute these transactions.

This activity is a niche that is not widely documented. Preqin (2017c) estimated that, as of 2016, 47 fund managers were active in this strategy. North America represents roughly 70 percent of the market and Europe the rest.

Risk-Return Profile

Turnaround operators aim at generating high absolute returns by **restructuring existing businesses** that have faced an exceptional event and have solid operations, a client base, and usually significant unclaimed assets on their balance sheet.

Turnaround is at the higher end of the private equity risk spectrum. The cost of the business acquisition is negligible, but undertaking a restructuring usually requires significant financial resources to be injected into the company. Moreover, in case of difficulties, the operator will have to handle a bankruptcy procedure with the legal and financial consequences attached to it. The loss ratio of turnaround capital is unknown, due to a lack of information, but is assumed to be notably higher than in the case of an LBO or growth capital and probably more akin to the failure rate of VC funds.

Turnaround capital is a very local activity, which requires an in-depth knowledge of regulations, notably of local social law, as well as business and cultural practices. Negotiating in a difficult context with unions and employees, as well as suppliers and customers, is part of the skill set of operators.

Use in a Portfolio Context

Investors usually include turn-around capital in their portfolio to diversify their industry exposure, as well as their return drivers. They also capitalize on a hands-on unique skill set that is developed by fund managers operating in the distressed space. In particular, distressed debt is far from being ubiquitous, notably due to a lack of adapted regulations (for example in Continental Europe). Turnaround capital is the only way to capitalize on opportunities offered during a macroeconomic downturn or when economic shocks uncover hidden sources of stress for some established businesses.

Performance

Due to a lack of specific data, we refer to the section on distressed debt for perspectives on performance of operators dedicated to hands-on turn-around of ailing businesses thanks to the acquisition of a controlling stake.

3.3.1.3 *Other Types of Private Equity Strategies*

Beyond capital increase and transfer of ownership, private equity aims at solving situations that are not usually addressed by public markets. One of them is to handle a partial transfer of ownership through **replacement capital**. This approach could be seen as the equivalent of an unleveraged buyout of a significant ownership in a firm. Replacement capital consists in providing an exit to a shareholder in a company that is not itself for sale. In that respect, it is a secondary transaction, as existing shares change hands. The buyer of these shares negotiates specific minority rights with other shareholders and, notably, an exit scenario. This strategy is often counted in statistics of LBO operations as the skill set is rather similar in replacement capital and usually operated by the same funds.

Other niche strategies could be listed but are less relevant from a strategic asset allocation strategy, especially since data about them is scarce or inexistent. We will therefore leave them aside in this book.

3.3.2 Private Debt: Senior/Direct/Unitranche, Mezzanine/Subordinated and Distressed Debt

PD funds provide financing when usual lenders do not and when the risk-return profile of the investment is not adapted to private equity. The involvement of PD fund managers can vary from moderately hands-on–relying on strong due diligence and strict covenants (and the rule of law to enforce them)—in the case of direct/senior lending funds, to very hands-on, in effect becoming the owners of the business and executing a turn-around with the help of the management. Three strategies are executed by PD funds active in distressed debt and non-performing loan investing (3.2.1), mezzanine/subordinated debt financing (3.2.2), direct/senior/unitranche lending (3.2.3), and niche strategies (3.2.4). Database provider Preqin estimated that, as of December 2017, PD funds managed $667 billion, of which more than $240 billion were of dry powder. The Alternative Credit Council estimates that it could reach $1 trillion by 2020.

3.3.2.1 *Distressed Debt (DD) and Non-Performing Loans (NPL)*

Definition

Distressed debt (DD) funds can be broken down into two categories: those specialized in debt for trading and those specialized in debt for control (also called loan-to-own). The former are in effect closer to hedge funds as they acquire the debt of an ailing business at a discount, expecting certain events to materialize so that the business recovers and eventually they can sell the debt at a higher price. These investors are essentially hands-off and need relatively liquid debt markets to operate.

DD investors dedicated to loan-to-own buy specific tranches of the debt of an ailing business at a discount with the target of eventually taking control of the business by converting some or all of this debt into equity. In the process, former investors will be washed out, and hands-on DD investors will implement a plan to restructure the company, make it profitable, and then sell it once its renewed viability is demonstrated. For the purpose of this book, when we refer to DD, we mean the hands-on loan-to-own strategy.

To operate, DD funds rely on the existence of appropriate bankruptcy procedures. Chapter 11 of the US Bankruptcy Code[97] is the most widely used in DD investing and thus provides the list of the desirable criteria to see the emergence of such strategies in other jurisdictions. Out of the 114 DD fund managers identified by Cumming and Fleming (2012), 72 are in the US (18 declare having a global investment mandate), 32 in Europe (4 declare having a global investment mandate), 9 in the rest of the world. The top 10 raised 67 percent of the total capital collected for DD investing between 2002 and 2012.

---

[97] As introduced in 1978 by the US Bankruptcy Reform Act.

First, Chapter 11 freezes all the debt repayment and interest due by the business placed in bankruptcy. This grants the business and its administrators a relief period during which it is possible to assess the options to restructure the business (or its liquidation, which falls under Chapter 7 of the US Bankruptcy Code).

Then, Chapter 11 places a judicial authority in charge of the process and notably to decide on specific issues related to the restructuring of the business. This authority can, remarkably, take specific actions such as approving a restructuring plan even if a minority of creditors do not. This authority can also reduce the capital of the company (thus washing out the former owners) and increase it by converting debt that was not originally designed to be convertible.

Furthermore, Chapter 11 does not create any hierarchy between creditors besides the contractual seniority of the different tranches of debt. This provides the potential buyers of the credit of the company a relatively clear picture of the tranches of debt to buy in order to have sufficient collateral in case of failure of the business, as well as to be able to force the restructuring of the business along a specific path. In the regard, the buyer of the credit has to acquire a specific quantity of debt to reach a given majority.

Some jurisdictions, such as France, make a distinction by granting privileges to administrative bodies (tax and social administration), for example. In this case, these administrative bodies are not inclined to sell their debt at a discount. As a consequence, it is impossible for potential credit buyers to acquire the relevant tranches of debt and lead the restructuring.

Most of the distressed debt market is located in the US. Some jurisdictions, such as the UK, offer a similar bankruptcy regime and could emerge as a potential market for DD investors. More recently, India has reformed its bankruptcy regime to facilitate operations, shorten the process, and possibly offer business under administration a way out of the process, notably thanks to the involvement of DD investors.

Some countries, particularly those without an equivalent of Chapter 11[98], have a limited activity in **turnaround capital** investing (see above). This type of operation is executed to avoid a formal bankruptcy procedure.

Whether with DD investing or turnaround capital, the new owner generally provides additional financial and specialist human resources (Cuny and Talmor, 2006), negotiates with the creditors, and restructures the business according to a specific plan. However, to be viable, this activity has to be undertaken early on, soon after the business starts to experience difficulties. Often, business owners acknowledge these difficulties late, beyond the point at which DD or turnaround investing remains potentially successful.

An emerging segment in the distressed debt world has been **non-performing loans**[99] **(NPL)**. The 2007–2009 financial crisis has led many banks, notably in Europe[100], to sell these loans at a discount. The new creditor then engages in active

---

[98] France is an example, having changed its bankruptcy laws to create a pre-bankruptcy process to facilitate out-of-court restructurings.

[99] The Basel Agreements define a loan as non-performing when the borrower is 90 days or more behind the agreed payment schedule. The borrower is deemed unlikely to pay the credit in full without an action from the bank to seize the collateral of the loan.

[100] According to Lehmann (2018), an estimated €870 billion of non-performing debt was present on the balance sheet of European banks as of mid-2018. On top of this, €1.1 trillion of "non-core

recovery strategies, which could be classified in three categories. First, a pressure to recover the backlog of interests and principal repayments. Second, a restructuring of the debt to adjust payments to the capacity of the borrower. Third, an action toward seizing the assets pledged as a collateral, later auctioned for repayment of the principal, interests, and damages. The first two strategies are at the core of active NPL investing (the third being the last resort solution).

DD represents roughly 32 percent of the PD fund investment universe and 6 percent of the PM investment universe. This does not include turnaround capital and NPL strategies.

Risk-Return Profile: Performance Drivers

DD funds are aimed at generating high absolute returns by **acquiring at a discount fundamentally sound businesses (or asset-backed loans) in order to restructure them** and make a profit out of the recovery of their value. They are therefore not dedicated to asset stripping and/or asset brokerage (so-called vulture investing).

DD funds acquire loss-making businesses affected by adverse events and bad management. Restructuring them is a difficult task, often involving a repositioning of the business, lay-offs, and shrinking the business. A significant number of operations do not succeed. DD fund managers have an extensive skill set in handling the risks associated with ailing businesses, operating under time pressure, and dealing with unexpected issues. Although some due diligence can be operated, fund managers essentially operate with limited information (examining the accounting books and discussing with the management, according to Cuny and Talmor, 2006). DD investing is a local activity, requiring an extensive legal knowledge, as well as an in-depth know-how of business turnaround.

DD funds usually target businesses with significant assets that can be sold if the restructuring fails and the company is liquidated. Fund managers therefore assess the assets carefully and their price on the secondary market. They calculate the liquidation value of businesses in order to set the price of the credit tranches they plan to acquire. This price will be inferior or equal to the value of the assets on the secondary market. The proceeds from the liquidation are expected to compensate the acquisition of the debt of the failed business. Risks are actively mitigated thanks to this analysis.

Use in a Portfolio Context

DD investing is a major source of diversification of the performance of a portfolio as a countercyclical investment strategy. This strategy provides investors with the opportunity to invest profitably in underperforming businesses. DD investing is probably the only investment strategy focusing on ailing businesses with the aim of pulling them out of difficulties. Other distressed investment strategies in effect try to anticipate by selling securities of businesses before the actual notice of these difficulties. They later buy these securities back when the difficulties are acknowledged and reflected in their

---

banking assets" could also be divested. He notes that "significant further supply might [...] come into the market as stricter supervisory guidelines are implemented, and as new accounting guidelines force higher provisioning levels." Lehmann estimates that in 2016 secondary loan transactions on NPL and non-core assets represented a turnover ratio of 7 percent (€146 billion, of which €118 billion was for NPL alone).

price, thus pocketing the difference between the inflated sale price and the deflated acquisition price.

In recession time, DD funds enjoy a significant flow of attractive investment opportunities[101]. Corresponding vintage years perform particularly well. However, deal flow remains significant regardless of macroeconomic conditions, as the source of difficulties for a business is often bad management.

Performance

According to Cambridge Associates, 110 US DD funds created between 1990 and 2008 collectively representing $94.2 billion generated a pooled average net IRR of 11.7 percent. Their pooled average MOIC is 1.56×. This has to be compared with a Public Market Equivalent[102] (PME) of 1.36×. The average time to liquidity is four years.

Top quartile funds on aggregate generated a pooled average net IRR of 17.4 percent (a 1.89× MOIC), the median is 10.4 percent (1.52×), and bottom quartile funds 5.5 percent (1.25×). Surprisingly given their focus on ailing businesses, the performance of DD funds is less volatile than for PE strategies: the top 5 percent of funds generated an IRR of 28.3 percent (2.58×), and the bottom 5 percent of funds barely lost capital on aggregate with an IRR of –0.5 percent (0.99×)[103]. Indeed, Cumming and Fleming (2012) note that the average default rate in DD investing is 0.04 percent and the median 0.025 percent (minimum 0.01 percent and maximum 0.13 percent). The use of bankruptcy procedures to purchase debt is proving effective to mitigate investment risk. On a risk-adjusted basis, DD funds generated in the past a very attractive performance.

3.3.2.2 *Mezzanine and Subordinated Debt Financing*

Definition

Mezzanine financing provides flexible subordinated loans to a borrower. In the case of mezzanine financing, the borrower is the owner of a business who pledges this business as the collateral of the loan. The profits distributed by this business are used to pay the

---

[101] Cumming and Fleming (2012). They notably identify four corporate distressed cycles in the US since 1980: the 1990–1991 junk bond crisis, the 1997–1998 Asian crisis, the 2001–2002 dot-com crisis, and the 2007–2009 global financial crisis. Default rate of non-financial speculative grade bonds jumped from a range of 0.5–5.1 percent before the crisis to 9.3–12.8 percent at peak corporate default rate.

[102] The index used is the Wilshire 5000 total market index. A PME using the Credit Suisse Distressed Loan index delivers a PME of 1.27× for vintage years 1992–2008 (versus 1.59× for DD funds over the same period).

[103] In Europe, 311 funds created between 1988 and 2008 and representing $312.1 billion generated a pooled average net IRR of 15.2 percent. Top quartile funds generated a net IRR of 22.2 percent and the bottom quartile 4.7 percent. MOIC are respectively 1.61× (pooled average), 2.14× (top quartile), and 1.23× (lower quartile). The PME of the pooled average is 1.17× based on the MSCI Europe. As for the rest of the world, 120 funds created between 1995 and 2008 representing $65.9 billion generated a pooled averaged net IRR of 9.4 percent, top quartile funds a net IRR of 19.6 percent, and the bottom quartile 1.5 percent. MOIC are respectively 1.53×, 2.02×, and 1.09×.

interests (and possibly some or all of the principal) to the lender. If the business fails to distribute these profits, the borrower can seize the business and auction it off. The proceeds are then used to compensate the lender.

Mezzanine debt is flexible as lender and borrower negotiate specifically the terms for each loan, depending on the capacity of repayment of the borrower. Mezzanine debt is subordinated in the sense that its interests are paid and the loan is refunded in order of priority after senior debt (see below the section on direct lending). The lender (or "mezzaner") therefore assumes a higher risk of default than the senior lender. The mezzaner also accepts that the repayment of his credit is deferred over a longer period of time, until the senior debt is repaid. For this higher risk and longer duration, the mezzaner is compensated by a higher interest rate and a right to convert the debt into equity. This right can be exercised upon the materialization of a liquidity event or bought back by the borrower (usually at pre-agreed terms). Mezzanine debt therefore generates a blend of yield and capital gains.

Thus, the terms negotiated between the borrower and the lender are the interest rate, the conversion rights (sometimes referred to as equity kicker), the duration of the loan and its repayment (usually *in fine*, that is at the term of the loan), and the covenants of the loan. Interests are usually defined as a margin over a base interest rate and can be paid ongoing and/or capitalized (and therefore accruing) to the principal. The covenants are the clauses of the lending contracts that define the information rights of the lender and its recourse in case the loan does not develop according to plan.

Mezzanine debt is often compared to leveraged loans, as both are provided to companies with no rating or rated below investment grade, such as the ones targeted by LBOs. However, leveraged loans are usually collateralized and thus senior, whereas mezzanine debt is not (as it is subordinated). Leveraged loans are usually provided by banks, which keep them to maturity or more frequently package and resell them (notably as collateralized loan obligations; see below). According to some estimates (Mackenzie, 2018, quoting S&P LCD and BofA Merrill Lynch), the leveraged loans market in the US has reached $1 trillion in 2018 and is on the verge of catching up with high yield bonds ($1.1 trillion).

Mezzanine debt can theoretically be provided by banks but is in practice provided by non-traditional lenders, such as mezzanine funds. The mezzanine debt can be "sponsored" if the equity provider is a financial institution, such as an LBO fund. The fund acquires a company (via one or multiple holding companies; see above) and places the mezzanine debt in the holding company (or one of the holding companies if there are more than one). However, the mezzanine debt can also be "unsponsored" if there is no intervention of a financial institution as an equity provider. The owner can be, for example, the management of the business.

Mezzanine debt is relatively expensive when compared to senior debt (see below). During the last credit cycle (until 2008), subordinated non-convertible debt emerged as an alternative: the **second lien** debt (sometimes referred to as junior debt). Unlike mezzanine debt, which aims to generate a gross IRR of 15 to 18 percent, second lien aims to a 10 to 12 percent gross IRR.

The current credit cycle has seen the quasi elimination of mezzanine debt as we know it in favor of so-called **unitranche debt**. This type of debt combines in one single tranche (hence its name) features of senior, second lien, and mezzanine debt. The expected gross IRR is between 9 and 11 percent. Unitranche debt diverges significantly from mezzanine financing as it is repaid and collects interests progressively and regularly and does not necessarily embed conversion rights. Therefore, we account unitranche debt funds in the direct/senior lending category.

Mezzanine financing (as well as unitranche and senior debt) are essentially available in developed markets, the US and Europe representing the bulk of it. Mezzanine debt represents roughly 11 percent of PD funds and 2 percent of PM funds.

Risk-Return Profile: Performance Drivers

Mezzanine debt funds are supposed to **combine the downside protection associated with debt securities** (albeit subordinated and high yield) **and the upside of capital gains** associated with equity conversion rights. Mezzanine debt is provided by active fund managers, who carefully assess the risk associated with the borrower and its business. This is not a credit-scoring approach but a full due diligence operated by the fund manager, in partnership with the equity provider in case of sponsored mezzanine. As a result, the loss ratio is supposed to be minimal or nil.

Although there is no certainty that each operation will lead to a success, the option to participate in that success also supports higher returns than senior or subordinated credits would normally generate. The overall IRR of mezzanine debt should thus be higher than the interest rate associated with leveraged loans and second lien debt.

Use in a Portfolio Context

Mezzanine debt provides an exposure to the upside of LBOs (in case of sponsored operations) while limiting the risks associated with this type of operation. This strategy provides investors with the opportunity to get an exposure to transfers of ownership of mid- to mega-size deals, including those that are not sponsored by LBO funds. The investment universe is, therefore, partially diverging from LBO funds.

Theoretically, mezzanine debt should be more resilient during adverse macroeconomic conditions than pure equity strategies. However, it usually shares the profit of an operation only if the latter hits a certain threshold of performance. Therefore, the dispersion of returns can be relatively high from vintage year to vintage year, as well as from fund manager to fund manager.

Performance

According to Cambridge Associates, 82 US mezzanine funds created from 1986 to 2008 collectively representing $30.8 billion generated a pooled average net IRR of 9 percent. The pooled average MOIC is 1.42×. This has to be compared to a Public Market Equivalent[104] (PME) of 1.38×. The average time to liquidity is 4.1 years.

---

[104]The index used is the Wilshire 5000 total market index. A PME using the BofA ML All U.S. Convertible index delivers a PME of 1.35× for vintage years 1988–2008 (versus 1.41× for mezzanine funds over the same period).

Top quartile funds on aggregate generated a pooled average net IRR of 11.9 percent (a 1.70× MOIC), the median 9.7 percent (1.48×), and bottom quartile 7.1 percent (1.29×). On aggregate, mezzanine funds can generate very attractive returns: top 5 percent funds generated an IRR of 22 percent (2.51×). They also do not lose capital: bottom 5 percent funds recorded on aggregate an IRR of 0.2 percent (1.01×)[105]. Nevertheless, the aggregate performance of the three funds tracked by Cambridge Associates of vintage year 1998 was negative (0.60×). The sample size limits generalizations but illustrates the fact that despite the use of credit instruments, mezzanine funds can in effect lose capital.

Given the significant changes experienced by the market of mezzanine funds and the emergence of unitranche debt that is still largely undocumented, these performances might not necessarily reflect the level of dispersion of current and future performances of private convertible debt strategies.

3.3.2.3   Direct/Senior and Unitranche Lending

Definition

Also called alternative credit, private credit, or senior debt, **direct lending** could be considered as equivalent to the senior lending activity operated by banks. The activity consists in providing usually small and mid-sized business with loans, but the difference with bank loans is that the purpose of the operation is specific. While banks provide loans to do more of the same, such as producing more or opening a new shop, direct lending usually finances unusual and often one-off operations.

As a result, the methods of analysis differ. Banks use scoring systems to determine if and how they should lend to businesses. These systems are applying statistical methods to determine the chances of success of the project to be financed by the loan and the economic and financial fitness of the borrower. Statistics are based on the past success of the business and its peer group.

Direct lending in effect finances the launch of a subsidiary abroad or of a new product/service or even an acquisition. This type of risk is difficult to assess for a bank, as it is very specific. Scoring is thus difficult or impossible. Direct lending fund managers apply techniques that are closer to the private equity toolbox. They undertake a due diligence, which implies meeting with management and going beyond a pure documentation analysis. The perimeter of this due diligence varies depending on the fund manager but can extend to market and competition analysis.

Kraemer-Eis (2014) states that there are different models of direct lending. First a bilateral lending, or private placement, in which the lender develops a dedicated expertise, as described above. Second, specialized loan funds, in which a fund manager pools

---

[105]In Europe, 311 funds created between 1988 and 2008 and representing $312.1 billion generated a pooled average net IRR of 15.2 percent. Top quartile funds generated a net IRR of 22.2 percent and the bottom quartile 4.7 percent. MOIC are respectively 1.61× (pooled average), 2.14× (top quartile), and 1.23× (lower quartile). The PME of the pooled average is 1.17× based on the MSCI Europe. As for the rest of the world, 120 funds created between 1995 and 2008 representing $65.9 billion generated a pooled averaged net IRR of 9.4 percent, top quartile funds a net IRR of 19.6 percent, and the bottom quartile 1.5 percent. MOICs are respectively 1.53×, 2.02×, and 1.09×.

loans together (see CLO in the next sub-section). Third, a "co-origination with a bank" model that is mostly prevalent in Europe and involves insurance companies. As a consequence, funds can be more or less diversified. Funds can be captive or independent.

Not surprisingly, direct lending fund managers operate essentially in countries with stable and low inflation rates, with strong and predictable legal environments, and where courts can rule relatively fast and judgments can be enforced without major hurdles. Developed markets, namely the US but also more recently Western Europe, are the main locations of this type of activity.

This activity has been developing fast, particularly since the financial crisis of 2008–2009. International regulatory frameworks such as the Basel II and Basel III Agreements, as well as major overhauls of national banking legislation, have redefined the perimeter of the lending activity of banks. Notably, these regulations have reset risk thresholds for banks and adjusted solvency ratios to these new assumptions. As a consequence, banks have retreated from lending activities and significantly reduced their lending activity to small and mid-sized businesses. Lending to these businesses was perceived as less profitable due to the increased costs of risk analysis and compliance, while risk assessments were less favorable to these businesses[106].

The US has a rather long history of providing alternative forms of credit to companies (Kraemer-Eis, 2014, p. 9), notably by using bonds, structured credit instruments, and securitization of loan portfolios. American direct lending fund managers have also offered an alternative to banks even before 2008. These fund managers also often offer mezzanine and **unitranche** financing, which complement direct lending activities. Their activity has increased since the financial crisis. Unitranche financing is a more flexible version of the straightforward direct/senior debt, combining different tranches of debt such as junior, subordinated and second lien tranches, and even possibly mezzanine debt.

Before the financial crisis, the Western European legal bank monopoly on lending essentially prevented the emergence of direct lending funds. Subordinated debt—and notably mezzanine funds—were, however, present. As the rules on lending were relaxed, fund managers launched direct lending strategies. This coincided with the erosion of the market for mezzanine debt associated with the fall of interest rates. Mezzanine fund managers not only reinvented themselves as unitranche lenders but also direct lenders.

Direct/senior lending funds expect a gross IRRs of 5 to 8 percent in Western Europe, which translates as 4 to 6 percent net IRRs (for Europe, see Kraemer-Eis, 2014, p. 30). These returns are based on a margin calculated on a risk-free or short-term market rate (such as the LIBOR). In the US, gross returns are expected to reach 7 to 9 percent (unlevered). Direct/senior lending funds can be leveraged (0 to 4.5× for direct debt funds and 0 to 6.5× for unitranche loans), a feature that enhances their IRRs and MOICs.

In the absence of actual data, it is difficult to estimate the market of direct and unitranche lending. We estimate that direct/senior/unitranche debt funds currently represent roughly 57 percent of the PD funds and 10 percent of PM funds. In 2017, $52.6 billion was raised by direct lending funds out of a total of $118.7 billion by private debt

---

[106] Kraemer-Eis (2014) lists as structural barriers to lending: "Limited scale of investment projects, lack of standardization, limited liquidity, and potential reputational harm in relation to specific projects and the need to spread risk."

funds, according to Cox and Hanson (2018). As a matter of comparison, mezzanine funds raised $14.9 billion that same year.

Risk-Return Profile: Performance Drivers

Direct/senior and unitranche debt funds are supposed to offer a **strong downside protection with higher returns than usual fixed-income instruments**. Returns are provided by the payment of interests.

Just like for mezzanine funds, direct/senior/unitranche debt is provided by active fund managers carefully assessing risks thanks to a due diligence. Besides active risk assessment and mitigation by the fund manager, the downside risk protection of direct/senior and unitranche debt funds come from the fact that they have a first claim on assets and strong covenants (that is, clauses to monitor and enforce the loan terms). These covenants are crucial to manage risks and act in case the borrower experiences financial difficulties.

When market conditions become more competitive for lenders, as interest rates are low and the access to capital is easy, it is tempting to lower the number and the strength of covenants. Borrowers can get access to lower interest rates, longer-term debt, larger amounts, and so-called covenant-light loans. If borrowers experience difficulties, the lender has to wait longer to act according to the lending terms, which might lead to a more difficult recovery of the principal and the interest.

Use in a Portfolio Context

Direct and unitranche debt provides a yield to income-oriented investors. As these debts are floating-rate instruments, they provide a relative protection against inflation and rising interest rates. They are an alternative to high-yield bonds and leveraged loans, providing a different exposure to small and mid-size businesses and thus a larger investment universe.

Performance

Unfortunately, there is no database providing comprehensive and solid data on the performance of direct/senior lending funds. Quoting Preqin (with sample calibration), Cunningham (2015) reports anecdotal global median annual returns between 2007 and 2012 ranging from 11.1 percent and 11.6 percent with "one of the lowest standard deviations of 5.8 percent."

These returns are high and capture the aftermath of the financial crisis and do not reflect the expected level and dispersion of returns of direct/senior lending. Reeve (2017), quoting a study from bfinance, states that "core senior debt in Europe now produces returns of 5–6 percent with average cash yields at around of slightly below 4 percent [. . . , a] noticeable spread compression since 2012."

According to Lanser et al. (2016), as of Q4 2016, in the US senior debt for middle market LBOs was priced as LIBOR + 450–525 bps, to be compared with second lien at LIBOR + 850–950 bps and mezzanine at 11 percent cash and 1 percent payment in kind (PIK). Unitranche was at LIBOR + 675–775 bps. In Europe, during the same period, senior funds had margins "sub 6 percent," while unitranche funds had margins of 6.5–7.5 percent. These are gross return figures.

3.3.2.4 Other Types of Private Debt Strategies

Private debt is the host of multiple niche strategies, which are sometimes gathered in funds under the label of "**special situations**." Fund managers are granted a broad mandate to deploy capital in a rather opportunistic manner, often across the capital structure (including possibly equity). Special situations can also encompass secondary opportunities.

Venture debt is another niche strategy. It could be described as the equivalent of mezzanine debt for mature start-ups. Usually, interests are capitalized, and funds get their capital, cumulated interests, and possibly capital gain upon a liquidity event. Venture debt activity has been limited to a few select markets, such as the US and more recently Europe and Israel. Venture debt funds usually provide convertible debt to late-stage start-ups, often as a complement or an alternative to a new round of financing. According to Preqin (2016), venture debt funds generated an average net IRR of 11.5 percent between 2007 and 2012. MOIC ranged from 0.83× to 1.43× and IRR from 1 percent to 60 percent. However, none of the funds observed were fully liquidated at the time of report, so these figures have to be used with caution. According to Devine (2015), venture debt funds were willing to raise $4.4 billion in 2015. This has to be compared with a total of $214 billion for private debt funds[107].

Litigation financing could also be seen as a form of private debt. The borrower can use it to finance pre-trial and trial proceedings (including lawyers' fees). In case of success, the fund gets a share of the financial compensation. In case of failure, the fund loses the investment. In certain instances, litigation financing can be used to finance the post-trial period, functioning as a receivable financing mechanism. The party that prevails in a legal proceeding gets the financial compensation from the fund in exchange for a discount. The fund then takes over the process of recovering the amount due.

Royalty financing, **aviation finance,** and even **trade finance** are also forms of private debt financing, which could potentially be seen as an overlap with private real asset debt. Each of these strategies uses either an asset (planes and parts) or claim on future cash-flow streams (royalties or payments) as a collateral to provide capital upfront. The fund manager takes over the task of recovering the capital or selling the asset/claim. According to Devine (2015), royalty-financing funds were willing to raise $2.5 billion in 2015, representing 1.16 percent of the total sought by private debt funds.

Other private-debt niche strategies, often gathered under the generic expression of specialty finance, include **asset-backed financing**. This could overlap with private real asset debt, as tangible or intangible assets are placed in a special purpose vehicle (SPV)

---

[107]Distressed debt funds (as defined in this book) were looking for $64 billion, mezzanine/subordinated debt $65 billion, direct/senior/unitranche funds $77 billion, royalty financing funds $2.5 billion, CLO funds $2.3 billion, and funds of private debt funds $1.3 billion (Devine, 2015).

structured with equity and debt. The benefit of the lender to the structure is that a specific asset is pledged as a collateral for a loan. The owner of the SPV can use the proceeds of the loan for other purposes while avoiding complex negotiations on the loan.

Collateralized debt obligations (CDO), which are a form of structured asset-backed financing security, and **collateralized loan obligations (CLO),** which bundle various business loans in a single security, sit at the border between private debt and asset management. In Figure 3.2 at the beginning of this chapter, it would be in the securitized segment, which is highly intermediated, of the private debt universe. The relationship between the fund manager and the borrower is only indirect.

3.3.3 Private Real Assets: Private Real Estate, Private Infrastructure, Timber/Farmland, Energy Assets and Other Niches

As illustrated by Figures 3.1 and 3.2 at the beginning of this chapter, private real asset (PRA) funds provide financing at every stage of the development of intangible or tangible real assets (fixed or not).

The equivalent of venture capital for PRA is called greenfield investing. This often implies acquiring assets (such as land in the case of real estate, infrastructure, natural resources, timberland, and farmland), securing the rights to build, managing the construction, and delivering the final asset. This strategy bears significant execution risks, compounded by potential foreign exchange, regulatory, and political risks associated with the geographical locations.

The equivalent of growth capital and LBO for PRA is most likely a combination of core, core-plus, and value-added investing. Assets are developed, of medium to high quality and variable levels of change. Core assets require less debt and transformation, while value-added assets support more debt and require more transformation.

The equivalent of distressed debt and turnaround capital for PRA is opportunistic (or brownfield in private infrastructure) as well as distressed (including non-performing loans) investing.

Private real assets differ substantially from companies financed by private equity and private debt in the sense that they represent a clear and direct access to predictable future cash flows associated with the collateral represented by the asset itself. For example, while a hotel management company is a company, the hotel itself is the asset. Sometimes, the two are combined in one entity, and unless the management of the hotel is very lean and passive, it is considered as a company first, with significant assets on its balance sheet.

PRA funds have been growing with an increased flow of investment opportunities. Multiple factors have contributed to this evolution. First, the trend toward a disengagement of states in the economy has led to the privatization of public assets, as well as the emergence of public–private partnerships (to develop new infrastructures, for example). Second, public and private companies have been keen to focus their activities and reduce the size of their balance sheet. Their assets were immobilizing financial resources that could be reallocated to compete more effectively. This led to the deconsolidation of assets from balance sheets, placed in special purpose vehicles (SPV) in need of equity providers. Third, as financial institutions have seen their regulatory framework overhauled against the provision of such equity to SPVs, PRA have seen an opportunity to jump in.

Private real asset funds finance assets through equity (PRA equity funds) or debt (PRA debt funds). Although PRA debt funds are emerging, most of PRA funds finance assets through equity. Just as in the PD sector, PRA fund managers can be more or less hands-on depending on the sub-strategies. PRA can be broken down into multiple categories: private real estate (3.3.1), private infrastructure (3.3.2), and investment niches (3.3.3).

Risk-Return Profile: Performance Drivers

PRA funds aim to generate a combination of income and capital gains, by **acquiring, managing, transforming, and selling assets over time.** The mix of income and capital gains delivered to the investors depends on the type of asset acquired and the transformation operated: the more transformation, the higher the potential capital gains.

Use in a Portfolio Context

The benefits of using PRA in a portfolio range from a diversification of return drivers, low historical correlations with traditional asset classes, a yield component that varies with the transformation, and some degree of inflation hedging associated with capital gains. Some PRA strategies are using debt, which means that they are sensitive to the evolution of interest rates. Moreover, there is a possible overlap with listed structures investing in real assets, leading to some competition on certain market segments.

3.3.3.1   *Private Real Estate*

Definition

Private real estate (PRE) funds represent roughly 36 percent of the PRA market and roughly 10 percent of the PM universe. These funds acquire real estate, such as office, commercial, industrial, or residential units, as well as a combination thereof, or more specialized assets, such as assisted living facilities or warehouses. Sub-strategies include core/core-plus, value-added and opportunistic, as well as distressed, debt, and secondary[108]. For the latter three strategies, little information is available. They differ significantly in focus, strategy, character of underlying assets, level of manager involvement, leverage, and other factors, all of which result in differing return and risk profiles.

---

[108] According to database provider Preqin, debt PRE funds raised $27.9 billion in 2017 (25.3 percent of the total raised by PRE excluding funds-of-funds), distressed PRE funds $2.9 billion (2.6 percent), and secondary PRE funds $0.7 billion (0.6 percent). As a matter of comparison, PRE funds-of-funds raised $1.2 billion, core PRE funds $3.6 billion (3.3 percent), core-plus PRE funds $3.7 billion (3.4 percent), value-added PRE funds $34.9 billion (31.7 percent), and opportunistic PRE funds $36.5 billion (33.1 percent).

Database provider Preqin estimated that as of June 2017, PRE funds managed $811 billion, of which 245 were of dry powder. North America represented 57.9 percent, Europe 25.9 percent, Asia 11.5 percent, and the rest of the world 4.7 percent. Opportunistic PRE funds had $98 billion of dry powder, value-added PRE funds $61 billion, debt PRE funds $49 billion, core PRE funds $16 billion, core-plus PRE funds $11 billion, and distressed PRE funds also $11 billion.

While listed real estate funds provide investors with an access to plain vanilla core real estate, PRE funds dedicated to core and core-plus differ. PRE implies a change of the assets, leading to a capital gain. **Core** PRE funds invest at the lower end of the risk spectrum, acquiring existing sound and stable assets (office, retail, industrial, and/or multi-family residential) in prime metropolitan locations and established markets. The strategy might consist in upgrading the tenant base, increasing the leasing rate further, shifting the duration of contracts, and/or operating mild improvements on the building. A pure buy-and-hold strategy is possible but limits the possible capital gains. Properties are already well maintained at acquisition time and require little or no capital injection. This strategy uses moderate leverage (15 to 30 percent of the value of the asset). Core PRE performance is primarily yield-driven (90 to 100 percent) with limited capital gain contribution (0 to 10 percent). Holding periods tend to be long (10 years or more).

Core-plus PRE funds invest in properties that are similar to the core sub-strategy but require more work and/or are located in prime or confirmed upcoming areas. The quality of buildings might be lower and require enhancements. Some buildings might need to be repositioned and their tenant base shifted. This strategy uses leverage (30 to 50 percent) and usually requires a moderate capital injection. Core-plus PRE performance is also primarily yield-driven (80 to 90 percent) with limited capital gain contribution (10 to 20 percent). Holding periods tend to be also rather long (7 years or more).

Performance data of core and core-plus PRE funds is difficult to come by. According to eFront Pevara (now Insight), 42 funds created between 1991 and 2008 representing $41.8 billion generated a pooled average net IRR of 6 percent. The pooled average MOIC was 1.52×[109]. The average time to liquidity is 7.2 years.

Top quartile funds on aggregate generated a pooled average net IRR of 10.6 percent (a 1.69× MOIC), the median is 4.7 percent (1.39×), and bottom quartile funds –2.1 percent (0.91×). Core and core-plus PRE show a certain dispersion of performance: top 5 percent funds generated an IRR of 19.1 percent (2.73×), and bottom 5 percent of funds lost capital on aggregate with an IRR of –7.5 percent (0.48×). Therefore, if core and core-plus PRE funds present some attractive features, they can also suffer from losses due to a drop in real estate prices. In that respect, the limited potential for improvement means that it is difficult to mitigate price movements.

Value-added[110] (VA) PRE funds focus on properties located on prime or secondary locations and that require a more active involvement from the fund manager. The purpose of the intervention is to upgrade the building by redeveloping, refurbishing, or repositioning it and/or changing the tenant base (lease-up). Fund managers need to be

---

[109]eFront Insight does not provide PME benchmarks at the time of writing.
[110]Value-added is sometimes referred to as value add. We will use both interchangeably.

able to identify and source appropriate target assets, implement relevant property and physical improvements and tenant-level strategy, and provide ongoing asset management. Beyond the plain vanilla assets described above, value-added strategies can be applied to specialty types including, notably, hospitality, healthcare-related properties, student housing, or self-storage. Performance is driven by a combination of income (30 to 50 percent) and capital gains (50 to 70 percent). Fund managers can use debt in the range of 40 to 70 percent of the value of the asset.

According to Cambridge Associates, 217 US VA PRE funds created between 1986 and 2008, collectively representing $78.2 billion, generated a pooled average net IRR of 6.1 percent. Their pooled average MOIC is 1.30×. This performance appears rather low, especially given the higher intensity of work required from the fund manager and the higher level of risks associated with this type of investment. Overhauling a building entails delays and risks of failure in some of the tasks or even of the whole project. These returns, as well as for the whole PRE market, might be affected by the real estate downturn experienced at the end of the period considered and notably 2007 and 2008. We estimate that over the long term, the expected return for such strategy should be 8 to 10 percent.

A PME based on the NACREIF Property[111] delivers at 1.46× MOIC. The PME based on the Dow Jones Real Estate Index over 1993–2008[112] delivers a 1.55× versus a 1.29× for VA PRE funds. The average time to liquidity is 4.4 years, but a significant share of the funds of vintage years 2005-2008 are still holding significant assets. Their performance has yet to be materialized by exits, and time to liquidity might increase.

Top quartile funds on aggregate generated a pooled average net IRR of 16.6 percent (a 1.76× MOIC), the median is 8.4 percent (1.52×) and bottom quartile funds 1.6 percent (1.12×). Top 5 percent funds recorded a performance of 28.9 percent (2.29×) and bottom 5 percent an IRR of -10.3 percent (0.51×)[113]. The risk associated with VA PRE investing is significant.

Opportunistic PRE funds are at the higher end of the risk spectrum. They target lower quality buildings in prime, secondary, or peripheral markets across the whole range of real estate markets, including niches. Properties require significant overhaul to upgrade them to the higher level of quality or even ground-up (re-) development. Fund managers are very hands-on in this type of situation involving complex turnaround and redevelopment. Performance is driven by capital gains, with possibly some little income

---

[111]The NACREIF Property is a private real estate index, gross of fees. It uses quarterly appraised values to generate total returns of unlisted real estate commercial buildings acquired on the private market for investment purposes only.

[112]The index is not available for the years before 1993.

[113]In Europe, 18 funds created between 2005 and 2008 and representing $11.9 billion generated a pooled average net IRR of −6.1 percent and a MOIC of 0.75×. This poor performance might be related to the limited size of the sample in terms of vintage year and number of funds. The sample has mostly been affected by the 2007–2009 crisis and remains to be liquidated. Top quartile funds generated a net IRR of 8.8 percent, and the bottom quartile −15.5 percent. MOICs are respectively 1.32× (top quartile) and 0.32× (lower quartile). The PME of the pooled average is 1.39× based on the FTSE EPRA/NAREIT Developed Europe Real Estate Index. There is no data available for the rest of the world.

(0 to 10 percent). Fund managers can use debt in the range of 60 to 80 percent of the value of the asset.

According to Cambridge Associates, 186 US opportunistic PRE funds created between 1994 and 2008, collectively representing $136.3 billion, generated a pooled average net IRR of 7.9 percent. Their pooled average MOIC is 1.38×. This performance appears as rather low, especially given the expertise and intensity of work required from the fund manager, as well as the high level of risks. These returns, just as for VA PRE funds, might be affected by the real estate downturn experienced in 2007–2009. We estimate that over the long term, the expected return for such strategy should be 12 to 18 percent.

A PME based on the NACREIF Property[114] delivers at 1.44× MOIC. The PME based on the Dow Jones Real Estate Index delivers a 1.54×. The average time to liquidity is 4.3 years, but a significant share of the funds of vintage years 2005–2008 are still holding significant assets. Their performance has yet to be materialized by exits, and holding periods might increase.

Top quartile funds on aggregate generated a pooled average net IRR of 13.5 percent (a 1.64× MOIC), the median is 8.8 percent (1.39×), and bottom quartile funds 0.25 percent (1.01×). Top 5 percent funds recorded a performance of 27.6 percent (2.19×) and bottom 5 percent an IRR of −11.5 percent (0.46×)[115]. Therefore, the risk is even higher than with VA PRE funds.

3.3.3.2 Private Infrastructure

Infrastructure investing supports the construction, development, operation, and overhaul of permanent structures facilitating economic activities. Among the sectors included are transportation (toll roads, ports, airports, bridges, tunnels, railroads), regulated utility and energy infrastructures (water, wastewater, electricity, and gas and oil networks), and communications infrastructures (phone and fiber networks, transmission towers). Infrastructures benefit from a local (or national) monopoly in their activities, which makes them less sensitive to economic cycles than other investment strategies. They are usually regulated and rely on long-term contracts with their

---

[114]The NACREIF Property is a private real estate index, gross of fees. It uses quarterly appraised values to generate total returns of unlisted real estate commercial buildings acquired on the private market for investment purposes only.

[115]In Europe, 34 funds created between 2005 and 2008 and representing $23.7 billion generated a pooled average net IRR of −3.3 percent and a MOIC of 1.13×. This poor performance might be related to the limited size of the sample and the impact of the 2007–2009 crisis. Most funds retain significant assets to be liquidated. Top quartile funds generated a net IRR of 11.7 percent and the bottom quartile −8 percent. MOICs are respectively 1.42× (top quartile) and 0.74× (lower quartile). The PME of the pooled average is 1.39× based on the FTSE EPRA/NAREIT Developed Europe Real Estate Index. For the rest of the world, 51 funds created between 2005 and 2008 and representing $31.4 billion generated at 1.24 percent pooled average IRR and a MOIC of 1.06×. Funds of vintage year 2006–2008 retain significant assets to be liquidated. Top quartile funds generated a net IRR of 9.1 percent and the bottom quartile −3.1 percent. MOICs are respectively 1.39× (top quartile) and 0.84× (lower quartile). The PME of the pooled average is 1.40× based on the MSCI World Index.

clients. Some authors include in infrastructures so-called social infrastructures, such as education, recreation, correctional, health care, fuel storage, and warehouse facilities. These facilities are closer to private companies or real estate in their characteristics, so we exclude them from the definition.

In general, infrastructure funds provide investors with fairly stable and predictable income, a relative protection against inflation (as prices are indexed), and a low correlation with other investment strategies. Although the disengagement of states in the financing of infrastructure has paved the way to public–private partnerships and the opportunity of infrastructure investing, the financing gap of new infrastructures remains largely open. This is because infrastructure investing supports specific risks, such as regulatory and sovereign risk (even in developed countries such as Norway[116]), and construction risk (for greenfield investments).

Although infrastructure is a recent sector of investment for institutional investors, private infrastructure funds invest in these tangible fixed assets in equity or debt. These funds can be classified in sub-strategies along the lines of real estate (see above) with **core, value-added,** and **opportunistic,** which are sometimes blended and referred to as **brownfield** when already built. **Greenfield** finances the design and construction of infrastructure projects and is an additional strategy. They represent roughly 41 percent of the PRA market and 11 percent of the PM universe. As in PRE, infrastructure debt funds have emerged as well. According to Pitchbook, private debt infrastructure funds raised $7.2 billion in 2017. Database provider Preqin estimated that, as of June 2017, private equity infrastructure funds managed $388 billion, of which 149 were dry powder. The US represents 38 percent of the total, Europe 30 percent, Asia 12 percent, and the rest of the world 20 percent. The sector is quite concentrated, and the average fund size is $1.3 billion.

Core infrastructure is expected to generate a net return of 6 to 8 percent, value-added 10 to 12 percent, and opportunistic above 14 percent (Rosenbaum, 2017). Unfortunately, a lack of detailed data prevents such empirical analysis.

According to Cambridge Associates, 29 infrastructure funds created between 1998 and 2008, collectively representing $40.6 billion, generated a pooled average net IRR of 6.4 percent. Their pooled average MOIC is 1.44×. This has to be compared to a Public Market Equivalent[117] (PME) of 1.40×. The average time to liquidity is 5.9 years.

Top quartile funds on aggregate generated a pooled average net IRR of 9.7 percent (a 1.62× MOIC), the median is 6.9 percent (1.46×), and bottom quartile funds 1.6 percent (1.12×). Top 5 percent funds generated an IRR of 14.4 percent (2.12×) and the bottom 5 percent –15.8 percent (0.37×).

3.3.3.3 *Investment Niches*

PRA includes a lot of investment niches, often gathered under the umbrella of **natural resources**. This generic expression can be broken down into multiple investment areas,

---

[116]Karagioannopoulos and Fouche (2018).
[117]The index used is the MSCI World total market index. A PME using the S&P Global Infrastructure index delivers a PME of 1.40× for vintage years 2003–2008 (versus 1.44× for infrastructure funds over the same period).

revolving around **energy** and **commodities production**. Another way to classify them is to differentiate between renewable and non-renewable production.

In the area of **non-renewable energy**, **oil and gas** has drawn recent interest for equity and debt (including convertible investments). Private energy funds can invest in the upstream (exploration and extraction), midstream (transport and pile-lines), and downstream (refineries, storage, and distribution) segments. The focus of private energy funds is usually on midstream and downstream assets. The advantage of such funds is to provide investors with an exposure to the growing need for international energy while reducing the exposure to the volatility of oil and gas prices.

Private energy funds focused on oil and gas represent roughly 22 percent of the PRA market and roughly 6 percent of the PM universe. According to Cambridge Associates, 96 American energy funds created between 1994 and 2008, collectively representing $96.5 billion, generated a pooled average net IRR of 10.5 percent. Their pooled average MOIC is 1.34×. This has to be compared to a PME[118] of 1.23×. The average time to liquidity is 2.91 years.

Private energy funds are likely to invest more and more in **renewable energy**, produced by solar farms, wind farms, biomass plants, and wave and tidal facilities, as well as hydroelectric dams. Unfortunately, there is limited data on this emerging field.

Renewable commodities production includes private **farmland** funds, for which there is limited data. Fortunately, their risk-return-liquidity profile can be compared to **timberland**. These two strategies are largely dominated by the US, although more recently some funds have started to deploy capital in the rest of the world. They provide a combination of yield, as crops and trees are sold, and capital appreciation as the land gains in value. They also provide a certain hedge against inflation. In many respects, they could be compared with private real estate, except that the yield depends on market prices for the commodities they produce and not on regular rents (although for farmland, this could be an option as well).

US timberland funds represent roughly 0.7 percent of the PRA market and an estimated 0.2 percent of the PM universe. According to Preqin, farmland and timberland funds represented 5 percent of unlisted natural resources capital in 2016. According to Cambridge Associates, 24 timberland funds, created between 2002 and 2008 and representing $8 billion, generated a pooled average of 4.2 percent and a MOIC of 1.36×. The average time to liquidity is 7.49 years. Over 2004–2008, the PME based on the S&P Global Timber delivered a 1.23× while timberland funds generated a 1.30×.

Non-renewable commodities funds include private **mining** funds, for example. There is unfortunately limited information available about this investment strategy.

CONCLUSION: BLURRY BORDERS

It would be tempting to conclude from this chapter that private markets are an investment universe on their own, to be considered as such and isolated from the rest of the

---

[118]The index used is the Wilshire 5000 Energy index.

financial markets. Even within private markets, sub-strategies are often described as "sub-asset classes," with their own characteristics to consider when investing. In reality, the borders within and between categories can be blurry.

Private markets strategies can overlap. For example, there is a rather fine line between an LBO fund investing in a company managing real estate units and a private real estate fund investing in real estate units and managing them actively. Likewise, oil and gas pipelines can be considered as an infrastructure investment as much as a private energy one. The classification depends mostly on the characteristics of each asset and the type of strategy applied to grow the company or the asset.

There are also **blurry borders between private and public markets**. The most obvious link between them at the moment is when assets shift from one to another. This is the case when an asset is taken private (a public-to-private transaction), through a delisting or the sale of an asset by a public company. This is also the case when an asset is listed on public markets, for example, when a company goes through an initial public offering (IPO). The main difference between private and public markets lies in the hands-on active ownership in private markets, as explained throughout this chapter.

Private market investors, and notably fund managers, also **refer to the public markets when valuing assets**. Valuation methods routinely use listed comparables as a basis for establishing the value of an asset. They also refer to key variables, such as discount rates (when applying the discounted cash-flow method) used to value listed assets. Although interactions are indirect, the fact that private assets are regularly appraised through a comparison with listed assets means that they tend increasingly to co-variate. The potential for diversification provided by the integration of private market assets decreases with this co-variance: assets tend to increase and decrease in concert more frequently.

Private assets could also appear as artificially riskier as they are re-evaluated along with listed assets (as required for quarterly reports by the IPEV). Somehow, private market investors import the volatility associated with the trading of listed assets every time they assess the value of a private asset through a comparison. This artificial volatility could in return magnify the risks associated with private market investments. Fortunately, the rules to value private assets still provide investors with room to eliminate some of the noise associated with the tradability of listed assets.

As the tradability of assets is very variable within public markets themselves, it could be argued that some of the listed assets actually belong to the private markets' universe. The IPO of a biotech firm that does not generate significant sales and is cash-flow negative could be seen as a financing event similar to a late-stage venture capital round. Along these lines, a PIPE is in fact a private equity financing provided to a listed company. More recently, the set-up of a very large fund of $100 bn by the listed Japanese conglomerate Softbank to finance late-stage, growth-stage, and mature technology companies further questions the nature of public and private markets investing.

Our view (see Introduction) is that setting a liquidity target, or a time horizon, is a dimension of investing, as well as setting risk thresholds and return targets. Along these lines, it is possible to compare the performance of indexes of listed stocks[119] with

---

[119]A rigorous approach would require a comparison of the performance of active funds of listed assets (mutual, thematic, and hedge funds) with private equity funds, after fees. Unfortunately,

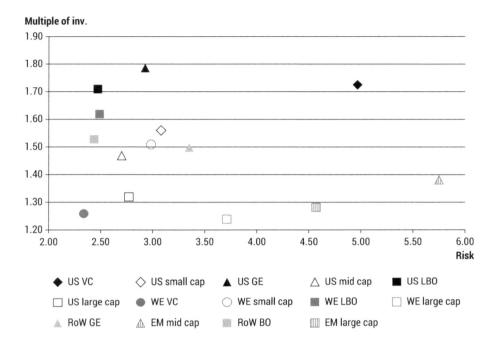

Multiple of inv.

◆ US VC	◇ US small cap	▲ US GE	△ US mid cap	■ US LBO
☐ US large cap	● WE VC	○ WE small cap	☐ WE LBO	☐ WE large cap
▲ RoW GE	⛰ EM mid cap	▨ RoW BO	▥ EM large cap	

FIGURE 3.20   Risk-return profile of listed and private companies over similar time-to-liquidity periods
Note: the period considered is 1981–2008 for consistency. Indexes for listed assets are MSCI. Performance of private equity funds is net of any fees. Performance of listed indexes is gross of any fees. Risk is measured as the TVPI spread between top 5 percent and bottom 5 percent of funds for private equity. For listed companies it is the difference between the minimum and maximum annualized performance.
Source: Cambridge Associates (as of December 2016), Bloomberg, Authors.

private equity strategies. Assuming similar time to liquidity, the risk-return profile of private and public portfolios of companies (Fig. 3.20) shows that US VC and GE funds have in general a higher level of returns and a higher level of risk than indexes of listed stocks. There are exceptions. Western European VC is less risky and less profitable than an index of listed Western European small caps. LBO funds from any region, as well as growth capital funds from the rest of the world, record a higher level of return and lower level of risk than the index of listed large caps.

Focusing on returns, while using similar time-to-liquidity periods (Fig. 3.21), it is clear that PE funds on aggregate outperform indexes of listed stocks, with the exception of Western European VC funds. This approach is similar to a PME benchmark, except that there is no timing of cash flow involved: the analysis is over the long term and regardless of the ability of fund managers to buy low and/or sell high. What appears

---

there is no easy way to track the actual average exposure of active funds to their underlying listed assets. Therefore, we resort to the use of indexes, gross of fees.

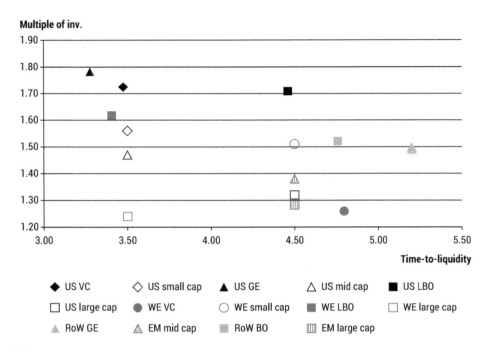

FIGURE 3.21   Return profile of listed and private companies over similar time-to-liquidity periods
Note: the period considered is 1981–2008 for consistency. Indexes for listed assets are MSCI. Performance of private equity funds is net of any fees. Performance of listed indexes is gross of any fee.
Source: Cambridge Associates (as of December 2016), Bloomberg, Authors.

also clearly is that listed stocks can deliver significant performance over longer periods of time. Investors able to set an asset allocation beyond the calendar year as a period of reference are compensated by multiples within the range 1.20×–1.60×. The question is therefore: are the resources mobilized to invest in private equity funds sufficiently rewarded by the return spread between PE funds and their benchmark index of listed stocks?

The answer might be positive when factoring extreme risks (Fig. 3.22). PE funds appear as clearly less risky than indexes of listed stocks, with the exception of US VC funds (for the reasons explained in the VC section of this chapter, namely the exceptional performances of the decade 1990 and the associated dispersion of fund performances). A deeper perspective could be drawn by comparing loss ratios and frequency of losses with listed stocks but also the performance of active strategies (through mutual funds) and their dispersion.

This has consequences in terms of asset allocation, as will be explored in Chapter 4. Assuming that investors set a target risk-return and time-to-liquidity horizon, the output of the strategy of investors could significantly shift in terms of composition of portfolios, performance generation, risk levels, and liquidity horizon.

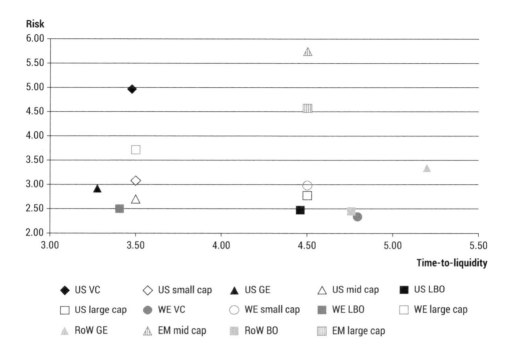

FIGURE 3.22 Risk profile of listed and private companies over similar time-to-liquidity periods
Note: the period considered is 1981–2008 for consistency. Indexes for listed assets are MSCI.
Risk is measured as the TVPI spread between the top 5 percent and the bottom 5 percent of
funds for private equity. For listed companies it is the difference between the minimum and
maximum annualized performance.
Source: Cambridge Associates (as of December 2016), Bloomberg, Authors.

SUMMARY

Throughout this chapter, we have pointed out that:

– Private markets (PM) investing aims to finance private companies or assets
  through the provision of debt and/or capital. This is a local activity requiring
  significant expertise and know-how, thus qualified as an **active investment
  strategy**.
– Investors have now a large choice to fine-tune the **design of their instruments** according to their needs and the analysis of investment opportunities.
  The determination of the type of instrument as well as the strategy adopted
  depends on the **risks and potential returns** associated with each private market
  intervention.
– To invest efficiently, it is necessary to diversify investments, and thus **intermediation and delegation** are necessary. Levels of intermediation vary depending on
  the level of non-financial commitment of investors.

- **Funds** are the main conduit for intermediated investments. They are set up and managed by fund managers that first design funds and then sell them to fund investors who might decide to sponsor funds in exchange for a share of the proceeds of the funds they sponsor. Fund structures vary depending on the jurisdiction they are registered in.
- **Securitization and funds of funds** offer investors a further degree of intermediation and are useful for investors with limited experience to select GPs and fund managers.

- PM investing is associated with enhanced performance and risk diversification.
  - This performance can be measured through three methods, each presenting benefits and drawbacks: the internal rate of return (IRR), the multiple of invested capital (MOIC), and the Public Market Equivalent (PME).
  - The **persistence of returns** of fund managers remains a fundamental feature of PM investing: fund investors exhibit, depending on their skill set and resources, an ability to generate an outperformance thanks to their asset allocation and their fund manager selection.
  - PM investing provides **attractive drivers of diversification**: wider investment universe, range of industries financed by PM funds, intervention at every stage of the life of a company, and wider geographical exposure for institutional investors.
  - PM investing also presents **numerous risks,** which fall below two categories generally speaking: **systematic** (interest rate risk, market risk, and inflation risk) and **idiosyncratic** risks (liquidity risk, credit risk, and operational risk). Besides, five type of risks can be associated with PM investing: macro, selection, reporting, strategic, and tactical asset allocation risks. Further, we can make a distinction between risks associated with PM strategic asset allocations (SAA risks), risks associated with PM tactical asset allocation instruments, risks associated with secondary investments, and risks associated with direct and co-investments.

- However, PM investing remains challenging due to **lack of transparency** and **information asymmetries**.
  - The requirements in terms of information disclosure are much lower; regulators have, therefore, only a limited role, and auditors are often not mandatory.
  - Thus, prospective investors run a **due diligence process** checking the information provided to them by the owners and managers of a given private company. This leads to the structuring of a **shareholders' agreement** defining the rights and duties of investors in the private company.
  - The **valuation of private companies** is also tricky: a few corporate finance methods (divided between intrinsic method and method by analogy) can help investors to determine the price of private companies, but valuation of private assets suffers from **stale pricing**, a result of the lower liquidity level associated with private assets. This generates issues in terms of asset allocation.
  - **Intermediated private market investing** can help to handle those challenges by ensuring lower risk thanks to intermediaries' expertise, by using an investment vehicle supporting the construction of a coherent and diversified portfolio, and by reducing the cost that is shared among all investors. But investors tend

to be uncomfortable with blind pool investing (for some unknown reason being associated with private asset investing), they dislike the fact that fund cash flows are difficult to predict for an established period of time, and they are afraid of the principal-agent dynamic and the risk of abuses and frauds (additional fees, conflicts of interest).

– Even though it is difficult to quantify the total size of PM investments globally, there are **three distinct strategies in PM investing:**
  - **Private equity**: PE funds can finance companies at virtually each and every stage of their development through:
    - **Capital increase**: **venture capital (VC) funds** finance companies from inception until they reach profitability or until they are acquired or listed on the stock exchange. They aim at generating high absolute returns, but this entails significant risks also. **Growth capital (GC) funds** finance companies already profitable that can be private or public. In the latter instance, the operation is a private investment in public equities (PIPE). As companies are already profitable, risks are more limited, but the returns generated are relatively high, making GC one of the most attractive PM strategies.
    - **Transfer of ownership**: this concerns profitable companies that have established their operations and can self-finance their development. Two different sub-strategies exist: first **the leveraged buyout (LBO)** to manage and finance the transfer of ownership of a company by using a combination of capital and debt. There are different types of LBOs (IBO, MBO, MBI, OBO). The risk is moderate to low, but LBO funds aim to generate relatively high absolute returns by using financial leverage and by implementing a plan to change significantly the acquired company; second, **turnaround capital**, a niche activity not widely documented, aims at acquiring ailing business before they enter bankruptcy. Turnaround capital benefits from a tax leverage but is present at the higher end of the private equity risk spectrum.
  - **Private debt**: PD funds provide financing when usual lenders do not, and when the risk-return profile of the investment is not adapted to private equity through:
    - **Distressed debt and non-performing loans (DD and NPL)**: DD investors dedicated to loan-to-own buy specific tranches of the debt of an ailing business at a discount with the target of eventually taking control of the business by converting some or all of this debt into equity. An emerging segment in the distressed debt world has been non-performing loans (NPL) as the 2007–2009 financial crisis has led many banks, notably in Europe, to sell these loans at a discount.
    - **Mezzanine and subordinated debt financing** essentially in developed markets: mezzanine financing provides flexible subordinated loans to a borrower and is subordinated in the sense that its interest is paid and the loan is repaid in order of priority only after some senior debt has been paid. This combines the downside protection associated with debt securities and the upside of capital gains associated with equity conversion rights. Mezzanine debt is relatively expensive when compared to senior debt; thus second-lien debt or unitranche debt have emerged now as alternatives.

- **Direct/senior and unitranche lending** are supposed to offer a strong downside protection with higher returns than usual fixed-income instruments.
- **Other PD strategies**: venture debt, litigation financing, royalty financing, aviation finance, trade finance, asset-backed financing, CDO, and CLO.

- **Private real assets**: PRA funds provide financing at every stage of the development of intangible or tangible real assets (fixed or not). PRA differ substantially from companies financed by PE or PD as they represent a clear and direct access to predictable future cash flows associated with the collateral represented by the asset itself. The sub-strategies include:
- **Private real estate**: core, core-plus, value-added, and opportunistic funds.
- **Private infrastructure** (same sub-strategies).
- **Investment niches:** natural resources, including farmland and timberland funds.

CHAPTER 4

The Three Dimensions of Investment

In a nutshell

This chapter will provide readers with applicable and concise guidance to build a portfolio of listed and private assets throughout three major steps: (i) assessing the investment horizon of the investor, jointly with the expected payout schedule to survey the investment universe of the investor; (ii) defining the risk appetite of the investor by delimiting the constraints within which the investor must structure his investment program; (iii) then, structuring multiple potential investment programs, which combine performance expectations and probabilities of reaching them. Some constraints might be adjusted, notably if the risk appetite is reviewed, to match return expectations or increase the chances of reaching these return expectations.

Investing means taking specific risks with the hope of generating returns, which in effect will reward these risks. Investing also requires a varying degree of patience, ranging from microseconds for high-frequency trading to decades for infrastructure investments. The compensation of the investor, his investment performance, can therefore be broken down into two elements: a **reward for the creation of value either directly by the investor or indirectly by his agent** and the **compensation of the investor accepting to defer the use of his capital**.

These two sources of performance are not mutually exclusive. In fact, to create value, a specific amount of time is needed. When an investor supports a start-up through a capital increase and sits on the board of that start-up, his value creation is clear: he will choose the company managers and delegate to them the application of the business plan of the company. His role will then be to monitor and control the execution. The investor chose to invest in this specific start-up, for a rather long period of time (five to seven years on average). If the management succeeds, and the company is ultimately sold or listed on the stock exchange at a significant mark-up, then he will reap the reward of his value creation. If the management fails, he will have to reshuffle them and possibly design a new business plan. Therefore, the risk is that the business does not execute the plan and that the investor cannot correct course. The performance is variable and related to the active and successful mitigation of the risk.

Likewise, a creditor can decide to lend to a company via a bond. His value creation is limited to providing capital against some form of collateral that he can seize to be repaid if the company cannot. The selection of borrowers and the monitoring of the credit are the main sources of activity of a creditor. The performance is fixed and essentially related to the duration of the credit and, to a certain extent, to the nature of the collateral and the clauses attached to the contract of the credit.

These two examples can be seen as two extremes of a financing spectrum, with an active value creation at one end and the compensation of a credit duration at the other. This is of importance, as some confusion appears when discussing the notion of risks, the sources of performance, and thus of portfolio construction. This confusion is largely due to the fact that the standard framework used by investors (illustrated notably by Marston, 2011) has been designed on a fundamental assumption: that the assets acquired by investors are tradable immediately, on an organized market, at low (or no) cost, with willing third parties. This can apply to listed stocks and bonds but excludes de facto assets such as direct real estate investments and, of course, private market funds. As this framework gained in popularity, it became de facto the main reference point, enticing its users to force other asset classes into it.

The consequences have been dire. Private market assets do not fit in this framework as they are not matching the fundamental assumption. To make things worse for the proponents of the standard framework, private market funds deliver consistently a higher performance than their listed peers, with a lower level of risk (measured as loss ratio). As private market assets require significant time to let investors create value, the proponents of the standard framework have declared the excess performance of private assets over listed ones as an "illiquidity premium." This is a conceptual mistake.

Some LBO fund managers acquire large companies, and sometimes even delist them, to transform and resell them at a higher price. Investors in listed companies, including activist funds, deliver performances that are much lower than those of LBO specialists. Attributing the excess net performance of LBO fund managers to the duration of their investments confuses a mean (duration) for a result (performance). If there was an "illiquidity premium," investors on the stock exchange would simply have to extend their holding periods to match those of LBO fund managers and reap the rewards. This is not the case, as regularly demonstrated by Public Market Equivalents (PME, see Chapter 3) calculations.

Do active and activist investors in listed companies suffer from a "liquidity discount"? This is probable but difficult to quantify. Investors in listed companies suffer from their lack of control on the management of these firms, as well as the volatility of the shares traded. Moreover, the price per share of a company integrates elements of appreciation that can be irrelevant to its specific situation: political, economic, and other events might affect the price of a company but not its specific situation. The price per share is also a function of supply of—and demand for—the shares. This has a specific consequence: the whole company is not bought or sold every time one of its shares is. Assuming that the value of a company is a function of the number of its shares and its price per share is a mental shortcut and at best an imperfect proxy. Sellers of blocks of shares know that they will have to trade their blocks out of the open market (via dark pools) and at a discount or that they will have to deploy complex strategies to dispose of their blocks anonymously in small portions in the open market. The logical consequence is that active and activist investors cannot create the same value as LBO fund managers as they do not control the companies they invest in. Even if they did, some of the value they created would not be fully reflected in the value of price per shares, which would suffer from some form of "leakage."

A counterargument could be made when it comes to private debt and specifically comparing high-yield debt (traded debt) and direct-lending (private debt) strategies. If the value creation of the creditor is too limited, and high-yield debt and direct-lending strategies have the same durations, they should generate the same level of performance. This would be true if the risks taken were similar. However, high-yield debt is often provided to fairly large companies that already have a high level of leverage and/or face a challenging situation. Direct lending provides debt to small and mid-sized companies for projects that are not financed by banks, such as the launch of a subsidiary abroad or a cross-border acquisition. The work operated by the private debt fund manager is therefore closer to a private equity investor, as the due diligence is more extensive than for the emission of a high-yield bond. The performance of a direct lending fund is the result of an active risk mitigation based on the strict selection of the borrowers and an in-depth analysis of their projects and collateral.

To effectively build an investment program encompassing less tradable assets, it is, therefore, necessary to change the perspective underlying this standard framework. The first step is to assess what is the investment horizon of the investor jointly with the expected payout schedule (Section 1). It is then possible to assess the composition of the investment universe of the investor. The next step is to assess the risk appetite of the investor (Section 2). This risk appetite defines the constraints within which the investor must structure the investment program. The result of this effort is the definition of multiple possible investment programs, which combine performance expectations and probabilities of reaching them (Section 3). Some constraints might be adjusted, notably if the risk appetite is reviewed, to match return expectations or increase the chances to reach these return expectations. This might be necessary to build an investment program that includes private markets (PM, Section 4).

4.1 SETTING UP AN INVESTMENT HORIZON

Listed stocks *can* be owned for a long time and traded bonds held to maturity. The investor has also the option to trade them. Private market assets *have to* be held until they are sold by the funds holding them. The investor can, under the right circumstances, sell fund stakes on the informal secondary market (see Chapter 3).

4.1.1 Differentiating the Investment Horizon and the Payout Schedule

To build a portfolio of listed and private assets, the starting point is that the investor should set up an investment horizon. A high net worth individual (HNWI) could assume that the time horizon of his investments is virtually infinite as his wealth will be passed on to multiple successive generations of descendants. Although this could be true, some crucial milestones have to be planned: investment in the individual through education and for the individual through residential real estate, for example. Retirement and succession are other milestones. Then the recurring (and thus plannable) expenses of the HNWI have also to be covered, and the unexpected ones should also be integrated in the planning (thus leading to the setup of some cash reserves). This series of analyses defines, in essence, the **investment horizon** of the investor and also his **payout schedule**.

Likewise, a pension fund manager can assess key milestones for the investment of the capital that he is in charge of. A pensioner has a recruitment date and an expected exit date. The exit date can be the consequence of the retirement of the person (assuming that he would cash out the entire pension at that date) or, if this is an occupational pension program managed by the employer, the departure of the person from the workforce. The investment horizon is theoretically easy to assess: the difference between the recruitment date and the exit date. However, the exit date can shift due to a change in regulations governing the retirement age, for example. As retirement age is usually extended, and the process to adopt such measures is long, this can be anticipated.

The person might also opt to stay in the pension system and require a regular payout instead of cashing out. It can also be difficult to anticipate the departure of the person before the retirement age. Statistical analyses can help pension fund managers anticipate and quantify departures: these become milestones and interim investment horizons.

Pension fund managers have also to handle payouts, to some extent. The obvious case is when pensions are paid as a rent. They also have to cover the costs of managing pensions.

4.1.2 Theoretical and Actual Investment Horizons

According to this brief analysis, pension funds could assess fairly clearly their theoretical investment horizon. They should therefore have a very large portion of their assets invested for the very long term, some assets yielding some regular and predictable distributions, and a fairly limited portion of their assets invested with different maturities to face unplanned exits. Surprisingly, this is not the case.

Pension fund managers tend to invest in assets with a shorter duration than the theoretical time horizon would warrant. In particular, they tend to focus on listed stocks and bonds, which suffer from a liquidity discount (see above) and largely ignore private market assets, which yield higher performance.

For example, in Switzerland, pension funds are allowed to invest up to 15 percent in alternative assets (Art. 55 of the Ordonnance sur la prévoyance professionnelle vieillesse, survivants et invalidité[1]). According to Swisscanto (2019), they invested on average 5.6 percent over the period 2009–2018 to alternatives (including commodities), of which 0.77 percent went to private equity and 0.31 percent to infrastructure.

The consequence is that the level of the pension payments is lower than it could be and the retirement age keeps increasing. For example, the legal retirement age for workers in Switzerland is 65 for men and 64 for women and discussions are ongoing to increase these. Another possible consequence, notably for American pension funds, is that liabilities are significantly and durably higher than their assets. The shortfall means that American pensioners might not get the capital or payout at retirement age that they were expecting.

---

[1]https://www.admin.ch/opc/fr/classified-compilation/19840067/index.html.

The discrepancy between theoretical and actual investment horizons could be explained by regulations, which might encourage pension managers to adopt a conservative approach in terms of investment durations. The reason for that might be to keep a margin of safety to handle significant unplanned exits from the pension fund. However, regulations alone do not explain the significant discrepancies between theory and practice.

The second possible reason is that the models to manage assets and liabilities matching (ALM) are ill-designed to handle longer time horizons and to integrate private market assets. Indeed, ALM models often use the standard framework referred to above. However, it is possible to change the perspective and decide that each asset should be by default held to maturity. This date is easy to assess for fixed-income products, although some might have a very long time horizon.

As for listed stocks, which by definition do not have a pre-set duration, it is possible to assign them one, which would match the time horizon of the investor, adjusted by regulatory buffers. The standard framework would thus shift from a yearly perspective (the implicit default timeframe) to the time horizon of the pension plan. This approach also works for individual pension programs.

The maturity date is also fairly easy to assess for private market funds, as it is possible to compute an average time to liquidity for private market strategies (Fig. 4.1). Private equity and private debt strategies record an average time to liquidity of three to six years. Private real asset strategies have a longer time to liquidity, above seven years, with the exception of private equity energy, which has the shortest one, slightly above three years.

It is then possible to assess the maximum deviations (Fig. 4.2) from this time horizon. This would be the equivalent of a "liquidity risk." Not surprisingly, secondaries have the shortest time to liquidity. Private equity has the highest dispersion of time to liquidity. It could be tempting to read into this that the average has the lowest return, but this is related to the fact that the average is also the less mature of the three

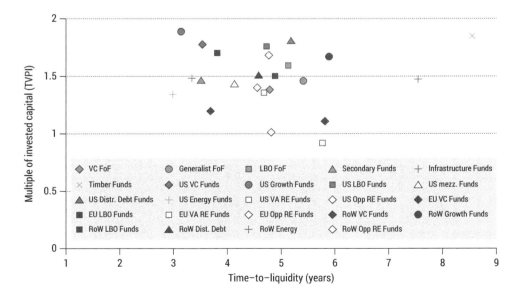

FIGURE 4.1 Average time to liquidity of realized private markets funds, by investment strategy
Source: Wellershoff & Partners (2019).

measurements (Fig. 4.3). As funds mature, their performance tends to increase (the NAVs are measured conservatively—see Chapter 3).

The logical conclusion from the three figures mentioned above is that investors in private markets should have a time horizon of at least four to five years. If not, the logic of integrating them in an investment portfolio should be questioned, and maybe private market fund investments should be excluded altogether.

In the case of private equity funds, the duration can go as high as eight years (Fig. 4.2). Private debt funds provide a fairly straight reading: their minimum duration is of roughly 3.5 years, their average duration of five years, and their maximum duration of six years (Figs 4.2 and 4.3). As their maturity is directly correlated to their duration, it is possible to conclude that the average exposure is in fact six years (Fig. 4.3).

At first glance, private real asset funds have a larger dispersion of time to liquidity (Fig. 4.2), somehow similar to those of private equity funds. This could appear as incoherent with Figure 4.1, but Figure 4.3 provides an explanation: only the funds with the longest duration are close to full maturity. Therefore, Figure 4.2 provides an insight on funds that are largely immature for the minimum and average time to liquidity.

Funds of funds are still in the making, given their longer time frame. At the moment, their minimum and maximum durations are close to those of private debt funds (Figs 4.2 and 4.3). Their average duration is even shorter. However, their maturity is also lower (Fig 4.3), and the pooled average includes funds that are still immature, hence dragging its performance down when compared to the minimum and the maximum. Nevertheless, they offer a higher performance than private debt funds for a similar average duration.

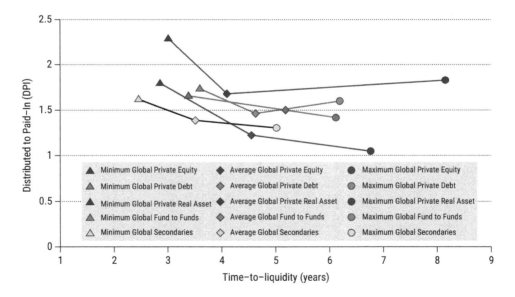

FIGURE 4.2   Average time to liquidity of realized private markets funds, by type of investment strategy
Source: Wellershoff & Partners (2019).

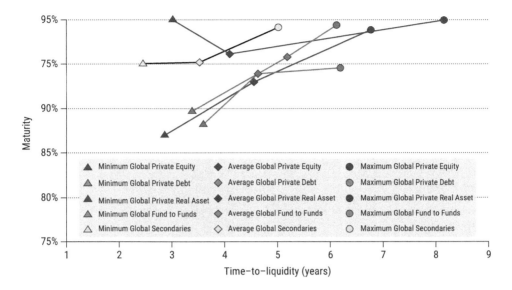

FIGURE 4.3 Average time to liquidity and maturity of realized private markets funds, by type of investment strategy
Source: Wellershoff & Partners (2019).

4.1.3   Payout and Distribution Patterns

There is therefore a discrepancy between the term of private market funds (eight to ten years in the case of private debt, usually ten for private equity funds, and ten to fifteen for private real asset funds) and their average time to liquidity. Two reasons explain it.

First, funds deploy capital during their investment period of three to five years. Investments are never planned to be made over the full term of the fund but for a shorter time. Second, some funds distribute interim proceeds (interests in the case of private debt funds, rents in the case of private real estate and infrastructure funds) and the result of their exits (trade or secondary sale or in some cases IPOs).

A possible explanation for the wide gap of minimum and maximum time to liquidity in the case of private equity funds is that these funds usually do not distribute interim proceeds, except in the case of dividend recaps for large and mega LBO deals (see Chapter 3 for more details). This could appear as a deterrent for portfolio construction. Another way to analyze the set of figures above is that it is possible to plan for the average and extreme scenarios of time to liquidity. In particular, it is possible to identify the potential explanations of the maximum deviation of time to liquidity. This wealth of information will then inform the construction of portfolios (Chapter 5).

Therefore, knowing the minimum, average, and maximum time to liquidity of individual private markets strategies supports the matching of payout and distribution patterns. To manage the variation around the average time to liquidity, investors have to structure cash reserves. These reserves act as a buffer to absorb the risk associated with divergences from the expected time to liquidity.

TABLE 4.1　Predictability of the Payout of Individual Private Market Strategies

Private market strategy	Predictability of interim payout	Predictability of final proceeds
Direct and unitranche lending	high	high
Mezzanine lending	high (if any)	moderate
Core real estate and infrastructure	high	low
Value add real estate and infrastructure	moderate (if any)	low
Timber and farmland	moderate	low
LBO	low (if any)	moderate
Growth capital	—	moderate
Private equity energy	—	moderate
Opportunistic real estate and infrastructure	—	low
Distressed debt and turn-around capital	—	low
Venture capital	—	low

Source: Authors.

Individual strategies can match very diversified payout schedules. Direct lending funds provide regular and predictable interest payments, as well as a predefined duration. The investment period is usually short (two years), and funds deliver cash payments shortly after the investments date. Although there is a risk of default of individual loans, the diversification associated with multiple loans in the funds reduces the overall risk. Thus, direct lending would match a shorter term of investment and demanding payout schedules.

Core private real estate or infrastructure funds would also provide some predictable distributions, but the term of investment is less clear. This implies that the investor has flexibility when it comes to that specific dimension. It is then possible to rank individual private markets strategies depending on their ability to match regular payouts and to provide predictable payment dates (Table 4.1). This, in return, can inform the process of portfolio construction.

4.1.4　The Secondary Market

The secondary market is informal and there is very limited information about it. It can be broken down into two segments: the secondary market for fund stakes and the secondary market of direct investments. The former represents the lion's share of the overall secondary market. Fund stake transactions are equivalent to roughly 10 percent of the amounts raised by funds on the primary market.

The secondary market is intermediated and requires a fair amount of expertise from investors willing to trade. Specialist intermediaries, such as Greenhill and Setter Capital, provide regular updates and estimates of the level of capital invested on this market, the number of transactions operated, and the overall discount (or premium) on NAV at which fund stakes have been exchanged. It is estimated that the effective transactions represent roughly a third of the assets on offer. There is, therefore, a significant pool of assets for sale that do not find any takers.

The secondary market provides assets for opportunistic buyers able to seize opportunities fast (in a matter of a few weeks). These buyers have to dispose of significant market knowledge (often gained by investing on the primary market), with significant resources and a specific skill set.

Sellers of private market fund stakes can find potential buyers, but this comes at a cost. Most of the fund stakes are exchanged at an average discount of 10 to 30 percent on the NAV of funds. The latter is conservative and does not represent the full potential of the assets in the portfolio of funds (see Chapter 3).

Therefore, the secondary market cannot be considered as a reliable route to dispose of private markets assets. The discount on NAV increased to 50 percent of NAV during the 2008–2009 period for LBO funds and went above 70 percent for VC funds. Moreover, there is never any certainty that a given fund stake will find a buyer.

In a context of portfolio construction, the use of secondary investments is fairly clear: it is essentially for marginal adjustments. Investors willing to dispose of assets due to a specific overallocation to one strategy, the need to reduce the number of relationships, or because a fund manager no longer matches the requirements set by the investor can selectively use the secondary market to dispose of the fund stake. This represents a significant cost, which means that the reasons have to be pressing and serious.

Investors willing to ramp up their portfolio can seize an opportunity to get access to a fund manager, to over-weight opportunistically a specific segment of the market, or to use an information advantage to exploit market inefficiencies. Unlike on the primary market, investment opportunities on the secondary market are unpredictable. Their use in a portfolio construction can therefore only be marginal.

4.1.5   Structured Financing and Other Liquidity Instruments

Investors could be tempted to use the secondary market to sell fund stakes in a period of financial stress. Those who did not plan their payout schedule correctly or who face unexpected requirements might see their private markets stakes as a reserve of value to mobilize through a secondary sale. As explained above, this is a suboptimal option. However, there is an alternative.

Structured financing presents a double advantage. First, the fund investor does not have to sever the relationship with the fund manager. If the need for the payout is unexpected and significant but is a one-off event, the prospects for the investor are that he will return to investing. Having the opportunity to re-commit with a known manager who has been through a full due diligence saves resources for the investor.

Second, structured financing can help investors either to commit to new funds or to face the upcoming capital call from a fund. In the first scenario, an investor has established a private market investment program and owns a portfolio of fund stakes. Investors regularly face the prospect of either committing to the new generation of funds from their managers, or losing the opportunity to do so in the future. This can represent a challenge if available capital is temporarily insufficient to maintain the program.

A solution consists in **structuring a loan** (or in case of a large portfolio of fund stakes, a bond) against a portfolio of private market assets. This solution is expensive, as interest rates reflect the risk taken by the lender. However, they are far lower than the discount on the conservative NAV supported by the investor selling on the secondary market. One of the limits of using this solution is that the value of the loan represents a fraction of the NAV of the portfolio of funds or even single funds.

Indeed, for smaller portfolios or single funds, it is also possible to structure loans. In that context, the value of the loan usually represents around 30 to 40 percent of the NAV of the fund stake. For large (but below $1 billion), diversified and mature portfolios of stakes in funds managed by established and reputable managers, it could be possible to get a loan representing up to 50 percent of the NAV of the funds.

For portfolios of assets with a NAV above $1 billion, another option consists in **securitization**. Structuring such a solution is time and resource intensive. Investors can use this solution to face a predictable need of significant payout within a period of six to twelve months. The portfolio of funds has to be sufficiently large and diversified and has to show some maturity to support the structuring of such loan. This has been done by Temasek, for example, in 2006 with the help of Capital Dynamics (in a transaction named Astrea[2]). The proceeds collected represent around 50 to 60 percent of the NAV of the portfolio.

The last option consists in **preferred equity**, which can represent up to 75 percent of the NAV of the portfolio. The provider of preferred equity financing offers liquidity to the owner of the portfolio, allowing the latter to retain the majority of the upside. This solution is much more flexible than a loan but is expensive. The preferred equity provider in essence has a priority claim on the cash flows of the assets until his principal and his expected return are paid out.

4.2 SETTING UP THE RISK THRESHOLDS

Once the payout schedule and the time horizon(s) of investments are defined, it is necessary to set a target in terms of risks. This is fairly challenging, for two reasons.

First, one of the most commonly used measures of risks for listed assets do not apply to private markets: the volatility of asset prices. Once acquired, private market assets are appraised on a quarterly basis and are often conservatively marked to market with a substantial time lag (see Chapter 3). For that reason, asset prices fluctuate fairly modestly and sparsely.

Second, risk measures that could be applied to listed and private markets, such as value-at-risk, deliver very different outputs, which are not necessarily comparable. For example, the closest instrument to an index tracker that private markets have is the fund of funds. Although it is expensive (while an index tracker usually is not), a fund of funds is fairly diversified and takes in effect a snapshot of some parts of private markets. A sample of funds of funds is therefore the best possible picture we can get of the situation in private markets.

Looking at how many lose capital, actually only a few do (Fig. 4.4), and when they lose capital, the amounts are limited. As a matter of fact, only 8.48 percent of the fully realized funds of funds lost money, and their IRR in case of loss was −2.35 percent.

---

[2]For a summary, see http://www.alacrastore.com/s-and-p-credit-research/Presale-Astrea-LLC-528003.

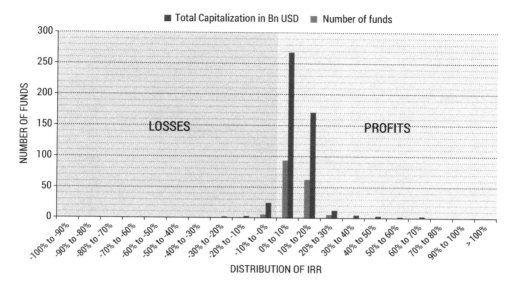

FIGURE 4.4   Distribution of private equity funds of funds based on their IRR
Note: 489 funds of funds in sample.
Source: Wellershoff & Partners (2019).

This differs quite substantially with portfolios of listed stocks, which can record more significant losses more frequently.

However, a true comparison is difficult to establish as funds of funds invest over three years in funds, which themselves invest over the course of an investment period of five years (Chapter 3). To compare listed assets, it would be necessary to run simulations with indexes of listed stocks. These simulations would apply the time exposures and cash-flow patterns of funds of funds to index stocks in the same historical environment. Only then would it be possible to draw meaningful conclusions. To do this, it would be necessary to access the individual data of each fund of funds, which is not possible due to restrictions of access from database providers.

4.2.1   Diversification and Correlations: Private Markets and the Rest of the Universe

The same reason explains the difficulty of running correlation tests between private markets funds and other assets. Fund managers have significant discretion when deploying capital, as well as when it comes to the duration of investment. It is challenging to assess the correlation between the evolution of the GDP growth, for example, and private market strategies. It is also challenging to assess what the link is between the evolution of prices of listed stocks and private market fund performances.

It is possible to assess the link between the performance of a specific fund manager and some macroeconomic and financial data. The most telling way is probably by establishing a value bridge analysis. Figure 4.5 is an illustration, with the application

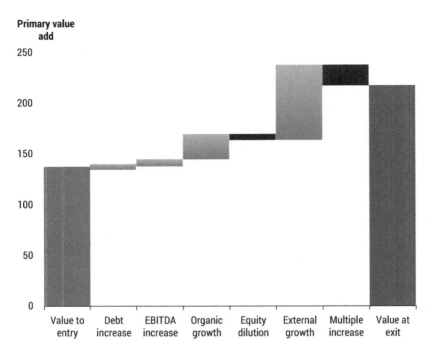

FIGURE 4.5 Example of value bridge analysis
Source: Authors.

of this type of analysis to a fictional LBO fund. In this specific case, it is possible to see the difference between the entry price and the exit price, broken down in multiple segments. The dark gray elements contributed negatively to the performance of the fund manager. In particular, the multiple of EBITDA at entry was higher than the multiple of EBITDA at exit. This means that the fund manager paid, all else being equal, a higher price when acquiring than when selling. It would theoretically be possible to look at the effect of interest rates by assessing the contribution of financial leverage.

However, this analysis is limited to a single fund. It would be necessary to apply this reasoning to a large sample of funds to be able to draw correlations. Unfortunately, this granular information is not widely accessible and obtaining it would require significant resources. It is also difficult to apply when assessing the link between macroeconomic data and the performance of fund managers.

Empirically, a few elements have emerged. In private equity specifically, it appears that venture capital funds tend to perform better when they invest at the end of a recession and sell or list their portfolio companies when the economy grows robustly. The reasons are difficult to pinpoint precisely, but a few potential factors could explain this link. First, start-up valuations are fairly low at the end of a recession, as companies have been battered by adverse conditions. Moreover, the intensity of competition is lower as many competitors failed during the recession. This gives more room for upstarts to capture market share. Second, in a period of recovery, existing clients start to renew their equipment and increase their consumption. This stimulates the demand for new products provided by start-ups. Third, when an economic cycle reaches maturity and the demand slows down, consolidation starts. This is the moment when buyers compete for the best assets and are ready to pay high prices to secure a position on a given market. This reasoning applies fairly well to venture capital financing IT start-ups.

Growth capital financing has a similar connection to GDP growth. However, the link to performance is less clear cut. Growth capital can finance growing companies in a recession when they acquire weaker competitors, during a recovery time when they see their market expand and grow organically, or expand internationally at any time of the cycle.

LBO financing tends to perform when assets are acquired just after the peak of a macroeconomic cycle. Overindebted owners are under pressure to sell companies, subsidiaries, or business units. Prices tend to be lower, and the assets sold are usually not the core business of the sellers. Often, as these assets have been overlooked, they offer an opportunity for improvement. As the recession unfolds, these companies gain an edge as they start to change before their competitors. They can then gain market share and selectively acquire competitors. They can be sold when the economy recovers.

Distressed debt is a clear case of an investment strategy that performs when the price of listed stocks and GDP growth suffer. Although companies can go bankrupt at any given point of a macroeconomic cycle and therefore be attractive acquisition targets for loan-to-own investors (see Chapter 3), recessions generate a particularly high volume of deal opportunities. Sound businesses can be pushed over the edge by defaulting clients, bad management, or imbalanced financials. If anything, distressed debt investing is anti-correlated with venture capital and to some extent LBO investments.

The purpose of this empirical exploration is to illustrate that investors would have a very hard time balancing precisely their exposure across their whole portfolio of listed and non-listed assets. It is therefore advisable to build a diversified portfolio of private market funds, with differentiated and complementary strategies. Fund managers can be assessed individually based on their investment strategy and their way to respond to specific macroeconomic events. This can be cross-checked with their track record. Moreover, value bridge analyses also help to understand reactions to past events such as shocks on asset prices or interest rates. In any instance, as we will see in Chapter 5, investors should avoid, at all costs, to timing the market with private market funds.

4.2.2   Risks Associated with Direct Funds and Funds of Funds/Mandates

In private markets, the choice of the instruments determines the type of risk taken. As explained above, the risk associated with funds of funds is fairly low. The probability of losing all the capital in funds of funds, but also in funds, is equal to zero (Fig. 4.6). European VC funds have a higher chance to lose money than funds of funds overall, and their average loss is also higher. Direct investments are the riskiest level of investment but also potentially the most lucrative.

Figure 4.6 illustrates two facts. First, direct investments are challenging, and there is no reward in investing randomly and frequently. There is no normal distribution in this case, and the extreme outcomes dominate the others.

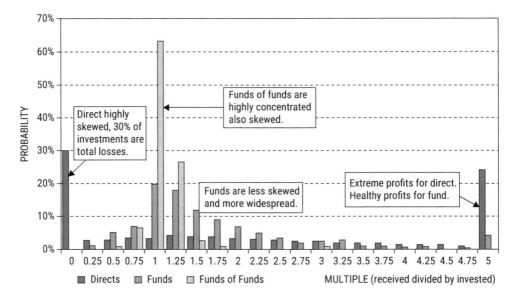

FIGURE 4.6   Dispersion of returns of American direct start-up investments, European VC funds and generalist funds of funds
Note: 5000 direct investments and 300 European VC funds extracted from VentureXpert, and 618 funds of funds extracted from Cambridge Associates.
Source: Weidig & Mathonet (2003), Wellershoff & Partners (2019).

Second, a normal distribution (potentially drawing a so-called Gaussian, or bell, curve) appears when fund managers select direct investments. This normal distribution means that there is a value creation when using funds and fund managers by pooling capital (diversification), eliminating some of the worst opportunities systematically and selecting some of the best ones (selection). This distribution is asymmetric and skewed towards the right (the break-even point being at a multiple of invested capital of 1). This means that fund managers are on aggregate creating a net performance. Fund of fund managers replicate and concentrate the normal distribution, while maintaining the asymmetry and the skewness toward the right. However, they do not amplify the movement toward the right significantly. This could be the result of management and performance fees paid to fund of funds managers and/or over-diversification.

Depending on their risk appetite, investors can choose which level(s) of intermediation are appropriate for them, ranging from no intermediation (direct investment) to a high level (funds of funds). The level of risk is inversely correlated with the degree of control of the investor on the effective capital deployment.

The logical conclusion is that the fund structure is not a simple artifact. Setting up a fund and mandating a fund manager directly and significantly modifies the risk taken by investors and their return expectations. The wide dispersion of performance of fund managers (see Section 3) is also testament: that this value creation requires significant and fairly scarce selection expertise, a large network, and a strong know-how in terms of execution, monitoring, and exit[3] of investments.

4.2.3 Myths: "De-Smoothing" LBO Returns and LBO as a Leveraged Listed Index

This conclusion is significant. The fund structure is often discarded as a technical feature or a mere annoyance. It is tempting to eliminate it in the grand scheme of analyzing private markets in the framework defined by and for listed assets. Some authors decided to force private market assets into the listed markets framework by "de-smoothing" their returns (Franzoni, Nowak, and Phalippou, 2012). Focusing on LBOs, proponents of this approach then argue that private equity investing does not create value and is essentially a leveraged index of listed small- and mid-sized companies (L'Her et al., 2016). That would be an error.

Listed markets have yet to prove their efficiency. Lo (2004), among others, tries to address the issue and create a comprehensive theory. We will not enter this debate but simply point out that listed markets are far from being efficient, pure, and perfect, as recognized by scholars themselves.

Nevertheless, private markets are seen as a degraded version of listed ones. Under this vision, private markets would be a "sticky" version of listed ones, flawed by stale pricing due to a lack of frequent reporting. The lack and asymmetries of information characterizing private markets would be the survival of symptoms, which used to affect listed ones. Regardless of the opinion of these authors, the facts are stubborn.

First, large stakes in companies cannot easily be sold in a fast and orderly transaction to a third party in an open market. This type of operation requires preparation and confidentiality. Significant stakes have to be traded on their own. Around a third of the transactions on listed stocks are operated separately from stock exchanges in venues called dark pools, specifically organized to trade significant blocks of listed shares.

Thus, the formation of prices on the open market is not a pure and perfect summary of the offer and demand of shares. A consequence is that calculating market capitalizations by multiplying the price per share by the number of shares is at best a distant proxy of the value of a company. In reality, if that whole company were sold, the price would likely be very different from market capitalizations. Market prices are at best a proxy of the value of companies.

This point is of particular importance and explains why the fair value of any asset differs from its transaction price. Appraising the fair value of an asset is more than a question of mimicking a supposed equilibrium price as the proponents of de-smoothing assume.

Fund managers apply majority premiums or minority discounts to their holdings. Two funds can co-own a company and value their respective stakes differently. When they acquire companies, LBO fund managers routinely negotiate **warranties**. Getting them implies paying a higher price, as some of the risks stay with the seller. If not, the transfer of risks implies a lower transaction price. A single company can thus

---

[3]Except for senior/direct lending, for which the duration is predetermined at investment time.

simultaneously have different prices: **the framework of the transaction is what matters**. Likewise, venture capital fund managers know that valuations do not matter much. They are an ego contest between entrepreneurs. What matters is the nitty-gritty in **shareholders agreements** such as **veto rights and liquidation preferences**.

The fair value method is the result of regular appraisals of company stakes by fund managers with different views and shareholder rights. It is therefore a subjective exercise. De-smoothing the returns of LBO funds by computing a more frequent proxy simply increases the noise and the biases embedded in the valuation of the companies, especially since NAVs are appraised conservatively (Chapter 3).

The proponents of private markets as "listed markets plus leverage" argue that the performance of LBO funds can easily be replicated by leveraging an index of listed stocks. This is also misguided, for multiple reasons.

First, the scholars and practitioners (usually from the hedge fund world) analyze data ex post and replicate the sector, size, and exposure of private market funds with a bespoke index. Applying ex ante the approach of these proponents would therefore be particularly difficult. The reality is that LBO fund managers are opportunistic and do not know ex ante where they will invest. Moreover, some of the sectors of investment of LBO are not represented on the stock exchange. It would therefore be necessary to buy a total market index ex ante, excluding some sectors that are excluded systematically by LBO fund managers (such as, probably, banks, some real estate portfolios, and regulated sectors).

Second, LBO fund managers invest in small, mid-size, large, and mega operations. Focusing on small and mid-sized listed companies introduces an analytical bias, which is not justified by the scholars. Likewise, their approach usually uses the US and LBOs as a reference point but is in effect inapplicable to the rest of private markets and outside of the US.

Third, the performance of LBO fund managers can be split (see Fig. 4.5 above for an illustration) and has been well documented (see Chapter 3). The financial and tax leverage account for roughly a third of the total performance of LBO funds. Multiple arbitrage (buying an asset at a low multiple of EBIT and selling it for at a higher multiple) contributes to this performance in a range of ±10 percent. The rest comes from the operational value creation within the assets acquired by these fund managers. A buy-and-hold strategy on listed stocks does not achieve this.

Fourth, leveraging a portfolio of listed stocks requires a collateral. In an LBO, the collateral of the loan contracted to acquire a business is that business itself. This is not the case with listed stocks, except maybe hedge funds, which can use leverage to buy listed assets. None so far has been able to replicate the performance of LBO funds.

Fifth, the risk associated with the "listed markets plus leverage" approach is much higher than the risk from investing in listed stocks. The risk associated with LBO investing, as explained above, is much lower. Default rates are low, and overall the performance is relatively stable.

Sixth, the acid test of the thesis of the proponents is already provided thanks to the PME method. If LBOs did not create any value beyond the application of a financial leverage, then the PME would show a very limited and normative outperformance versus indexes of listed assets. There would also not be any dispersion of performance between fund managers. In practice, LBO funds **outperform listed indexes**

significantly on a capital-weighted average basis, far beyond the contribution of the financial leverage. As we have seen in Section 3, there is a significant dispersion of performance between fund managers.

4.2.4   Dealing with Foreign Exchange Fluctuations

As explained above, investors in private markets usually deal with fairly unpredictable investment durations. The exception is in the case of senior/direct lending. However, the duration of this type of loan is often of five to seven years. There is no option to easily sell them if needed. For investors, the investment duration associated with private markets is thus of three to eight years, depending on the investment strategy considered and the geographical region in which this strategy is applied.

The direct consequence for investors is the difficulty of handling the consequences of the variation of currencies on their investments. Investments are made in local currencies. Funds use a specific currency of reference, which often is aligned with the local currency when it comes to developed markets—but not always. It is rarely the case when it comes to emerging markets (usually, funds are denominated in US dollars). The currency of reference of investors usually depends on where their tax residence is.

Long durations mean that the cost of hedging currency variations, that is, cancelling the effect of the relative movement of two currencies, is very expensive. This is why private market fund managers do not do it if the currency in which they invest and the currency of reference of their fund diverge.

This is also why fund investors are reluctant to do so for each of their private market fund investments. In theory they could do it, but a more logical approach would be to consider their whole portfolio of investments and hedge the undesirable exposure ("currency overlay").

For example, an American investor might invest in a euro-denominated private market fund, investing in British pounds, euros, and northern and eastern European currencies. The fund will effectively act as a barrier to hedge the underlying exposure by the American investor, due to the recurring delays and lack of detailed information about the activity of the fund. However, it could be possible to neutralize the exposure to the euro. But the American investor might in fact want this exposure, anticipating an appreciation of the euro. By looking at the overall exposure of all the assets to the euro, it is possible to eliminate only the unwanted exposure (for example, if the American investor is exposed beyond his wish and risk appetite).

Although this looks like an appealing proposition, it is difficult to set up in practice. To do so, it would be necessary to compare the duration of investments. In private markets, the relative unpredictability limits the options of our American investor. Knowing statistically the average investment durations of strategies, the actual maturity, and the theoretical maximum time exposure could help set up a currency overlay. However, practicalities will limit the precision of this approach and will imply setting up brackets of expected exposure.

This also means that the performance of private market funds in emerging markets will necessarily be more volatile than in developed markets. The fluctuation of currencies can reduce or increase the performance beyond the value created in each and every single asset. As funds distribute proceeds of investments usually within 10 days after realizing investments, this means that fund investors will register these fluctuations without recourse.

4.3 SETTING UP RETURN EXPECTATIONS

Return expectations for a portfolio of private market strategies are the direct conse-quence of investors' choices in terms of time horizon and levels of acceptable risks. Once these two dimensions are defined, it is possible to list the strategies available within these combined constraints. As a result, investors can assess possible headline returns from private market funds measured as IRRs, MOICs, and PMEs gathered from com-mercial databases (possibly supplemented by their own data and those communicated by fund managers).

4.3.1 The Limits of Performance Data

However, these are aggregated historical returns based on limited samples, generating a series of challenges for investors in terms of interpretation and use. First, providers of higher quality disclose data that is aggregated and anonymized, to comply with their confidentiality obligations. Second, samples are limited and possibly biased (see Introduction and Chapter 3). Third, data reflects the more or less distant past of a fast-evolving asset class.

Performance figures are provided to investors only if the sample reaches a certain population threshold (usually six or eight funds per vintage year). They are usually available on a capital-weighted basis, offering investors the opportunity to virtually "buy the market." Additional elements, such as a median performance, and quartile, decile, or even top and bottom 5 percent brackets can be provided, although not systematically. Data is anonymized. Investors can only guess the representativeness of the sample of funds they use (see Chapter 3). In return, this means that aggregated figures cannot precisely be analyzed.

Investors have then to make scenarios for the future and see how their portfolio of private market funds would react to these events. By assigning probabilities to these scenarios, they can decide which portfolio is the most likely to perform according to their expectations. However, this is only part of the exercise. Swensen (2009) explains that 20 percent of the performance of the Yale endowment comes from its unique asset allocation and 80 percent from the implementation and notably the selection of private market fund managers. Being able to select the latter is thus of particular importance. This is especially challenging due to the dispersion of performance of funds within each vintage year.

4.3.2 Performance Dispersion

Indeed, the dispersion of the performance of fund managers is significant across time and within a peer group. The variation and dispersion of performance have led Demaria and He (2019) to design specific instruments to measure the risk[4] and the performance of private market strategies.

One of the instruments they have designed is to monitor the **investment strategy risk and performance**. This instrument measures, vintage year by vintage year, the evolution of the pooled average multiple of the invested capital of funds of a specific strategy. The result is a spread between the highest and the lowest points for the risk measure and the pooled average multiple of invested capital over the same period. This type of instrument is particularly useful when building a portfolio of private market funds. It addresses the 20 percent of performance that Swensen attributes to his asset allocation. This is a top-down perspective.

However, it is difficult to use when funds are not largely realized. In the case of US VC (Fig. 4.7), for example, vintage years 2008 and younger are still largely unrealized. As the NAV of active funds is appraised conservatively, their performance could appear as low and be misinterpreted. Moreover, some years are exceptional and could skew the results. Figure 4.7 shows an illustration, as US VC recorded exceptional performances in the second half of the decade of 1990. These performances are unlikely to be repeated. It is, therefore, necessary to filter the outliers. Demaria and He (2019) provide some solutions for that matter.

Another challenge of using this instrument is to identify what is strategy-specific and what is idiosyncratic to the sample of the funds captured by the statistics. As

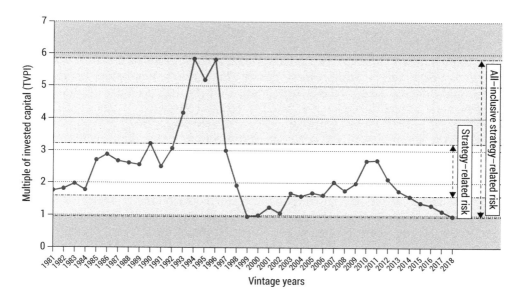

FIGURE 4.7 Pooled average multiples of investment of US VC funds over time
Source: Wellershoff & Partners (2019).

---

[4]They have designed five instruments to measure the risk associated with private markets investments.

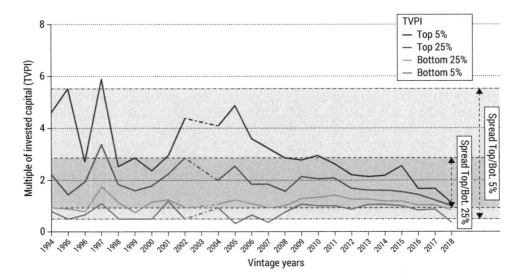

FIGURE 4.8 Top/bottom 5 percent and 25 percent TVPI of global growth capital over time
Source: Wellershoff & Partners (2019).

managers raise funds every two to three years, the variation of performance from one vintage year to the other might be related to the presence or not of the best managers in the sample.

Another instrument that Demaria and He (2019) have designed is to assess the skill set of a fund investor: the **fund selection risk**. This instrument measures the spread of the multiple of invested capital of two groups of funds, such as the top and bottom quartile (the most frequent selection risk) and the top and bottom five percent (the extreme selection risk), as shown by Figure 4.8. This instrument can prove to be useful to assess the risk-return profile of a given strategy, possibly computing a simplified Sharpe ratio. It addresses the 80 percent of performance that Swensen attributes to his fund selection. This is a bottom-up perspective.

This approach has multiple advantages, helping investors sorting the market to specific phenomena. This type of instrument can also support the analysis of losses, in their frequency. However, it depends heavily on the availability of data and can be sensitive to outliers (setting intervals of confidence is recommended). It is also difficult to use when funds are not largely realized, just like the previous instrument. The dispersion of performance increases with the maturity of funds, as shown by Figure 4.9.

Thanks to Figures 4.7 to 4.9 , it is clear that the dispersion is not symmetrical. Bottom-quartile funds fluctuate much less than top-quartile ones. The dispersion is also not constant, as the spread varies significantly over time.

4.3.3 Persistence of Performance

Kaplan and Schoar (2005) have established that there is a persistence of performance in private equity: fund managers who have ranked a fund in a specific quartile tend to

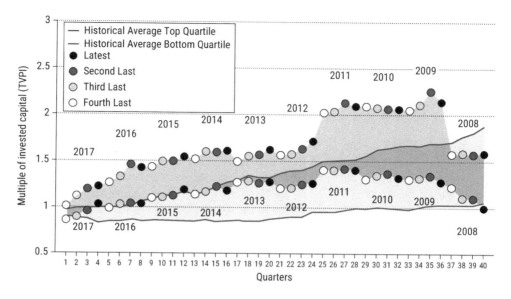

FIGURE 4.9 Quarterly TVPI of active top- and bottom-quartile global growth funds and historical average capital over time
Source: Wellershoff & Partners (2019).

reproduce this ranking over time. For example, if a fund manager has ranked a fund in the top quartile of its peer group, there is a fairly high chance that this is going to happen again. The extent and durability of this effect has been heavily debated (notably in Harris, Jenkinson, and Stucke, 2012; Robinson and Sensoy, 2013; Li, 2014; Harris, Jenkinson, and Kaplan, 2014; and Korteweg and Sorensen, 2015). Overall, the image is that this persistence is confirmed, although it might be less prevalent than in the initial academic study. Empirically, this phenomenon is still considered as valid, not only by Swensen (2009) but by practitioners themselves.

A few elements explain why this phenomenon is discussed. First, this persistence is unique in the financial world. According to academic literature, good investors cannot beat the average regularly and over an extended period of time. The fact that this could exist in private markets questions the validity of these academic conclusions. Second, some authors have declared that this effect is wearing off and have attributed it to a historical anomaly. The challenge comes from the indirect observation of this persistence of performance.

The analysis of persistence of returns (and its critics) have focused on quartiles, a rather rough and arbitrary instrument. Quartiles are a proxy, in effect, for performance analysis as it is not possible to get more granular data. However, fund samples are not constant, which means that quartiles are not either. Funds are raised every two to three years and benchmarked according to their vintage years (a notion which is subject to interpretation; see Chapter 3). The peer group of a fund can fluctuate a lot in terms of number, one vintage year counting more funds than another, and in terms of quality, one vintage year counting more strong funds than another. As a consequence, a fund manager with a constant performance can be or dropped from a quartile simply because the peer group is fluctuating.

For example, a manager created two successive LBO funds, both of which record exactly the same performance (say, a 1.5× multiple). The performance is therefore persistent. However, the first fund might rank in the top quartile of its peer group because the performance of other funds is weak. Then, the subsequent fund might be in the second quartile because the peer group is stronger that vintage year.

In 2005, using this instrument made sense because of the high dispersion of returns (see above) and the scarcity of data available. These conditions have changed. The dispersion of performance between fund managers has narrowed, as private markets are getting more efficient and competitive. Moreover, the lowest performers are being eliminated over time.

As performance dispersion decreases, fund managers can drop out from a quartile faster and for reasons that are not related to their actual performance (and ultimately value creation). For example, the use (or not) of credit lines to boost the IRRs (if the quartile analysis is based on this measure). The analysis should use cash-on-cash analysis and a PME analysis.

Another factor compounding the difficulty of analyzing the persistence of returns is that fund managers change over time: individuals retire, and others spin off. Ewens and Rhodes-Kropf (2015) and Braun et al. (2019) show that the performance of a fund manager is largely related to its individual components. If they move or retire, this can affect a specific fund manager. The analysis of the persistence of returns should also focus on individuals.

A new trend is emerging: the larger end of the market is more competitive and therefore abrasive for returns. Funds have been getting larger in LBOs, VC, and select other private market strategies. Fund sizes are directly correlated to deal sizes. The number of opportunities is essentially independent from the capital on offer. More capital for a pool of given opportunities means more competition. More competition means higher prices, which translate ultimately in the long term to lower performance.

There could also be another reason to the lower performance of established managers (who are often the managers of large funds): they reduce their risk appetite to preserve their track record. This might imply that they could drop from a quartile to another, for example. Also, the strategy of fund managers might evolve over time, and this could trigger some shifts in performance.

Assessing the performance of fund managers is, thus, a particularly intense process. It is even more so when considering that private markets evolve very fast, with the compounding factor that there is a recurring time lag and lack of information. As a result, what was considered as established empirical knowledge can age and be irrelevant. Other trends can emerge without notice.

4.3.4   Analyzing Performance to Set Targets

To set performance targets, fund investors have first, therefore, to assess their payout requirements. Then, they have to clearly assess their risk appetite. Then, within this double perimeter of constraints, they can determine what could be the returns ranges they could expect. These return ranges are the result of the construction of portfolios combining investment strategies, geographical regions, industrial exposure, and fund manager selection.

The variation of returns is higher for top-quartile funds than for bottom-quartile funds. The lower the performance is, the more predictable it is as well. This explains why some fund investors aim at more conservative and predictable returns and thus why there is a persistence of returns in the bottom-quartile segment.

The performance analysis is decomposed in three tasks. First, building theoretical portfolios of private market strategies (see Chapter 5) to assess their payout, risk, and performance. Second, analyzing from a top-down perspective each investment strategy and matching it with the investment universe (bottom-up), to see if there are funds offered. For example, there might not be any distressed debt fund option in continental Europe or any LBO fund in emerging markets.

Third, once there is a list of bottom-up options, the analysis of the performance of fund managers starts. The process consists in an intrinsic analysis, then a benchmarking exercise, and finally a value creation analysis.

The **intrinsic analysis** analyzes how a manager has built his past performance. How did the successes emerge, what were the reasons for the lack of success of some deals, and how did the manager apply the initial strategy and adapt it to new conditions? This intrinsic analysis is documenting the ability of the manager to replicate the performance in the future. It is helpful to assess how the fund managers have learnt from past mistakes and how the team has evolved and handled unexpected events.

The **benchmarking exercise** consists in comparing a specific fund manager with a peer group but also with public markets thanks to the PME method of analysis (see Chapter 3). This can be fairly challenging as data is hard to come by, and keeping track requires a lot of resources. This is not only about ranking the fund manager but also about understanding his positioning and differentiation against the competition. Regardless, investors should get access, upon request, to the detailed cash flows of past funds of the manager. Thanks to this information, they can assess the recurrence and amplitude of the outperformance against an index of listed assets.

The intrinsic analysis and the benchmarking exercise will lead the investor into the **value creation analysis**. The systematic application of an investment strategy by a manager leads to value creation in a pool of portfolio companies. These companies are chosen according to investment criteria, explained in the private placement memorandum of each fund. Once the companies are elected to join the portfolio, the fund manager applies the investment strategy on them. This should result in a measurable value creation, which can be notably broken down and analyzed by the investor (see Fig. 4.5 as an illustration of the value bridge analysis).

The value creation analysis loops back to the intrinsic analysis as it can support investors in their assessment of the replicability of the performance, and to a certain extent the persistence of performance of the manager. It also should provide some perspective for the benchmarking exercise. If a manager systematically manages to benefit from an increase from the multiple at entry to the multiple at exit, then this is not luck but a built-in feature of the investment strategy. This part of the value creation can be cross-checked with the PME analysis, as the latter reflects the ups and downs of the price of listed assets.

Ultimately, the value creation analysis should be the one that aligns the top-down analysis, bottom-up matching, and fund manager selection. As private market funds are difficult to combine with listed assets in a standard asset allocation, the analysis of the value creation could in effect support the choice of the drivers of return generation and risk mitigation. To some extent, it could be possible to reconcile the value creation analysis with factor investing, although with limited quantitative modeling due to data limitations.

4.4 ADDRESSING PRIVATE MARKET SPECIFICITIES

Investors have to deal with specific constraints related to the nature of private markets. Unfortunately, it is not easy to assess and quantify the effect of these constraints and even less to mitigate their consequences.

4.4.1 Facing Opportunity Costs

When investing in private markets, investors face opportunity costs, that is, the cost of unused capital. When committing to a fund, investors promise to pay a certain amount, but this amount will only progressively be invested and for an unknown quantity of time. The opportunity cost is the cost of capital for the time it sits idle on the balance sheet of the investor. Moreover, a regulated private market investor faces a solvency cost for the full amount, adding up to the cost of capital.

Opportunity costs appear when the capital is committed but not yet invested and when the proceeds from an investment are distributed and not yet reinvested. It is challenging to quantify these opportunity costs as the timing and duration of investments are essentially unknown.

They can, however, be modeled. First, there are limits to the annual amount that can be called by a fund manager. Second, capital calls can be statistically modeled. Opportunity costs can be minimized by investing unused capital in low-risk fixed-income products matching with the expected duration for which the capital is idle.

Nevertheless, even when they can be minimized, opportunity costs create a performance lag that has to be considered in the total cost of ownership of private market funds. Chapter 5 will provide illustrations of opportunity costs through modeling.

4.4.2 Underachieving Deployment Targets

As primary funds deploy capital progressively, investors can be tempted to compensate for the lack of exposure in the early stages of funds by committing to secondary funds, co-investing, or investing directly in private companies or assets in a more tactical approach. The challenge is to handle the exposure provided by these tactical instruments (see Chapter 5). In particular, they could increase the concentration risks in the portfolio of the investor.

Due to the progressive deployment of capital over three to five years, but also to the progressive distribution of capital after three to eight years, it is very unlikely that an investor will have at any given point in time a 100 percent exposure to the investment strategy within a fund. As we will see in Chapter 5, the net cash exposure varies between 45 and 65 percent at the portfolio level. Fund investors could be tempted to overcommit to funds to increase their net exposure (see Chapter 5). This could, however, backfire if the calibration is not precise enough. It also involves some solvency costs, as investors get to cover their legal exposure to a fund, not their actual capital at risk.

4.4.3 Dealing with Equity Bridge Financing Facilities

Fund investors are also exposed to a specific risk due to the use of leverage by managers. The practice was originally tried out by managers specializing in the acquisition of large and diversified portfolios of private market funds. More recently, the practice has gained momentum with managers of single funds, who could borrow capital to finance the acquisition of new assets or companies or to anticipate distributions. The purpose of the use of these credit lines (also called equity bridge financing) was to boost internal rates of returns, which are computed only when the capital is called. Managers essentially borrowed against the ability of fund investors to answer capital calls.

The practical consequence is that fund investors might be liable to pay significant amounts in a rather short amount of time without explicitly knowing it, for example, in the event that the lender to the fund would restrict or cancel the use of the credit line (or substantially increase the costs of its use). This creates additional risks if investors do not actively track their actual exposure versus the targeted exposure and do not build cash reserves to potentially face unusually significant and abrupt capital calls. These cash reserves would then translate into further opportunity costs (see Section 4.1), which are even more difficult to mitigate (except by using short-term money market instruments).

This also changes the cash-flow pattern of funds, which no longer behave as their historical peers did. As investors might use historical data to reduce their opportunity costs (see Section 4.1) or to reach their deployment targets (see Section 4.2), the use of equity bridge financing facilities can in effect reduce the efficiency of the strategies used by fund investors.

Finally, the use of equity bridge financing facilities can increase the contagion risks. Some investors might simply not be able to answer unusually high capital calls abruptly and might default on the call. This, in return, will affect negatively all the other investors in the fund.

SUMMARY

Throughout this chapter, we have pointed out that:

To effectively build an investment program encompassing less tradable assets and to avoid the confusion when discussing the notion of risks around sources of performance and portfolio construction, **it is essential to change the perspective underlying the standard framework.** The latter is based on the fundamental assumption that the assets acquired by investors are tradable immediately, in an organized market, at low or no cost with willing third parties. Yet, private markets are not matching this assumption as they require significant time to let investors create value, and the two sources of performance, which are not mutually exclusive, remain the reward for the creation of value and the compensation of the investor accepting a deferment of the use of his capital.

Three steps are essential to build a portfolio of listed and private assets:

- Setting up an investment horizon by:
  - **Differentiating this investment horizon** (difference between the investment date and the exit date even if the exit date is sometimes difficult to predict) **and the payout schedule.**
  - **Taking into account the discrepancy between theoretical and actual investment horizons,** as pension fund managers tend to invest in assets with a shorter duration than the theoretical time horizon would warrant. Thus, the level of pension payments is lower than it could be, and retirement age keeps increasing. This discrepancy can be explained by regulation and ill-designed models managing assets and liabilities matching. Investors should have a **time horizon of at least four to five years** to integrate private markets in an investment portfolio.
  - Knowing the minimum, average, and maximum time to liquidity of individual private markets strategies to **support the matching of payout and distribution patterns** and thus to overcome the discrepancy between the term of private markets funds and their average time to liquidity.
  - **Using the secondary market marginally, as secondary investment opportunities are unpredictable**: investors willing to dispose of assets due to a specific overallocation to one strategy, the need to reduce the number of relationships, or because a fund manager no longer matches the requirements set by the investor can selectively use the secondary market to dispose of the fund stake. They can also use the secondary market for direct investments to ramp up their portfolio by seizing an opportunity to get access to a fund manager, to use information advantage to exploit market inefficiencies.
  - **Using structured financing** (by structuring a loan against a portfolio of private market assets), **securitization** for portfolios of assets with a NAV above one billion, or **private equity,** which can represent up to 75 percent of the NAV of the portfolio.

- **Setting up the risk thresholds:**
  - **Diversification and correlations, private markets, and the rest of the universe**: it is challenging to assess what the link is between the evolution of prices of listed stocks and private market fund performance. It is possible to assess the link between the performance of a specific fund manager and some macroeconomic and financial data, but this analysis is limited to a single fund. Empirical evidence shows that investors have to build a diversified portfolio of private market funds with differentiated and complementary strategies.
  - **Risks associated with direct, funds, and funds of funds:** setting up a fund and mandating a fund manager directly and significantly modifies the risk taken by investors and their return expectations. Depending on their risk appetite,

investors can choose the appropriate level of intermediation for them. The level of risk is inversely correlated with the degree of control of the investor.

▪ **De-smoothing LBO returns and seeing LBOs as a leveraged listed index to eliminate their specificity is counterproductive:** private markets are often seen as a "sticky" version of listed ones. Some observers state that private equity investing does not create value and is essentially a leveraged index of listed small- and mid-sized companies. This is a mistake.

▪ **Foreign exchange fluctuations:** investors in private markets deal with unpredictable investment durations, and it is thus difficult to handle the consequences of the variation of currencies on their investments made in local currencies. Long and unpredictable durations mean that the cost of hedging is too high. Thus, the performance of private market funds in emerging markets will be more volatile than in developed markets.

- **Setting up return expectations:**

▪ **The limits of performance data:** the classic return measures of performance are based on limited samples of aggregated historical returns, which are difficult to quantify and analyze. Investors have to define scenarios for the future and see how their portfolio of private market funds would react to these events, assigning probabilities to these scenarios. The selection of fund managers is paramount but challenging especially due to the dispersion of performance of funds.

▪ **Performance dispersion:** some specific instruments to measure risk and performance have been developed. One consists in monitoring the investment strategy and performance. Another measures fund selection risk, measuring the spread of the multiple of investment capital of two groups of funds, for example.

▪ **Persistence of performance:** managers are subject to a persistence of performance in private equity, though the extent is discussed. This analysis is based on quartiles, with the limits that this entails. Moreover, fund managers change over time. Assessing their performance is a demanding process as private markets evolve fast.

▪ **Analyzing performance to set performance targets:** the performance analysis is then split into three tasks: building theoretical portfolios of private market strategies (to assess payout, risks, and performance), analyzing from a top-down perspective each investment strategy, and matching it with the investment universe. Once there is a list of bottom-up options, the performance of fund managers can start, and the process consists in an intrinsic analysis, a benchmarking exercise, and a value creation analysis.

Finally, and beyond those three steps, addressing private markets specificities is essential for portfolio construction and management. First, when investing in private markets, investors face **opportunity costs**, but we can only model them as they are difficult to quantify (timing and duration of investments are essentially unknown). Those costs create a **performance lag** that needs to be considered in the total cost of ownership of private market funds.

Besides, due to the progressive development of capital, fund investors could be tempted to overcommit to funds to increase their net exposure and compensate the lack of exposure in the early stages of funds, but this could involve **solvency costs** for regulated investors.

Finally, fund investors are exposed to additional risks due to **the use of leverage (like credit lines) by managers**. This use of equity bridge also changes the cash-flow pattern of funds reducing the efficiency of strategies used by fund investors. This use of leverage also increases contagion risks for fund investors.

CHAPTER 5

Portfolio Construction and Management

In a nutshell

This chapter will guide readers through the process of portfolio construction within private markets. This process is specific. It relies on the combination of top-down and bottom-up approaches. Some rules have emerged and apply specifically to private markets. In that respect, knowledge gained on listed markets is not applicable to private markets without a strict and detailed scrutiny and a healthy dose of caution.

O ver the course of the last four decades, private markets have emerged as an asset class, providing a differentiated source of enhanced returns and risk diversification to the portfolio of investors. This change has notably been initiated by a landmark interpretation of ERISA rules by the US Department of Labor in 1979 (Demaria, 2015). Since then, investors have tried and tested different approaches, forging investment rules as they explored how to build private markets portfolios (Section 1).

These rules are derived from the experience of practitioners, although some of them have eventually been confirmed by academic literature. Once the program is up and running, monitoring and controlling investments help investors to learn and adjust the program (Sections 2 and 3). In particular, long-term trends change the environment in which programs are built and managed. It is therefore important to analyze, discuss, and possibly anticipate some of them (Section 3).

5.1 BUILDING PORTFOLIOS OF PRIVATE MARKETS FUNDS

In private markets, portfolio construction is the result of the confrontation of top-down and bottom-up approaches (Fig. 5.1).

5.1.1 The Top-Down Perspective

The **top-down perspective** itself is the fruit of macroeconomic analyses resulting in scenarios in which assets are expected to behave in a specific way. Private market strategies react differently to macroeconomic events. They also generate variable levels of returns, and the risk associated with their investments can fluctuate significantly.

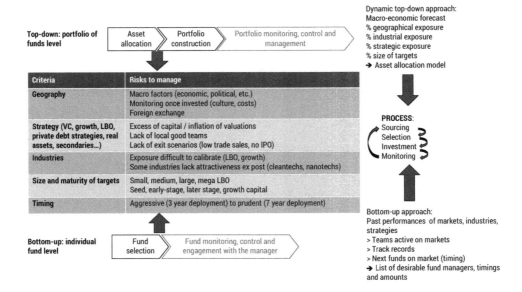

FIGURE 5.1   Meeting of the top-down and bottom-up approaches
Source: Authors.

The output of the top-down approach is an investment matrix with multiple dimensions. One of them is the expected **geographical** exposure, which is a function of economic and political analyses and anticipations. Often, targets are assigned to these dimensions, which are expressed as a percentage of the pool of capital to be allocated.

Another is the exposure to **investment strategies** (such as venture capital, distressed debt, or timberland), which are functions of capital available, deal flow, valuations, exit opportunities, and other specific dimensions.

At times, investors want to add more granularity and add **specific asset sizes** (from small to very large assets) and **maturity** (from inception to established assets). These characteristics are usually used to refine the exposure of investors to investment strategies, possibly compensating an exposure to large listed assets, for example.

Some investors might want to add targeted **industrial** exposures, such as information technologies or biotechnologies. This might prove to be difficult to implement. Fund managers often want to retain a relative freedom to invest and choose to scout the market for attractive opportunities in a wide range of industries (for example, in LBOs).

One dimension, however, is not determined by the top-down approach: market timing. Indeed, the first rule of portfolio construction in private markets is "Do not try to time the market."

5.1.2   First Rule: Do Not Try to Time the Market

Private equity performance is described as "highly cyclical" (Brown et al., 2019). Investors could be tempted to establish a correlation between past performance (and risks) and specific macroeconomic conditions. They could try to take advantage of the link they would have established by assessing where national economies stand at the time of the launch of their program and build a program maximizing profits or minimizing risks.

This is not advised, as confirmed by Brown et al. (2019), who state that they "find modest gains, at best, to pursuing more realistic, investable strategies that time capital commitments to private equity." Multiple cumulative reasons explain this strong empirical and academic conclusion.

Specific Fundraising Features and Capital Deployment Patterns

First, establishing strong correlations between macroeconomic events and the performance of private markets funds is fiercely difficult. Fund managers can count on investment periods of three to five years to deploy in private markets the capital that they have collected (Chapter 3). They benefit from ample margins for action. This latitude, in effect, cancels attempts to time the market by fund investors, who have no say in the capital deployment.

Second, it is exceedingly difficult to anticipate even major macroeconomic events multiple months in advance. Private market funds are raised over a period of six to eighteen months. Even if a fund is closed before such an event, it is difficult to assess the likelihood that the fund manager will be able to take advantage of (or will suffer from) these conditions.

Third, fund managers raise funds on average every two to three years. This means that even if investors can manage to clearly identify in advance a macroeconomic event, there might simply not be any fund from a specific manager on offer at the required time. This is possible, but being aware of it implies a thorough bottom-up analysis (see next subsection) from investors. In any case, investors are never in position to decide when a fund should be raised.

Fourth, fund managers might adapt their strategy to macroeconomic conditions as they unfold, avoiding the detrimental consequences of these changes on their assets or even capitalizing on the changes to move ahead. These actions cannot be foreseen by fund investors.

Waves of Performances and Cycles

Fifth, the performances of individual vintage years tend to be correlated (forming "waves" of performance) but show significant differences in terms of absolute performance. It is exceedingly difficult to identify which year will benefit (or suffer) the most from a specific macroeconomic event.

Sixth, private markets cycles are starting to emerge, but most of the strategies are too recent to have documented patterns, which are also changing over time. US VC starts to show some patterns, and LBOs as well, but these would require longer time series of data to lead to conclusions. Moreover, these cycles evolve as macroeconomic and political events unfold. It is only after funds are liquidated that the data can be crunched and lead to some conclusions.

The conclusion is thus that investors should deploy capital regularly to try to mitigate the impact of economic and political events on their portfolio of private markets funds.

A sound approach is to start to invest over a planned multi-year period of time, for example, five (empirically the most frequent approach) to seven (a more conservative approach) years, deploying regularly the capital with the fund managers identified through the bottom-up analysis (see below). Seven years should provide investors with the ability to deploy at least twice with the same manager and to be able then to fund the next funds in the program thanks to the distributions of the funds already in the program.

5.1.3   A "Market Neutral" Top-Down Matrix

Table 5.1 provides a picture of a "market neutral" (defined in Chapter 4 as a replication of the overall regional and strategic breakdown of private markets) portfolio from a top-down perspective. Using data from Cambridge Associates and Preqin, and including some market dynamics to fill the blanks, we have established a strategic and geographical breakdown of a portfolio that would reflect the capital historically and expected to be invested in private markets worldwide.

There is a strong tilt toward equity strategies, which are the longest running (notably VC and LBOs in the US) and the most developed. Real assets come next, while private debt strategies still represent a smaller proportion of assets managed in private markets.

This market-neutral portfolio is theoretically investible. In practice, executing this plan would require full access to each fund raised in the world pro rata to the capital raised by these funds. This is a tall order, and in practice very few investors would be able to do so.

TABLE 5.1   Market-neutral capital-weighted allocation to private markets

RegionStrategy	North America	Europe	Rest of the World	Total
Venture capital	8%	1%	2%	**11%**
Growth Capital	4%	3%	3%	**10%**
Leveraged buyout	25%	11%	2%	**38%**
Private equity	**37%**	**15%**	**7%**	**59%**
Direct lending, unitranche, mezzanine	6%	5%	3%	**14%**
Distressed debt	2%	1%	0%	**3%**
Private debt	**8%**	**6%**	**3%**	**17%**
Private real estate	5%	4%	4%	**13%**
Infrastructure	3%	2%	2%	**7%**
Private equity energy	3%	0%	0%	**3%**
Timber and farmland	1%	0%	0%	**1%**
Private real assets	**12%**	**6%**	**6%**	**24%**
Total	**57%**	**27%**	**16%**	**100%**

Source: Authors, based on Cambridge Associates, Preqin, and own estimates. This does not include funds of funds or secondary funds, as they are considered as pass-through vehicles of investment. Distressed debt includes turn-around capital.

Nevertheless, we will use this grid and combine it with our bottom-up access to data to test a market-neutral portfolio with our model.

5.1.4 The Use of Secondary Investments

Some investors might consider the seven years mentioned above as too long a period to commit capital. It is possible to reduce this period to five years, but the risk is that investors could be caught in a major and durable macroeconomic event, such as a recession, and allocate a significant proportion of their capital during vintage years that would suffer from the consequences of this event. Below five years, the risk increases that investors are overexposed to underperforming vintage years.

To ramp up the exposure over a shorter time frame, investors could resort to secondary investments. The logic is that an investor willing to commit a specific amount over three years would only allocate some of this amount to funds newly created (primary commitments). This investor will simultaneously scout the market to identify funds stakes for sale (secondary investing). With this approach, the investor hopes to get the exposure to past vintage years through these secondary commitments. However, this approach bears its own risks.

First, there is no guarantee that a significant volume of secondary investment opportunities will come to the market. The motivations for existing investors to sell vary, and the quality and number of fund stakes for sale depends on who sells and for what reason. More often than not this information is not available.

Second, the investment opportunities might not match the requirements of the top-down approach of the investor. For example, investment opportunities on the secondary market might come heavily from venture capital investments in emerging markets or funds dedicated to private equity energy. Maybe these two segments of the market are not part of the investment strategy of the investor. This means that the investor will not be able to deploy the capital reserved for secondary investments and the portfolio will bear significant risks as it will be less diversified.

Third, secondary investments themselves are subject to a specific risk as they have their own cycles. Fund stakes are sold on the informal secondary market at an average discount of 20 to 30 percent on the net asset value of the fund. At times, the average discount increases, which was the case in 2008. It can also shrink below 20 percent, as we have seen since 2010, or even in a range of 8 to 11 percent, as it has been since 2014. As this is an average, this means that some fund stakes trade at a premium. The investor willing to invest on the secondary market will have to accept these levels of discount (or premium). This has significant consequences.

An investor could deploy aggressively in a short time frame (for example, three years) significant amounts at the top of an economic cycle. This investor would invest significantly on the primary market in funds that would ultimately underperform. Deploying capital in the secondary market at the top of the cycle implies a reduced or no discount. As a result, the benefit of investing "retroactively" is significantly reduced or vanishes altogether. This will be explored through our model in this chapter.

Therefore, unless the investor has superior forecasting and selection skills, as well as an unprecedented ability to source fund investment opportunities, it is not advisable to try to time the market and to significantly reduce the time frame of the program construction below five to seven years. It has to be noted that selection and sourcing are a function of the experience of the investor. Initiating a completely new program implies that the investor has not developed these skills. It is therefore recommended to stick to principles that have proven time and again to be empirically sound.

5.1.5   The Bottom-Up Perspective

The **bottom-up perspective** is the result of canvassing the investment field to identify existing investment opportunities. Fund managers raise capital regularly and contact prospective investors. As they come back, it is possible to anticipate their next fundraising effort. Fund investors can source opportunities through different channels (Fig. 5.2). They then engage in fund selection, with their own resources or with the help of external providers. Once fund managers have been selected, some terms can be marginally negotiated between investors and managers. As indicated in Chapter 3, the options of investors to act are limited at the time of investment and even more so after they have invested (see also Demaria, 2015, Introduction).

As private market strategies are more or less developed, the number of investment opportunities can vary significantly in number, quality, and granularity. For example, there is ample choice for an investor willing to invest in US VC funds dedicated to information technologies. The choice might be more restricted if that investor wants to invest in US VC funds specializing in environmental technologies or new materials, and there might not be any equivalent in Japan.

Another example might be that some growth capital funds dedicated to emerging markets are pan-regional, focusing on Asia-Pacific, or Africa, or Latin America. Fund managers might want to allocate specifically to a country, for example, Indonesia or Vietnam, but there might not be any fund manager focusing only on this country. If

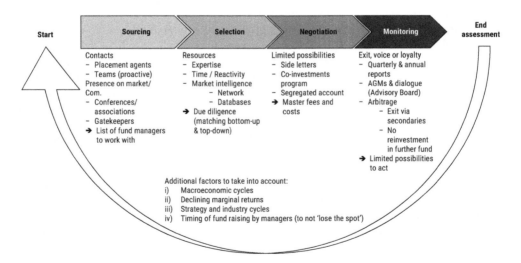

FIGURE 5.2   Bottom-up approach
Source: Authors.

there are, their track record might not be long or convincing enough to match the selection criteria of the investor.

Once investors have chosen their base case scenario, they choose from the investment opportunities they have identified. At times, there is no opportunity matching the requirements. A typical example would be the lack of distressed debt funds in Continental Europe. Local bankruptcy procedures are not adapted to the intervention of this type of fund. Another example is the lack of LBO funds in emerging markets. High inflation and a lack of sophistication prevent the structuration of the financial leverage necessary for such buyouts. Rules limiting foreign ownership can also prevent such operations.

As a result of the bottom-up analysis, it could be tempting to focus on specific fund managers and to allocate a significant amount to their funds. This would be a mistake. The second rule of fund investing is diversify.

5.1.6   Second Rule: Diversify

A lack of diversification substantially increases the selection risk of the investor. Even though fund managers regularly show a relative persistence of their performance (see Chapter 3), there is no certainty that this will remain true for the future.

This performance is largely driven by some of the individuals working for the fund manager. These individuals can move to another fund manager or create a new one. This is the reason why so-called key man clauses are set up in fund regulations, to prevent further investments until specific individuals are replaced, often with the approval of fund investors. If the departure of key individuals happens, the investor might end up being invested in a fund without the talents required to drive the performance up.

Moreover, even the most reputable fund managers can ultimately fall. The example of the demise of the largest Middle Eastern private equity fund manager Abraaj Capital is a cautionary tale (Demaria, 2020, Chapter 7) that illustrates the necessity of diversifying—not only among multiple funds but also multiple fund managers.

Therefore, whenever possible, investors are advised to invest regularly every year in two funds or more fitting in a given category of investment. The latter is the result of the matrix of the top-down perspective, that is, a combination of the dimensions (for example, US early-stage VC dedicated to software).

5.1.7   The Use of Overcommitment

Investors might find this rule challenging to apply for multiple reasons. First, screening the market requires significant resources. Identifying high quality fund investment opportunities is therefore expensive. Monitoring and managing these investments also involves significant resources. Therefore, the initial and ongoing costs have to be taken into account.

Second, securing an access to funds is challenging. Investors can see their offer to invest turned down, or the amounts they plan to invest can be significantly downscaled by the fund manager.

Third, the net capital used at any given point in time by fund managers will not match the target exposure. Funds call capital as opportunities arise and distribute the proceeds of these investments whenever they collect them. For that reason, the net exposure of an investor in a given private equity fund is at best between 40 and 60 percent of the total committed.

The temptation for the investor facing one or more of the issues above could be to overcommit to the funds that he has managed to get in—assuming that regulations allow it (see Chapter 1). Overcommitting consists in signing up for an amount that is higher than the effective amount targeted. If the investor expects his commitment to be called on a net basis at 60 percent, a possible solution to increasing the amount of capital at work could be to increase the commitment by 20 percent. The net exposure would then increase to 72 percent. Likewise, if an investor expects to commit 20 million to a highly selective fund and the fund manager eventually downscales by half the commitments of all the investors, then the overcommitment strategy will allow him to effectively deploy more capital in the fund.

The obvious drawback to this strategy is that the net exposure of the investor could exceed his target. This could happen if a fund calls capital and does not distribute any proceeds for an extended period of time. The next exposure will increase and might exceed the contribution capacity of the investor.

Another drawback comes from the fact that the overcommitment of the investor has to be registered as such according to solvency rules. Therefore, if the effective capital deployment can increase, the cost of the unused capital (even if some of it is virtual) will also increase correspondingly. Some regulations might simply forbid any form of overcommitment.

A third drawback is that overcommitment amplifies any sudden shift in terms of cash flow in the fund. Fund managers might use credit lines (also called equity bridge financing) to invest and delay capital calls and still distribute proceeds from investments. Fund investors might even get net positive distributions from their private market program. In the event that credit lines are no longer a viable financing option, investors will face a sudden wave of capital calls from their funds. An overcommitment increases the scale of this wave of capital calls.

Therefore, investors should consider using overcommitment selectively and test their portfolio accordingly. This will be explored through our model in this chapter.

5.1.8   Modeling: Setting Up of a Market-Neutral' Investment Program

For the purpose of illustration, we have set up a model using historical data from Cambridge Associates. We have retrieved the cash flows of each available private market strategy by vintage year and by geographical region (see Table 5.2). In essence, this is the high-level equivalent of a bottom-up review of what is available in terms of data. This differs significantly from the top-down analysis (Table 5.1 above). Multiple strategies are not available in specific regions.

We then assign the historical cash flows that we retrieved to four performance buckets: low, medium, high, and very high. This exercise is based on performance brackets that we have identified and correlation analyses among vintage years. The purpose of this classification is to be able to consciously choose a historical environment to test the behavior of a set of private markets funds.

TABLE 5.2 Matrix of the cash flows used in the model

	North America	Europe	Rest of the World	Global
Venture capital	X	X	X	
Growth capital	X	X	X	
Leveraged buyout	X	X	X	
Mezzanine financing	X			
Distressed debt	X			
Real estate opportunistic	X	X	X	
Real estate value-added	X	X		
Private equity energy	X			
Timberland				X
Infrastructure				X
Secondary				X
Funds of funds				X

Source: Authors, based on Cambridge Associates (data as of Q1 2018).

We include overcommitment and secondary investment tools. The latter is set by "buying" at a premium or a discount funds that are anterior to the reference date of the program that we manually set. To account for the cost of unused capital, we manually input a risk-free rate that applies to this idle cash. We are then able to compute a new performance metric: "complete annualized return." This is what investors want to measure when evaluating their private markets investments in their entirety, including the performance drag of the unused capital.

Assessing a Market-Neutral Portfolio

We try to apply the relative weights described in Table 5.1 with the available data listed in Table 5.2. The result is relatively easy to implement when using recent vintage years for private equity. However, some limitations appear.

For private debt, the lack of data on senior and unitranche debt forces us to allocate the whole chunk of 14 percent to US mezzanine debt funds. This means that the overall absolute performance that we get is probably higher than with more conservative private debt strategies but also that the time-sensitive and the complete annualized return are different (as senior and unitranche debt distribute proceeds earlier). The capital deployment and distribution of proceeds is also different. As for distressed debt (which includes turn-around capital), we have to allocate the whole three percent to US funds as we do not have enough data for other geographical regions.

As for private real assets, the situation is contrasted. Data is more granular for private real estate than in Table 5.1. We decide to allocate two-thirds to "real estate opportunistic" and one-third to "real estate value add" (if available). As for timberland and infrastructure, data is available only at the global level. The input is summed up in Table 5.3. We choose the vintage year 2003 as a reference year. This is the most recent vintage year with which we can compute three- to seven-year programs.

We start with a five-year deployment period for the program. The risk-free rate is initially set to zero. The result is an IRR of 7.06 percent with a multiple of committed

TABLE 5.3   Market-neutral portfolio: dimensions of investment and output

Input

	North America	Europe	Rest of the World	Global
Venture capital	8%	1%	2%	
Growth capital	4%	3%	3%	
Leveraged buyout	25%	11%	2%	
Mezzanine financing	14%			
Distressed debt	3%			
Real estate opportunistic	5%	4%	4%	
Real estate value-added	2%	2%		
Private equity energy	3%			
Timberland				1%
Infrastructure				3%
Year of reference	2003			
Risk-free rate	0%			
Pace of deployment **Output**	3 years	5 years	7 years	
IRR	7.94%	7.06%	7.21%	
TVPI	1.44×	1.41×	1.41×	
DPI	1.38×	1.34×	1.34×	
Multiple of committed capital	1.38×	1.35×	1.34×	
Complete annualized return	3.56%	3.46%	3.36%	
Maximum exposure	−49.38% (Q 20)	−46.93% (Q 27)	−43.58% (Q 31)	
Break-even point	Q 42	Q 47	Q 50	

Source: Authors.

capital of 1.35×. The latter is chosen as this is a return computed on the capital set aside by fund investors. Taking into account the cost of unused capital and annualizing the returns, the complete annualized return is 3.46 percent. Our calculation is conservative for two reasons.

First, we stop the program when the residual value of funds is equal to 0.05×. Theoretically, this residual value would not significantly change the overall outcome of the program. Nevertheless, some proceeds might come after and are not accounted for. It is important to note that with this model, we stop new commitments after five years. This means that the program will distribute capital, and these proceeds are not used in our model.

Second, we include the cost of the unused capital, but we do not include the revenues from the reinvestment of the proceeds (not even invested at the risk-free rate). This creates a significant drag on the performance of the program, which does not correspond to reality. In particular, the proceeds from private market funds are usually committed to new funds or invested in other financial instruments.

Figure 5.3 provides a graphical illustration of the result of the portfolio. What appears clearly is that the maximum net exposure is of 46.93 percent in quarter 27. The program breaks even in quarter 47.

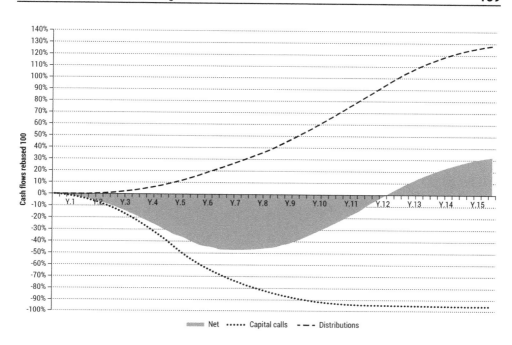

FIGURE 5.3 Market-neutral portfolio (0 percent risk-free rate, reference year: 2003)
Source: Authors.

Measuring the Impact of the Deployment Period

To invest in private markets, 2003, 2004, and 2005 were mixed vintage years, 2006 was not favorable, and 2007 was more favorable. Deploying capital more conservatively over seven years (from 2003 on) has a mixed effect on the performance of the program. The IRR *increases* to 7.21 percent (from 7.06), illustrating the value of diversifying in a challenging environment. The complete annualized return drops to 3.36 percent (from 3.46). The multiple of committed capital slightly decreases to 1.34× (from 1.35×). The maximum net exposure reaches 43.58 percent in quarter 31. The break-even point is reached in quarter 50. The program spans 17 years.

Accelerating the deployment of the capital over three years (from 2003 on) increases the IRR to 7.94 percent (from 7.06). This is a fairly marginal increase compared to the programs built over five or seven years considered above. The complete annualized return reaches 3.56 percent (from 3.46) and the multiple of committed capital 1.38× (from 1.35×). The maximum net exposure reaches 49.38 percent in quarter 20. The break-even point is reached in quarter 42. The program spans 14 years.

Thus, accelerating the capital deployment of the program can provide a marginally higher performance, but a much longer period can increase the time-sensitive performance. In the next section, we will stress-test these capital deployment scenarios to see what the risk really is.

Measuring the Effect of the Risk-Free Rate

The level of the risk-free rate has significant consequences. With a 1.5 percent compensation of the unused capital, the performance of the 5-year program increases to an IRR of 9.65 percent and a complete annualized return of 4.17 percent. The multiple of committed capital is 1.42×.

If the risk-free rate is set at –0.75 percent, the IRR decreases to 5.96 percent and the complete annualized return drops to 3.09 percent. The multiple of committed capital drops to 1.31×.

The level of the risk-free rate has a much larger effect on the overall performance of the program than the pace of deployment (at least in a relatively benign environment). This also means that the opportunity cost of unused capital is a significant concern for fund investors.

Stress-Testing a Market-Neutral Portfolio

We switch the year of reference to 1997, which was the run up to the boom and bust of the so-called Internet bubble. Unfortunately, the restricted availability of data limits our asset allocation by excluding fairly small allocations in growth capital in Europe (we redirect it to North America and the rest of the world), in private real estate in North America (we redirect it to North America), and in infrastructure and timber (we redirect it to real estate). The result is a different allocation as illustrated in Table 5.4.

With a capital deployment over five years, the IRR reaches 8.06 percent. The multiple of committed capital is 1.41×. The complete annualized return is 3.54 percent. The maximum net exposure is higher and reaches 50.73 percent in quarter 24. The break-even point is reached in quarter 44 for a program lasting 16 years (Figure 5.4).

We then run the same exercise over three years and seven years (Table 5.5). The longer the capital deployment, the higher the performance and the lower the maximum exposure.

We then test the same portfolio with a reference year set in 1994, which, with the following years, was a very favorable environment to invest in (Table 5.6). Unfortunately, distressed debt does not have enough data, so we allocate the three percent to mezzanine financing. If the capital deployment is the shortest, then the performance is the best. This assumes the perfect timing of investment in 1994.

Strikingly, the maximum net exposure with a seven-year capital deployment is only 27.62 percent. The early distributions compensate a significant part of the capital calls.

We systematically test an adjusted (to take into account available data) market-neutral portfolio invested over three, five, and seven years (Table 5.7). The variation of complete annual return for the shortest deployment is 476 bps. This program records not only the highest (8.08 percent) but also the lowest complete annual return (3.32 percent) of the overall results. The longer the capital deployment, the lower the dispersion of returns and also the higher the minimum performance. This limits the overall top performance as well.

We run the same exercise, this time to measure the maximum net exposure. Not surprisingly, in line with previous findings, the shortest capital deployment leads to the

TABLE 5.4 Market-neutral portfolio adjusted to the reference year 1997

Input

	North America	Europe	Rest of the World	Global
Venture capital	8%	1%	2%	
Growth capital	**6%**		**4%**	
Leveraged buyout	25%	11%	2%	
Mezzanine financing	14%			
Distressed debt	3%			
Real estate opportunistic	**16%**			
Real estate value-added	**5%**			
Private equity energy	3%			
Timberland				
Infrastructure				
Pace of deployment	5 years			
Year of reference	1997			
Risk-free rate	0%			
Output				
IRR	8.06%			
TVPI	1.48×			
DPI	1.41×			
Multiple of committed capital	1.41×			
Complete annualized return	3.54%			
Maximum exposure	−50.73%	In quarter	24	
Break-even point		In quarter	44	

Source: Authors.

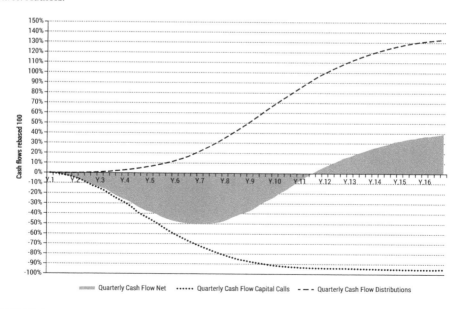

Quarterly Cash Flow Net   •••••• Quarterly Cash Flow Capital Calls   – – – Quarterly Cash Flow Distributions

FIGURE 5.4 Market-neutral portfolio (0 percent risk-free rate, reference year: 1997)
Source: Authors.

TABLE 5.5   Market-neutral portfolio (reference year: 1997) deployed over 3, 5, and 7 years

Input

	North America	Europe	Rest of the World
Venture capital	8%	1%	2%
Growth capital	6%		4%
Leveraged buyout	25%	11%	2%
Mezzanine financing	**17%**		
Distressed debt			
Real estate opportunistic	16%		
Real estate value-added	5%		
Private equity energy	3%		
Year of reference	1997		
Risk-free rate	0%		
Pace of deployment **Output**	3 years	5 years	7 years
IRR	6.00%	8.06%	8.92%
TVPI	1.36×	1.48×	1.53×
DPI	1.30×	1.41×	1.45×
Multiple of committed capital	1.30×	1.41×	1.45×
Complete annualized return	3.30%	3.54%	3.65%
Maximum exposure	−58.04% (Q 22)	−50.73% (Q 24)	−41.50% (Q 28)
Break-even point	Q 42	Q 44	Q 47

Source: Authors.

TABLE 5.6   Market-neutral portfolio (reference year: 1994) deployed over 3, 5, and 7 years

Input

	North America	Europe	Rest of the World
Venture capital	8%	1%	2%
Growth capital	6%		4%
Leveraged buyout	25%	11%	2%
Mezzanine financing	**17%**		
Distressed debt			
Real estate opportunistic	16%		
Real estate value-added	5%		
Private equity energy	3%		
Year of reference	1994		
Risk-free rate	0%		
Pace of deployment **Output**	3 years	5 years	7 years
IRR	18.29%	14.07%	12.58%
TVPI	1.87×	1.67×	1.61×
DPI	1.78×	1.59×	1.53×
Multiple of committed capital	1.80×	1.60×	1.54×
Complete annualized return	6.24%	4.83%	4.54%
Maximum exposure	−45.57% (Q 16)	−36.60% (Q 20)	−27.62% (Q 27)
Break-even point	Q 29	Q 38	Q 44

Source: Authors.

TABLE 5.7 Comparison of the performance depending on the pace of deployment

Input

	North America	Europe	Rest of the World
Venture capital	12%	2%	3%
Growth capital	6%		5%
Leveraged buyout	36%	16%	3%
Mezzanine financing	9%		
Real estate value-added	8%		
Risk-free rate	0%		

Output

Pace of deployment Complete annual return	3 years	5 years	7 years
1993	8.08%	6.74%	5.13%
1994	7.64%	5.90%	4.36%
1995	6.36%	4.58%	4.17%
1996	5.02%	3.80%	4.64%
1997	3.32%	3.92%	4.14%
1998	3.41%	4.33%	4.32%
1999	4.35%	4.83%	4.48%
2000	5.49%	5.21%	4.95%
2001	5.69%	5.10%	4.63%
2002	5.23%	4.46%	4.90%
2003	4.58%	4.55%	4.27%
Min–Max	3.32%–8.08%	3.80%–6.74%	4.14%–5.13%
Variation	476 bps	294 bps	99 bps

Source: Authors.

highest level of net capital deployment and the longest to the lowest level of net capital deployment (Table 5.8). Interestingly, the variation of maximum net exposure increases with the time used to deploy the capital.

We test for a correlation between the complete annual return and the maximum net exposure. It reaches –0.79 for the 3-year program and –0.85 for the 5-year program, hinting at a strong negative correlation between performance and maximum net exposure. However, the negative correlation is only –0.34 for the 7-year program. This indicates that the diversification introduced by a long capital deployment supersedes the link between performance and exposure.

Exploring Overcommitments

At least 35 percent of investors' capital is never put to work. Moreover, some of the capital is used fairly late and bears significant opportunity costs. Assuming that investors are authorized to do so, it could make sense to overcommit to funds systematically.

TABLE 5.8 Comparison of the maximum exposure—depending on the pace of deployment

Input

	North America	**Europe**	**Rest of the World**
Venture capital	12%	2%	3%
Growth capital	6%		5%
Leveraged buyout	36%	16%	3%
Mezzanine financing	9%		
Real estate value-added	8%		
Risk-free rate	0%		

Output

Pace of deployment	3 years	5 years	7 years
Maximum net exposure			
1993	43.04% (Q 16)	31.07% (Q 19)	22.19% (Q19)
1994	45.03% (Q 16)	33.66% (Q 19)	24.04% (Q19)
1995	49.84% (Q 18)	38.72% (Q 20)	28.72% (Q 23)
1996	55.54% (Q 19)	43.05% (Q 20)	35.73% (Q 31)
1997	61.32% (Q 22)	50.94% (Q 26)	41.98% (Q 29)
1998	56.73% (Q 20)	47.70% (Q 25)	38.54% (Q29)
1999	53.69% (Q 21)	45.31% (Q 25)	37.68% (Q 29)
2000	44.81% (Q 20)	38.77% (Q 24)	33.92% (Q 31)
2001	43.86% (Q 20)	41.36% (Q 25)	35.96% (Q 29)
2002	44.85% (Q 20)	45.47% (Q 25)	39.79% (Q 33)
2003	50.92% (Q 21)	48.20% (Q 28)	44.79% (Q 31)
Min–Max	43.04%–61.32%	31.07%–50.94%	22.19%–44.79%
Variation	1828 bps	1987 bps	2260 bps

Source: Authors.

We test this with a 35 percent overcommitment first (Table 5.9). The complete annualized return increases by 99 to 191 basis points for the 3-year program, 108 to 167 basis points for the 5-year program, and 114 to 139 basis points for the 7-year program. Interestingly, the variation of performance increases the most for the 3-year program and the least for the 7-year program.

The maximum net exposure is 61 percent for a 3-year program starting in 1997 (Fig. 5.5). An overcommitment of 35 percent led to a maximum net exposure of 82 percent (Fig. 5.6). This assumes that the underlying funds accept this higher commitment.

Next, we set a targeted net maximum exposure of 90 percent. We then determine the overcommitment necessary to reach this target depending on the time frame of the program. When the targeted 90 percent cannot be reached, we select the closest increment of exposure before exceeding this threshold. The results (Table 5.10) are quite enlightening.

The 3-year program can support a range of 46 to 109 percent of overcommitment. The complete annual return reaches on average 8.57 percent for the eleven years considered, ranging from 4.63 percent to 13.26 percent (863 basis points).

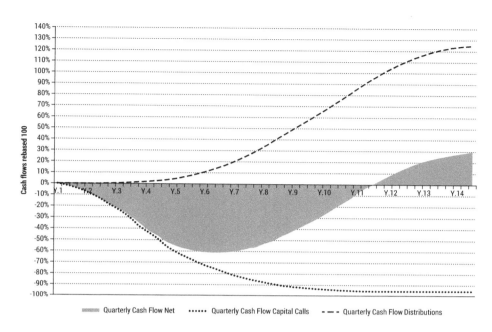

FIGURE 5.5   Market-neutral portfolio (0 percent risk-free rate, reference year: 1997, 3-year deployment)
Source: Authors.

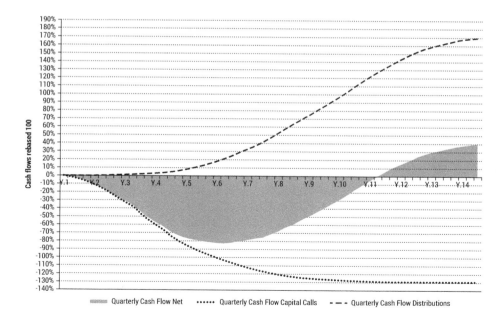

FIGURE 5.6   Market-neutral portfolio (0 percent risk-free rate, reference year: 1997, 3-year deployment, 35% overcommitment)
Source: Authors.

TABLE 5.9 Comparison of the performance with an overcommitment of 35%

Input

	North America	**Europe**	**Rest of the World**
Venture capital	12%	2%	3%
Growth capital	6%		5%
Leveraged buyout	36%	16%	3%
Mezzanine financing	9%		
Real estate value-added	8%		
Risk-free rate	0%		

Output

Pace of deployment	3 years	5 years	7 years
Complete annual return			
1993	9.99% (+191 bps)	8.41% (+167 bps)	6.46% (+133 bps)
1994	9.49% (+185 bps)	7.42% (+152 bps)	5.52% (+116 bps)
1995	8.03% (+167 bps)	5.83% (+125 bps)	5.31% (+114 bps)
1996	6.42% (+140 bps)	4.88% (+108 bps)	5.92% (+128 bps)
1997	4.32% (+100 bps)	5.04% (+112 bps)	5.29% (+115 bps)
1998	4.40% (+99 bps)	5.53% (+120 bps)	5.52% (+120 bps)
1999	5.56% (+121 bps)	6.15% (+132 bps)	5.72% (+124 bps)
2000	6.94% (+145 bps)	6.61% (+140 bps)	6.32% (+137 bps)
2001	7.20% (+151 bps)	6.49% (+139 bps)	5.93% (+130 bps)
2002	6.65% (+142 bps)	5.71% (+125 bps)	6.29% (+139 bps)
2003	5.88% (+130 bps)	5.85% (+130 bps)	5.48% (+121 bps)
Min–Max	4.32%-9.99%	4.88%-8.41%	5.29%-6.46%
Average compl. ann. ret.	9.06%	6.17%	4.74%
Average excess perf.	+143 bps	+132 bps	+125 bps
Variation	567 bps (+91 bps)	353 bps (+59 bps)	117 bps (+18 bps)

Source: Authors.

The 5-year program supports higher overcommitment, ranging from 76 to 189 percent. The average complete annual return reaches 8.85 percent, and the range of returns decreases to 762 basis points, ranging from 6.24 to 13.86 percent.

The 7-year program is not for the fainthearted. The program can support an overcommitment ranging from 100 to 305 percent. This means that investors applying this strategy would commit between double and quadruple their reference program to reach a 90 percent maximum net exposure. The average complete annual return reaches 9.56 percent, and the range of returns drops to 588 points. The minimum performance reaches 7.48 percent.

Not surprisingly, overcommitments boost returns. They are higher on average, but also the minimum achievable return is higher. What is somewhat surprising is that the variation of returns continues to be lower as the program is deployed over a longer period of time.

TABLE 5.10 Overcommitment and resulting complete annual return for a targeted 90% net maximum exposure

Input

	North America	Europe	Rest of the World
Venture capital	12%	2%	3%
Growth capital	6%		5%
Leveraged buyout	36%	16%	3%
Mezzanine financing	9%		
Real estate value-added	8%		
Risk-free rate	0%		

Output

Pace of deployment	3 years	5 years	7 years
Overcommit. (comp. ann. ret.)			
1993	109% (13.26%)	189% (13.86%)	305% (13.36%)
1994	99% (12.31%)	167% (11.92%)	274% (11.08%)
1995	80% (9.92%)	132% (8.76%)	213% (9.73%)
1996	62% (7.41%)	109% (6.86%)	151% (9.41%)
1997	46% (4.63%)	76% (6.24%)	114% (7.55%)
1998	58% (5.01%)	88% (7.15%)	133% (8.33%)
1999	67% (6.56%)	98% (8.23%)	138% (8.80%)
2000	100% (9.24%)	132% (9.84%)	165% (10.48%)
2001	105% (9.77%)	117% (9.29%)	151% (9.47%)
2002	100% (8.92%)	97% (7.68%)	126% (9.42%)
2003	76% (7.25%)	86% (7.57%)	100% (7.48%)
Min–Max overcommit.	46%–109%	76%–189%	100%–305%
Average complete ann. ret.	8.57%	8.85%	9.56%
Variation of complete ann. ret.	863 bps	762 bps	588 bps

Source: Authors.

In practice, it is impossible to forecast the next three to seven years. Logically, investors able and willing to overcommit would use a margin of safety (the 10 percent difference between our 90 percent maximum net exposure and a theoretical 100 percent) and would apply systematically the lowest overcommitment that was historically validated, that is, 46, 76, and 100 percent for respectively the 3-, 5-, and 7-year program. We run this with the same portfolio and a zero percent risk-free rate (Table 5.11).

By overcommitting 46 (3-year program) to 100 percent (7-year program) more than the initial target, fund investors would be able to generate an average complete annualized return of 7.22 to 7.83 percent. The variation is particularly low in the case of a 7-year program as returns are within a range of 7.14 to 8.59 percent. The returns are therefore fairly predictable with a prudent deployment of capital.

The logical conclusion is that if fund investors can overcommit without any constraint or additional regulatory cost, they should choose the 7-year time frame and

TABLE 5.11 Highest overcommitment applied systematically and the resulting complete annual return

Input

	North America	Europe	Rest of the World
Venture capital	12%	2%	3%
Growth capital	6%		5%
Leveraged buyout	36%	16%	3%
Mezzanine financing	9%		
Real estate value-added	8%		
Risk-free rate	0%		

Output

	North America	Europe	Rest of the World
Pace of deployment (overcommit.)	3 years (46%)	5 years (76%)	7 years (100%)
Comp. ann. ret. (max net exp.)			
1993	10.53% (62.83%)	10.11% (54.68%)	8.56% (44.38%)
1994	10.02% (65.74%)	9.00% (59.25%)	7.36% (48.09%)
1995	8.52% (72.76%)	7.16% (68.14%)	7.14% (57.43%)
1996	6.83% (81.08%)	6.02% (75.78%)	7.99% (71.46%)
1997	4.63% (89.53%)	6.24% (89.66%)	7.18% (83.96%)
1998	4.70% (82.82%)	6.80% (83.96%)	7.46% (77.08%)
1999	5.91% (78.39%)	7.54% (79.75%)	7.75% (75.37%)
2000	7.36% (65.42%)	8.08% (68.23%)	8.56% (67.85%)
2001	7.64% (64.03%)	7.96% (72.80%)	8.04% (71.92%)
2002	7.06% (65.48%)	7.05% (80.03%)	8.59% (79.58%)
2003	6.26% (74.34%)	7.25% (84.83%)	7.48% (89.57%)
Min–Max compl. ann. ret. (diff.)	4.63%–10.53% (590 bps)	6.02%–10.11% (409 bps)	7.14%–8.59% (145 bps)
Average compl. ann. ret.	7.22%	7.56%	7.83%
Variation of net exposure	62.83%–89.53%	54.68%–89.66%	44.38%–89.57%

Source: Authors.

significantly overcommit. The level of overcommitment is determined by the relative weight of the strategies and the targeted net maximum exposure (see above).

Using Secondary Investments

If investors cannot overcommit and if they have to bear negative interest rates, the weight of the uncalled capital can add a significant drag to the performance. It could be

TABLE 5.12 Use of secondary investments and resulting complete annualized return

Input

	North America	Europe	Rest of the World
Venture capital	12%	2%	3%
Growth capital	6%		5%
Leveraged buyout	36%	16%	3%
Mezzanine financing	9%		
Real estate value-added	8%		
Risk-free rate	0%		
Year of reference	2003		
Program deployment	3 years		
Output: compl. ann. ret. (max. net exp., multiple of comm. cap.)			
Pricing	0%	−15%	+15%
Exposure to secondaries			
0%	4.58% (50.92%, 1.52×)	4.58% (50.92%, 1.52×)	4.58% (50.92%, 1.52×)
10%	3.92% (50.23%, 1.41×)	3.97% (49.90%, 1.42×)	3.87% (50.53%, 1.40×)
20%	3.49% (49.71%, 1.36×)	3.60% (49.07%, 1.38×)	3.38% (50.29%, 1.35×)
30%	2.88% (49.40%, 1.33×)	3.04% (48.57%, 1.35×)	2.73% (50.14%, 1.31×)
40%	2.56% (49.95%, 1.30×)	2.79% (48.84%, 1.32×)	2.36% (50.94%, 1.27×)
50%	2.18% (50.50%, 1.26×)	2.53% (49.12%, 1.29×)	1.92% (51.73%, 1.23×)

Source: Authors.

tempting to deploy capital on the secondary market. In effect, an investor with a 3-year program could buy stakes in funds created before the launch of the program.

We investigate the use of secondaries with a 3-year program, allocating from 0 to 50 percent to secondaries. The price of the fund stake is at NAV (0 percent discount) or at a 15 percent discount or premium. In our example, we assume that the fund stakes are acquired over the three years of the investment program. The exposure is the same then for the primary program, but the funds were created five years before they are acquired on the secondary market (Table 5.12).

Figure 5.7 shows the minimum exposure to secondaries in our set of scenarios (10 percent, without discount). The shape is very similar to one of Figure 5.5. It is a significant contrast with Figure 5.8, which depicts a portfolio where secondaries represent 50 percent of the total size. The "staircase" deployment in secondaries is clearly visible in this figure.

What appears clearly is that, in fact, the use of secondaries reduces the amount of capital at work. This is because secondary investments distribute capital immediately. As a consequence, they also reduce the multiple on committed capital. Acquiring stakes

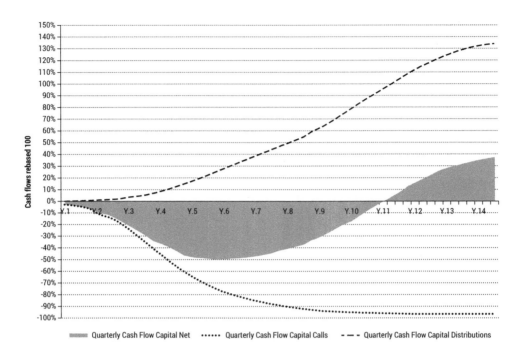

FIGURE 5.7 Market-neutral portfolio (0 percent risk-free rate, reference year: 2003, 3-year deployment, 10 percent secondaries, no discount/premium on NAV)
Source: Authors.

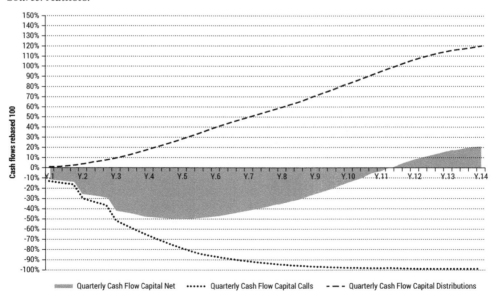

FIGURE 5.8 Market-neutral portfolio (0 percent risk-free rate, reference year: 2003, 3-year deployment, 50 percent secondaries, no discount/premium on NAV)
Source: Authors.

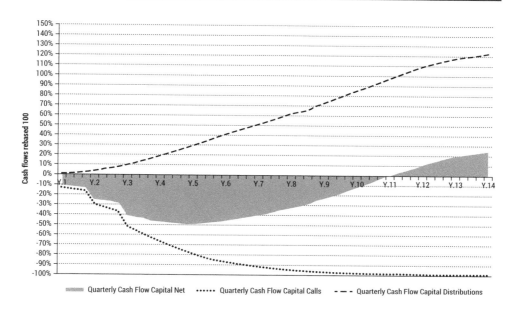

FIGURE 5.9 Market-neutral portfolio (0 percent risk-free rate, reference year: 2003, 3-year deployment, 50 percent secondaries, 15 percent discount on NAV)
Source: Authors.

at a 15 percent discount reduces, not surprisingly, the capital put to work. The discount also marginally improves the performance of the program for a given exposure to secondaries. Figure 5.9 illustrates the small difference with an exposure at 50 percent and a discount of 15 percent on NAV.

If fund stakes are acquired at a premium, returns fall significantly when compared to a purely primary program. Figure 5.9 illustrates the small difference with an exposure at 50 percent and a premium of 15 percent on NAV. Not surprisingly, the capital effectively put to use increases, but the returns are overall lower than when investing at a zero percent premium/discount or at a 15 percent discount.

Table 5.13 shows that secondaries are of no help when an investor tries to mitigate the impact of negative interest rates. The profile of the cash-flow curves is identical, so the returns are just proportionally lower due to the effect of negative interest rates.

It could theoretically be possible to combine the use of secondaries and overcommitment. However, this construct reaches a practical limit: in reality it is not possible to replicate exactly the primary exposure that fund investors target on the secondary market. The latter provides fund stakes that can only be acquired opportunistically.

The case for including secondary investments in a private market program relies on their use opportunistically, to acquire high-quality fund stakes at an attractive discount and support the matching of the bottom-up and the top-down approaches.

5.1.9 Setting Up and Assessing a Defensive Portfolio

We run a "defensive portfolio" by allocating 18 percent of the capital to equity strategies, 34 percent to debt strategies, and 48 percent to real asset strategies. In effect, we reduce

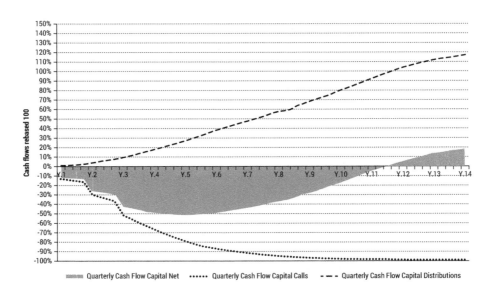

Quarterly Cash Flow Capital Net   Quarterly Cash Flow Capital Calls   Quarterly Cash Flow Capital Distributions

FIGURE 5.10 Market-neutral portfolio (0 percent risk-free rate, reference year: 2003, 3-year deployment, 50 percent secondaries, 15 percent premium on NAV)
Source: Authors.

TABLE 5.13 Use of secondary investments and resulting complete annualized return (with negative interest rates)

Input

	North America	Europe	Rest of the World
Venture capital	12%	2%	3%
Growth Capital	6%		5%
Leveraged buyout	36%	16%	3%
Mezzanine financing	9%		
Real estate value-added	8%		
Risk-free rate	−0.75%		
Year of reference	2003		
Program deployment	3 years		
Output: compl. ann. ret. (max. net exp., multiple of comm. cap.)			
Pricing	0%	−15%	+15%
Exposure to secondaries			
0%	4.33% (50.92%, 1.49×)	4.33% (50.92%, 1.49×)	4.33% (50.92%, 1.49×)
10%	3.65% (50.23%, 1.38×)	3.71% (49.90%, 1.39×)	3.60% (50.53%, 1.37×)
20%	3.23% (49.71%, 1.34×)	3.35% (49.07%, 1.35×)	3.13% (50.29%, 1.33×)
30%	2.66% (49.40%, 1.31×)	2.83% (48.57%, 1.33×)	2.51% (50.14%, 1.29×)
40%	2.36% (49.95%, 1.27×)	2.58% (48.84%, 1.30×)	2.15% (50.94%, 1.25×)
50%	1.98% (50.50%, 1.24×)	2.33% (49.12%, 1.27×)	1.72% (51.73%, 1.21×)

Source: Authors.

the equity exposure by two-thirds, double the debt exposure and the real asset exposure. The year of reference remains 2003 (Table 5.14).

The performance of this portfolio is lower when compared with a market-neutral portfolio, whether time-sensitive returns or cash-on-cash. The complete annualized return also drops significantly, by about a third. The maximum exposure is reached slightly faster, but the break-even point of the program is postponed by two to three quarters.

5.1.10 Setting Up and Assessing an Aggressive Portfolio

We then run an "aggressive portfolio" by allocating 82 percent of the capital to equity strategies, 8 percent to debt strategies, and 10 percent to real asset strategies. The equity exposure increases by 45 percent, and the debt and real asset exposures are halved. We keep 2003 as the year of reference (Table 5.15).

As expected, the time-sensitive returns and cash-on-cash performance of this portfolio are higher than the market-neutral ones. The IRR increases from 7–8 percent to 8.5–10 percent, and the multiple of invested capital from 1.35–1.4× to 1.45–1.5×. The complete annualized return also increases significantly from 3.36–3.56 percent to 4.03–4.48 percent. The maximum exposure increases slightly, and the break-even point of the program is reached faster.

TABLE 5.14   "Defensive" portfolio: dimensions of investment and output

Input

	North America	Europe	Rest of the World	Global
Venture capital	3%	0%	0%	
Growth capital	1%	1%	1%	
Leveraged buyout	8%	4%	0%	
Mezzanine financing	28%			
Distressed debt	6%			
Real estate opportunistic	10%	8%	8%	
Real estate value-added	5%	4%		
Private equity energy	5%			
Timberland				2%
Infrastructure				6%
Year of reference	2003			
Risk-free rate	0%			
Pace of deployment **Output**	3 years	5 years	7 years	
IRR	4.42%	3.61%	4.20%	
TVPI	1.25×	1.21×	1.24×	
DPI	1.19×	1.16×	1.18×	
Multiple of committed capital	1.19×	1.15×	1.17×	
Complete annualized return	1.90%	1.64%	1.96%	
Maximum exposure	−50.85% (Q 20)	−48.67% (Q 26)	−44.68% (Q 31)	
Break-even point	Q 45	Q 51	Q 53	

Source: Authors.

TABLE 5.15   "Aggressive" portfolio: dimensions of investment and output

Input

	North America	Europe	Rest of the World	Global
Venture capital	3%	0%	0%	
Growth capital	1%	1%	1%	
Leveraged buyout	8%	4%	0%	
Mezzanine financing	28%			
Distressed debt	6%			
Real estate opportunistic	10%	8%	8%	
Real estate value-added	5%	4%		
Private equity energy	5%			
Timberland				2%
Infrastructure				6%
Year of reference	2003			
Risk-free rate	0%			
Pace of deployment **Output**	3 years	5 years	7 years	
IRR	9.83%	8.67%	8.91%	
TVPI	1.56×	1.51×	1.52×	
DPI	1.49×	1.43×	1.45×	
Multiple of committed capital	1.49×	1.45×	1.45×	
Complete annualized return	4.48%	4.31%	4.03%	
Maximum exposure	−51.68% (Q 20)	−46.16% (Q 27)	−42.98% (Q 31)	
Break-even point	Q 39	Q 46	Q 49	

Source: Authors.

Unlike the defensive portfolio, the aggressive one is closer to the market-neutral one. This is because the market-neutral portfolio has a strong tilt toward private equity, as mentioned above. This notably explains why the maximum exposure is reached in the same quarter for the market-neutral portfolio and the aggressive one.

5.2   CONTROLLING AND ADJUSTING

Once the top-down approach has been used to set up a target allocation, fund investors have to apply the bottom-up approach. The latter is not only the application of the asset allocation but also a feedback loop that informs adjustments to the asset allocation (see Fig. 5.2 above). In their bottom-up approach, fund investors face three types of tasks: select fund managers, operationally manage their commitments to funds, and adjust their program if and when needed.

5.2.1   Selecting Fund Managers: Intrinsic, Comparative, and Extended Analyses

First, investors need to **effectively select fund managers**. This task consumes a lot of resources. According to Preqin, there were 2296 PE funds marketed in 2018. Investors screen 145 funds each year on average, of which 15 are selected for a second-round screening and four are selected for an investment. Fund sourcing is a mix of internal sourcing and direct external approach (73 percent). Twenty-one percent of investors do internal sourcing only, and 6 percent rely on a direct external approach only.

The analysis of fund investors consists in a wide array of analyses summed up as "performing a due diligence." The intensity and the extent of this effort depend on the resources and experience of fund investors. A due diligence is generally composed of an intrinsic analysis that capitalizes on the information provided by fund managers, a comparative analysis based on data provided by external specialists or accumulated over time by fund investors, and an extended due diligence thanks to the patient and systematic collection of market intelligence.

Intrinsic Analysis

Investors usually apply a self-made analytical grid to sets of qualitative and quantitative data about fund managers raising new funds. Investors analyze the investment thesis of fund managers, assess their investment sourcing capacity, and understand the origin of their past performance, their ability to replicate it or to adjust to new market conditions, and ultimately the ability of the managers to deliver on their promises. In this effort, investors will try to identify sources of risks and challenge managers on the way they mitigate them.

The track record focuses a lot of attention. The lack thereof was cited in 62 percent of the cases of rejection, while unfavorable fund terms were mentioned in 56 percent of the cases and a below-average team track record 52 percent of the time.

Each fund manager provides data in a specific format, although investors often issue due diligence questionnaires and ask managers to fill them in. The purpose is to feed the analytical grid referred to above and to be able to analyze systematically the information.

Investors also apply a bespoke approach, but their due diligence questionnaires and analyses ultimately share a lot of common questions and concerns. Some investors, such as funds of funds managers and consultants, can be more sophisticated and enter much more into the details of the analyses.

Additionally, reference calls are made with managers of portfolio companies (past and present), business partners, co-investors, former employees, and the overall ecosystem of the fund manager.

Depending on the nature of and the constraints applicable to a given investor, the focus on the analysis can shift. Some investors might be particularly keen on deploying capital fast, while others might be concerned by the time to liquidity, for example. As these preoccupations diverge, the questions asked and the interpretation of the answers will lead investors to decide whether or not to commit to the fund.

This analytical challenge is compounded when investors have to analyze emerging fund managers or existing managers launching new investment strategies, as there is limited or no quantitative information available. In that case, reference checks and deeper analyses are required, and a specific expertise has to be developed by investors for that matter.

Comparative Analysis

This intrinsic analysis is supplemented with a comparative analysis. Fund managers are benchmarked by fund investors. This is an equally difficult task as there is a recurring lack of information about private markets and fund managers. Even performance figures provided by independent data providers reflect at best 10 to 15 percent of the fund investment universe.

Long-standing and meticulous fund investors would have collected a significant pool of data they can tap. As fund managers contact them to raise the next generation of funds, there is an opportunity to collect data. However, this opportunity is a window that opens (if at all) when fund managers need to raise new capital. Fund investors are therefore constrained and limited in their ability to benchmark fund managers.

Another limit lies in the fact that fund managers are not necessarily comparable. Some have an industry expertise that their competitors do not have, such as LBOs on technology companies. Others engage in specific value-creation techniques, such as carving out corporations or building them up. These specificities imply specific risks and return potential, as well as differentiated time-to-liquidity patterns. They might simply not provide any ground for benchmarking.

Extended Due Diligence

The due diligence that investors operate on managers implies going beyond the limits of the pre-packed and polished information provided by fund managers (and, somehow, data providers). Managers control fund information, and there is little independent input to cross-check this information.

To perform a comprehensive analysis and generate valuable information, investors have to gather so-called gray information, that is, elements that are not public but are not confidential either. Indeed, the most seasoned fund investors gather a lot of informal market intelligence, to counterbalance the asymmetries of information, which benefit fund managers. This extended due diligence is possible thanks to the ongoing gathering of market intelligence. Investors go to conferences, annual general meetings, and other types of events. Networking and discussions lead to exchanges of views and information but also rumors that can be material and helpful to make informed decisions on whether to invest with a fund manager.

Fund investors also have to survey various sources, ranging from the executives of the assets fund managers invested in, competitors of these managers, former employees, and service providers to fellow current or prospective fund investors. Some forums, such as the International Limited Partners Association (ILPA), encourage the exchange of views and information.

One of the main challenges that fund investors encounter is the confidentiality that surrounds private markets and to which they have to strictly adhere, as they routinely sign confidentiality agreements when examining new commitments or when handling existing ones.

5.2.2   Operationally Manage the Commitments to Funds

The second task that fund investors have to handle is **the operational management of their commitments to funds**[1]. The involves the recurring analysis of the quarterly reports and the frequent meetings with fund managers but also the analysis of the deployment of capital, type of investments done, and other parameters as fund managers execute their mandates, provide fund investors with a deeper understanding of specific fund managers, but also their sectors and the overall asset class.

This knowledge is useful as it helps investors control their program, steer, and adjust it. Although the options are limited once fund investors have invested (Chapter 3), there is still some room for action. Investors can engage with fund managers to understand and possibly suggest some course of action ("voice," Demaria, 2015). They can then act, possibly buying or selling ("exit," Demaria, 2015) fund stakes on the secondary market. As mentioned above, the secondary market can be seen as an opportunistic tool to adjust the course of a program. Fund investors can use their accumulated knowledge to shift the operational course of their program to match it with their targeted allocation.

Disappointed investors can simply not commit again ("re-up") to the next generation of fund raised by the managers (which is a softer form of "exit"). One of the consequences of this exit is that investors have to find a new manager as a replacement. Assuming that this is not possible, or that funds do not include new investors, investors are facing the choice of sticking with the current manager ("loyalty," Demaria, 2015) in order to apply their asset allocation or to revise their allocation, thus challenging their top-down approach.

Therefore, at times, investors can invest in a series of two to three successive funds to provide managers with the time to apply their investment strategy and correct course if the developments are not satisfactory. Though some investors act fast and cut their relationships early, a large majority of investors tend to stick to their bottom-up analysis for some time. The alternative is to accept that the resources invested to select the disappointing manager did not bear fruit and that this effort has to be renewed with uncertain results. Fund investors often would rather know (and try to circumvent) the evil they face than simply roll the dice another time.

5.2.3   Adjust Their Programs If and When Needed

The operational management of investments can also help investors to **adjust their program**. As political and economic events unfold, investors adjust their expectations in terms of risks, returns, and liquidity. These adjustments also lead to changes in terms of allocations to private markets.

---

[1] Other operational duties include processing capital calls and distributions, cross-checking data, reporting, etc.

However, these changes have to capitalize on the accumulated knowledge of investors, witnessing directly the effect of events on their funds. This might lead them to counterintuitive decisions as fund managers adapt their behavior. For example, unless regulatory or governance rules force the investor to act otherwise, it might make sense to increase the exposure to private markets funds in the case of a downturn such as 2008, for multiple reasons.

First, investors selling on the secondary market might be forced to sell high-quality fund stakes and accept a higher discount. By being opportunistic, an investor might be able to significantly increase the performance of his portfolio, while reducing the time to liquidity and some of the risks associated with the program.

Second, fund managers will greatly benefit from a crisis environment as the price of assets will decrease. Competition from strategic and other investors will decrease. Moreover, new assets will be offered for sale as owners feel the pinch of the crisis unfolding and need capital to handle the consequences.

Third, fund managers are well equipped to weather crises (Chapter 3). Their companies usually fare better than the competition in a downturn, given the expertise provided by managers but also the additional capital that they can provide to their assets.

Thus, the bottom-up approach can usefully complement a more theoretical top-down one. The latter often assumes that investment strategies will evolve in a particular direction given specific macroeconomic and political events. However, each crisis is unique and has differentiated consequences on assets. Gathering factual data from the bottom-up perspective can challenge the assumptions of the top-down approach and the scenarios drawn as its output.

For example, in 2008 a sensible approach would have been to avoid fire-selling private market funds. Listed assets saw their valuations vary dramatically over a short period of time, while private market funds reacted with a significant delay and only partially reflected the variations of listed assets. Although at the time it was particularly difficult to assess how the crisis would unfold and the consequences of the liquidity squeeze affecting some parts of the market, the experience shows that private market funds remained a sound investment. The safest course of action was to set brackets for asset allocations until valuations settled down. It also showed the importance of setting up cash reserves at all times, although they might be expensive in terms of performance lag.

5.3   PORTFOLIO CONSTRUCTION: THE CONVERGENCE OF TOP-DOWN AND BOTTOM-UP APPROACHES

Top-down approaches are specific to each investor and confidential. It is difficult to illustrate this process in that context. Even the resulting portfolio is often elusive (Table 5.16) and difficult to comment on, as there is no indication of how this decision was made. Indeed, the information is often limited to the percentage of total assets under management allocated to PE and the deployment of capital over a year.

The process of portfolio construction often starts with a "house view" of the current macroeconomic situation, at times broken down by regions. Table 5.17 provides a simplified version of a snapshot done in 2014 as an example. This house view is useful

TABLE 5.16 Example of allocation to private equity by large pension funds, as of 2013

Pension	Country	Total invested over a year (% of assets under management)	Primary	Secondaries & co-inv.	Advisor
CPPIB	Canada	3.99 (17.8 %)	3.2 (80.2%)	0.79 (19.8%)	Internal team
CalPERS	USA	3.3 (12.4%)	NC	NC (managed funds)	Grove Street (PE) State Street (Cust.)
WSIB	USA	3.23 (17.5%)	NC	NC (managed funds)	Hamilton Lane (PE) State Street (Cust.)
PSERS	USA	3.17 (21%, planned to go down to 16% over the next 10 years)	NC	NC	Portfolio Advis. (PM) BNY Mellon (Cust.)
TRS Texas	USA	3.14 (12.3%)	NC	NC	Hamilton Lane (PE) State Street (Cust.)
NYCERS	USA	2.1 (6.1%)	NC	NC	Muller & Monroe AM
Florida SBA	USA	2.07 (5%)	NC	NC	Hamilton Lane (PE)
CalSTRS	USA	1.85 (11.5%)	NC	NC	Invesco B. Of A. (Cust.)

Note: All figures are in billions of dollars. "Cust." refers to custodian.
Source: Authors, based on website of institutions and secondary sources, 2013.

TABLE 5.17 Example of "house view" on macroeconomic cycles, as of 2014

	2014	2015	2016	2017	2018	2019
USA	Peak/Crisis	Crisis/Recovery	Recovery	Growth	Peak	Crisis
EU	"Growth"	"Peak"	Crisis	Recovery	Growth	Peak
APAC	Slow-down	Crisis	Restructuring	Recovery	Growth	Peak
MENA	Restructuring	Restructuring	Recovery	"Growth"	"Growth"	Crisis
LatAm	Peak/Crisis	Restructuring	Recovery	Growth	Peak	Crisis

Source: Authors, for illustration purposes, 2014.

in the sense that it provides a base case scenario, in which specific investment strategies will perform better than others.

For example, the vintage years of venture capital funds associated with economic growth and peak phases tend to perform well. For LBO funds, especially large and mega funds, it is recovery time, while small and mid-size funds are more resilient and appear as an "all weather" type of investment. The best vintage years for distressed debt and turn-around funds are associated with crises as companies of good quality are affected by adverse events and can be acquired fairly cheaply.

The translation in a top-down approach (simplified in Table 5.18) is expressed in the intensity of the investment (here ranging from minus to double plus) and the type of fund manager who should be looked for. As mentioned before, **it is not a matter of timing the market but trying to put more emphasis on the teams that would thrive in the expected environment**. For example, venture capital in the rest of the world at peak time would be opportunistic: an exceptional team would still justify the selection or a high-quality fund sold on the secondary market at a significant discount.

The next step is matching the results of bottom-up scouting (Table 5.19, with names provided for illustration purposes only). The planning is possible as fund managers communicate on their expected fundraising efforts. The choice of the strategy for

TABLE 5.18 Example of simplified top-down approach, as of 2014

	Venture Capital	Growth Capital	LBO-Mezzanine	Special Situations
USA	+ *Top team only*	++ *Limited risk* *Stable teams*	++ *Small to large* *Expert/niche teams*	+ *Opportunistic* *Strong expertise*
EU	= *Opportunistic* *secondaries* *Top team only*	+ *Select markets* *Top teams only*	++ *Small and mid* *Select markets*	++ *Top teams* *Strong expertise*
ROW	− *Opportunistic* *secondaries* *only*	+ *Select markets* *Top teams only*	= *Opportunistic* *Secondaries*	+ *Opportunistic* *Secondaries*

Source: Authors, for illustration purposes, 2014.

TABLE 5.19 Simplified combination of top-down and bottom-up approaches, as of 2014

	2014	2015	2016	2017
USA	*VC*	*Growth-BO*	*LBO*	*Distressed*
	Ex: Sequoia/KPCB	*Ex: TA Ventures*	*Ex: Bain Capital*	*Ex: Sun Capital*
EU	*Distressed*	*VC*	*Growth*	*LBO*
	Ex: Endless	*Ex: Index Ventures*	*Ex: Axa Cap. Dev.*	*Ex:*
				InverstIndustrial
APAC	*Distressed A-NZ-J*	*VC SK-JA_NZ*	*Pre-IPO*	*Opportunistic*
	PIPE CN	*Growth CN-Frontier*	*CN-Frontier*	*secondaries*
LatAm	*VC - Growth*	*VC - Growth*	*Opportunistic*	
	Ex: Advent	*Ex: Advent*	*secondaries*	

Note: 'A-NZ-J' refers to Australia-New Zealand-Japan. 'CN' refers to China. 'SK' refers to 'South Korea'. 'LatAm' refers to Latin America. 'APAC' refers to Asia-Pacific. Axa Private Equity is now known as Ardian. *Source:* Authors, for illustration purpose, 2014.

emphasis and the illustrative names should guide the executives of the investor in their screening of the market. If the team is not raising, or the fund is oversubscribed, the idea is to look for the direct competitors and try to invest in their funds. A very favorable environment might also help investors test an emerging strategy or fund manager.

As illustrated in Table 5.19, at times (2017 for Latin America, for example), there is no obvious strategy to address the phase of the cycle expected to strike the geographical area. The deployment would then purely be market neutral (see above). In other cases (APAC, for example), there would be teams corresponding to the strategy and the geographical regions, but the names were not known at the time of the construction of the table. The team of the investor would then have to start to survey the market to see if there is any corresponding match.

5.3.1 Preliminary Questions

Fund investors have to assess honestly and lucidly their **experience** when it comes to invest in private markets. It is easy to overestimate it, especially since the asset class is usually wrongly perceived as an "illiquid extension" of listed equity and bond markets. Experience is measured by the time spent in the asset class and the amounts invested. These are the criteria applied by fund managers when selecting fund investors (Chapter 3). An experience that spans less than five years is essentially irrelevant. Investors with ten or more years of experience can start to be perceived as knowledgeable. This implies that they have in effect deployed at least 500 million or more during this period of time.

The second question that fund investors have to solve is **their expectations in terms of returns, risks, and time to liquidity**. We refer to prior developments on these questions. Fund investors often struggle to set clear targets to each dimension and to document them carefully. As a result, these targets become contingent to other factors that are unclear and can lead to suboptimal or even irrational decisions.

The third question is the **resources available to set up and manage the program**. Fund investors underestimate the time and financial and human resources necessary to do so. Due diligence captures the mind, but managing a program is an ongoing effort spanning more than a decade and is also expensive. This includes validating capital calls and distributions, tracking valuations and the evolution of funds, regularly meeting with fund managers, going to annual general meetings, going to industry events, gathering gray information (see above), generating new contacts to canvass the market and updating the bottom-up approach, reporting internally, dealing with difficult situations in funds, and handling relationships with auditors, custodians, risk management officers, and the back office in general.

The fourth question for investors is assessing their **internal political constraints**. Despite setting specific return, risk, and time-to-liquidity targets, additional dimensions could influence the construction of the portfolio. One of them is criteria for investing sustainably, by excluding specific countries, industries, or investment strategies. Another is the involvement of specific executives with a differentiated agenda, which might steer the portfolio in directions to satisfy this agenda.

The last question is the **clear identification of pain and pressure points**. Is there an issue with fees and costs that the investor might have to report on? If so, portfolio construction will have to include this as a variable, maybe by negotiating with managers that fees should be computed and reported in a specific way to satisfy the requirements of the investor. Another classic example is that some American pension funds are not supposed to generate unrelated business taxable income (UBTI) to retain their tax-exempt status. They routinely negotiate side letters to the fund regulations to make sure that fund managers actively prevent any issue on this specific topic.

5.3.2 What Tickles Fund Investors?

Fund investors have to systematically make choices in terms of cash management (over-commitment or not), in the use of secondary investments (or not), the frequency of portfolio rebalancing, and the level of reporting and monitoring that they apply to their private market programs.

What Investors Like

Fund investors would generally say that their bottom-up approach requires them to be given **enough time** to analyze deal flow and that managers should provide them with a **clear timeline**. The right balance is difficult to strike. Too much time means that managers fall in the list of priorities, too little means that they have an incentive to decline immediately.

Fund investors also appreciate **consistency in the strategy** and **stability of the team of the fund manager**. They need a **clear differentiation** of fund managers so that they can position fund managers within their bottom-up universe. The questions usually are, "Why this strategy, why now, and why with you?"

Given the importance of the track record in their assessment, fund investors expect a **clear and complete communication on the performance and activity metrics of managers**, that is, net figures (and often also the gross to compute the fee charges), benchmarks, and breakdown by asset, by partner in charge, by exit scenario, and so forth. As explained in Chapter 3, performance figures are combining IRR and TVPI but also increasingly PME.

Fund investors also **appreciate standard structures and terms**, which might prove to be in conflict with the pressure toward lower costs and fees. Indeed, the most popular jurisdictions, notably onshore in the EU, have recorded a significant inflation of fund structuring and operational costs. Investors nevertheless routinely expect special treatments and therefore still require side letters and other supplementary documents.

Some fund investors perceive the **brand** developed by fund managers as a form of insurance against bad surprises. This comes at a cost, as fees and other terms are less negotiable, and it is far from being a silver bullet against any mismanagement by private market fund managers, as the long list of fines issued to them by the Securities and Exchange Commission (Demaria, 2020, Chapter 7) has illustrated.

Additional benefits that fund investors might expect are some form of education by managers, as well as information, market intelligence, or co-investment and secondary investment opportunities, among other non-financial outcomes.

What Investors Do Not Like

In general, fund investors are **reluctant to be among the first ones to invest in a fund**. The reputational concern is that they might have chosen "the wrong one" or that the manager might not be able to collect the total fund size and therefore that the investment strategy will only be partially applied. Fund managers often address the issue by identifying a fund investor accepting to be a sponsor (providing a branding and operational support to the fund managers) or an anchor (providing a significant amount to the fund).

Fund investors also usually **avoid the unknown, sources of unforeseen developments, and any form of surprise**. Their main concern is usually to identify and carefully mitigate risks, since they have little or no say in the management of the funds that they invest in.

They also try to **avoid investment niches that are too narrow**, as this might lead to an overcrowded market, inflated valuations, or a lack of partners to syndicate investments.

They **carefully avoid markets characterized by a lack of information**. They also tend to avoid fund managers with returns that are perceived as too volatile and/or even too high. High unexpected returns might signal higher risks than expected or that managers were lucky and might not be able to replicate the performance going forward.

5.3.3 Setting Up a Program in Practice

The parameters to set up an investment program are fairly well known and documented.

Institutional Parameters

The **size of the institution and the growth of its assets under management** as well as its **ability to refinance itself (if necessary) on the markets** are the first defining parameters.

Constraints

Then, the constraints set the framework. The **maturity of the liabilities** and the **liquidity requirements** are two fundamental questions to address. This can exclude specific investment strategies. For example, infrastructure and timberland require investors to wait seven to eight years to get back the capital invested but might distribute interim streams of cash flow matching the liquidity requirement and the maturity of the liabilities of a pension fund.

Another constraint is the **tax status** of the investor. Some investment strategies might match the liabilities and liquidity requirement of investors, but the proceeds might be deemed taxable by the jurisdiction in which they are registered or the jurisdiction in which the investments are done (leading to withholding taxes). The investment strategy might ultimately not be attractive anymore due to the tax treatment. A clear example is investing in American real estate funds for specific non-US investors.

Other constraints can come from investment limitations in specific geographical areas or industrial sectors.

Expectations

Finally, the expectations in terms of returns (time-sensitive or not), level of acceptable risk and payout frequency and level will complement the list of parameters to set up an investment program.

Set up

A viable program also has to be designed from a bottom-up perspective. The minimum amount to invest in a given fund is set by the manager. For a small fund of $100 to $150 million, it would be a million, but often larger funds require $5 or even $10 million. To be considered as an important investor that the manager will listen to and often cater to specific needs, it is often necessary to commit five to ten percent of the fund size. Above this threshold, and up to 20 percent of the fund size (which is the maximum usually authorized by fund regulations), the investor might be able to get special rights such as a seat on the advisory board or co-investment rights.

The expenses are not only related to the due diligence (see above) but also cultivating the knowledge of the market, monitoring (whether insourced or outsourced), and the operational aspects of controlling, cash management, and so forth.

Funds of Funds

Fund investors can choose from various options, such as a turnkey program provided by a funds of funds manager. The management fees are of 0.5 to 0.8 percent per year on average, and the carried interest ranges from 5 to 10 percent. These structures are created for 13 years in general. The minimum to invest in such program is generally low and can start at one million for institutional investors. If investors commit a significant amount, they might benefit from special conditions.

Mandates

Mandates or segregated accounts can be set up for programs usually reaching a minimum of $35 to $50 million in size. The format is bespoke to the investor, and the management fees are usually lower. The consultant ("gatekeeper") operating the mandate or account can, however, take on additional roles such as controlling and reporting, thus pushing up the cost of the program. Mandates can be set up to advise the investor ("non-discretionary" mandate), who ultimately takes investment decisions, or to be fully acting in the name of the investor ("discretionary mandates"). Depending on the size and scope of the mandate, the management fees usually are 0.25 to 0.35 percent, and the carried interest (if any) is between 0 and 5 percent. For the large mandates, it can be a flat fee or budget, and a performance fee can be calculated above a specific benchmark.

Gatekeepers belong to essentially three categories: banks and asset managers (such as J.P. Morgan, BlackRock, UBS, and Pictet), funds of funds managers (such as Ardian, Partners Group, HarbourVest, and AlpInvest), and specialized consultants (such as StepStone, Hamilton Lane, Mercer, Portfolio Advisors, Grove Street, and Cambridge Associates). Investors usually choose them by issuing a request for proposal with specific criteria and questions. Once the first screening is done, a round of interviews is organized so that the candidates can present their credentials and the investment strategy. Often, investors choose two or more gatekeepers, with complementary mandates.

The selection criteria range from the geographical coverage, knowledge of the investment strategies, and ability to match the performance and risk targets to the costs and the type of service provided and the flexibility of the offering. The latter includes the sourcing of investments, the advice and expertise (including education), the negotiation capacities, the quality of the reporting, the aptitude for getting access to high quality primary and secondary opportunities, and additional services (structuring, cash management, hedging, etc.).

Structuring options range from pure advisory to full delegation. The advisory model means that the investor puts the investment on its balance sheet. It is a simple solution, with rather low external costs. However, the investor has to support the middle- and the back-office duties. The investor also has to make the investment decisions. At the other end of the delegation spectrum, the mandate or single account protects the investor in terms of reputation and liabilities but adds costs and reduces control from the investor. A mandate can alleviate the workload for the investor and facilitate a sale on the secondary market as the fund stakes are usually lodged in a specific structure.

In-House Programs

In-house programs require significant human resources. Investment offices can monitor on an ongoing basis 10 to 15 funds and analyze 5 to 10 investments per month at best. Fund investors meet their managers once or twice a year, attend annual general meetings, and report. They also execute due diligence, which takes from two to four months for primary investments (secondary investments take two to three weeks). Expenses include traveling, database (such as Cambridge Associates) and information (such as Preqin) access, specific software subscription (such as eFront), training, conference attendance, as well as legal and tax advice, and middle- and back-office services.

Application

A defined benefit pension fund managing $15 billion of assets decides to allocate five percent to PE only. The program of $750 million will be invested with commitments of $20 million per fund over seven years. This implies the selection of five to six fund managers per year. The pension fund, which lacks experience and know-how, decides to focus on developed markets and LBO and growth capital. The annual commitments would be of roughly $150 million per year and the program should be cash-flow positive after ten years. The initial capital is committed after nine years.

In the case of a funds of funds program, the cost would be $2.5 to $4 million per year over 13 years, that is, a total of $30 to $50 million overall, plus a carried interest of 5 to 10 percent (if any). A discretionary mandate would cost $15 to $20 million over 13 years, plus performance fee (if needed), but there will also be custody fees (0.05 to 0.1 percent of total assets per year) and other fees (audit and possibly reporting). A non-discretionary mandate would be cheaper ($10 to $15 million and no performance fee), but some fixed costs (such as an investment committee) would add up.

To further illustrate the challenges of portfolio construction, we focus on and discuss four questions that illustrate the top-down and bottom-up dynamics at the heart of portfolio construction. These are long-term trends that should remain topical for some time for readers interested in private markets and portfolio construction.

5.3.4   What Is the Right Number of Fund Manager Relationships?

In the example above, the pension fund manager decided to be a significant investor in future funds in its portfolio. This in return defined the number of fund manager relationships.

Large institutional investors, such as the one in our example, have an advantage in the sense that they can commit larger amounts and therefore get access to these large funds. Indeed, there is a direct correlation between fund sizes and investment sizes. If a mega LBO fund operates investments of $1 billion and does 15 deals, the fund size should be of $20 billion (including management and other fees to be paid). This conditions the ticket size for prospective fund investors, as it will be difficult for the fund manager to accommodate commitments of $1, $5, or even $10 million.

However, this opportunity has its own drawbacks, such as reduced diversification and a higher exposure to selection and reputational risks. In fact, it can be challenging to find the right number of relationships, as this is a compromise. A higher number diversifies the selection risk but could also lead to a dilution of returns. It could also increase the selection and monitoring costs.

The Pros and Cons of a Higher Number of Fund Manager Relationships

Building a large roster of fund manager relationships can be beneficial, as investors could fine-tune their portfolio, select the best managers in each of the segments they target, and identify the right team for their need. Moreover, if a fund manager fails to match expectations, the investor can always reallocate some of the capital to other managers while scouting for a replacement. Smaller fund managers are also usually more receptive to investors' requests.

Nevertheless, their fixed costs constrain their aptitude to decrease management fees. An increased number of relationships might lead to a dilution of returns, and the costs of selection and monitoring increase substantially.

This approach could match investors with superior selection skills, able to scout niches willing to execute a fairly granular portfolio construction.

The Pros and Cons of a Smaller Number of Fund Manager Relationships

It is tempting to reduce the number of relationships by investing with multiple teams placed under the same umbrella brand (a kind of one-stop shop). As the fund manager would collect more capital from the same investor, it could be possible to negotiate costs (maybe through a mandate covering multiple strategies). The brand provides the investor with some form of validation, although this could disappear fairly quickly (Demaria, 2020, Chapter 7).

The drawback of this approach is that fund managers are not usually the best at every single strategy they host. They create their reputation with series of flagship funds and then attract emerging managers willing to capitalize on the brand to mutualize marketing and middle- and back-office costs. Worse, some fund managers exercise at times some arm-twisting on their fund investors, granting access to the flagship fund if investors commit to the other strategies on offer. The cost savings associated with a one-stop shop might also be rather small and essentially cosmetic, especially considering that strong brands usually command higher fees than average. Finally, established brands could over time lead their teams to adopt a more conservative approach toward risks. This, in return, leads to potentially lower returns.

This approach is more adapted to conservative and more risk averse investors. It is adapted to large investors, while smaller ones would need to pool their commitments through feeder funds (usually offered by asset managers, or wealth managers in the case of high net worth individuals) or funds of funds.

5.3.5 Will Private Equity Deliver Lower Returns Going Forward?

Regularly, the press and fund investors raise the prospect of potentially lower performance generated by managers going forward. If this happened, the logic would be that the risks associated with private market fund investing would also decrease, notably the dispersion of fund manager returns.

Two main sets of arguments are listed to support the thesis of lower future returns. First, the increasing maturity of private markets, which is a long-term trend. Second, the excess of capital available and the high valuation of assets, which is a more pressing concern as it is more current.

Lower Returns Due to an Increased Maturity of the Asset Class

Private markets are characterized by a recurring lack and significant asymmetries of information. However, over time as fund managers execute more investments, information is produced and communicated. In particular, buyers, sellers, and intermediaries learn from their private market counterparts. Some techniques, such as the use of financial leverage, become standard knowledge. Prices on private markets are also more readily known.

Likewise, fund investors gain knowledge as they analyze, invest, and monitor funds and fund managers. The increased number of transactions on the secondary market of fund stakes also contributes to the wider knowledge of fund investors.

Following this logic, private markets are becoming more efficient, and therefore, the performance related to the exploitation of market imperfections is expected to decrease. The question is how fast and by how much? There is no easy answer.

Private markets are not a solid block that is more or less transparent. They have to be seen as a continuum of different investment strategies and geographical regions. A clear example is large and mega LBOs in the US. The sector has collected vast amounts of capital as fund sizes have increased significantly. Observers have assumed that the overall sector of LBOs is overheating. This is not necessarily true.

First, LBO investments are not fungible: if large and mega LBOs collect more capital, this is not necessarily true for small and mid-size LBOs. Moreover, the capital collected for large transactions cannot be easily transferred in smaller deals, although fund managers can try to buy a series of marginally smaller assets and assemble them in so-called buy-and-build strategies. Thus, the contagion from one investment strategy to others is not warranted, and blanket statements such as "Private equity is overheating" are essentially wrong.

Second, LBO investing is essentially a local activity. If American fund managers collect significant amounts, they are expected to deploy them locally. European companies would be targeted by funds raised to specifically invest in them. The geographical contagion is thus more tenuous than generally thought and comes from fund investors willing to reallocate capital from one region to another as they struggle to deploy it.

Third, even large and mega American LBOs are not necessarily maturing as fast as the capital is collected. Only a handful of fund managers are able to collect vast sums. This means that even if the capital collected increases, the number of operators able to execute these large deals might not increase or could even have decreased (as the process of collecting $20 billion in 12 to 18 months is more challenging than collecting a tenth of it, for example). The amount of capital raised is only one element to consider; the number of deals and the average capital deployed have to be taken into account as well.

Fourth, the investment universe itself changes. Managers of large and mega American LBO funds receive new investment opportunities from sellers who have grown accustomed to this type of buyer. Moreover, funds can sell companies to other funds in secondary, tertiary, and subsequent buyouts. The number of opportunities increases correspondingly. A crucial missing piece of information is thus the number of investment opportunities examined every year and the evolution over time.

Fifth, fund managers themselves evolve over time. As one strategy becomes more mature, some fund managers explore further by targeting new types of industries and assets and applying innovative strategies. The buy-and-build strategy is an example, but corporate carve-outs or technological LBOs can also serve as an illustration.

Some fund managers will stick to the original strategy and patiently build barriers to entry, for example, by building in-house consulting practices to improve the companies. Some fund managers provide the equivalent of headquarter services to their portfolio companies, ranging from centralized purchasing services and specialized human resource functions to access to dedicated industry experts. By developing such services, fund managers are able to compete with strategic buyers. The latter can count on the synergies they will create after a merger or an acquisition to amortize some of the price paid. Fund managers replicate some of these synergies with the centralized functions that they deploy across their portfolio.

Therefore, the maturity of large and mega US LBOs might lead to some reduction of performance as market imperfections are rarer, but the market dynamics might provide other sources of value creation that could compensate or even increase the performance going forward.

Lower Returns Due to Increased Capital Available and Higher Valuations

Preqin regularly releases its estimates of capital collected and yet to be invested by fund managers (the so-called dry powder). Each release triggers fears that the amounts collected might have detrimental effects on the market, leading to excesses and ultimately to lower returns. The essential reasoning is that if more capital is collected by fund managers who are buyers of assets, this will tip the balance of negotiations in favor of sellers. As a result, the price of these assets would durably increase, which in turn would lower the returns of funds. Usually, the average price of the acquisitions operated by fund managers is called in as a support to this reasoning, under the form of multiples of EBITDA.

Although this reasoning has some merits, it relies on multiple assumptions that are not clearly established. First, fund managers acquire companies to significantly change them and resell them at a profit. Although the price of companies can increase, notably because capital from fund managers and strategic investors is abundant, the translation into an inflation of valuations is not automatic. Some assets are sold because they underperform, are rudderless, or because they are not strategic anymore for the seller. Others are delisted because they languish on the stock exchange. It is not only the price but the potential for improvement that matters and justifies an acquisition. A typical example is a delisting by an LBO fund. Listed corporations are usually acquired at an average premium of 20 to 30 percent on the listed price, and fund managers still manage to generate performance.

Fund managers are only marginally "buying low and selling high." Although this could contribute to their performance, the core contribution is the transformation of companies. Moreover, a way to reduce the marginal price of an acquisition by a fund is to buy smaller and cheaper assets and combine them. This is one of the rationales of buy-and-build strategies.

Second, the investment universe is not constant. Corporations buy and sell subsidiaries and divisions at all times. They might hold on to them for a shorter time as well. As private market funds are interim holders of assets, what matters is not the number of opportunities per year but the frequency at which assets come back to the market. As funds sell to funds, this frequency tends to increase correspondingly.

It is therefore difficult to conclude that private equity returns, and namely large and mega US LBOs, are going to decline. Notably, US LBOs perform when investing during and after crises. Depending on the nature and the duration of these crises and the urge of sellers to dispose of assets, the performance of LBO funds might in fact increase for a certain period of time.

In that context, portfolio construction requires a significant analysis of market dynamics and a deep understanding of private markets. What appears clearly is that knowledge gained on listed markets is not applicable to private markets without a strict and detailed scrutiny and a healthy dose of caution.

SUMMARY

Throughout this chapter, we have pointed out that:

- **Portfolio construction** in private markets combines **two complementary approaches** and must comply with specific major rules:
  - **The top-down perspective**, which notably depends on macroeconomic analyses and supports the construction of investment portfolios based on multiple dimensions (geographical, investment strategies, asset sizes and maturity, and industrial exposures). In that respect, unless the investor has superior forecasting and selection skills, as well as an unprecedented ability to source fund investment opportunities, investors should:
    - **Not try to time the market.** Private equity and, along with it, private markets in general are highly cyclical. Investors should deploy capital regularly to mitigate the effect of economic and political events on their portfolios.
    - **Invest their program over a period of seven years**. This provides investors with the ability to deploy at least twice with the same manager and to be able to diversify carefully. If investors wish to reduce their portfolio ramp-up to less than five years, they could resort cautiously to **secondary investments.**
  - **The bottom-up perspective** is the result of canvassing the investment field to identify fund investment opportunities. When selecting fund managers, investors should:
    - **Focus on diversification**, by regularly investing every year in two funds (or more) fitting in a given category of investment. Indeed, allocating a significant amount to a specific fund is risky as there is no certainty that the performance will persist.
    - **Be careful with the use of overcommitment**, which can result in exceeding the contribution capacity of the investor. Moreover, this mechanism is de

facto forbidden by many regulations due to solvency costs increase. It can also amplify the drawbacks of the use of credit lines by fund managers.

■ Using a simplified top-down approach, we **set up a model** illustrating a **market-neutral investment program.** The main conclusions are the following:

■ The **level of the risk-free rate has much more impact on the overall performance of the program than the pace of deployment,** meaning that the opportunity cost of unused capital is a significant concern for fund investors, much more than the time to actually deploy capital.

■ The **longer the capital deployment is, the higher the minimum performance, the lower the maximum exposure, and crucially, the lower the dispersion of returns.** These results depend on the reference year during which the program is launched as a few sequences of years are particularly favorable to launch a program.

■ The **diversification introduced by a long capital deployment supersedes the link between performance and exposure.**

■ **Overcommitments boost returns**, the minimum achievable return is also higher, **and the variation of returns continues to be lower as the program is deployed over a longer time period**. If fund investors can overcommit without any constraint or additional regulatory cost, they should choose the 7-year time frame.

■ **If investors cannot overcommit** and if they have to bear negative interest rates, the weight of the uncalled capital can add a significant drag to the performance. The **use of secondary investments could be tempting**. In reality, replicating exactly the primary exposure that fund investors target with secondary investments is difficult. The case for including secondary investments in a private market program relies on their use opportunistically, to acquire high-quality fund stakes at an attractive discount and to support the matching of the bottom-up and the top-down approaches.

■ A **"defensive" portfolio** rather than a market-neutral one will prove to have a lower performance; an **"aggressive" portfolio** will be closer to the market-neutral one even if returns will be slightly better.

– Once the top-down approach has been used to set up a target allocation, fund investors apply the bottom-up approach by:

   Selecting fund managers through:

   ■ **Intrinsic due diligence**, an analytical grid to sets of qualitative and quantitative data about fund managers raising new funds.

   ■ **Comparative analysis**, as fund managers are benchmarked by investors.

   ■ **Extended due diligence**, thanks to the ongoing gathering of market intelligence. Investors gather gray information, which is not public but is not confidential either, and survey various sources.

   Operationally managing the commitment to funds. Fund investors gain a deeper understanding of specific fund managers, their sectors, and the overall asset class to control and adjust their programs.

- The bottom-up approach is essential. It challenges the top-down approach, which often assumes that investment strategies will evolve in a specific direction. Investors adjust their expectations in terms of risks, returns, and liquidity thanks to these insights. The top-down view evolves and results in a potential change in portfolio construction.
- Monitoring and controlling further feed the bottom-up filtering by providing high-quality information for due diligence on fund managers.

– **Finally, portfolio construction requires a significant self-analysis, as well as of market dynamics and a deep understanding of private markets:**

Before investing, fund investors need to consider their **experience** (ten years or more can start to be perceived as knowledgeable), their **expectations in terms of returns, risks and time to liquidity**, the **resources available** to set up and manage the program, their **internal political constraints**, and a clear identification of **pain and pressure points**.

In practice, to set up an investment program in private markets funds:

- **Some institutional parameters** are required: the size of the institution and the growth of its assets under management as well as its ability to refinance itself on the markets; the expectations will complement the parameters.
- **The constraints** set the framework: maturity of liabilities, liquidity requirements, tax status of the investor.

A viable program also has to be reconciled from a **bottom-up perspective**: the minimum amount required to invest in a fund is set by the manager.

- Sometimes, the **funds of funds** option is the most efficient, although this comes at a cost.
- **Mandates or segregated accounts** can be set up for programs reaching $35 to $50 million in size. Structuring options range from pure advisory to full delegation to the gatekeeper.
- **In-house programs** are an option but require significant human resources.

It can be challenging to find the right number of fund manager relationships: a large number can be beneficial as this diversifies the selection risk, but it also means a dilution of returns. A small number bears a higher selection risk but can fit the perspective of some investors.

The increasing maturity of private markets could give the impression **that managers will deliver lower returns going forward.** Explanations range from higher efficiency and reduced market imperfections to the excess of capital available, as well as high valuation of assets. However, the case remains to be built. It is, in fact, difficult to conclude that private equity returns and notably large and mega US LBOs are going to decline.

General Conclusion

Adding private markets to a classic asset allocation framework is challenging (see Introduction, Chapters 2 and 4). Investing in private markets (Chapter 3) implies adding complexity to the setup of investment programs, adding new dimensions. In fact, investors should reassess their liabilities (Chapter 1) and set targets in terms of liquidity horizon, risk thresholds, and return expectations (Introduction, Chapters 3 and 5).

It is possible to tiptoe around such an arduous task. The incentive is high, given the significant amount of resources investors put in the current standard: the Capital Asset Pricing Model (CAPM), derived notably from Markowitz's research (1952) and its application in multiple variations. Countless product and service providers have a vested interest in propagating, reusing, and refining it—but not to change it or ditch it altogether. The scale of the endeavor that breaking away from the CAPM represents could deter investors.

Breaking up with this standard mold also requires courage. As Keynes (1936) wrote, "Worldly wisdom teaches that it is better for reputation to fail conventionally than to succeed unconventionally." This assertion is now true more than ever. However, the wedge is already in: Fama and French (2004) stated that "the failure of the CAPM in empirical tests implies that most applications of the model are invalid." As a consequence, adopting a less conventional approach is necessary, and including private markets in these new asset allocation frameworks is no longer a matter of if but how.

The clear challenge is that many instruments for this new asset allocation framework have yet to be designed. The conceptual field of asset allocation has to move away from a reference to listed assets to focus on investment durations. From there, it is necessary to rethink the measurement of risks and performance. These instruments have to apply to various asset classes without frictions. The PME (see Chapter 3) is an attempt to bridge the gap of performance measurement between the listed and private asset worlds. It could probably be significantly refined and improved. Better information from private market operators would also help significantly.

Investors should guard themselves against the temptation of reproducing existing investment strategies (Section 1). By importing an asset allocation designed by another institution, investors might think that they are spared the time, effort, resources, and agonizing process of rebuilding a strategy from scratch. This would be a mistake. Allocations are essentially a compromise between conflicting targets, either explicit (such as liquidity horizon, risks thresholds, and return expectations) or implicit (such as strategic and political goals; Section 2), as well as Environmental, Social, and Governance concerns (ESG; Section 3).

Likewise, the operational setup of investors has a very significant influence on their asset allocation (see the Introduction, of Demaria, 2015). The sensitivity of investors to fees and costs (Section 4) and their choice between internal operations or external advice (Section 5) both have an influence on their allocations.

1. THE RISK OF REPRODUCING INVESTMENT STRATEGIES

When leaving the reassuring shores of the CAPM-centered asset allocations, investors could be tempted to adopt a famous ready-made one. When it comes to significant allocations to private markets, the approach of the Yale University endowment (also referred to as the endowment model, although only Yale effectively applies it) is frequently mentioned (see Chapter 1 for more details). According to its annual report, as of June 2019 the endowment was allocating 15.9 percent of its capital to LBO, 21.1 to venture capital, 10.1 to real estate, and 4.9 to natural resources. The market value of the endowment that year reached $30.3 billion (from $16.3 billion ten years earlier), having increased by 11.5 percent in 2015, 3.4 in 2016, 33.2 in 2017, 33.1 in 2018, and 5.7 in 2019. The annual returns of the endowment have reached 11.1 percent over ten years.

At least five characteristics distinguish Yale's endowment: its long-standing presence in private markets, its infinite investment horizon, its tax-exempt status, its sheer size, and its significant yearly payout requirement ($1.5 billion). These characteristics are crucial in understanding how the current allocation of Yale was built and why it is impossible to replicate as such.

Its long-standing presence in private markets provides the Yale endowment with a crucial factor of success: an access to some of the best fund managers (showing a persistence of high performance; see Chapter 3). The reputation of Yale as a successful private market investor opens doors, as fund managers screen their investors (see Introduction of Demaria, 2015).

Moreover, Yale has accumulated expertise and know-how in investing in these markets, giving it an edge, as well as the connection to managers through its alumni network. This advantage is particularly difficult to replicate, as private market investors are competing to invest with these managers. In fact, historically the power of Yale was so high that it could negotiate investment terms, fostering alignment of interests. This was particularly true when it started to invest significantly in the asset class, when the latter was still a cottage industry. This is no longer the case. Very few private market investors are in the same situation as Yale, except long-standing funds of funds managers, some family offices, and a few financial institutions.

An important characteristic singles out the Yale endowment: it has an infinite investment horizon. The donations to the endowment should not be spent but invested. Yale is only allowed to use the proceeds from the investments of the endowment. This is a fairly unique situation only effectively shared by sovereign wealth funds (SWF). Even pension funds and family offices have to face some redemptions, the former to pay the pensions of their retirees, the latter to face life events (notably the succession) of their beneficiary owners.

Part of the success of Yale is also related to the fact that it is tax exempt. The lack of taxation plays a role in the strong progression of its assets under management, as well as its annual performance. This is difficult to replicate for multiple investors, except foundations and charities, some SWF (but not all), and pension funds.

The size of Yale also has a fundamental consequence on its operations: it has the resources to operate in less liquid markets. It can also require mandates, and possibly co-invest with funds, if it wishes to do so. Thanks to its size, no private market fund is out of reach, as the Yale endowment can match the minimum commitment to get in. Few financial institutions can do so.

Finally, the payout schedule of the endowment to Yale is also very specific. In 2019, 32.4 percent of the proceeds were spent by the University. This creates a specific constraint for Yale: a mandatory annual significant payout. Otherwise, the endowment is largely unconstrained: it has no solvency ratio to observe, no limitation on its freedom to invest, and no specific regulatory constraint to observe, other than a legal minimum yearly payout to keep its tax exempt status, expressed as a percentage of its proceeds.

The effective payout from the endowment to Yale is significant. It has forced Yale to cut its costs, delay some campus investments, and issue an emergency bond during the 2008 financial crisis, as its proceeds could not match its payout requirements.

Therefore, the constraints weighting on the endowment can be summed up as a recurring and fairly inflexible yearly payment of $1.5 billion. This is also quite unique, as most of the investors have to fulfil specific regulatory obligations and match specific liabilities. The current asset allocation of Yale's endowment is the direct result of the specific constraints weighting on it.

Investors inspired by it should analyze its evolution over time and see how it was adjusted as the university relied more on its endowment to finance its operations.

In general, replicating asset allocations from other institutions is not advisable. At best, existing examples can serve as thought experiments, cautionary tales, or illustrations of what is possible. Ultimately asset allocations should be tailored to the liabilities and needs of each investor. Smaller investors might struggle to achieve such an objective and resort to investment consultants, which have a vested interest in directing them in specific directions (see Section 5). Off-the-shelf asset allocations are routinely used as a support to match the investor's risk appetite. They are, then, fine-tuned as the investor expresses additional preferences to its consultant. Regardless of the fine-tuning, such approaches embed significant hidden risks: concentration and contagion.

As investors adopt similar asset allocations, they react in concert and contribute to the propagation of market movements. Investors have increasingly adopted passive instruments such as funds replicating indexes (exchange-traded funds, or ETFs) to invest on listed markets. By doing so, they have concentrated their investments in specific assets selected by index providers. When these indexes move, they affect investors using them, triggering movements that are amplified by investors using similar asset allocations. This can prove to be detrimental to investors, especially if their specific constraints such as a regular payout or a legal requirement are not properly factored in.

2. STRATEGIC AND POLITICAL GOALS

Asset allocations are the result of a view of the world. Investors assess the future using scenarios to which they assign probabilities. Based on these views, it is possible to steer the portfolio in a direction, which can be adjusted as events unfold. In that respect, asset allocations are political as they are the result of a vision.

Investors have multiple—sometimes conflicting—strategic and political goals. Some might want to push an agenda dedicated to complying with religious goals (Sharia-compliant, for example) or the equivalent in the matter of environmental and/or social concerns (ESG, see next section). Others, such as development finance institutions, might want to foster the development of emerging markets. Some governmental agencies may want to apply industrial policies, supporting specific industrial sectors in their rise or their restructuring. Some corporations might develop an asset allocation to provide them with a vantage point on some corners of the industry, such as in venture capital. Investing through venture capital funds could also give them a head start in acquiring strategic upstarts in their sector.

Strategic and political goals can be more or less explicitly formulated and can shift over time. As a result, asset allocations have to be carefully documented and regularly revised, notably as the views of the investor have changed. This can prove to be challenging when steering private market investments, as programs ramp up and decrease rather slowly (see Chapters 3, 4, and 5). Lerner (2012b) illustrates the challenges of financing innovation, for example, when financial and strategic ambitions collide. He has also shown (2012a) the result of political ambitions facing harsh financial realities, notably when nations attempt to replicate industrial clusters such as Silicon Valley.

Investors face hard legal and regulatory constraints on their activity. Political and strategic goals have to be ranked among the soft (self-directed) constraints. They are investor-specific, cannot be ignored, and have to be introduced into the mix of asset allocations. At times, the ultimate beneficiaries of the asset allocation, such as pensioners or students, can express the wish to skip some industries as a target of investment, such as gun manufacturing (Sicilia, 2018) or coal, oil, and gas (Stannard, 2017). To a certain extent, these wishes can influence asset allocations.

Therefore, asset allocations are multi-dimensional. Investors have to set a time horizon, thus applying a first filter and potentially eliminating some investments. Legal constraints, political targets, and other constraints have to be integrated next. They define the range of possible options. Only then can investors set their risk thresholds, through maximum drawdowns and value-at-risk approaches. This has to be done at the portfolio level. Multiple portfolios can be generated, with the associated performance expectations. This is when investors choose a risk-return mix over the other options.

3. ESG AND IMPACT INVESTING

Sustainable development concerns, which sum up some environmental, social, and ethical concerns from various parts of the civil society, have emerged during the 1970s and 1980s and have developed in the following decades. The expression was popularized by the report of the Bruntland Commission (1987) established for the United Nations, which famously stated that "sustainable development is development that meets the needs of the present without compromising the ability of future generations to meet their own needs."

To some extent, the Environmental, Social, and Governance (ESG) framework is synonymous with the original sustainable development. To apply this approach, investors have progressively defined applied ESG criteria to their strategy and asset allocation. The application tends to be bespoke, as illustrated by the large variety of concepts that have emerged around ESG.

Some investors apply a filtering approach, eliminating specific sectors from their asset allocation such as weapons and armament, or addiction-related industries (such as tobacco, alcohol, or gambling). Others promote "best in class" companies in any sector, ranking them according to specific metrics in matters of environmental, social, and/or governance topics, in a so-called triple bottom line[1] (people, planet, profit) or an "impact investing[2]" approach.

ESG is among some of the most preeminent political goals that investors have set for themselves over the course of the last decades. The challenge is to integrate these targets in asset allocation, for multiple reasons.

First, sustainability indexes underperform mainstream indexes and have a higher risk, a conclusion drawn in 2003 (Demaria) that still holds true today. The Dow Jones Sustainability World index grew at a compound annual rate of 0.38 percent from its inception in 1999 to 2019. Its maximum drawdown[3] over the same period of time is 42.4 percent. As a matter of comparison, for the Dow Jones Industrial Average, the figures are respectively 0.59 percent and 40.7 percent. In Europe, the STOXX Sustainability Index grew at a compound annual rate of 0.18 percent from its inception in 1998 to 2019. Its maximum drawdown is 47 percent. As a matter of comparison, the STOXX 600 figures were respectively 0.26 and 41 percent over the same period. In both instances, the mainstream index had a more robust performance and registered a lower risk.

Sustainability indexes have a narrower investment universe, limiting their diversification—and therefore increasing their risk. This risk could be compensated if investors could actively mitigate it through governance rights in which they could decide the strategy and enforce it. As passive instruments, sustainability indexes do not lead to such governance framework. They do not add specific value. There is thus no clear compensation for the additional risk associated with the use of sustainability indexes. This has to be acknowledged and documented in an asset allocation exercise, as a consequence of specific political targets.

Second, adding constraints to an asset allocation, such as reducing carbon emissions, has a direct, clear, and isolated cost for the investor. There is no systematic equivalent in terms of benefits, except possibly in measurable resource or emission savings as for environmental concerns. A common argument is that the diffuse ESG value (positive externalities) cannot be captured by indexes. This is not convincing.

Only a rigorous analysis from cradle to cradle[4] (McDonough and Braungart, 2002) provides the certainty that only necessary resources were used optimally to reach a

---

[1]In 1994, John Elkington referred to the triple bottom line as a framework in which the financial, social, and environmental performance of a given company or activity are evaluated and integrated in a "full cost" accounting exercise.

[2]This expression refers to investments made with the intention of generating a measurable, beneficial social and/or environmental impact alongside a financial performance.

[3]Measured from the start of the considered period.

[4]The cradle-to-cradle approach requires a holistic economic, industrial, and social framework that seeks to create systems that are efficient and waste free.

specific goal, the latter also being analyzed along these lines. This circular approach is the acid test of sustainability to investments, that is, the application of ESG criteria.

Third, if ESG targets are already difficult to formulate, and assessing their impact is challenging, applying ESG criteria to them is even more challenging. On the face of it, PE and ESG could be a match. The PE investment universe is larger than the stock exchange, as explained in Chapters 3 and 4. Comprehensive and detailed PE due diligence offers the opportunity to apply a full circular ESG analysis. LBO managers set up powerful governance frameworks to steer their investments. Jensen (1989, 1997) famously made the case for the superiority of the ownership by LBO funds. However, the LBO governance is ruthlessly efficient because of its unique aim: extracting cash flows from a business to refund the debt contracted to acquire it, a far cry from sustainability. Reconciling it with a cradle-to-cradle approach is challenging, to say the least.

As demonstrated by Demaria (2015, Chapter 1), even private market investors themselves put financial performance above other non-financial targets. The illustration comes from investors in PE funds focusing on businesses owned by ethnic, gender, and/or social minorities. When these funds did not match the return expectations of investors, then their support from investors was discontinued. Some of the managers effectively stopped investing in such businesses to back mainstream businesses.

With a few exceptions, such as with emissions and resource consumption, environmental and social performances are particularly hard to measure. Even filtering out undesirable sectors, which could appear as rather straightforward, is fairly difficult. For example, the hospitality industry, often a target of LBO investments, sells alcohol and falls foul of the anti-addiction criteria.

Even the VC industry, often presented as the poster child of ESG investing, struggles to qualify in a cradle-to-cradle approach. The recreational cannabis industry, which has recently been gathering significant VC investments, is connected to tobacco and addiction. Video games can embed some gambling features ("loot boxes," for example). The information technology (IT) industry, which gathered 43 percent of the capital allocated to VC funds since 2000, is itself related to military contracts. Drones, 3D printing, semiconductors, software, GPS, and telecommunication are dual-use technologies, with both civil and military applications.

Moreover, IT is not environmentally friendly, consuming staggering amounts of electricity and water and generating substantial quantities of carbon dioxide. The consequences of planned obsolescence, the environmental liabilities due to lack of recycling chains (for example in nanotechnologies) but also the detrimental social consequences of some innovative products and services (for example, the gig economy) are difficult to address from an asset allocation perspective.

Fourth, setting governance targets can also add up costs and potential risks for the investor. ESG requires extra work and thus increases the costs. This is not only true when it comes to choosing products but also in the operational set up of the investor. Setting an ESG program implies monitoring, controlling, and potentially sanctioning it. The governance set up to undertake these tasks, whether in-house or outsourced, will eventually lead to specific costs.

Setting ESG targets also adds some potential fiduciary risks for the investors who manage third-party capital. Under an ESG framework, financial returns will decrease to a certain extent. There is no free lunch: higher operational and governance costs alone will have consequences. Giving way to improved environmental and social performance will also have a negative impact on the financial performance and/or the risk supported by the investor. This could lead to a conflict with the mission given to institutional investors, such as pension fund managers: generating the best financial performance for a given level of risk, within the regulatory constraints applying to the investor. ESG is a voluntary effort and thus does not qualify as a regulatory constraint.

As an illustration, the largest American pension fund, CalPERS, has debated the idea of investing again in tobacco, after it stopped in 2001. According to Wilshire Associates, this decision cost $3.6 billion to CalPERS until June 2018, which is around 1 percent of its total asset value. Overall, all the divestments have cost the fund about $2.4 billion (Venteicher, 2019). As a consequence, the management of the fund was changed (Atkins, 2018). A $1.2 billion class action lawsuit was filed by the policyholders after CalPERS notified an 85 percent increase of their long-term insurance premium, as result of the overall performance shortfall of the fund.

4. TOTAL COST OF OWNERSHIP AND FEES

Chapter 3 details the fee and cost structure associated with investing in private market funds. This fee structure has regularly been criticized for multiple reasons.

First, the level of fees and costs is significant, representing a difference of 500 to 600 basis points (see Chapter 3) between gross and net IRR (with all the reservations attached to the use of the IRR as a measure of performance; see Chapter 3).

Second, the performance fee of fund managers appears as a pure option, with limited or no actual skin in the game. Fund managers are required to invest at least 1 percent of the fund size from their own resources, but this amount is easily recouped with the management fees that they receive. Even a commitment of 3 percent, which is the average observed by MJ Hudson at the time of writing, does not significantly dent the income of fund managers in case of bad fund performance. The fund manager can recoup this amount from management fees, which represent 15 to 20 percent of the fund size.

Despite an ongoing and long-term pressure from fund investors to lower the fees collected by managers, there have been limited adjustments. A fairly limited number of fund managers match the requirements of investors in terms of fund size, track record, and brand (see Chapters 3 and 4, and the Introduction of Demaria, 2015). This has sparked a wave of initiatives.

Large investors can set up investment mandates (Chapter 3), with a negotiated fee structure. This could reduce, to some extent, the cost of investing in private markets for these investors but triggers questions in terms of alignment of interest between the principal (investors) and the agents (fund managers). Moreover, the incentives of fund managers remain essentially unchanged, with a significant portion of their income derived from management fees and the performance fee being a pure option.

Other investors have tried to reduce their investment costs by co-investing with funds. This has also triggered questions about alignment of interests, anti-selection, and hidden direct costs and risks for co-investors (Chapter 3). The SEC has also stepped in to preserve the equality between investors, thus dampening the enthusiasm associated with co-investing.

In practice, these initiatives did not change the fundamental structure of fund fees (see Chapter 3). Taking the example of Swiss pension funds, the challenge for investors can be broken down into multiple elements.

First, there is a fee level issue. Swiss pension funds are benchmarked against each other, and the level of fees that they pay (the total expense ratio, or TER) is compared, regardless of their exposure to asset classes. A pension fund with a pure exposure to listed markets through passive instruments and therefore with low costs, is compared with a pension fund exposed to private market funds charging higher fees and thus with higher costs.

This reasoning has multiple consequences, notably because the costs are considered in isolation from the performance generated and from the risk taken. Moreover, indirect costs (such as spreads) are often not captured in the TER. As explained by Morkoetter and Wetzer (2016), the TER of the 81 participating Swiss pension funds is 0.58 percent (of which 75 percent are portfolio management costs). The average net stock return is 0.3 percent and net bond return is –0.1 percent. According to them the average investment costs in private equity is 5.8 percent. Gross returns are 12.1 percent, leading to net returns of 6.4 percent. Their conclusion is that "high costs are not necessarily a bad sign" and that "correlations between portfolio net returns and portfolio management costs are strongly positive."

Second, there is an operational issue. Besides the opportunity costs associated with the committed but uncalled capital (see Chapters 3, 4, and 5), the TER and its equivalents can be magnified when management fees are charged on the capital committed but the capital does not generate the associated returns. Some pension funds have addressed the issue by calculating an overall fee charge to be collected by fund managers and then paid progressively as the capital is deployed. The idea is not to reduce the TER but to maintain it as a proportion of the capital effectively put to work. This solution can partially bridge the gap of expectations between fund investors and managers.

5. DEALING WITH AGENTS, CONFLICTS OF INTEREST, AND NOISE

The last operational element that investors have to take into account is the agenda of their internal agents (employees and executives) and external agents (consultants and advisors). Demaria (2015, Introduction) explains that agents usually have a vested incentive to aim at a more conservative investment program than the actual investors constraints dictate. This is related to the nature of their interest: keep the relationship active. Lowering the risks gives them a lead in that matter, even if this means reducing the actual performance.

The principal–agent dynamic has been widely documented and debated. The issue boils down to control, incentives, and alignment of interests. This is not limited to private markets, but specific factors compound the issue, such as lack and asymmetries of information, as well as behavioral biases from the principal side and the agent side.

Although some of the performance will be absorbed by such a setup, investors are advised to run a competitive process (such as a request for proposal) and to regularly assess if their agents are delivering on their promises. Many investors also split mandates in multiple components and have two or three different agents running each component. By doing so, not only can they compare the service provided to them, but they also have a backup in case one of the providers has to be replaced at short notice.

Empirical evidence shows that it is possible to set a viable and fruitful investment program in private markets. Though setting up an allocation to private markets is still a work in progress, tackling this effort is delivering results and could contribute, to a certain extent, to help pension fund managers matching their assets and their liabilities, for example.

In the long run, a continued success of private markets should lead to a significant capital inflow. As the asset class matures, market imperfections, such as asymmetries of information, will decrease. Risk and return should be reduced accordingly. The effect is difficult to quantify, and some segments of the market will mature faster than others. Fund managers tend to be creative and innovative and explore new corners of private markets. Private markets are expected to provide a rather extensive range of choices to investors in terms of risk-return-liquidity profiles. Investors should benefit from these options, especially if the overall information context improves with the maturity of private markets.

Glossary

100-day plan   Series of measures and dispositions that a company acquired through an **LBO**[1] is expected to execute after its acquisition. It includes back-up measures in case the original plan fails to deliver the expected results. *See also* Leveraged buyout (LBO).

A

Accelerated monitoring fees   At time of investment, the **LBO fund manager** determines an annual monitoring and control fee charged to a portfolio company along an expected holding period. If the portfolio company is sold or listed ahead of the planned schedule, the remaining amount due is then charged all at once by the **LBO** manager before the exit: it is the accelerated monitoring fee. *See also* Fund manager; Leveraged buyout (LBO).

Accelerator   Also referred to as **start-up** accelerator. Six- to eighteen-month program dedicated to supporting entrepreneurs at the inception of their company. Accelerators usually provide a mix of lectures, workshops, mentorship, and events with the aim of supporting the start-up in its fundraising. Most programs culminate in a final event where start-ups can **pitch** themselves to potential investors. *See also* Pitch; Start-up.

Accredited investor   An investor deemed sufficiently informed and sophisticated, who benefits from a satisfactory knowledge of investments and is thus able to handle private market investments, which do not benefit from the protection offered by the stock exchange regulations. In the US, this status is defined by the Investment Company Act of 1940.

Aborted deal costs   *See* Broken deal costs.

Acquiror due diligence   Also known as buy-side due diligence. *See* Due diligence.

Acquisition   The take-over of a portfolio company by another industrial or financial company.

Active ownership   For a shareholder, it consists in exercising dutifully her rights and fulfilling all associated duties and actively advising the management of a firm. If the shareholder is a board member of a company, this includes exercising the rights and duties of a board member.

Activism   In finance, it consists in a series of actions supporting a campaign to bring significant change in the management and governance of a company. An activist investor usually acquires a minority stake in a listed company, launching a communication campaign to get the support for a bid to get one or multiple board seats. The purpose is to act decisively to change the strategy of the company by convincing or changing the management of a firm. Activist investors are compensated by the resulting increase of the price of the shares they own and/or distribution of dividends.

Add-on transaction   Direct or indirect acquisition of a firm by a private equity fund, to be further merged or associated with a company already in the portfolio of the fund: the **platform**. *See also* Platform deal.

---

[1]Terms that are defined in this glossary appear in **bold** type.

Adverse selection   Any situation when an investor systematically gets investment opportunities of lower quality or return potential due to a disadvantage when interacting with a better-informed party.

Advisory board   Group of fund investors or third parties advising a fund manager on a specific fund. The powers of this board are limited to simple advice on topics ranging notably from valuation of assets to solving conflicts of interests.

Advisory committee   Informal group of individuals advising a fund manager on specific questions.

Agency theory   A branch of economic theory that deals with the question of asset owners (i.e., principals) and their agents. An agency relationship exists when the principal pays the agent to make decisions in his place. The contract plays an important role in ensuring that the agent acts in the best interest of the owner. Agency costs are evidenced by the fact that contracts are costly and difficult to enforce. They include structuring costs, management costs, and the application of multiple contracts between agents with different interests.

AIFMD   *See* Alternative Investment Fund Managers Directive.

Alignment of interests   Usually refers to an arrangement between an agent and a principal in which the agent stands to benefit more from a cooperation with the principal than if the agent tries to maximize his own single outcome.

Alternative assets   If traditional investments refer to listed stocks, listed bonds, and cash, alternative assets refer to non-traditional investments. This category includes notably private market investments, hedge funds, commodities, and derivatives.

Alternative Investment Fund Managers Directive   EU-wide regulation introduced in 2011 to provide a common regime for managers of funds dedicated to non-traditional assets, namely hedge funds and private market funds. To market their funds within the European Union, alternative investment fund managers have to obtain an authorization from at least one national EU regulator. This authorization is delivered upon compliance with transparency and investor protection provisions.

American waterfall   Variant of the schedule of distribution of the performance fee (**carried interest**) of a fund manager. According to this one, the carried interest (if any) is distributed to the fund manager each time an investment has been sold profitably by the fund and the "**hurdle rate**" has been paid. If the fund sold investments at a loss, some or all the carried interest distributed to the fund manager has to be recalled according to a "**claw-back clause**" to compensate the investors for their loss. *See also* Carried interest; Claw-Back clause; Hurdle rate.

Anchor investor   *See* Cornerstone investor.

Angel investor   A high net worth individual who invests in venture capital to help companies and let them benefit from his experience, his network, and his know-how. Also called business angel.

Anti-dilution clause   Clause in a **shareholders' agreement** (usually of a **start-up**) that entitles some investors to maintain their ownership percentage in a company by buying additional shares of a company in subsequent financing rounds. If the subsequent round of **fundraising** is done at a lower valuation than the current one (a "**down round**," the option will compensate beneficiary investors with additional shares to maintain their ownership percentage). *See also* Down round; Fundraising.

Asymmetry of information   Situation in which an economic agent has better information than another, placing the second at a disadvantage compared to the first one when choosing an investment. For example, an entrepreneur can benefit from a higher level of information than an investor in a company. The entrepreneur extracts this information from his day-to-day activities while the investor relies on the summary provided by the entrepreneur for his information. Current investors in a company also benefit from better information than prospective ones, which is why the latter undertake a **due diligence** to reduce or eliminate the asymmetry of information. *See also* Due diligence.

Asset allocation   Breakdown of a portfolio between different categories of assets. For an institutional investor, this usually involves listed stocks, listed bonds, local and foreign currencies, hedge funds, commodities, gold, and private market investments. For a fund manager, this usually involves companies of different sectors and possibly geographical regions.

Asset stripping   Process of selling off part of a company with the hope that the proceeds from this sale will be higher than if the company were sold as a whole.

Asset under management   The sum of all the assets managed (that is to say, those available for investment and those already invested) by an investment team in private market deals.

Auction   Process to sell a company potentially involving multiple competing buyers. The purpose of this process is usually to maximize the proceeds for the seller.

AuM   *See* Asset under management.

B

Balance sheet   The picture of the financial situation of a company at a given time. The balance sheet is the synthesis of the value of assets, debts, and capital of the company.

Balanced fund   An investment strategy in **private equity** designed to build a portfolio of companies at different stages of development (**venture capital**, **growth capital**, and/or **leveraged buyout**). *See also* Private equity investing.

Bankruptcy   Legal status declared by a special court under which a company which is either **insolvent** or has sustained accumulated losses superior to its total capital for a prolonged period of time (usually two years) is placed under administration and supervised by an independent third party. The debt (interest and principal) repayment of the company is suspended for the length of the bankruptcy procedure (usually of 6 to 18 months), which usually ends by the restructuring of the company or its liquidation. *See also* Insolvent.

BDC   *See* Business Development Company.

Beauty contest   Competitive process in which each potential buyer of a business/asset tries to convince a seller (and his agents) and outcompete other potential buyers. This process can be compared to an auction, except that the decision factors are not only the price offered but also other elements such as reputation, credentials, or a track record.

Benchmark   Metrics of performance, risk, and liquidity of a fund or a company, to support a comparison with a **peer group**. *See also* Peer group.

Blocker   Structure set up in a specific country to gather commitments in a fund located in another country. *See also* Feeder fund.

Blind pool   Feature of a fund according to which investors do not know at the time of investment which assets will be acquired and have no influence on the choice of these assets. Investors usually know at least the detailed investment strategy applied by the fund, that is, the criteria such as the geographical area, the type of investment strategy applied, the size and type of asset, and sometimes, the industrial sectors targeted.

Bolt-on transaction   *See* Add-on transaction.

Book value   Using the balance sheet of a company, it is computed as the total value of the assets (after depreciation) minus the outstanding liabilities.

Bottom quartile   Lowest 25 percent of a sample according to specific criteria, such as a performance metric.

Bottom-up   Progressing from the lowest (or most granular) to the highest (or the least granular) level of an analytical process. In the context of asset allocation, this consists in analyzing the microeconomic factors of an asset to draw specific conclusions and build a portfolio from this analysis. The positive side of this approach is that it is empirically verifiable and can be concretely applied. The negative side of this approach is that it depends on observable samples and therefore might not be systematic. A complementary approach is **top-down**. *See also* Top-down.

Break-up fee   Financial sanction that the seller of a company in an LBO transaction has to pay when walking away from the transaction. If it is the prospective buyer who walks away, then the fee is called a "reverse break-up fee."

Bridge financing   Short-term financing generally provided as a credit to a company expecting a financing event (IPO or further round of financing) in the coming six to twelve months. The bridge financing can combine debt and equity features. If so, this debt instrument is then generally converted into shares at the time of the liquidity event.

Bridge loan   *See* Bridge financing.

Broken auction   Competitive sale process of a company that failed to effectively translate in an effective acquisition.

Broken deal costs   *See* Broken deal fees.

Broken deal fees   Buy-side expenses associated with the analysis of an investment opportunity that did not materialize into an effective investment. These expenses are supported by the potential buyer with no associated investment to recoup them.

Brownfield   Refers to **real assets**, such as **real estate** or **infrastructure**, that have been already developed and are not currently in use. The underlying land can be contaminated.

Bullet payment   Feature of a loan according to which the principal and the accumulated interests are paid all at once, usually at the end of the duration of the loan.

Burn rate   Measure of the net cash spent by a start-up at a given time occurrence (usually monthly). It is notably used to assess how many months the **start-up** can operate before it runs out of funds (and therefore plan for a new **round of financing**).

Business angel   *See* Angel investor.

Business Development Company (BDC)   Listed US closed-end investment vehicle created in 1980 through an amendment of the Investment Company Act of 1940. If a company elects to be a BDC and matches the criteria, it pays little or no corporate income tax as it is a pass-through tax structure.

Business plan   Document prepared by the management of a company, often with the help of advisors, detailing its past, present, and expected future performance and activities. This document contains not only a detailed analysis of the human, financial, and physical resources of the company but also its history, its competitive position, and its pricing scheme, as well as financial projections for the next three to five years following its last exercise. It details the strategy, defines the targets, and is used to monitor future performance.

Buy-and-build   LBO strategy in which a fund buys companies from a given sector with the aim of combining them and capitalizing on their synergies. The initial transaction is called the **platform transaction** and the subsequent acquisition the **add-on transaction**. *See also* Add-on transaction; Platform transaction.

Buy-in   *See* Leveraged buy-in (LBI).

Buy-In Management Buyout (BIMBO) A **leveraged buyout** that involves current managers (**management buyout**) and new coming managers (**management buy-in**).

Buyout *See* Leveraged buyout (LBO).

Buy-side due diligence *See* Due diligence.

C

Capital account Report on the position held by an investor in a private market fund, including committed capital, capital **paid in**, investments, **valuations**, and distributions.

Capital call Operation through which the fund collects a portion of the **commitments** of its fund investors to invest in **portfolio companies** and pay for its expenses (and notably the **management fees**). *See also* Management fees.

Capital increase Operation in which investors provide additional resources, in cash or in-kind, to a company in exchange for shares. As a result, the equity of the company increases.

Capitalization table List of the current and future shareholders of a company, usually detailing the percentage of ownership, number of shares, and stock options owned by each of them.

Captive manager A private market fund manager that is totally (captive) or partially (semi-captive) owned by a large group or a financial institution.

Carried interest The share of the profit generated by a fund manager that is dedicated to the investment team (fund manager) without any initial financial contribution to the fund. It is generally 20 percent of the profits generated by the fund ("whole fund carried interest," also called **European waterfall**), or sometimes by each of the investments of a fund ("deal-by-deal carried interest," also called **American waterfall**). *See also* American waterfall; European waterfall.

Carve-out Conversion of an activity, a business unit, or a division of a company into an independent company, which can subsequently be sold by the corporation it originates from.

Catch-up Mechanism entitling the fund manager to collect the pro rata of the **hurdle rate** collected by fund investors. *See also* Hurdle rate.

Cherry-picking Choosing only the best opportunity from what is available.

Chief investment officer Board-level executive of an institutional investor (or a family office) in charge of overseeing the **asset allocation**, the investment selection, monitoring, and reporting. *See also* Asset allocation.

CIO *See* Chief investment officer.

CLO *See* Collateralized loan obligation.

Claw-back clause Requires the fund manager to return distributions to fund investors. This provision is associated with the early distribution of **carried interest** to the fund manager under an **American waterfall**. The carried interest distributed with the successful realization of early investments could be clawed back if successor deals fail to generate sufficient performance to return the capital to fund investors (and associated potential hurdle rate). If a fund distributes carried interest deal-by-deal and registers highly successful exits initially and weaker ones later on, this provision ensures that fund investors will ultimately get back what is owed to them according to fund regulations. *See also* American waterfall; Carried interest.

Closed-end Feature of a fund according to which it is created and dissolved at a predetermined specific date. The life span of the fund is thus set at the start. It is not opened to new investors after the end of its **fundraising period**, and investors have no redemption right before the dissolution. *See also* Fundraising period.

Closed-ended *See* Closed-end.

Closed-end fund *See* Closed-end.

Closing During the creation of a fund, the fund manager accumulates the **commitments** of the investors who are interested. The closing is the effective gathering of a critical volume of commitments and the signature of **subscription agreements** to the **Limited partnership agreement**. The **fundraising** can last a year or more, and the fund manager can make multiple closings (initial, intermediate, and final) to indicate the progress of the process, set up its operations, and begin to invest rapidly.

The term also applies to the materialization of an investment in a portfolio company. The closing is the signature of the transfer of ownership (**LBO**) or of the capital increase (**venture capital** and **growth capital**).

See also Fundraising; Limited partnership agreement.

Club deal **Leveraged buyout** operated by a group of **private equity** funds.

Cluster of financing Geographical aggregation of **venture capital** investors that have reached a critical mass to attract companies and entrepreneurs and have developed a sector expertise. The most emblematic cluster is the American Silicon Valley in information technologies.

Co-investment Option or right offered to invest alongside a **private market** fund directly in a **portfolio company** or asset. The investor is usually also investing in the private market fund itself and hence can choose to increase his exposure in select companies or assets.

Co-investment fund **Private market** fund investing in **portfolio companies** or assets jointly with other vehicles managed by a fund manager. This fund is usually offered to specific investors only and supports lower **management fees** and **carried interest** than usual.

Co-lead investor Prospective investor (usually in a **start-up**) who negotiates jointly with another one (the **lead investor**) the terms of a **capital increase** in a start-up with usually the management of the firm (representing existing investors).

Collateral An asset from a borrower pledged so that a debt or a security will be repaid or refunded. This can be linked to a specific debt or a series of transactions. For example, entrepreneurs must sometimes provide personal collateral for the loans provided to their company.

Collateralized loan obligation Securitization vehicle often rated by an independent agency, in which a large number of loans are pooled together and then sliced in tranches with various levels of seniority (and therefore of risks). These tranches are then sold to investors, who are entitled to the payment of interests and the repayment of the principal. The interest rate varies upon the risk supported by the investor in a given tranche.

Commingled fund Investment vehicle that gathers capital from different sources and blends them together. Private market **fund of funds** are commingled funds as opposed to **mandates**. *See also* Fund of funds (FOF); Mandates.

Common equity *See* Common shares.

Common shares Group of securities representing the ownership of a company that embeds one voting right and one dividend right per share. Any divergence from this rule qualifies these securities as **preferred shares** if they have more rights. Common shares are usually held by entrepreneurs and employees of a company. *See also* Preferred shares.

Committed capital *See* Fund size.

Commitment The obligation for an investor to provide a certain amount of capital to a fund. By extension, it is the amount committed by an investor in a fund or **fund of funds**, including those that are agreed on but not yet called. The sum of the commitments of all investors equals the fund size.

Companion fund *See* Parallel fund.

Concerted action   Shareholders acting in concert according to a (formal or informal) agreement for the acquisition of the shares of a company, to achieve, maintain, or increase their control over this company.

Conflict of interests   Position in which an economic agent has competing professional or personal motivations, leading to a risk of unethical or improper actions.

Consulting fees   Compensation paid to the provider of services to a portfolio company.

Conversion rights   An option or financial right attached to debt financing instrument, notably the **mezzanine debt**. Under specific pre-negotiated conditions, this guarantees the owner of this financing instrument to get access to an equity stake in the company and hence a share of the profits. In that respect, subordinated debt providers can be paid for the higher risk that they take, compared to other debt providers. *See also* Mezzanine debt.

Convertible debt   Often subordinated, this tranche of debt can be converted (optional conversion) or has to be converted (mandatory conversion) into a given company's equity by the creditor upon the materialization of certain events (and/or the wish of the creditor).

Cornerstone investor   Financial institution (or sometimes family office) supporting the **fundraising** effort of a fund manager by committing a significant percentage of a private market fund. This investor often supports the fund manager notably with branding, introduction to other investors, and even operational support. Cornerstone investors receive, in exchange, **advisory board** seats and possibly additional rights such as **co-investment** rights.

Consultant   Agent operating for institutional investors, providing asset allocation and fund selection services. If the consultant is specialized in fund selection and has a discretionary **mandate**, he is a **gatekeeper**. *See also* Gatekeeper.

Core   Conservative investment strategy applied in **private real estate** and private **infrastructure**, essentially aiming at delivering income to investors, and possibly a capital gain. This strategy is characterized by a rather low risk-return profile. Assets are stable, in top locations, fully leased and held for a rather long period, require low or no management from investors, and are often characterized as high quality. Tenants rent these assets on long-term leases and are usually of high quality. The debt used to acquire these assets is 30 to 40 percent of the value of the assets.

Core-plus   Investment strategy with a low to moderate risk applied in **private real estate** and private **infrastructure**. It aims at delivering a mix of income and capital gains to investors. Assets are held for a rather long period and are of high quality but require light improvements and/or an increased management efficiency and/or an increase in the quality of tenants. Similar to the core strategy, tenants rent these assets on long-term leases and are usually of high quality. The debt used to acquire these assets is 40 to 60 percent of the value of the assets.

Cornerstone investor   Financial institution or family office that acquires a significant stake (between 15 and 30 percent) in a **private market** fund. This institution usually supports the **fundraising** effort of the fund manager in various ways, such as branding, serving as a reference, and actively marketing the fund.

 The expression is sometimes used in **venture capital** when an investor acquires a large stake in a start-up and serves as a **due diligence** reference.

See also Fundraising.

Corporate governance   Principles, mechanisms, and processes of direction and management control of corporations by their owners. The rights and responsibilities of the owners are usually defined legally and contractually, in the latter case in the **shareholders' agreement**. The aim of corporate governance is to reduce and eliminate **conflicts of interests** among corporate owners, as well as between corporate owners and managers. In **private markets**, corporate governance plays a central role in the value creation of investors in the assets they control. *See also* Shareholders' agreement.

Corporate venture capital   *See* Corporate venturing.

Corporate venturing   Large companies can buy a stake in, or establish a joint venture with, a smaller company in order to help it develop new products, services, or technologies and benefit from certain synergies. The large company can thus not only provide capital but also managers or marketing resources. Corporate venturing can also support **spin-off** processes. *See also* Spin-off.

Cost of capital   Rate of return expected by the shareholders of a company. It is usually measured by the CAPM model, which states that the capital cost equals the risk-free rate plus a premium, which varies according to the systemic risk (which cannot be diversified by the portfolio construction) and the market price of risk (around 6.5 percent by unit of beta).

Cost of debt   Interest rate requested by the banks from a company.

Cost of liabilities   Rate of return expected for the different means of financing. The total cost of liabilities is the compounded average rate of return of all the sources of financing used by the company.

Covenants   Restrictions imposed by a lender on a borrower. It is generally associated with the necessity of maintaining a certain level of cash, certain ratios, or certain levels of investment in an LBO.

Covenant-light   Qualification applied to a loan whose contract includes a lower number of clauses protecting the lender than in a usual contract. The borrower thus benefits from a higher flexibility, often without incurring a higher interest rate. The flexibility can be related to the repayment schedule, the ability to contract additional debt, make investments, pay dividends, forgo and accumulate the payment of interests for a certain period of time, or any other form of flexibility that would usually be limited or prohibited.

Covenant-lite   *See* Covenant-light.

Covenant-loose   Qualification applied to a loan whose contract includes a very low number (usually one or two) of clauses protecting the lender, providing the borrower with a high flexibility.

Credit line   *See* Equity bridge financing.

Cross investment   Process in which two funds managed by the same fund manager invest in the same underlying asset. Cross investments can create a conflict of interest for the fund manager if the two funds have different time horizons (one might have to sell its assets earlier than the other, for example).

Crowdfunding   Mechanism matching a company in fundraising mode with a multitude of potential investors (often retail or **business angels**), notably over the Internet, hence disintermediating the process of **private market** investing. The company can raise capital (equity crowdfunding), debt (crowdlending), or collect money as a donation or against a product or a service.

Crowdlending   *See* Crowdfunding.

Custodian   Specialist institution dedicated to the certification of cash-flow movements of funds. It acts as a trusted third party to guarantee that the fund manager handles the cash of a private market fund in a specific way.

D

Data room   Large series of detailed documents gathered by the seller of a company to prepare the **due diligence** of (a) prospective buyer(s).

Deal-by-deal carried interest   *See* American waterfall.

Deal flow   Investment opportunities presented to a financial institution.

Debt-for-trading Distressed debt investment strategy usually applied by hedge funds and consisting in acquiring at a discount listed bonds or loans of a distressed company. Once the company has solved its issues, bonds or loans recover their value and investors can then sell and book a profit. *See also* Distressed debt investing.

Decile The segment of a sample representing a sequential ten percent. Thus, the first 10 of 100 funds are the first (or top) decile and the last 10 are the last (or bottom) decile.

Default Event in which a promise to pay out a financial obligation (such as repaying a loan or answering a capital call) has been breached.

Defaulting investor Fund investor who does not answer a **capital call**.

Delisting A **private equity** transaction implying an offering on the total of the capital of a listed company to take it private.

Development fund **Venture capital** fund dedicated to later stage **start-ups**. *See also* Expansion capital.

Dilution A process through which the percentage of participation of an investor in a company is reduced by the issue of new shares.

Direct alpha *See* Public Market Equivalent.

Direct investment Capital increase in or acquisition of a company with no intermediate investment vehicle. A direct investment can be a **co-investment** or a **solo investment**. *See also* Co-investment; Solo investment.

Direct lending **Private debt** strategy similar to traditional bank lending. A lender provides a borrower with an amount of debt that is progressively repaid along with the interests computed on the outstanding amount still due. Also known as senior lending.

Direct secondaries *See* Secondary investing.

Discount rate Price value of time. It is notably used to determine the present value of future cash flows in the formula $PV = FV_t/(1 + K)^t$, where PV is the present value, FV_t is the future value at the end of the year t, and K is the cost of capital.

Discounted Cash Flows (DCF) A method of evaluating investments by compounding the value of the future cash flows of a company by the actual value of these flows. When it is necessary to decide whether to invest or not in a given project, the future cash flows of an investment are discounted to get a value at the time the project would be initiated. The discount rate is the expected rate of return from the investors. In theory, if the actual value of future cash flows is higher than the invested amount, the investment should be made.

Dissolution of a fund Point of the life span of a fund at which its assets have all been sold, it is free from any warranty or obligation, and can be effectively wound up.

Distressed debt investing Acquisition at a discount of some of the debt of a company in financial trouble. This strategy is a case where hedge funds and **private debt** funds can overlap in their activities. Distressed debt hedge funds acquire the debt and hold it until the value increases (debt-for-trading). Private debt funds focusing on distressed debt acquire the debt and convert some or all of it into shares. They restructure the company and sell it once the company is back on track (loan-to-own).

Distribution Payment made by a fund to its fund investors, usually in cash. If not, it is a **distribution in-kind**. *See also* Distribution in-kind.

Distribution in-kind Although very restricted, or outright forbidden, some fund regulations allow the distribution of securities to fund investors, instead of cash. These securities are usually traded on an organized and regulated financial market with a minimum threshold of liquidity.

These securities can be subject to a **lock-up period** if they are distributed after an **initial public offering**. *See also* Initial public offering; Lock-up period.

Distribution to Paid-In (DPI)　Ratio between the amount distributed by the fund (from the proceeds of its divestments) and the total of **capital calls** (paid-in).

Distribution waterfall　Schedule of distribution of the performance fee (**carried interest**) of a fund manager. Two variants are usually differentiated: the **American waterfall** and the **European waterfall**. Each variant can involve different features such as a **claw-back clause** for the American variant, or a **catch-up clause** in the European variant. *See also* American waterfall; Catch-up clause; Claw-back clause; European waterfall.

Divestment　The sale of a part or all of an investment through a trade sale or an **initial public offering (IPO)**. *See also* Exit (of an investment); Initial public offering (IPO).

Divestment period　Subsequent to the **investment period**, the divestment period represents a five- to twelve-year timeframe during which a fund develops and sells or lists its investments. If necessary, this period can be extended by one to three years if the fund regulations allow it. At the end of the divestment period, the fund is supposed to have sold all its holdings and be free of any warranties. If not, the fund manager has the choice to sell the assets on the secondary market (**direct secondaries**) or to other investors, transfer these assets in a new fund (**GP-led restructuring**), or extend the life span of the fund beyond the initial plan. *See also* Direct secondaries; GP-led restructuring.

Dividend recapitalization　Partial or full refund of the capital injected in an **LBO** thanks to the payment of a special dividend by the holding. This dividend is usually the proceeds of an increase of its debt or, more rarely, the disposal of an asset of the underlying portfolio company.

Down round　**Venture capital** investment round where the valuation of the company is inferior to the previous one.

Downstream　Generally refers, in the oil and gas industry, to the refining of crude oil and the processing and purifying of natural gas, as well as the distribution of derived products.

DPI　*See* Distribution to Paid-In.

Drag along clause　Disposition of a **shareholders' agreement** according to which the majority shareholder can force minority shareholders to sell their shares at the same price as his/hers to a third party, unless minority shareholders buy his/her shares at the price offered by this third party.

Drawdown　*See* Capital call.

Dry powder　At a fund level, it is the portion of the **fund size** that has not been called yet. At the **private market** industry level, it is the sum of all the capital committed but not deployed yet.

Due diligence　Investigation resulting in independent and detailed analysis process preceding an investment. It is realized by or for investors of a given target company or a fund. In the case of a company, this includes a detailed analysis of the hypothesis of a **business plan**, as well as checking material facts (client accounts, contracts, bills, etc.) and opinions. Applied to a fund, this consists in determining the attractiveness, the risks and issues of an investment strategy, a **track record**, and the setup of the fund and its manager. *See also* Business plan.

Duration of a fund　*See* Lifespan of a fund.

Duration of an investment　*See* Holding period.

E

Early stage financing　This includes seed investments and the first **rounds of financing** of a company.

Earnings before interest and taxes (EBIT)   This measure is calculated in the profit and loss statement of a company. Depending on the accounting methods, it can be calculated from the turn-over from which inputs such as costs of goods and services sold: wages; marketing, general, and administrative expenses; and depreciations and amortizations are deducted. *See also* Earnings before interest, taxes, depreciation, and amortization (EBITDA).

Earnings before interest, taxes, depreciation, and amortization (EBITDA)   This measure is calculated in the profit and loss statement of a company. Depending on the accounting methods, it can be calculated from the turn-over from which the inputs such as costs of goods and services sold: wages; and marketing, general, and administrative expenses are deducted. Depending on the financial structure and the activity of the company, it can be relevant to use a multiple of EBIT (or EBITA for telecom companies) or EBITDA, or any other financial instrument of measurement (EBITDAR—R standing for rental of aircrafts—for airlines, for example).

Earn-out clause   The final price to be paid to the vendor by an acquirer depends on the realization of results announced in the **business plan**. To ease negotiations, the vendor and the buyer can settle on a temporary price and simultaneously negotiate a future potential complementary payment (the earn-out) to the vendor. This complementary payment to the vendor is triggered by the realization of certain results by the company. These results are the fruit of efforts initiated before the transaction by the vendor, but which will be materialized after the acquisition and hence attributed to the buyer. Thanks to this mechanism, the vendor can retain an interest in the company for the compensation of efforts he has undertaken and results that he has contributed to but whose proceeds are difficult to evaluate at the time of the sale. *See also* Business plan.

Employee buyout (EBO)   An **LBO** in which the employees have the opportunity to acquire a significant number of shares in the company. *See also* Leveraged buyout (LBO).

Employee stock-option plan (ESOP)   Program enabling a firm's employees to become owners, as a compensation for work done.

Endowment   Process of transferring the ownership of assets to a nonprofit structure. By extension, it designates the tax efficient structure in which assets are transferred to a beneficiary owner, which can be an institution (such as a university). Assets can be in cash or in-kind. The endowment is managed independently and invests these assets whenever possible. The endowment can then spend the proceeds of these investments and only these. The assets bequeathed to the endowment cannot be spent. To keep their tax-exempt status, endowments have to respect specific rules.

Enterprise value (EV)   Sum of the equity value and the net debt of a firm.

Entry multiple   Valuation ratio set when an investor acquires or invests in a company or an asset (the entry). It is usually computed by dividing the enterprise value of the company or asset at entry by a subtotal from its profit and loss statement (such as **EBIT**) or cash flow statement. *See also* Earnings before interests and taxes (EBIT).

Environmental, Social, and Governance (ESG) criteria   Set of informal standards used by investors to screen opportunities to invest in projects and companies. Environmental criteria support the analysis of a company's or an asset's stewardship of nature. Social criteria support the analysis of a company's or an asset's relationship with the community in which they operate, such as employees, suppliers, clients, partners, and stakeholders. Governance criteria support the analysis of a company's or an asset's ownership framework, including management control and sanction and owners' rights and duties.

Equalization mechanism   Process consisting in establishing a strict equality between investors joining the roster of a fund at different **closing dates**. Investors joining after the **first closing** have to compensate initial investors, usually by paying initial investors an interest.

Interests are in effect collected by the fund manager and paid pro rata to investors in the first closing.

Equity   Sum of capital provided by shareholders plus the sum of undistributed profits or losses.

Equity bridge financing   Also known as credit line, subscription line facilities, or capital call facilities, these financing instruments are short-term (less than 365 days) loans provided to private market funds backed by the commitments of fund investors. Capital calls can then be delayed, along with the start of the computation of the IRR associated with them. Distributions can also be anticipated, thus affecting the computation of the IRR.

Equity crowdfunding   *See* Crowdfunding.

Equity kicker   *See* Conversion right.

End of life   Point at which a closed-end fund reaches its maximum contractual life span.

ESG   *See* Environmental, Social, and Governance criteria.

ESOP   *See* Employee stock-option plan.

European waterfall   Variant of the schedule of distribution of the performance fee (**carried interest**) of a fund manager. According to this one, the carried interest (if any) is distributed to the fund manager only once the capital of the fund has been returned to investors and the **hurdle rate** and **catch-up** have been paid. *See also* Carried interest; Catch-up; Hurdle rate.

EV   *See* Enterprise value.

Evergreen vehicle   An open-ended private market investment vehicle (often a holding company), usually listed on the stock exchange. An evergreen vehicle can be a fund, a fund management company, or a combination of the two.

Exit (of an investment)   A means by which investors in a portfolio company sell part or all of their stakes. Common means of exit are initial public offerings or trade sale to an industrial group. Other options such as **secondary buyouts** are becoming increasingly frequent. *See also* Divestment.

Exit multiple   Valuation ratio set when an investor sells or divests a company or an asset (the exit). It is usually computed by dividing the enterprise value of the company or asset at exit by a subtotal from its profits and losses statement (such as **EBIT**) or cash flow statement. *See also* Earnings before interest and taxes (EBIT).

Exit process   Series of steps leading to the **initial public offering (IPO)**, trade sale to a company, financial secondary sale to an investment group, sale to the management, or liquidation (**write-off**) of a stake in a company. This therefore excludes **dividend recapitalizations**. *See also* Initial public offering (IPO); Write-off.

Expansion capital   Financing provided to a **start-up** company at a later stage of its development.

F

Fair market value   Estimate of the **net asset value** of a fund using the assumption of what a buyer would pay in an open market operation for an asset (or a group of assets such as portfolio companies of a **private market** fund).

Fair value   Company or asset price agreed upon by willing market participants in an orderly transaction at the transaction date.

Fairness opinion   Evaluation given by a trusted third party on the situation and value of a portfolio or a portfolio company. This service is often used when a potential **conflict of interest** is perceived by a fund investor in the valuation of a portfolio or a company by a fund manager.

Farmland   Subcategory of **private real asset investing**, referring to agricultural space used for raising crops or livestock.

Family office   Independent and professionally managed private structure dedicated to the management of the wealth of very or ultra **high net worth individuals** or families. *See also* High net worth individuals.

Fee offset mechanism   **Distributions** from **portfolio companies** (for example dividends, service fees, board attendance fees) are often not tax efficient if made to the fund. However, they are not theoretically payable to the fund manager as the latter is paid (thanks to the **management fees**) to manage the fund and its portfolio. The mechanism is hence set up to direct the **distributions** to the fund manager, and these distributions will be compensated to the fund by reduced **management fees**. *See also* Distribution; Management fees.

Feeder fund   Local legal structure used by investors to invest in a fund, often used for tax and regulatory purposes.

Finder's fund   Small fund used to source investment opportunities for the account of the investors who then usually finance the investment or the acquisition themselves directly.

First closing   Operation handled by a fund manager, materializing the creation of the fund and the beginning of its investment period. A fund can hold a single closing (first and final) or multiple subsequent ones, usually over a period of twelve to eighteen months since the beginning of the **fundraising period**. *See also* Fundraising period.

First lien   Highest legally enforceable claim on the collateral of a loan in case a borrower defaults.

First round of financing   The first investment made by external professional investors.

First-time fund   Initial investment vehicle of a series launched by an established or emerging fund manager. The fund manager usually capitalizes on a preexisting **track record**, for example, built in a previous institution. *See also* Track record.

Follow-on investment   Reinvestment by a venture capitalist in an existing portfolio company.

Fonds Commun de Placement dans l'Innovation (FCPI)   French **FCPR** dedicated to venture capital investment and retail investors. An FCPI is created for eight years and its fund investors are entitled to a tax break on the amount committed to the FCPI (up to a certain amount). *See also* Fonds Commun de Placement à Risque (FCPR).

Fonds Commun de Placement à Risque (FCPR)   Predecessor in French Law of the *Fonds Professionnel de Capital Investissement*. The FCPR can be authorized by the French *Autorité des Marchés Financiers* (AMF, the regulator of French financial markets), declared to the AMF, or simply contractual. The FCPR's management company has to be duly authorized by the AMF to create such funds.

Fonds d'Investissement de Proximité (FIP)   French **FCPR** dedicated to regional **private equity** investment and retail investors. An FIP is created for eight years, and its fund investors are entitled to a tax break on the amount committed to the FIP (up to a certain amount). *See also* Fonds Commun de Placement à Risque (FCPR); Private equity investing.

Fonds Professionnel de Capital Investissement (FPCI)   Equivalent of the limited partnership in French Law. The FPCI is managed by a management company (equivalent of the fund manager). The FPCI is contractual and does not have to be authorized by the French regulator (*Autorité des Marchés Financiers*, AMF). However, its management company has to be duly authorized by the AMF to create such funds.

For cause   Preestablished conditions for the termination of the fund manager's mandate. These conditions usually refer to an agreed upon level of negligence or **key-man clauses**. *See also* Key-man clause.

Foundation   Refers to a nonprofit organization usually created to support a specific cause. Foundations can collect capital or invest capital. In the latter case, some or all the proceeds are then used for charitable purposes. Foundations can use their financial resources to support other organizations through donations or for their own charitable purposes. They are a legal category that notably benefits from tax incentives.

Fund   A **private market** fund is an investment vehicle created to pool capital from investors and invest it in equity or debt in different companies or assets. The fund can be a registered vehicle (most of the time for tax reasons), such as a French **FCPR**, or a non-registered vehicle, such as a limited partnership. *See also* Fonds Commun de Placement à Risque (FCPR).

Fund administrator   Service provider in charge of the operational aspects of the management of a fund, such as handling cash inflows and outflows, calculation of fees and **carried interest**, and reporting. *See also* Carried interest.

Fund investor   Investor in a **private market** fund. A fund investor is responsible for an investment in a private market fund only up to its initial **commitment**, not more. An investor in a **limited partnership** is called **limited partner** (abbreviated as LP). *See also* Commitment; Limited partner; Limited partnership.

Fund management company   *See* Fund manager.

Fund manager   A group of **principals** managing a fund or a **fund of funds**, and by extension the staff working for these principals. If the fund is a **limited partnership**, the fund manager is called **general partner** (abbreviated as GP). The fund manager sources, structures, executes, and monitors investments. Additional responsibilities include operational fund management, as well as reporting to and communication with **fund investors**. *See also* Fund of Funds; General partner; Limited partnership; Principal.

Fund of funds (FOF)   A financial instrument whose purpose is to acquire stakes in private market funds. Funds of funds can be classified as primary, secondary, or balanced: those investing mainly in new funds are primary funds of funds, those acquiring mainly stakes in existing funds are secondary funds of funds, and those combining primary and secondary investments are balanced funds of funds.

Fund regulation   Contractual agreement between investors and the **fund manager** of a **private market** fund. This agreement defines the rules governing the management of the fund, the relations between the fund and its investors, and the rights and duties of the **fund manager**. Fund regulations are an instruction manual of the fund in the sense that they describe all the legal elements, the fees, the structure, and other elements agreed upon by the investors and the **fund manager**. They can be at times amended and completed by **side letters**. An example of fund regulation is the **Limited partnership agreement**. *See also* Fund manager; Limited partnership agreement; Side letter.

Fund secondary   *See* Secondary investing.

Fund size   The sum of the **commitments** of all investors in a given fund.

Fund sponsor   *See* Sponsor.

Fundraising   A process during which the **fund manager** accumulates the commitment of **fund investors** to create a **private market** fund. These funds are raised from private investors, institutions, and companies, which become **fund investors** of the fund that will be invested in by the **fund manager**. *See also* Fund investors; Fund manager.

Fundraising period   Refers to the time between the beginning of the marketing of a **private market** fund and its final **closing**. It can be as short as a few weeks and as long as 12 to 18 months.

G

Gatekeeper   Advisor to fund investors dedicated to the selection of **private market** funds. A gatekeeper has usually a **discretionary mandate**. *See also* Discretionary mandate.

General partner   *See* Fund manager.

Goodwill   The difference between the price of acquisition of an asset and its net market value at a given time.

Government agencies   Permanent or semi-permanent public organizations in charge of specific functions, established by legislation or executive powers. Their autonomy, independence, and accountability can vary significantly. Their functions are normally executive and encompass financing of outside bodies or organizations supporting their goals, if necessary.

GP-led restructuring   Proactive liquidation of a **private market** fund heading toward the end of its **life span** by its manager. This involves the transfer of the remaining assets of the fund to be liquidated to a new fund managed by the same manager. This new fund is not allowed to make new investments and is purely dedicated to the management of the existing assets.

Greenfield   Refers to the construction of a new real asset, such as **infrastructure** or a piece of **real estate**, on virgin land.

Growth capital   Financing provided by funds that are targeting companies already established on the market that need additional financing in order to exploit growth opportunities.

H

Hands-on/hands-off   Depending on the degree of involvement of investors in **private market** in the management of their portfolio company/assets, they can be qualified as hands-on or hands-off investors. A hands-on investor is generally a non-executive director on the board of portfolio companies. A hands-off investor will have only a low degree of involvement in the management of a portfolio company. European continental laws limit the degree of involvement of a **private equity** investor in a **portfolio company** (not crossing the management line is interpreted strictly). *See also* Portfolio company.

Harvesting period   *See* Divestment period.

Hedge fund   Alternative investment vehicle employing strategies and instruments to provide specific exposure to their investors. Managers often use derivatives to actively seek high absolute or relative returns. Hedge funds are accessible to accredited investors, are less regulated than mutual funds, and are often leveraged.

High net worth individuals (HNWI)   Natural person with a net wealth evaluated at more than $1 million (excluding the value of their primary residence). An alternative definition includes natural persons with a lower net wealth but earning at least $200,000 per year. Very high net worth individuals (VHNWI) often refer to a subset of this category with a net wealth of at least $5 million. Ultra-high net worth individuals (UHNWI) refer to an even more exclusive subset with a net wealth of at least $30 million. HNWI are deemed to be accredited investors, able to invest in private markets funds.

Historical cost   The value of assets as shown by the financial statements of the company but not necessarily reflecting the market value of these assets.

HNWI   *See* High net worth individuals.

Holding period   Amount of time during which a portfolio company remains in the ownership of a private market fund.

Hurdle rate   *See* Preferred rate of return.

I

ICM   *See* Index comparison method.

Impact investing   Investment philosophy combining financial performance with other targets, such as social, environmental, or other aims. The financial performance of impact investing is therefore usually lower than the performance of traditional investments.

Incubators   Structures supporting entrepreneurs or start-ups in their effort to launch their operations. They usually provide the fledging ventures with access to operational resources, such as facilities, at low or no cost. They also foster networking opportunities, experience sharing, and at times access to sources of capital. Some of them require payment for these services, in cash and/or stocks.

Index comparison method   Proposed in 1996 by Austin M. Long and Craig J. Nickels, this performance benchmarking approach consists in comparing private market investments or funds with an index. *See also* Public Market Equivalent (PME).

Indemnification   Agreement between fund investors and the fund manager to provide security, protection, and/or compensation for unplanned circumstances that might arise over the course of the partnership's duration.

Infrastructure   Fixed tangible assets supporting productive activities, such as roads, highways, bridges, airports, ports, or networks (telecom, water, sewer systems). At times, this definition is stretched to so-called social infrastructure, such as prison and school systems.

Initial public offering (IPO)   First listing on a stock exchange of existing or new shares of a private company.

Institutional buyout (IBO)   A **leveraged buyout** in which an institution is involved. *See also* Leveraged buyout (LBO).

Institutional investor   An investor, such as an investment company, an insurance group, a bank, a pension fund, an endowment, or a foundation, which generally manages substantial assets and benefits from a significant investment experience. In many countries, institutional investors are not protected by stock exchange regulations, as small investors are, because they are supposed to have a deep knowledge of finance and to be better able to protect their own interests.

Internal rate of return (IRR)   The discount rate that equals the future cash flows with initial investments of a project, that is to say the discount rate at which the **net present value (NPV)** of a project is equal to zero. This is the way to express in percentage terms the (annual) rate of return of an investment project. The calculation takes into account the amounts invested, the amounts earned, and the impact of time on these operations. This measure can be net or gross (of fees). *See also* Net present value (NPV).

Investee company   *See* Portfolio company.

Investor(s)   *See* Fund Investor.

Investment committee   When applied to a fund manager, group of executives deciding on behalf of a **private market** fund to invest in private companies or assets. When applied to an institutional investors, group of executives deciding to invest in private market funds.

Investment period   Initial three- to five-year time frame during which a fund is allowed to make new investments. If necessary, this period can be extended, usually by one year, if the fund regulations allow it. After the end of the investment period, the fund is not allowed to make new investments but can reinvest in existing portfolio companies if needed, and if the fund regulations allow it.

Investment strategy   Rules and processes designed to support the choice of assets by an investor, usually along the lines of potential returns, risk, and liquidity (or duration) dimensions.

By extension, this term refers to unique sets of rules and processes clearly differentiated from others, such as **venture capital** and **leveraged buyouts**. An investment strategy is usually refined thanks to additional dimensions such as the maturity of the underlying asset, its industrial sector, its geographical location, and the type of expected plan to be applied to it to create value and generate profit. *See also* Leveraged buyout (LBO); Venture capital.

Investor protection   Rules and processes designed to prevent capital providers from being misled in the process of selecting assets, thereby supporting them in preventing financial losses. This ranges from fraud prevention to the provision of certified information, and can include guarantees, warranties, or insurance schemes.

IPEV   *See* International Private Equity and Venture Capital Valuation Guidelines.

International Private Equity and Venture Capital Valuation Guidelines   Set of recommendations issued by a large group of international, regional, national, and local private equity associations, designed to support their members in the task of valuing private markets investments.

IPO   *See* Initial public offering (IPO).

IRR   *See* Internal rate of return (IRR).

J

J-Curve   The curve generated when tracing the cash flows of a private market fund as time goes by from its inception to its liquidation has the form of a J. The reason for the initial downward evolution is that the management fees and setup costs are paid from the initial capital call and are followed by further capital calls for management fees and investments. This means that the fund will first show negative accumulated cash flows. When the first **distributions** are made, the curve will change direction. After four to seven years, the fund will usually break even and start to record net positive accumulated cash flows. *See also* Distribution.

Junior debt   Form of subordinated debt. The payment of its principal and interests are second to the senior debts. It can be secured or not. It has the priority on more subordinated forms of debt such as **mezzanine** debt. It is usually not convertible to equity.

K

Key-man clause   Clause of a fund regulation that states that (a) fund manager(s) specifically named have to participate in the fund management. Should this/these manager(s) be impeached, the fund would be prohibited from making new investments and would pursue its activity only toward its winding down.

Key person clause   *See* Key-man clause.

L

Later stage investing   **Venture capital** financing dedicated to the development of a **start-up** once it has reached a certain number of milestones and notably to help it grow abroad, and/or by launching new products/services and/or to acquire competitors.

LBI   *See* Leveraged buy-in (LBI).

LBO   *See* Leveraged buyout (LBO).

LBU   *See* Leveraged build-up (LBU).

Lead investor   In syndicated investments, this is the investor who identifies, structures, and plays the main role in negotiating the terms of an investment. Large **leveraged buyouts** can involve a lead equity investor and a lead debt investor. *See also* Leveraged buyout (LBO).

Letter of confidentiality *See* Non-disclosure agreement.

Letter of intent (LOI) The letter from an investor expressing an interest, the will, or the intention to go into a form of transaction. It usually precedes the negotiation of a full agreement and is generally structured so as not to be legally binding.

Leveraging Practice consisting in borrowing debt to acquire a company or an asset, in order to increase the performance of the capital also used for this acquisition. This also results in increasing the risk of the capital investment.

Leveraged build-up (LBU) An operation in which capital is provided to a holding company in order to finance the acquisition of initially one (**platform** deal) and then other companies (**add-ons**). This is a source of consolidation in certain industries. *See also* Add-on transaction; Platform transaction.

Leveraged buy-in (LBI) An operation of a company by an investor, or a group of investors, through an **LBO** in which the investor(s) bring in a new management. *See also* Leveraged buyout (LBO).

Leveraged buyout (LBO) The acquisition of a company by an investor, or a group of investors, owing to a dedicated structure (holding company) and to a significant borrowed amount (generally 60 to 70 percent of the total). The debt of acquisition is then repaid from the cash flows generated by the company or the help of asset sale. LBOs are generally financed by means of so-called junk bonds. Generally, the assets of the target company are used as collateral for the debt structured by the acquirer. This structuring can also be used by the management team to take control of the company it operates (**management buyout**). *See also* Management buyout (MBO).

Leveraged loan Type of loan used in an LBO for highly leveraged takeovers. They are therefore considered as riskier than most of the credit instruments. Leveraged loans are usually split and held (thus syndicated) between multiple lenders.

Leveraged recapitalization *See* Dividend recapitalization.

Life span of a fund For a **closed-end** fund, the start of the life span of a private market fund is determined by either its first or its last closing, depending on the fund regulations. The end is usually determined by the fund regulations as well and include extensions. At times, the life span of a closed-end private market fund can extend beyond what was planned by the fund regulations. For an **evergreen** fund, the life span starts at the creation of the structure and is indefinite. *See also* Closed-end; Evergreen vehicle.

Limited partner *See* Fund investor.

Limited partnership A legal structure used by most of the **private market** investment vehicles. A limited partnership is created for a given time. It is advised by a **general partner** (the **fund manager**, who bears unlimited liabilities). The general partner manages the limited partnership according to the policy that is described in the **Limited partnership agreement**. The **limited partners** are investors who have a limited responsibility and are not involved in the day-to-day activity of the limited partnership. *See also* Fund investor; Limited partnership agreement (LPA); Fund manager.

Limited partnership agreement (LPA) Form of **fund regulation**. The Limited partnership agreement defines the relationships between the **fund investors**, as well as between the **general partner** (**fund manager**) and the **limited partners** (**fund investors**). *See also* Fund investor; Fund regulation; Fund manager; Fund investor.

Liquidation preferences Organization of the priority claims that shareholders might have upon the exit from a private market investment. A category of shareholders might have a priority claim on getting its capital back before any other category, and at times this claim extends to a minimal return on capital as well.

Liquidity   Degree of speed with which a private market asset can be sold to a third party without negatively affecting the asset price.

Listed private market funds   Investment structure listed on the stock exchange, which is most of the time **evergreen**. This structure is dedicated to **private markets** investments and usually has limited or no organizational expenses. Investors in these structures theoretically have access to the proceeds (capital gains or dividends) generated by these investments. An example of listed private market fund is the **master limited partnership**. *See also* Evergreen vehicle; Master limited partnership; Private markets investing.

Listed private market fund managers   Private markets **fund managers** listed on the stock exchange, theoretically providing their investors with access to the cash-flow streams generated by **management** and other **fees**, as well as the **carried interest** of the team. Most of listed private market fund managers do not hold private market assets and therefore do not provide access to capital gains (only funds, listed or not, do).

Loan-to-own   *See* Distressed debt investing.

Loan-to-value   Measure of risk that provides a lender with a ratio of the total lent divided by the value of the collateral pledged for the loan.

Lock-up period   The time during which the shareholders of a company have agreed not to use their right to sell the shares they own in a listed company after an **IPO**. Investment banks in charge of managing the initial public offering generally insist that the lock-up period lasts at least 180 days for the main shareholders (who own at least 1 percent of the capital) in order to let the floating part of the shares acquire the characteristics of a normal flotation and notably find an equilibrium price. *See also* Initial public offering (IPO).

LOI   *See* Letter of intent.

LP Secondaries   *See* Secondary investing.

LPA   *See* Limited partnership agreement (LPA).

LPX   Sponsor of a series of indexes of listed alternative investment vehicles. By extension refers to the indexes produced, such as the LPX 50. It is in substance an index of listed financial institutions, highly correlated with usual indexes of listed stocks.

Living dead company   *See* Zombie company.

M

Majority ownership   In the case of a majority control ownership, an investor or a group of investors collectively own half plus one of the political (voting) rights in a company. In the case of simple or qualified majority, an investor or a group of investors collectively reach a preset threshold of political rights in a company. Thresholds are often set by the shareholders' agreement to make specific decisions.

Management buy-in (MBI)   The transfer of a company where the new management team, which has control, did not work for the company before and where the current management does not necessarily have a common previous experience. The transaction generally implies the acquisition of a part of the company by the new management and the financial backers.

Management buyout (MBO)   The transfer of a company from its current owner to a new group of owners where the existing management and staff play an active part. In large buyouts, managers have little chance to have a minor part of the company owing to the size of the operation. If the operation is open to all employees, it is then an employee buyout.

Management company *See* Fund manager.

Management fees Financial remuneration for the service provided by a **fund manager**, usually paid quarterly by the fund to the fund manager. The fund manager uses management fees to cover its operational costs, such as wages, office space rent, and other costs. Management fees usually range from 0.5 to 1 percent for a **fund of funds** manager, 1.25 to 2.5 percent for a private equity **fund manager**, 0.4 to 2 percent for a private debt fund manager, and 0.8 to 2 percent for a private real asset fund manager. Management fees are determined notably by the size of the fund raised, the size of the fund managed, the type of strategy, and the region where the manager is based. Macroeconomic conditions and the relative bargaining power of the fund manager and fund investors during the **fundraising** also influence the level of fees. Management fees can be reduced by a **fee offset mechanism**. *See also* Fee offset mechanism; Fund manager; Fundraising; Fund of Funds.

Management team A group of managers in charge of a company, for example, a **start-up**, who can initiate the contact with one or multiple **fund managers** that then leads to an operation of **private equity**.

Mandate Investment delegation to a **gatekeeper** by an investor to define and invest a certain amount in **private market** funds according to the preferences and objectives of the investor. *See also* Gatekeeper.

Market value The value of an asset once it has been reevaluated at a current price.

Marketing of a fund *See* Fundraising.

Master limited partnership (MLP) **Private market** investment structure listed on a stock exchange. It combines the benefits from the tax transparency of a private market fund with the liquidity associated with a listing. MLPs are most frequently used in the energy sector, for example, to invest in oil and gas pipeline operators. They could also be used in the **real estate** sector.

MBI *See* Management buy-in (MBI).

MBO *See* Management buyout (MBO).

Mezzanine debt The most **subordinated** form of debt; it is convertible to equity. It is ranked above equity but after every other form of debt, according to the priority of repayment. Its interests can be capitalized and repaid as a **bullet payment** or distributed regularly. The forms of mezzanine debt vary from senior mezzanine debt, which is less flexible and therefore cheaper, to junior mezzanine debt, which is more flexible and, for example, bears no regular interest payments. *See also* Bullet payment; Subordinated debt.

MFN *See* Most favored nation clause.

Midstream Refers, in the oil and gas industry, to the transportation (by any means) to refineries, storage, and handling of crude oil and unrefined natural gas.

Milestone Preset target for a company to reach, to raise a new round of financing or release a tranche of an existing financing facility.

Minimum commitment Lowest threshold to reach for an investor to be accepted in a **private market** fund.

Minority ownership Literally any investor who does not reach an ownership threshold of half plus one shares. Different levels of minority ownership can be differentiated, such as a significant minority ownership or a blocking minority ownership, which entitles the owner(s) to have special rights in the **shareholders' agreement**.

Minority protection rights Set of legal and contractual provisions protecting the minority shareholders. Contractual provisions are essentially set in the **shareholders' agreement**, which notably defines information, monitoring, control, and action rights for minority shareholders.

These rights are targeted to handle relationships with other shareholders, whether minority or majority owners, as well as with the management of their investment. *See also* Minority ownership.

MLP   *See* Master limited partnership (MLP).

MOIC   *See* Multiple of invested capital (MOIC).

Monitoring   A process by which investors follow the actions of the **portfolio company's** management directed at the realization of preset targets, such as sales, cash situation, and (if applicable) debt service and repayment. Methods of monitoring include presence on the board, regular reports, and meetings. These methods should provide investors with a way of identifying any problems early and taking corrective action rapidly. This provides management with access to new ideas, contracts, and a certain amount of help from investors.

Monitoring fees   To monitor and control a portfolio company, **LBO** fund managers can decide to charge to the company an annual fee. This fee can be attributed to the **fund manager** or the **fund investors** or shared between the fund manager and the fund investors. *See also* Monitoring.

Most favored nation clause   Provision of a **fund regulation** in which the **fund managers** agrees to automatically provide each **fund investor** with the best terms negotiated by any other investor in the fund, including by way of direct negotiation with the fund manager in a **side letter**, for example. *See also* Side letter.

mPME   *See* Public Market Equivalent (PME).

Multiple expansion   One of the sources of performance generation for a **private market** fund. It is the difference between the **entry multiple** and the **exit multiple** and therefore can be positive or negative. *See also* Entry multiple; Exit multiple.

Multiple of invested capital (MOIC)   The ratio between the proceeds from the realization of an investment and the amount invested.

N

Natural resources   Materials or substances readily available as raw input that are extracted and exploited for profit.

NAV   *See* Net asset value (NAV).

Net asset value (NAV)   Estimate of the value of the companies or assets held by a **private market** fund as of a given date.

NDA   *See* Non-disclosure agreement (NDA).

Net cash flows   The difference between the incoming and the outgoing cash flows of a company over a certain period of time. In a **leveraged buyout** operation, the cash flows are a better indication than the net result of a company for an assessment of its capacity to repay its obligations toward its debtors.

Net debt   Total value of the liabilities of a company minus the available cash and cash equivalent.

Net present value (NPV)   The present value of future cash flows of an investment, less the initial investment. In theory, if the net present value is above zero, the investment should be made.

No-fault divorce clause   Provision of a fund regulation such as a **Limited partnership agreement** allowing the **fund investors** to change the **fund manager**, even if the latter has not mismanaged the fund. *See also* Limited partnership agreement (LPA).

Non-disclosure agreement (NDA)   Legally binding document between two economic agents, who agree to actively not disclose and prevent the disclosure of information described and proven confidential. This document is often signed between a prospective portfolio company (represented by its management) and a **VC/growth fund manager** or between a business owner and an **LBO** fund manager. *See also* Fund manager; Growth capital; Leveraged buyout (LBO); Venture capital.

Non-performing loan   Amount due by a borrower that is not repaid and/or whose interests are not paid. The debt is in default or close to it.

NPL   *See* Non-performing loan.

O

Open-end   *See* Evergreen vehicle.

Open-ended   *See* Evergreen vehicle.

Open-end fund   *See* Evergreen vehicle.

Operating partner   Executive paid by a **fund manager** whose role is to work with the **portfolio companies** to increase their value.

Operational costs   Costs associated with the operations of a **private market** fund, such as audit, accounting, fairness opinions, and other expenses that are not covered by the **management fees**. This encompasses notably the **custodian** fees and the **broken deals** expenses. *See also* Broken deal fees; Custodian; Management fees.

Operational improvements   Effort of a **portfolio company** to increase its efficiency in sales and/or profitability.

Opportunistic   Theoretically, the riskiest investment strategy applied in **private real estate** and **private infrastructure**, essentially aiming at delivering capital gains to investors. Assets require significant improvements, sometimes being entirely redeveloped or repositioned. The debt used to acquire these assets is 70 percent or more of the value of the assets.

Overcommitment   Operation leading a **fund investor** to promise to contribute to a **private market** fund a higher amount than effectively planned. The expected result is to help the **fund investor** deploy on a net basis more capital—if possible, close to the planned target. Thus, the purpose of overcommitting is to compensate the early distributions of a fund to reach a higher level of net exposure.

Oversubscription   Situation in which demand from investors significantly exceeds the supply of a financial instrument, such as a **private market** fund.

Owner buyout (OBO)   **Leveraged buyout** operated on a company by its current owner, either to get full control (exit of a co-owner) or to prepare the transition of ownership to an heir.

P

P2P   *See* Public-to-private transaction.

Paid-In   Sum of the capital called by a **private market** fund.

Parallel funds   Investment vehicles set up to accommodate investors with specific legal and/or tax needs. They usually operate on a **pari passu** basis with the main fund that they are mimicking. Some parallel funds are set up for employees or close business relations of fund managers, usually with more favorable terms than the main fund. *See also* Pari passu.

Pari passu   Latin expression that means "at an equal rate or pace," referring to the equality between parties. In the context of credit, lenders whose loans have a pari passu status should collect any amount on an equal footing, including the case of insolvency.

Partial exit   An investor receives proceeds from the exit of an investment but still remains partially invested. This happens, for example, during a **dividend recapitalization**, or when an investor sells part of its stake in a **portfolio company** but also keeps some of it. *See also* Dividend recapitalization.

Partner   *See* Partners.

Partners   The owners of the fund management company or **fund manager**. *See also* Fund manager.

Payment in-kind   Feature of a loan according to which interests are capitalized and paid, usually along with the principal, not in cash but with securities.

Peer group   Sample of funds that are similar in their investment strategy (including target maturity and size), geographical reach, industrial specialization (if any), and vintage year.

Pension fund/plan   Organization collecting employer and/or employee contributions to invest them and later distribute these contributions and the eventual investment proceeds to the employees upon and/or during their retirement.

Performance fee   *See* Carried interest.

Persistence of performance   Refers to the ability of a **private market fund manager** to either perform within a specific subset of a peer group or to perform consistently above or below a specific threshold.

Pitch   Refers to the rather short and condensed form of commercialization of an investment.

Placement agent   Intermediary specialized in the support and services to **fund managers** willing to raise a private market fund. Its services can be regulated (or even banned) in some jurisdictions.

Platform transaction   In the context of a **buy-and-build** strategy, refers to the first and/or largest of a series of investments leading to the creation of a larger company thanks to **add-on transactions**. *See also* Add-on transaction; Buy-and-build.

Pledge fund   Investment vehicle designed so that investors can finance specific deals along the lines pre-agreed with the **fund manager**. Investors have to approve the transaction.

Portfolio company (also known as investee company)   A company or entity in which a fund invests directly.

Post-money value   The valuation of a company after the most recent **round of financing**. The value is calculated by multiplying the total number of shares by the price of a share applied at the most recent round of financing.

PME   *See* Public Market Equivalent (PME).

PME+   *See* Public Market Equivalent (PME).

PPM   *See* Private placement memorandum.

PPP   *See* Public private partnership.

Pre-marketing   Series of actions undertaken by a **fund manager** with no actual or immediate fund to sell, aimed at testing and assessing the idea of raising a new fund with investors. This usually implies describing in broad terms the strategy, aim, and operations of this new fund. This activity can be regulated in specific jurisdictions.

Preemption right   Shareholders have the right to maintain a certain percentage of ownership in a company by buying shares on a pro rata basis in case new shares are issued. This can also be exercised in the case of the sale of shares to an existing shareholder, before opening the sale to third parties.

Pre-money value   The value of a company before a planned injection of capital.

Preferred equity   In the **secondary** market, a tranche of financing sitting between debt and equity. This instrument is provided by a third party to an existing **fund investor** unable or not willing to answer current and upcoming capital calls. The third-party specialist provides the capital to answer the calls and gets some of the returns provided to the fund investor. The benefit for the fund investor is to stay invested and possibly keep the opportunity to reinvest in successor funds from the same manager. (For disambiguation, compare with Preferred shares.) *See also* Preferred shares; Secondary investing.

Preferred rate of return   The minimal yearly rate of return acceptable for the investors in a **private market** fund, which is often set at 8 percent on capital invested. It is therefore calculated as an **internal rate of return**. This rate has to be paid to investors before the **carried interest** is paid to the **fund manager**. *See also* Carried interest; Internal rate of return.

Preferred shares   The class of shares that includes specific rights, not attributed to **common shares**, such as a preferred redemption with a guaranteed minimal multiple of investment.

Principal   Key executives working for the **fund manager** and putting in place the strategy and who can claim a portion of the carried interest. In academic literature relative to **agency theory** (also referred to as "principal-agent problem"), these executives as a group are referred to as an "agent" (and fund investors as "principals"). The use of the term here is different to the way it is used in the academic context of the principal–agent problem. *See also* Agency theory.

Private debt investing   Institutional lending to businesses that is not done by banks. The purpose of this investment strategy is to lend, recover, or restructure the debt of a company to generate interests and/or capital gains. This investment strategy includes **direct lending** (also known as senior lending), **venture debt**, **unitranche**, **mezzanine** financing, **distressed debt**, non-performing loans investing, and other niches, such as litigation financing and trade finance. *See also* Direct lending; Distressed debt investing; Mezzanine debt; Unitranche debt; Venture capital.

Private equity investing   Capital infusion in a company or its transfer of ownership, with the intention of implementing a plan in this company to increase its value and eventually sell it, usually after three to seven years, at a significant profit. This plan is set up with the full support of the entrepreneurs/management of the firm. This investment strategy includes **venture capital**, **growth capital**, **leveraged buyout**, **turn-around capital**, and other niches, such as **private investment in public equities**. *See also* Growth capital; Leveraged buyout (LBO); Private investment in public equities (PIPE); Turn-around capital; Venture capital.

Private investment in public equities (PIPE)   A significant stake in a listed company is sold through a **private placement**. This is in general linked to a capital infusion in the listed firm. This operation leads to the sale by the company of shares at a discount compared to the public price of the shares. This discount is justified by the commitment of the owner of this stake to hold the shares for a minimum amount of time, usually at least 24 to 36 months. *See also* Private placement.

Private markets investing   Expression gathering **private equity**, **private debt**, and **private real asset investing**. *See also* Private debt investing; Private equity investing; Private real assets investing.

Private placement   Sale of securities at arm's length, that is to say, out of the stock exchange.

Private placement memorandum   Prospectus summing up the features of a private market fund to be created. This sales document notably includes an executive summary, a detailed investment strategy, a description of the operational capacity of the fund manager, its track record (if any), and its differentiating factors, as well as the key terms of the fund.

Private real assets investing Equity or debt investment in private assets, whether tangible or not and whether fixed or not, thus ranging from royalties to airports. The purpose of this investment strategy is to develop, structure, or restructure the asset to generate a mix of dividends and capital gains. The holding period is usually of 3 to 12 or even 15 years. This investment strategy includes **private real estate**, private **infrastructure**, the oil and gas value chain, **timberland** and **farmland**, and other niches, such as intellectual property and royalty financing, mining, or leasing. *See also* Private real estate; Infrastructure; Timberland; Farmland.

Privatization Acquisition of a state-owned company or asset by a private owner (or a group of private owners).

Proceeds Cash generated and collected from an investment activity.

Proprietary deal flow Sourcing technique in which the potential buyer is the first and the only one looking at an investment opportunity.

Prudent man rule American legal principle according to which an agent managing the asset of a client should apply the philosophy of an individual seeking reasonable income and the preservation of capital.

Prudent person principle *See* Prudent man rule.

Prudential ratio A regulatory ratio that defines the quantity of capital that a bank must keep in-house in order to cover the risk of its commitments.

Public Market Equivalent (PME) Performance benchmarking method to compare the performance of a private market investment or fund with an index. Different variations exist, such as the ICM (also referred to as PME or LN-PME), which essentially mimics the cash-flow pattern of a private market fund with an index. This method supports the comparison of the performance of a fund with equivalent investments in the index. It has a shortcoming though: if the cash distributions are significant, the index performance could be negative. The PME+ of Christophe Rouvinez and the mPME of Cambridge Associates regulate the distribution by computing either a factor adjusting the NAV of the fund (PME+) or the weight of the distribution in the fund (mPME). Additional variations around these three methods, such as the KS-PME by Steve Kaplan and Antoinette Schoar aim at determining a direct indicator of performance in a single figure. The Direct Alpha by Oleg Gredil, Barry E. Griffiths, and Rüdiger Stucke is another variation on this approach.

Public–private partnership Agreement between one or multiple governmental agencies and private sector companies, leading to the creation, improvement, or regeneration of a company or an asset.

Public-to-private transaction Acquisition of a listed company or asset by a private owner (or a group of private owners) and its subsequent delisting.

Q

Qualified investor Entity or person that invests large volumes in the securities market, which allows for better negotiation conditions, lower commissions, and so forth. The regulations generally provide them with lower levels of protection than small investors, given that, due to their institutional or professional nature, they have sufficient knowledge and experience to assess the risks they assume and make their own investment decisions. Qualified investors are considered to be institutional investors (banks and savings banks, insurance companies, investment fund management companies, pension fund management entities, funds and investment companies, and so forth), small businesses, and individuals who, in compliance with certain criteria, request to be considered qualified investors. They are allowed to invest in private market funds.

Quartile   The segment of a sample representing a sequential quarter (25 percent). Thus, the first 10 of 40 funds are the first (or top) quartile and the last 10 are the last (or bottom) quartile.

Quasi-equity   Instruments such as shareholders' loans, **preferred shares**, and so forth. These instruments are not guaranteed by collaterals and are convertible at exit.

R

RAIF   The Reserved Alternative Investment Fund, which is a legal form available in Luxembourg to create rapidly and flexibly private market funds to be marketed in the EU. The fund manager is regulated under the **AIFMD** that dispenses the fund to be. *See also* AIFMD.

Real assets   Tangible (and by extension intangible claims on tangible) properties that have value on a stand-alone basis due to their substance or features. This category notably includes real estate, infrastructure, and natural resources.

RCF   *See* Revolving credit facility.

Recapitalization   A change in the initial financing structure of a buyout to reschedule the debt payments or capitalize the structure further, because of insufficient results to pay the debt of acquisition or because of a capital need linked to further investments. Alternatively, a recapitalization could lead the initial investors to exit from a successful **LBO**, so as to enable the management team to continue without any **IPO** or trade sale. *See also* Initial public offering (IPO); Leveraged buyout (LBO).

Recycling of distributions   *See* Reinvestment of distributions.

Redemption   Withdrawal of an investor from a fund. The fund pays back the capital (and distributes the eventual losses or profit associated with it) to the investor.

Reinvestment of distributions   Provision of **fund regulations** allowing the **fund manager** to reinvest early **distributions**, as long as the fund is in its **investment period**. The aim is to allow the fund manager to effectively invest up to 100 percent of the fund size, thereby compensating for the fees paid by the fund. *See also* Distribution; Fund manager; Fund regulation; Investment period.

Removal of fund manager   Clause in a fund's regulations leading to the replacement of the manager with and/or without cause.

Reporting   Process supporting the regular and recurring information of investors by their agent. In the case of a private markets fund, the reporting is often a quarterly and is a written report from the **fund manager** to the **fund investors**. In the case of a private company or asset, the reporting is from the management to the investors and can be monthly, quarterly, or less frequent. *See also* Fund investors; Fund manager.

Representations   Series of contractual clauses usually used when a transfer of ownership of a given company or asset occurs (for example, in a **leveraged buyout** operation). It allows the buyer of a company to make sure that the means necessary for the company to operate belong to the latter. However, it does not cover an over- or under-valuation of the company. It is often combined with **warranties**. *See also* Leveraged buyout (LBO); Warranties.

Replacement capital   Financing provided by funds to buy out one or multiple shareholders. This can be the way for shareholders of a family business to sell their shares without necessarily obliging the family to lose control.

Residual value   Sum of the **net asset value** of all the assets held by a **private market** fund as of a given date.

Residual value to paid-in (RVPI)   Ratio between the **net asset value** of a fund (its **residual value**) and the total capital called by this fund (**paid-in**). *See also* Paid-in; Residual value.

Responsible investing   *See* Environmental, Social, and Governance (ESG) criteria.

Restart   Process of launching a new company out of the ashes of a failed one.

Restructuring   Series of actions undertaken by the management of a company to significantly or radically improve its financial and/or operational situation.

Retail investor   Nonprofessional, unqualified, or non-accredited individual purchasing financial instruments for his or her own personal account.

Reverse break-up fee   *See* Break-up fee.

Revolving credit facility   Permanent credit line from a bank.

Re-up   Process in which an investor in a fund decides to invest in the next fund from the same fund manager, with the same specific investment strategy.

Round of financing   Designation of a capital increase operation in a given **venture capital**-backed (or **business angel**-backed) company, which is usually supporting it to its next stage of development. Usually referred to as Series A, Series B, Series C, and so forth, until the company reaches profitability. As **growth capital** is not operated in stages, there is no round of financing.

RVPI   *See* Residual value to paid-in (RVPI).

S

Sale-and-leaseback   Financial transaction in which an asset, such as a machine or a building, is sold and immediately leased back for the long term. The seller is no longer the owner but continues to use it.

Scale up   Refers to the growth phase of a **start-up**, after the launch of its product or service (also known as "go to market" milestone). This includes the mass commercialization, internationalization, acquisition of competitors, and even the launch of additional products or services. *See also* Start-up.

Scheme of arrangement   Agreement between a company and its creditors that is approved by a bankruptcy court. This type of arrangement is usually undertaken to significantly alter the structure of a company and the rights of its creditors. It can be used to reschedule its debt or amend priorities of creditors or their claims on the assets of a company, for example.

Search fund   *See* Finder's fund.

Second lien   Debt subordinated to the repayment of the senior debt (first lien) but exempt of conversion rights. It is usually secured against the same collateral as the senior debt, but this collateral can only be claimed if the first lien rights are extinct.

Secondary buyout/buy-in   The exit path from an investment where the initial professional investors can realize all or part of their investment through the sale to another professional investor.

Secondary investing   Investment in a preexisting asset. This can lead to the acquisition of an existing stake in a portfolio company by a fund (direct **secondary**) or of an existing stake in a private market fund by a fund investor (**fund secondary**). Direct secondary investments differentiate themselves from direct primary investments in the sense that there is no new instrument created in the operation (no new shares in the case of direct VC secondary). *See also* Secondary investing.

Securitization   Bundling of assets into a fund vehicle further offered to investors under the form of notes or bonds that are often rated by independent credit rating agencies.

Seed investing   Initial funding used for the proof of a concept and eventually to develop the prototype of the product or service and initiate a formal or informal market study.

Segregated accounts   Investment conduit held by a single investor. The account can be managed discretionarily by a third party through a mandate or non-discretionarily.

Semi-captive   *See* Captive manager.

Senior debt   A loan used to finance the **leveraged buyout** of a company, which benefits from priority in the case of default of payment by the company or in the case of failure of the structuring. It is usually secured against the company as a collateral. *See also* Leveraged buyout (LBO).

Setup costs   Costs borne by a **private market** fund for its setup. They usually include lawyers' fees, sometimes **placement agents'** fees, and additional costs related to this initial operation. It can range from 0.5 to 3 percent of the fund size.

Shareholders' agreement   A contract between the shareholders of a company to establish their common and respective rights and duties. In particular, the agreement must determine the protection of minority holders against actions taken by the majority and which would be unfavorable to minority interests. This document is contractual and evolves with the ownership structure of the company.

SICAR (*Société d'Investissement en Capital Risque*)   Luxembourg investment vehicle dedicated to private equity investments, combining a fund and a fund management company in a single entity. A SICAR distributes dividends.

Side letter   Agreement signed between the **fund manager** and (a) **fund investor**(s) outside the **fund regulations**. This usually does not involve any significant change of the fund regulations, but adds precision, for example, to ensure compliance with specific tax regulations. Side letters are often generalized to all the investors in a given fund due to the **most favored nation clause**. *See also* Most favored nation clause.

Sidecar fund   Investment vehicle operated alongside a main fund but under different terms. This type of investment vehicle is usually reserved for the employees and specific partners of a **fund manager** and can operate without supporting any **management fee** or **carried interest**.

SIF (Specialized investment fund)   Luxembourg investment fund dedicated to private equity investments. An SIF distributes capital gains.

SLP   *See* Société de Libre Partenariat.

Société de Libre Partenariat   French equivalent of the limited partnership structure.

Solvency ratio   A regulatory ratio that defines the quantity of capital that an insurer must keep in-house to cover the risk of its commitments.

Solo investment   Form of direct investment in which the investor acts alone.

Sovereign wealth fund   Investment vehicle owned and operated by a state or governmental agency. The source of capital is often related to the exploitation of natural resources, the constitution of large foreign exchange reserves, or public savings.

Special purpose acquisition company   Investment trust created by a manager with the purpose of investing in a private company. The manager identifies a target, trust unit holders vote on the project, and if the vote is positive, the trust makes the acquisition and is converted into a listed special purpose acquisition company.

Special purpose vehicle   Legal entity set up for a particular function, such as owning an asset as a collateral for a loan.

Specialized fund An investment strategy in **private equity** designed to build a portfolio of companies that are specialized in some industrial sectors and possibly located in certain geographical areas.

Spin-off A group separates itself from a business unit but can maintain a significant ownership in the resulting company. This can happen when strong commercial relationships are maintained and/or the former business unit develops a new product that could be of interest to the group.

SPAC *See* Special purpose acquisition company.

Sponsor In the context of raising a **private market** fund, refers to the institution that owns a significant part or the entire **fund manager**. The sponsor also acts as a **cornerstone investor**. *See also* Cornerstone investor.

Sponsored LBO Transfer of ownership of a private company in which a fund or a financial institution is involved. An unsponsored LBO is a transfer of ownership of a private company without the involvement of a fund or a financial institution, such as a pure management buyout.

SPV *See* Special purpose vehicle.

Staple financing Form of **secondary investing** in which the acquisition of a stake in a fund is combined with the commitment of the next generation of fund (**successor fund**) from the same fund manager. *See also* Secondary investing; Successor fund.

Start-up The stage of development of a company, where it develops its product or service, reaches the prototype stage, and eventually starts to market the product or service. This company is usually structured or is only active for a short period of time (a year or less). Generally, this company has recruited key managers, designed a **business plan**, and attracted some seed financing. A start-up is generally considered to be five-years old or less. *See also* Business plan.

Structuring Process of setting up a financial transaction, instrument, or investment vehicle.

Subordinated debt Corporate credit whose repayment and interest payment are subject to the prior repayment of more senior credit. The claims of subordinated debt holders on the collateral of the debt are also subject to a priority from those of senior debt holders.
The concept of subordinated debt varies according to the legal regimes of different countries.

Subscription agreement Legal document signed by an investor to commit to a fund.

Successor fund Next generation of a series of funds dedicated to a specific investment strategy raised by a **fund manager**. The right to raise a successor fund can be limited by the **fund regulations** of the current active generation of fund. For example, the fund regulations can state that a successor fund cannot be raised if the current one is not invested at least at 70 percent of its fund size.

Subsequent closing Interim steps in the process of a **fund raising**, materializing the commitment of **fund investors** who were not part of the initial closing, also called **first closing**. *See also* Closing; First closing.

Sweat equity Shares given to the management and/or employees of a company in exchange of their work and/or their intellectual property.

Syndicate/syndication A means of financing a company by splitting the risk between multiple investors. In the case of large **buyouts** (**LBO**), there can be multiple syndicates for different forms of financial instruments (equity or debt).

T

Tag along Clause of a **shareholders' agreement** that protects the minority shareholder, in case of a sale by the controlling shareholder of their stake in a company. **Minority shareholders** have the right to sell their stake under the same conditions as the **majority shareholders**.

Take down   *See* Capital call.

Take private   *See* Public-to-private transaction.

Target company   Company that is to be acquired directly or indirectly by a **private equity fund**.

Term of a fund   End date of a **private market** fund. For **closed-end funds**, this ranges from 8 to 15 years. There is no term for **open-end funds**.

Term sheet   The synthesis of the main conditions proposed by the investor for a stake in a company.

Terms and conditions   Statements of the rights of the **fund investors** and duties of the **fund manager**.

Theory of agency   See Agency theory.

Timberland   Geographical area covered with marketable wood.

Top-down   Progressing from the highest (or least granular) to the lowest (or the most granular) level of an analytical process. In the context of asset allocation, this consists in analyzing macroeconomic factors to draw general conclusions and build a portfolio from this analysis. The positive side of this approach is that it is systematic and theoretically sound. The negative side of this approach is that it might not be applicable for the lack of actual assets in specific investment categories. A complementary approach is **bottom-up**. *See also* Bottom-up.

Top-line growth   Growth of the revenues of a given company.

Top quartile   25 percent of a sample which ranks the highest according to a specific criterion, such as for example a performance metric.

Total value to paid-in   *See* TVPI (Total value to paid-in).

Track record   Historical performance of a **private market fund manager**, which includes notably **multiples of investment** (TVPI) and **internal rates of return** (IRR) and at times, its **Public Market Equivalent** (PME). *See also* Internal rate of return (IRR); Multiple of invested capital (MOIC); Public Market Equivalent (PME).

Tranche of equity or debt   Defines the priority of payment of the holder of a security. The capital structure of a company may contain several tranches of both debt securities and equity securities.

Transaction fees   Expenses borne by a **private market** fund associated with investments or divestments.

Turn-around capital   Acquisition of ailing businesses by specialized funds, with the aim of turning around these businesses thanks to a change in their business model, financial structure, capital, management and/or product or services. This type of investment is executed before the company goes bankrupt.

TVPI (Total value to paid-in)   Ratio between the total value of the portfolio of a given **private market** fund (i.e., the sum of its **distributions** and the **net asset value** of the portfolio) and the total of the capital called (**paid-in**).

U

Undrawn capital   Capital not yet called by a **private market** fund. Also referred to as **dry powder**. *See also* Dry powder.

Unitranche debt   Single loan structure combining multiple layers of debt ranging from senior to subordinated ranks.

Unrealized value   *See* Residual value.

Unsponsored LBO   *See* Sponsored LBO.

Upstream   Also referred to as exploration and production, this refers to searching for crude oil and natural gas fields, drilling and operating wells.

V

Valuation   Analytical process leading to the current or projected estimation of the worth of a company or an asset.

Valuation date   Date on which a valuation applied to a given investment.

Value add   Moderate to high-risk investment strategy applied in **private real estate** and private **infrastructure**, essentially aiming at delivering capital gains to investors and possibly income. Assets require significant management from investors, solving vacancy issues, maintenance or operational issues, significant upgrading or renovation, and/or quality of tenants issues. The debt used to acquire these assets is of 60 to 75 percent maximum of the value of the assets.

Value-at-risk   Method to measure the probability of an investment loss and its extent during a set time period.

Value creation   Result of a set of actions undertaken to increase the worth of a company or an asset.

VCT   *See* Venture capital trust (VCT).

Vendor due diligence   Detailed report on a company or an asset provided by the seller to potential buyers.

Vendor financing   Financing in which the seller of a company accepts a deferred payment from the buyer.

Venture capital   Financing provided by funds targeting emerging businesses, notably **start-ups** with strong growth perspectives. The venture capital investor provides at the same time capital, a network of contacts, know-how, and additional experience. *See also* start-up.

Venture capital trust (VCT)   British investment vehicle allowing retail investors to gain exposure to venture capital investments. A tax incentive is associated with a commitment in this vehicle that is listed after its inception.

Venture debt   Financing provided to mid- to late-stage under the form of convertible debt and as a complement to equity financing. As most **start-ups** are usually free of debt, this type of loan is in practice senior and collateralized. *See also* Start-up.

Venture leasing   Investments in **venture capital** that are linked to the leasing of equipment or other fixed assets in a technology **start-up**. Compared to traditional leasing contracts (generally not available for start-ups), venture leasing implies some equity kickers to compensate for the risk borne by the leaser. *See also* start-up.

Venture philanthropy   Subset of impact or **ESG** investments aiming at investing in emerging projects or companies with the purpose of achieving charitable targets, often leading to lower or no returns on investment. This approach applies **venture capital** techniques and criteria to select and invest in these projects and companies. *See also* Environmental, Social, and Governance criteria (ESG).

Vesting (carried interest)   Procedure of attribution to each of the principals of the **carried interest** allocated to the **fund manager**. It can be immediate or progressive (over time). *See also* Carried interest.

Vintage year   Year of creation of a **private market** fund and usually of its first **capital call** (or in specific cases of its **final closing**) or its first investment. This is also a reference point for the funds created the same year for comparison purposes.

Vulture investing   Often confused with **distressed debt** or **turn-around** investing, this approach consists in taking control of ailing businesses with the clear target of shutting them down and selling their assets. Vulture investing thus differs from other strategies aimed at distressed businesses, as its only purpose is the liquidation of activities. *See also* Distressed debt investing; Turnaround capital.

W

Warranties   Series of contractual clauses usually used when a transfer of ownership of a given company or asset occurs (for example, in a **leveraged buyout** operation). It allows the buyer of a company to make sure that there are no hidden liabilities (or at least that the buyer will not support the financial consequences of past liabilities). However, it does not cover an over- or undervaluation of the company. It can be combined with representations. *See also* Leveraged buy-out (LBO).

Wash-out   In the context of a **distressed debt** investment, a wash-out is the complete elimination of the current shareholders from the capitalization table. In a more general context of capital increase, a wash-out round is when the entrepreneurs and managers of a company lose the control of the firm. *See also* Distressed debt investing.

Waterfall distribution   Mechanism attributing the cash generated by a given **private market** fund to its stakeholders according to priorities (for example, refund to the **fund investors** and the **fund manager** of their initial **commitments**, then distribution of the **hurdle rate**, then **distribution** of the **catch-up**, then distribution of the profits and **carried interest**). *See also* Carried interest; Commitment; Distribution; Fund investor; Fund manager; Hurdle rate.

Winding down of a fund   Process of completely terminating the operations of a private market investment vehicle. This includes liquidating any remaining assets, liquidating escrow accounts, and handling any outstanding right or duty, such as a warranty.

Write down   Accounting and reporting operation reflecting the impairment losses of a **portfolio company**.

Write-off   An action that changes the value of an asset/portfolio company to zero.

Z

Zombie company   In the context of **venture** and **growth** capital investments, these are **portfolio companies** that are break-even but do not provide attractive prospects for a potential buyer or listing. In the context of **LBO** and **private debt**, these are portfolio companies that generate sufficient cash flows to service their debt and operate their daily activity but cannot repay their debt. *See also* Growth capital; Leveraged buyout (LBO); Private debt investing; Venture capital.

Bibliography

BOOKS AND REPORTS

Brooke, Peter, and Daniel Penrice, 2009, *A Vision for Venture Capital – Realizing the Promise of Global Venture Capital and Private Equity*, New Ventures.

Bruntland Commission, 1987, *Report of the World Commission on Environment and Development: Our Common Future*, United Nations (https://sustainabledevelopment.un.org/content/documents/5987our-common-future.pdf).

Cornelius, Peter, Christian Diller, Didier Guennoc, and Thomas Meyer, 2013, *Mastering illiquidity – Risk Management for Portfolio of Limited Partnership Funds*, John Wiley & Sons.

Cummine, Angela, 2016, *Citizen's Wealth – Why (and How) Sovereign Funds Should Be Managed by the People for the People*, Yale University Press.

Demaria, Cyril, 2003, *Développement durable et finance*, Maxima.

Demaria, Cyril, 2015, *Private Equity Fund Investments*, Palgrave Macmillan.

Demaria, Cyril, 2020, *Introduction to Private Equity, Debt and Real Assets*, 3rd ed., John Wiley & Sons.

Hobohm, Daniel, 2010, *Investors in Private Equity Funds: Theory, Preferences and Performances*, Gabler Research.

Impavido, Gregorio, 2012, *Handbook of Key Global Financial Markets, Institutions, and Infrastructure*, Academic Press.

Keynes, John Maynard, 1936, *The General Theory of Employment, Interest and Money*, Palgrave Macmillan.

Kocis, James M., James C. Bachman, Austin M. Long III, and Craig J. Nickels, 2009, *Inside Private Equity: The Professional Investor's Handbook*, John Wiley & Sons.

Lerner, Josh, 2012a, *Boulevard of Broken Dreams: Why Public Efforts to Boost Entrepreneurship and Venture Capital Have Failed – and What to Do about It*, Princeton University Press.

Lerner, Josh, 2012b, *The Architecture of Innovation: The Economics of Creative Organizations*, Harvard Business Review Press.

Malkiel, Burton G., 2015, *A Random Walk Down Wall Street: The Time-Tested Strategy for Successful Investing*, 11th ed., W. W. Norton & Company.

Marston, Richard C., 2011, *Portfolio Design: A Modern Approach to Asset Allocation*, John Wiley & Sons.

McDonough, William, and Michael Braungart, 2002, *Cradle to Cradle: Remaking the Way We Make Things*, North Point Press.

Meyer, Thomas and Pierre-Yves Mathonet, 2005, *Beyond the J-curve – Managing a Portfolio of Venture Capital and Private Equity Funds*, John Wiley & Sons.

Swensen, David F., 2009, *Pioneering Portfolio Management: An Unconventional Approach to Institutional Investment*, Free Press.

Teall, John L., 2019, *Financial Trading and Investing*, 2nd ed., Academic Press.

Dates in brackets refer to the journal publication, but the text of the book refers to the first date and the working paper.

ACADEMIC PAPERS

Acharya, Viral V., Oliver Gottschalg, Moritz Hahn, and Conor Kehoe, 2009, "Corporate Governance and Value Creation: Evidence from Private Equity," *Review of Financial Studies*, 26(2): 368–402, European Corporate Governance Institute Working Paper No. 232/2009.

Allen, Franklin, 2001, "Do Financial Institutions Matter?" *The Journal of Finance*, 56(4): 1165–75.

Andonov, Aleksander, Yael V. Hochberg, and Joshua D. Rauh, 2018, "Political Representation and Governance: Evidence from the Investment Decisions of Public Pension Funds," *The Journal of Finance*, 73(5):2041–86.

Ang, Andrew, Dimitris Papanikolaou, and Mark M. Westerfield, 2014, "Portfolio Choice with Illiquid Assets," *Management Science*, 60(11):2381–617.

Anson, Mark, 2017, "Measuring Liquidity Premiums for Illiquid Assets," *The Journal of Alternative Investments*, Fall: 1–12.

Arias, Liliana, Mohamed El Hedi Arouri, Philippe Foulquier, and Stéphane Gregoir, 2010, "On the Suitability of the Calibration of Private Equity Risk in the Solvency II Standard Formula," EDHEC, April.

Barber, Brad M., Adair Morse, and Ayako Yasuda, 2015 (2020), "Impact Investing," SSRN Working Paper No. 2705556 *Journal of Financial Economics*, forthcoming.

Bortolotti, Bernardo, Veljko Fotak, William L. Megginson, and William F. Miracky, 2010, "Quiet Leviathans: Sovereign Wealth Fund Investment, Passivity and the Value of the Firm," SSRN Working Paper No. 1787191.

Bernstein, Shai, Josh Lerner, and Antoinette Schoar, 2013, "The Investment Strategies of Sovereign Wealth Funds," *The Journal of Economic Perspectives*, 27(2):219–37.

Braun, Alexander, Hato Schmeiser, and Caroline Siegel, 2014, "The Impact of Private Equity on a Life Insurer's Capital Charges under Solvency II and The Swiss Solvency Test," *The Journal of Risk and Insurances*, 81(1):113–58.

Braun, Reiner, Nils Dorau, Tim Jenkinson, and Daniel Urban, 2019, "Persistence in Private Equity Investments," SSRN Working Paper No. 3475460.

Braun, Reiner, Tim Jenkinson, and Ingo Stoff, 2017, "How Persistent Is Private Equity Performance? Evidence from Deal-Level Data," *The Journal of Financial Economics*, 123(2):273–91.

Broeders, Dirk W. G. A., Kristy A. E. Jansen, and Bas J. M. Werker, 2020, "Pension Fund's Illiquid Asset Allocation under Liquidity and Capital Requirements," *Journal of Pension Economics and Finance*, 1–23.

Brown, Keith C., Christian Ioan Tiu, and Lorenzo Garlappi, 2007, "The Troves of the Academe: Asset Allocation, Risk Budgeting, and the Investment Performance of University Endowment Funds," McComs Research Paper Series No. Fin-03-07, SSRN Working Paper No. 981436.

Brown, Gregory W., Oleg R.Gredil, and Steven N. Kaplan, 2017 (2019), "Do Private Equity Funds Manipulate Reported Returns?" SSRN Working Paper No. 2271690. *Journal of Financial Economics*, 132(2): 267–297.

Brown, Gregory, Robert Harris, Wendy Hu, Tim Jenkinson, Steve Kaplan, and David T. Robinson, 2019, "Can Investors Time Their Exposure to Private Equity?" Kenan Institute of Private Enterprise Research Paper No. 18-26, SSRN Working Paper No. 3241102.

Brown, Gregory, Wendy Hu, and Bert-Klemens Kuhn, 2019, "Why Defined Contribution Plans Need Private Investments," DCALTA/IPC Research Paper, October.

Cai, Ye, Merih Sevilir, and Xuan Tian, 2014, "Do Entrepreneurs Make Good VCs?" SSRN Working Paper No. 2021327.

Cao, Jerry, 2011, "IPO Timing, Buyout Sponsors' Exit Strategy and Firm Performance of RLBOs," *Journal of Financial and Quantitative Analysis*, 46(4):1001–24.

Cao, Jerry, and Josh Lerner, 2009, "The Performance of Reverse Leveraged Buyouts," *Journal of Financial Economics*, 91(2):139–57.

Cavagnaro, Daniel R., Berk A. Sensoy, Yingdi Wang, and Michael S. Weisbach, 2019, "Measuring Institutional Investors' Skill at Making Private Equity Investments," *The Journal of Finance*, 74(6): 3089–134.

Chamberlain, Trevor W., and François-Xavier Joncheray, 2017, "Reverse Leveraged Buyout Return Behaviour: Some European Evidence," *Eurasian Journal of Economics and Finance*, 5(4):142–75.

Chen, Henry, Paul Gompers, Anna Kovner, and Josh Lerner, 2009 (2010), "Buy Local? The Geography of Successful and Unsuccessful Venture Capital Expansion," NBER Working Paper No. 15102, *Journal of Urban Economics*, 67(1): 90–110.

Cumming, Douglas, and Grant Fleming, 2012 (2015), "Corporate Defaults, Workouts and the Rise of the Distressed Asset Investment Industry," SSRN Working Paper No. 2144912, *Business History Review*, 89(2): 305–30

Cuny, Charles J., and Eli Talmor, 2006 (2007), "A Theory of Private Equity Turnarounds," SSRN Working Paper No. 875823, *Journal of Corporate Finance*, 13(4), 629–46.

D'Angelo, Enzo, 2010, "Limited Partners' Perception and Management of Risk in Private Equity Investing," Kellogg School of Management.

Da Rin, Marco, and Ludovic Phalippou, 2013, "Investor Heterogeneity: Evidence from a Survey of Private Equity Investors," SSRN Working Paper No. 2379354.

Degeorge, François, and Richard Zeckhauser, 1993, "The Reverse LBO Decision and Firm Performance: Theory and Evidence," *Journal of Finance*, 48(4):1323–48.

Diamond, Douglas W., 1984, "Financial Intermediation and Delegated Monitoring," *Review of Economic Studies*, 51: 393–414.

Doidge, Craig G., Andrew Karolyi, and René M. Stulz, 2017, "The U.S. Listing Gap," *Journal of Financial Economics*, 123(3):464–87.

Doskeland, Trond M., and Per Strömberg, 2018, "Evaluating Investments in Unlisted Equity for the Norwegian Government Pension Fund Global (GPFG)," April.

Dyck, I. J. Alexander, and Adair Morese, 2011, "Sovereign Wealth Fund Portfolios," Chicago Booth Research Paper 11–15 / Rotman School of Management Working Paper 1792850, University of Toronto and University of Chicago.

Dyck, I. J. Alexander, and Lukasz Pomorski, 2016, "Investor Scale and Performance in Private Equity Investments," *Review of Finance*, 20(3):1081–106.

Ewens, Michael, and Matthew Rhodes-Kropf, 2015, "Is a VC Partnership Greater than the Sum of its Partners?" *Journal of Finance*, 70(3):1081–113.

Fama, Eugene F., and Kenneth French, 2004, "The Capital Asset Pricing Model: Theory and Evidence," *Journal of Economic Perspectives*, 18(3):25–46.

Fang, Lily, Victoria Ivashina, and Josh Lerner, 2015, "The Disintermediation of Financial Markets: Direct Investing in Private Equity," *Journal of Financial Economics*, 116(1):160–78.

Franz, Richard, and Stephan Kranner, 2019, "University Endowments – A Primer," *CFA Institute Research Foundation*, Brief.

Franzoni, Francesco, Eric Nowak, and Ludovic Phalippou, 2012, "Private Equity Performance and Liquidity Risk," *Journal of Finance,* 67(6):2341–73.

Gredil, Oleg, Barry E. Griffiths, and Rüdiger Stucke, 2014, "Benchmarking Private Equity: The Direct Alpha Method," SSRN Working Paper No. 2403521.

Harris, Robert S., Tim Jenkinson, and Steven N. Kaplan, 2014, "Private Equity Performance: What Do We Know?" *Journal of Finance*, 69(5):1851–82.

Harris, Robert S., Tim Jenkinson, and Rudiger Stucke, 2012, "Are Too Many Private Equity Funds Top Quartile?" *Journal of Applied Corporate Finance*, 24(4):77–89.

Hochberg, Yael V., Alexander Ljungqvist, and Yang Lu, 2007, "Whom You Know Matters: Venture Capital Networks and Investment Performance," *Journal of Finance*, 62(1):251–301.

Hochberg, Yael V., and Joshua D. Rauh, 2013, "Local Overweighting and Underperformance: Evidence from Limited Partner Private Equity Investments," *Review of Financial Studies*, 26: 403–51.

Holthausen, Robert W., and David F. Larcker, 1996, "The Financial Performance of Reverse Leveraged Buyouts," *Journal of Financial Economics*, 42: 193–332.

Hsu, David, 2004, "What Do Entrepreneurs Pay for Venture Capital Affiliation," *Journal of Finance*, 59(4):1805–44.

Ivashina, Victoria, and Anna Kovner, 2011, "The Private Equity Advantage: Leveraged Buyout Firms and Relationship Banking," *Review of Financial Studies*, 24(7):2462–98.

Jelic, Ranko, 2011, "Staying Power of UK Buy-Outs," *Journal of Business Finance & Accounting*, 38(7–8):945–86.

Jenkinson, Tim, Wayne R. Landsman, Brian Rountree, and Kasbi Soonawalla, 2016, "Private Equity Net Asset Values and Future Cash-Flows," SSRN Working Paper No. 2636985.

Jensen, Michael C., 1989, "Eclipse of the Public Corporation," *Harvard Business Review*, September–October, revised 1997.

Johan, Sofia A., April Knill, and Nathan Mauck, 2013, "Determinants of Sovereign Wealth Fund Investment in Private Equity vs Public Equity," *Journal of International Business Studies*, No. 44, 155–72.

Johan, Sofia, and Minjie Zhang, 2016, "Reporting Bias in Private Equity: Reporting Frequency, Endowments and Governance," SSRN Working Paper No. 2826839.

Kaplan, Steven N., and Antoinette Schoar, 2005, "Private Equity Performance: Returns, Persistence and Capital Flows," *Journal of Finance*, 60(4):1791–1823.

Kinlaw, William, Mark Kritzman, and David Turkington, 2013, "Liquidity and Portfolio Choice: A Unified Approach," *The Journal of Portfolio Management*, Winter, 39(2):19–27.

Korteweg, Arthur, and Morten Sorensen, 2015 (2017), "Skill and Luck in Private Equity Performance," SSRN Working Paper No. 2419299 and Rock Center for Corporate Governance at Stanford University Working Paper No. 179, *Journal of Financial Economics*, 124(3), 535–62.

Lehmann, Alexander, 2018, "Risk Reduction through Europe's Distressed Debt Market," Bruegel, Policy Contribution, 2, January.

Leland, Hayne E., and David H. Pyle, 1977, "Informational Asymmetries, Financial Structure and Financial Intermediation," *Journal of Finance*, 32: 371–87.

Leleux, Benoît, Joachim Schwass, and Albert Diversé, 2007, "Europe's Family Offices, Private Equity and Venture Capital," EVCA/IMD.

L'Her, Jean-François, Rossista Stoyanova, Kathryn Shaw, William Scott, and Charissa Lai, 2016, "A Bottom-Up Approach to the Risk-Adjusted Performance of the Buyout Fund Market," *Financial Analysts Journal*, 72(4):36–48.

Lerner, Josh, Jake Ledbetter, Andrew Speen, Ann Leamon, and Chris Allen, 2006, "Private Equity in Emerging Markets: Yesterday, Today and Tomorrow," *Journal of Private Equity*, 19(3):8–20.

Lerner, Josh, Antoinette Schoar, and Jialan Wang, 2008, "Secrets of the Academy: The Drivers of University Endowment Success," SSRN Working Paper 1271364, *Journal of Economic Perspectives*, 22(3): 207–22.

Lerner, Josh, Antoinette Schoar, and Wan Wongsunwai, 2007, "Smart Institutions, Foolish Choices? The Limited Partner Performance Puzzle," *Journal of Finance*, 62(2):731–764.

Li, Yi, 2014, "Reputation, Volatility and Performance Persistence of Private Equity," Federal Reserve Board of Governors, Working Paper.

Ljungqvist, Alexander, and Matthew Richardson, 2003, "The Cash Flow, Return and Risk Characteristics of Private Equity," SSRN Working Paper No. 369600 and NYU Finance Working Paper No. 03-001.

Lo, Andrew W., Constantin Petrov, and Martin Wiersbicki, 2003, "It's 11 PM – Do You Know Where Your Liquidity Is? The Mean-Variance-Liquidity Frontier," *Journal of Investment Management*, 1(1):55–93.

Lo, Andrew, 2004, "The Adaptive Market Hypothesis: Market Efficiency from an Evolutionary Perspective," *Journal of Portfolio Management*, 30(5):15–29.

Longstaff, Francis A., 2018, "Valuing Thinly Traded Assets," *Management Science*, 64(8), 3469–970.

Markowitz, Harry M., 1952, "Portfolio Selection," *Journal of Finance*, 7(1):77–91.

Morkoetter, Stefan, and Thomas Wetzer, 2016, "The Impact of Costs and Returns on the Investment Decisions of Swiss Pension Funds," University of St Gallen and SFAMA study.

Muscarella, Chris J., and Michael R. Vetsuypens, 1990, "Efficiency and Organizational Structure: A Study of Reverse LBOs," *Journal of Finance*, 45(5):1389–413.

Nadauld, Taylor, Berk Sensoy, Keith Vorkink, and Michael Weisbach, 2017 (2019), "The Liquidity Cost of Private Equity Investments: Evidence from Secondary Market Transactions," NBER Working Paper No. 22404, *Journal of Financial Economics*, 132(3), 158–81.

Nielsen, Kasper Meisner, 2010, "The Return to Direct Investment in Private Firms: New Evidence on the Private Equity Premium Puzzle," *European Financial Management*, 17(3):436–463.

Robinson, David T., and Berk A. Sensoy, 2013, "Do Private Equity Managers Earn Their Fees? Compensation, Ownership and Cash Flow Performance," *Review of Financial Studies*, 26(11): 2760–97, and NBER Working Paper No. 17942.

Rouvinez, Christophe, 2003, "Private Equity Benchmarking with PME+," *Venture Capital Journal*, 43(8):34–9.

Sensoy, Berk A., Yingdi Wang, and Michael S. Weisbach, 2014, "Limited Partner Performance and the Maturing of the Private Equity Industry," *Journal of Financial Economics*, 112(3):320–343.

Sharpe, William F., 1992, "Asset Allocation: Management Style and Performance Measurement," *Journal of Portfolio Management*, 18(2):7–19.

Sorensen, Morten, 2007, "How Smart Is Smart Money? A Two-Sided Matching Model of Venture Capital," *Journal of Finance*, 62(6):2725–62.

Sorensen, Morten, and Ravi Jagannathan, 2015, "The Public Market Equivalent and Private Equity Performance," *Financial Analysts Journal*, 71(4):43–50.

Stafford, Erik, 2107, "Replicating Private Equity with Value Investing, Homemade Leverage, and Hold-to-Maturity Accounting," SSRN Working Paper No. 2720479.

Strömberg, Per, 2008, "The New Demography of Private Equity," *in* Lerner, Josh, and Anuradha Gurung (ed.), *The Global Impact of Private Equity Report 2008, Globalisation and Alternative Investments,* World Economic Forum, 1:3–26.

Weidig, Tom, and Pierre-Yves Mathonet, 2004, "The Risk Profile of Private Equity," SSRN Working Paper No. 495482.

Welch, Kyle T., and Stephen Stubben, 2018, "Private Equity's Diversification Illusion: Evidence from Fair Value Accounting," SSRN Working Paper No. 2379170.

Winton, Andrew, 2003, "Institutional Liquidity Needs and the Structure of Monitored Finance," *Review of Financial Studies*, 16(4):1273–313.

NEWSLETTERS, PAPERS, PROFESSIONAL STUDIES, REGULATORY PAPERS, AND WHITE PAPERS

Aon Hewitt, 2016, *Global Report: Global Survey of Retirement Plan Accounting Assumptions*, July.

Bain & Company, 2017, "Global Private Equity Report 2017," 27/2.

Barton, Andrew, and Madison Kaur, 2019, "Unlocking investment by insurers in SMEs," MacFarlanes, 23 April (https://www.macfarlanes.com/what-we-think/in-depth/2019/unlocking-investment-by-insurers-in-smes/, last accessed July 30, 2020).

Bender, Jennifer, Remy Briand, Dimitris Melas, and Raman Aylur Subramanian, 2013, "Foundations of Factor Investing," MSCI, Research Insight, December.

British Business Bank and Oliver Wyman, 2019, "The Future of Defined Contribution Pensions – Enabling Access to Venture Capital and Growth Equity," September.

Cagnati, Roberto, and Joanna Asfour, 2017, "Adding Private Markets to DC Pension Plan Portfolios – a Case Study," Partners Group, Research Paper, January.

Cox, Dylan, and Bryan Hanson, 2018, "Welcome to the Private Debt Show," Private Equity Analyst Note, Pitchbook, Q1.

Dasgupta, Prikshit, 2017, "Dealing with 'Broken-Deal' Expenses: SEC Recent Action Shows its Continued Focus on Fee and Expense Practices of Fund Managers," Reed Smith, Client Alert, October 5 (https://www.reedsmith.com/en/perspectives/2017/10/dealing-with-broken-deal-expenses-sec-recent-action, last accessed, December 1, 2018).

Demaria, Cyril, 2015b, "How Do Co-Investments in Emerging Markets Compare with the Ones in Developed Markets?" UBS Chief Investment Office, June.

Demaria, Cyril, 2017a, "Is There Too Much Capital in Leveraged Buyouts?" *Critical Perspectives*, n°60, Wellershoff & Partners, August.

Demaria, Cyril, 2017b, "Private Markets Secondary Investments: No Free Lunch," *Critical Perspectives*, n°61, Wellershoff & Partners, November.

Demaria, Cyril, and Rémy He, 2019, "Beyond Volatility: Five Practical Ways to Measure Private Markets Risk," *Critical Perspectives*, n° 71, August.

Dobbs, Richard, Tim Koller, Susan Lund, Sree Ramaswamy, Jon Harris, Mekala Krishnan, and Duncan Kauffman, 2016, *Diminishing Returns: Why Investors May Need to Lower Their Expectations*, McKinsey Global Institute.

Fernyhough, Wylie, 2019, "Sovereign Wealth Funds Overview," Pitchbook, Analyst Note, 3Q.

Frei, André, and Michael Studer, 2011, "What Is the Optimal Allocation to Private Equity?" *Partners Group Research Flash*, Partners Group.

Henzler, Filip, 2008, "Alternative Routes to Liquidity: Securitising Private Equity," in *The Private Equity Secondaries Market – A Complete Guide to Its Structure, Operation and Performance*, PEI Media, pp. 35–36.

ILPA, 2017, "Subscription Lines of Credit and Alignment of Interests – Considerations and Best Practices for Limited and General Partners," June.

Invest Europe, 2017, "2016 European Private Equity Activity – Statistics on Fundraising, Investments and Divestments."

The Investment Association, 2019, "Investment Management in the UK 2018–2019 – The Investment Association Annual Survey," September.

Johnson, Paula D., 2018, "Global Philanthropy Report – Perspectives on the Global Foundation Sector," Harvard Kenney School's Hauser Institute for Civil Society and UBS.

Jones Day, 2007, "Comparison of Chapter 11 of the United States Bankruptcy Code with The System of Administration in the United Kingdom, The Rescue Procedure in France, Insolvency Proceedings in Germany, and The Extraordinary Administration for Large Insolvent Companies in Italy."

Kraemer-Eis, Helmut, 2014, "Institutional Non-Bank Lending and the Role of Debt Funds," European Investment Fund, EIF Research & Market Analysis, Working Paper 2014/25.

Lanser, Howard P., Paul Bail, and J. David Cumberland, 2016, "Global Leveraged Loan and High Yield Quarterly," Leveraged Capital Markets Analysis, Baird, Q4.

Leamon, Ann, Josh Lerner, and Maria Susana Garcia-Robles, 2012, *The Evolving Relationship Between LP and GPs*, September, Multilateral Investment Fund, Inter-American Bank of Development.

Marks, Howard, 2014–2015, "Risk Revisited" and "Risk Revisited Again," Oaktree Capital Management.

Marks, Howard, 2015, "Liquidity," Oaktree Capital Management.

Marks, Howard, 2017, "There They Go Again . . . Again," Oaktree Capital Management.

Massi, Markus, Alessandro Scortecci, and Pratik Shah, 2017, "Sovereign Wealth's Hunt for the Next Unicorn," The Boston Consulting Group.

Mooradian, Peter, Andrea Auerbach, and Michael Quealy, 2013, "Growth Equity Is All Grown Up," Cambridge Associates, June.

Norges Bank Investment Management, "Government Pension Fund Global – Annual Report 2019," No. 22.

Preqin, 2015, "Preqin Introduces 'Private Capital' for 2016."

Preqin, 2016, *The 2015 Preqin Global Private Debt Report.*

Preqin, 2017, *Asian Private Equity & Venture Capital*, Special Report, September.

Preqin, 2017b, *Private Equity and Venture Capital Spotlight*, Vol. 13, No. 8, November.

Preqin, 2017c, *2017 Global Private Equity and Venture Capital Report.*

Private Equity International, 2018, "PE Gets Schooled," Friday Letter, April 13.

Private Equity Wire, 2015, "Direct Lending Funds Offering Superior Risk/Return Profile," 17/04.

PwC, 2017, "Asset & Wealth Management Revolution: Embracing Exponential Change."

Reale, Anthony, 2010, "Endowment and Foundation Spending Policies: One Size Does Not Fit All," J.P. Morgan Investment Analytics and Consulting, 7/12.

Rice, Bob, 2017, "The Upside of the Downside of Modern Portfolio Theory," *Investment & Wealth Monitor*, Investment Management Consultants Association, January/February, pp. 13–18 and 55.

Rosenbaum, Kevin, Indradoot Dhar, and Daniel Day, 2017, "Digging in: Assessing the Private Infrastructure Opportunity Today," Cambridge Associates, Research Note, April.

SEC, 2017, "Private Funds Statistics – First Calendar Quarter 2017," Division of Investment Management, Risk and Examinations Office, 23/10.

StepStone, 2018, "Cracking the Illiquidity Code: Long-Term Partnerships, Short-Term Cash Flows," September.

Studer, Michael, and Marc Wicki, 2010, "Private Equity Allocations under Solvency II," *Partners Group Research Flash*, Partners Group.

Toll, David M., and Paul Centopani, 2017, "PE/VC Partnership Agreements Study 2018–2019," 5th ed., *Buyout Insider.*

Schilling, Lisa, 2016, "U.S. Pension Plan Discount Rate Comparison 2009–2014," Society of Actuaries, September.

Shukis, David, and David Thurston, 2016, "The 15% Frontier," Cambridge Associates.

Swisscanto, 2019, "Etudes sur les caisses de pension en Suisse," Swisscanto Prevoyance SA.

UBS and Campden Wealth, 2020, "The Global Family Office Report 2019."

Urdan, Jennifer, and Max Gelb, 2015, "Private Investments: Filling a Pension's Return Void," Cambridge Associates, Research Note, October.

Williams, Victoria, 2014, *Small Business Lending in the United States 2013*, U.S. Small Business Administration Office of Advocacy, December.

Willis Towers Watson, 2017, *Global Pension Assets Study* 2016.

Wilson, Cullen, and Brian Buenneke, 2017, "The Shrinking Public Market and Why It Matters," *Infocus*, Pantheon.

World Economic Forum, 2014, "Direct Investing by Institutional Investors: Implications for Investors and Policy-Makers," November.

The Yale Endowment, 2019 Report.

PRESS ARTICLES AND PRESS RELEASES

Atkins, Paul S., "California Public Employees Vote Against Pension-Fund Activism, *Wall Street Journal*, Opinion, 18/10/2018.

Bass, Matthew D., "The Illusion of Liquidity," *Pensions & Investments*, 24/09/2014.

Binham, Caroline, and Patrick Jenkins, "Watchdogs Exempt Sovereign Wealth and Pension Funds from Study," *Financial Times*, 16/06/2016.

Bradford, Hazel, "TPG Settles with SEC over Accelerated Monitoring Fees," *Pensions & Investments*, 22/12/2017.

DeLuca, Alexandra, "An Insider's Perspective on the Yale Endowment," *Chief Investment Officer*, 05/12/2016.

Devine, Anna, "He Who Dares," *Private Debt Investor*, June 2015, pp. 16–20.

Dixon, Mark, "Endowments Should Rethink the 5% Rule," *Pensions & Investments*, 8/05/2017.

The Economist, "The Princess and the Pearl," 6/12/2001.

The Economist, "Yale May Not Have the Key," Buttonwood, 12/03/2011.

The Economist, "Many Unhappy Returns," 21/11/2015.

Ford, Jonathan, "The Exorbitant Privilege Enjoyed by Private Equity Firms," *The Financial Times*, 8/9/2019.

Fixsen, Rachel, "Investors Gain Ground in Push for Lower Private Debt Costs," *IP&E*, 10/03/2017.

Hall, Jessica, "Private Equity Buys TXU in Record Deal," *Reuters*, 26/02/2017.

Investment & Pensions Europe, "Switzerland: SBA Calls for Investment Guidelines to Rejig to Boost Alternatives," February 16.

Jardine, Nick, "Report: Private Debt Fees on the Slide," *Private Debt Investor*, 16/05/2017.

Jost, Philippe, and Ivan Herger, 2013, "Robust but Adaptable," *Private Equity International*, February, pp. 54–56.

Karagiannopoulos, Lefteris, and Gwladys Fouche, "Norway's Supreme Court Rules in Favour of State in Pipeline Tariff Dispute," *Reuters*, 28/06/2018.

Klein, Matthew C., "Private Equity's Mark-to-Make-Believe Problem," *Financial Times*, 06/04/2016.

Mackenzie, Michael, "The Rise of Leveraged Loans as a USD 1 tn Asset Class," *The Financial Times*, 03/05/2018.

Martin, Timothy W., "CalPERS to Cut External Money Managers by Half," *The Wall Street Journal*, 08/06/2015.

McGrath, Charles, "Fewer Companies, Higher Valuations," *Pensions & Investments*, 23/06/2017a.

McGrath, Charles, "Fees on Committed Capital the Norm in Private Equity Funds," *Pensions & Investments*, 25/07/2017b.

Mendoza, Carmela, "DC Pensions: What's inside Pantheon and Partners Group's US Offerings?" *Private Funds CFO*, 15/07/2020.

Moyo, Dambisa, "Why Wall Street's Fear Index Remains Calm," *Financial Times*, Opinion, The Exchange, 18/10/2017.

Nicolaou, Anna, "Eminem Royalties Shares to be Sold in IPO," *Financial Times*, 25/09/2017.

Primack, Dan, "Why Persistence Matters," *Pro-rata*, Axios, 21/11/2017.

Private Equity International, "Reassuringly Expensive," 18/11/2016.

Private Equity International, "The Appeal of the Separate Account," 15/09/2017.

Reeve, Nick, "Consultant Warns on Changing Risks in Private Debt Sector," *Investment & Pensions Europe*, 13/03/2017.

Sicilia, Michael, "CalSTRS Moves Forward to Engage Firearms Makers and Retailers," 9/5/2018, CalSTRS press release (https://www.calstrs.com/news-release/calstrs-moves-forward-engage-firearms-makers-and-retailers).

Stannard, Ed, "Yale Stays Invested in Fossil Fuel Industries, Student Reports Say in New Haven," 17/5/2017, *New Haven Register* (https://www.nhregister.com/connecticut/article/Yale-stays-invested-in-fossil-fuel-industries-11312894.php).

Steinberg, Julie, and Kelly Greene, "Financial Advice, Served Rare," *Wall Street Journal*, 17/05/2013 (http://online.wsj.com/article/SB10001424127887323551004578441002331568 618.html, accessed, 21/7/ 2020).

Venteicher, Wes, "New CalPERS Leader Wants Pension Fund to Put Its Money Back into Yobacco," *The Sacramento Bee*, 19/03/2019.

Venteicher, Wes, "Settlement Talks over $1.2 Billion CalPERS Lawsuit Are Extended with a Retired Judge at the Helm," *The Sacramento Bee*, 28/01/2020.

Wall Street Journal, "From Buyout to Bankruptcy: Ranking the TXU LBO," Moneybeat, 29/04/2014.

Wall Street Journal, The Daily Shot, 20/06/2018.

White, Amanda, "Private Equity Persistence Slips," Top1000Funds.com, 9/11/2017.

DATA

eFront Pevara (now Insight) database (2017)
Preqin (2016)
Robert Shiller's online data (2016)
StepStone (2017)
Thomson Eikon's (now Refinitiv) Cambridge Associates database (2016–2017)

WHITE PAPERS

CBOE, *The CBOE Volatility Index – VIX*, White paper, (https://www.cboe.com/micro/vix/vixwhite.pdf, last accessed 10/08/2017).

IPEV, *International Private Equity and Venture Capital Valuation Guidelines*, December 2018, (http://www.privateequityvaluation.com/Portals/0/Documents/Guidelines/IPEV%20 Valuation%20Guidelines%20-%20December%202018.pdf?ver=2018-12-21-085233-863 &timestamp=1545382360113, last accessed 24/07/2020).

Index

Page numbers: Figures given in *italics* and Tables in **bold**